NIJIGAHARA HOLOGRAPH

Inio Asano

Fantagraphics Books

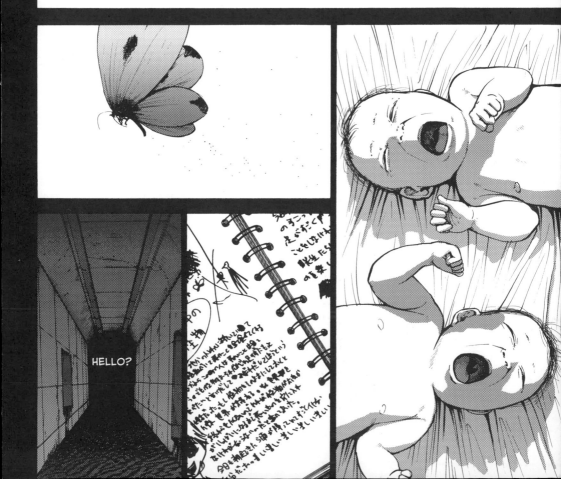

HELLO?

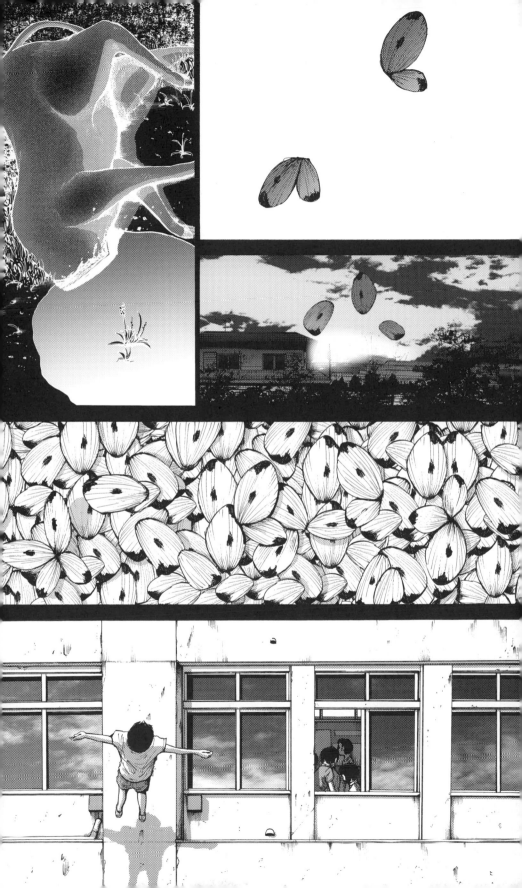

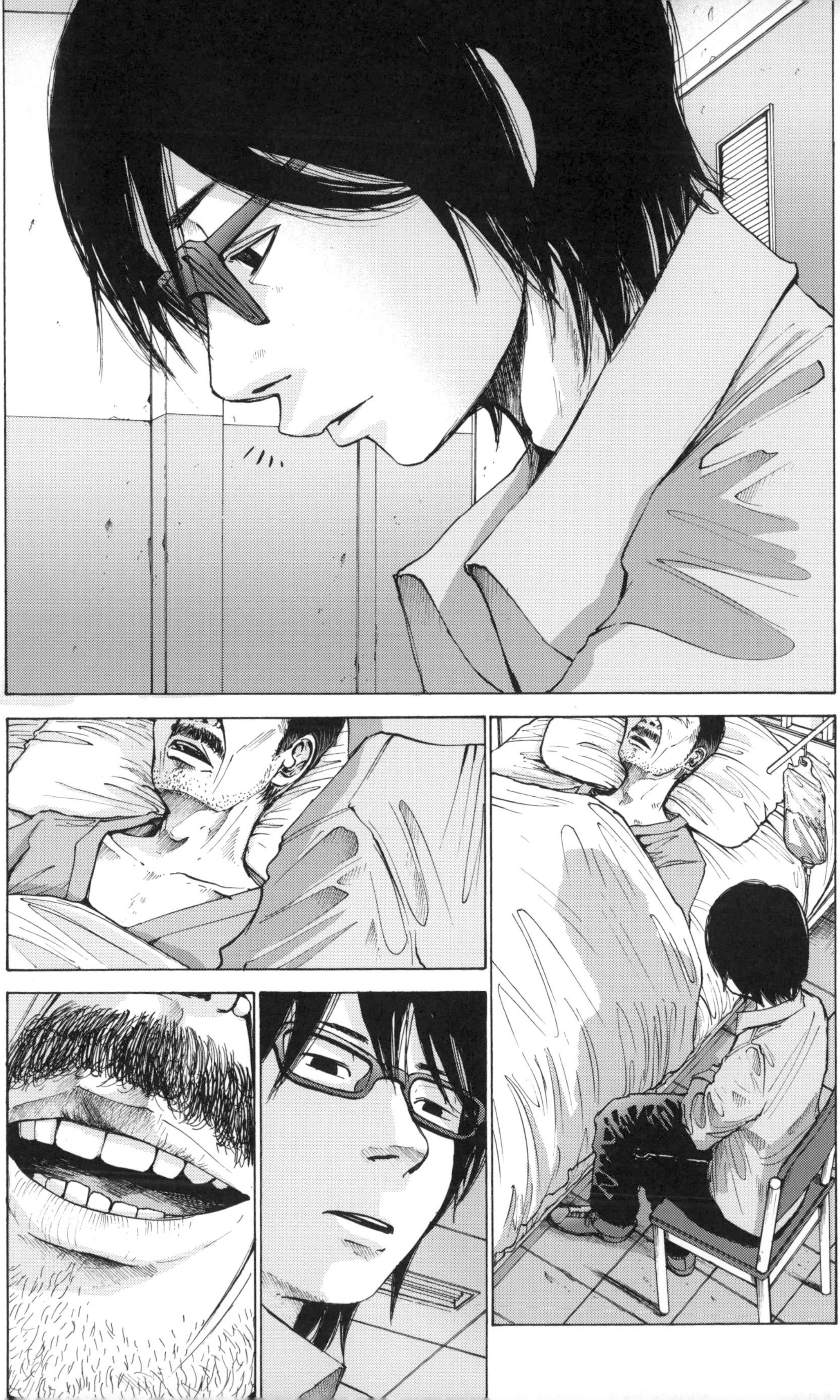

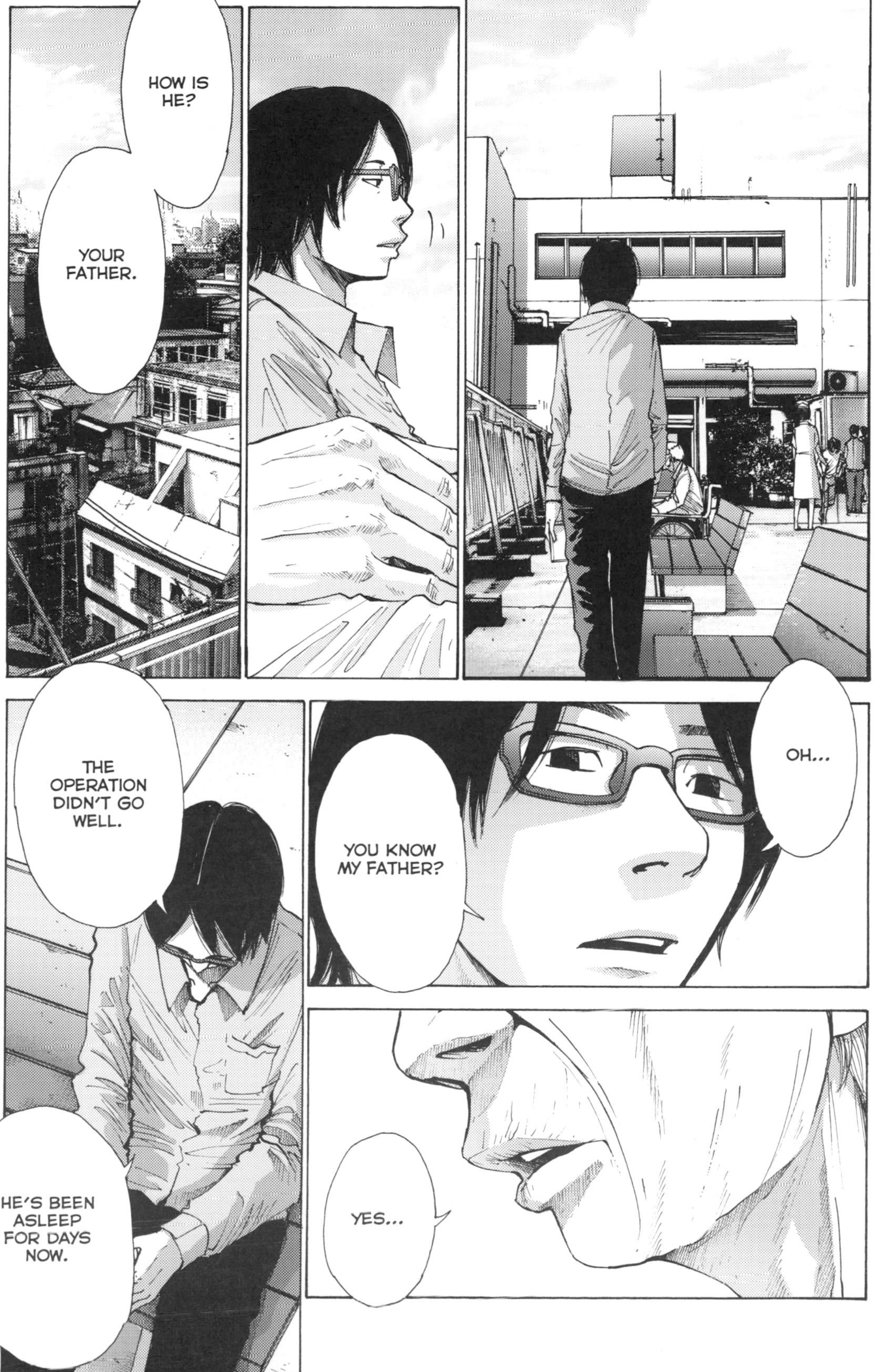
HOW IS HE?
YOUR FATHER.
OH...
YOU KNOW MY FATHER?
YES...
THE OPERATION DIDN'T GO WELL.
HE'S BEEN ASLEEP FOR DAYS NOW.

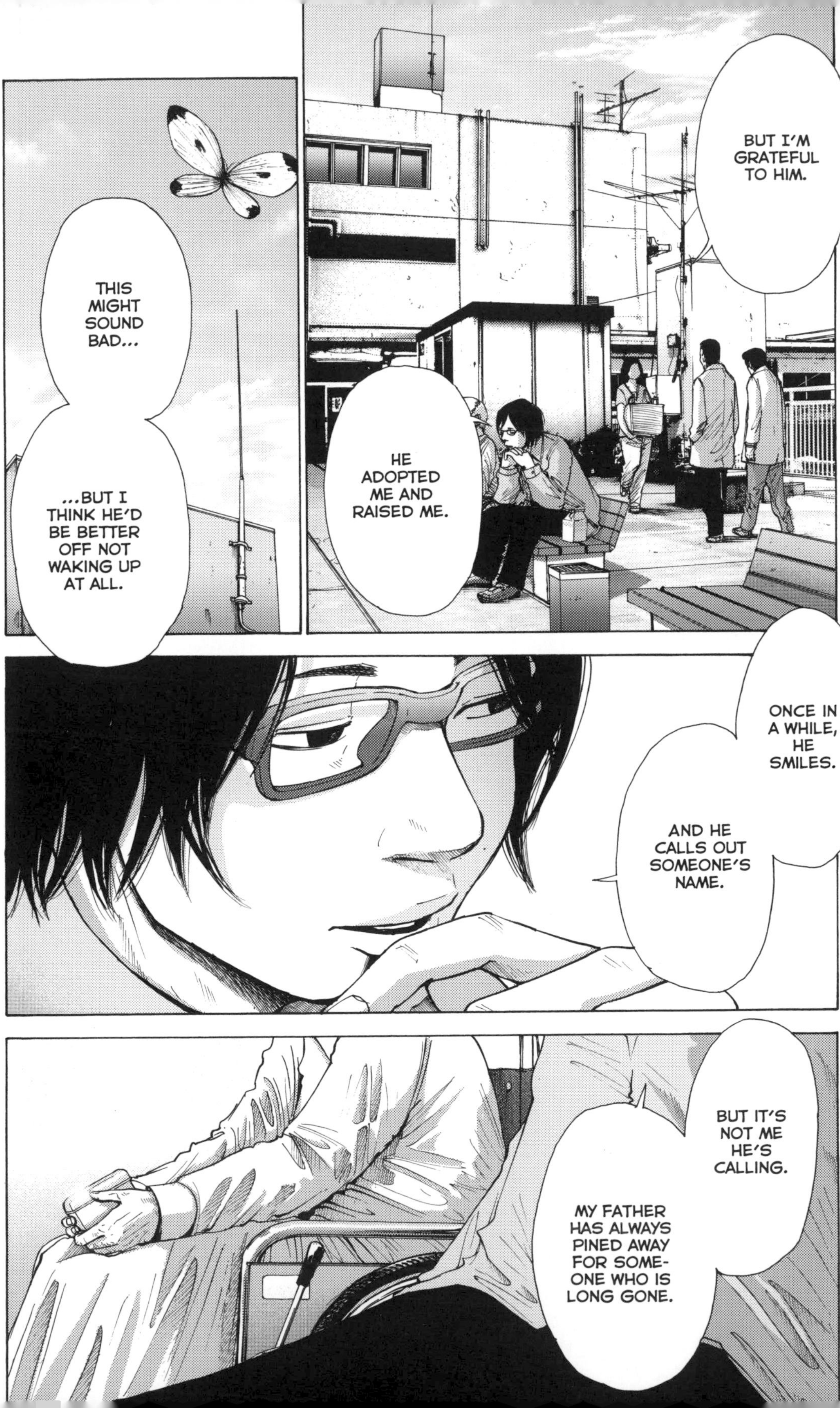
BUT I'M GRATEFUL TO HIM.
HE ADOPTED ME AND RAISED ME.
THIS MIGHT SOUND BAD...
...BUT I THINK HE'D BE BETTER OFF NOT WAKING UP AT ALL.
ONCE IN A WHILE, HE SMILES.
AND HE CALLS OUT SOMEONE'S NAME.
BUT IT'S NOT ME HE'S CALLING.
MY FATHER HAS ALWAYS PINED AWAY FOR SOME-ONE WHO IS LONG GONE.

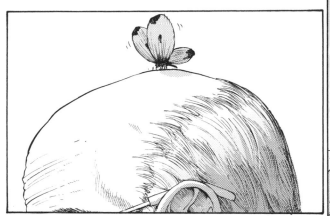

THESE DAYS... I HAVE DREAMS.

IT MAKES ME WONDER IF WHAT I'M SEEING NOW ISN'T REALLY JUST A DREAM.

EACH DAY, THE DREAMS BECOME MORE AND MORE REAL.

AND YET...

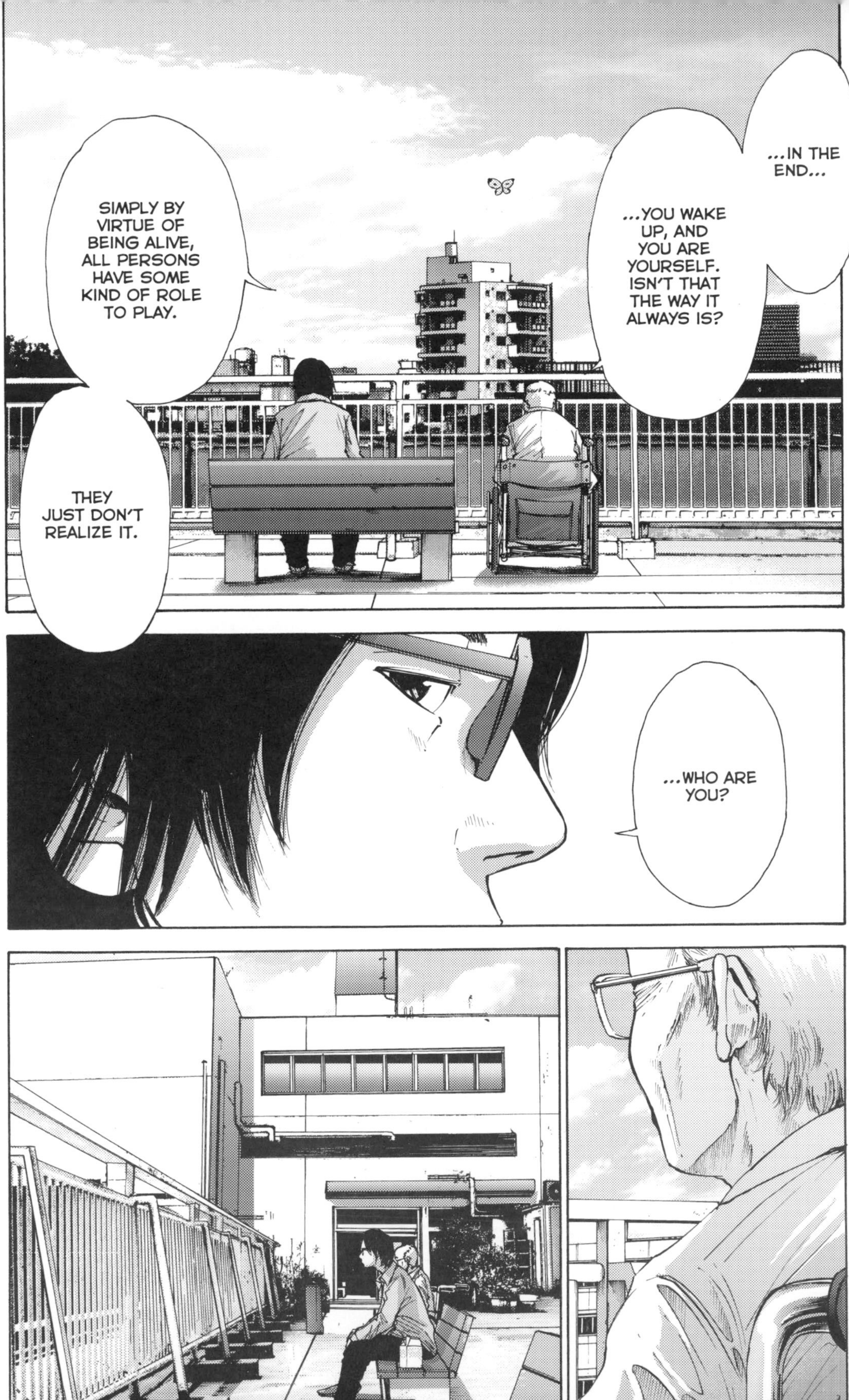
...IN THE END...
...YOU WAKE UP, AND YOU ARE YOURSELF. ISN'T THAT THE WAY IT ALWAYS IS?
SIMPLY BY VIRTUE OF BEING ALIVE, ALL PERSONS HAVE SOME KIND OF ROLE TO PLAY.
THEY JUST DON'T REALIZE IT.
...WHO ARE YOU?

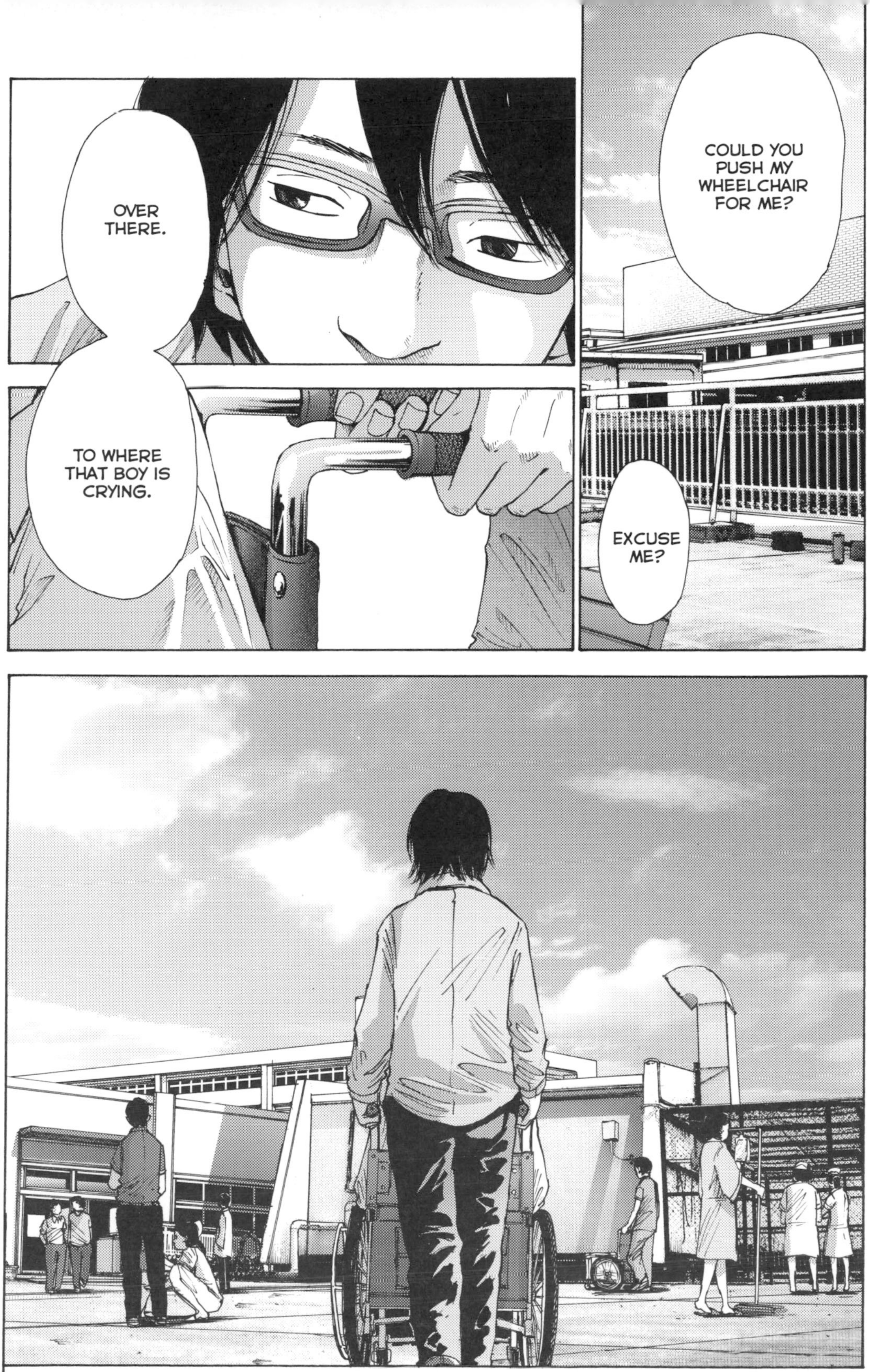
COULD YOU PUSH MY WHEELCHAIR FOR ME?
EXCUSE ME?
OVER THERE.
TO WHERE THAT BOY IS CRYING.

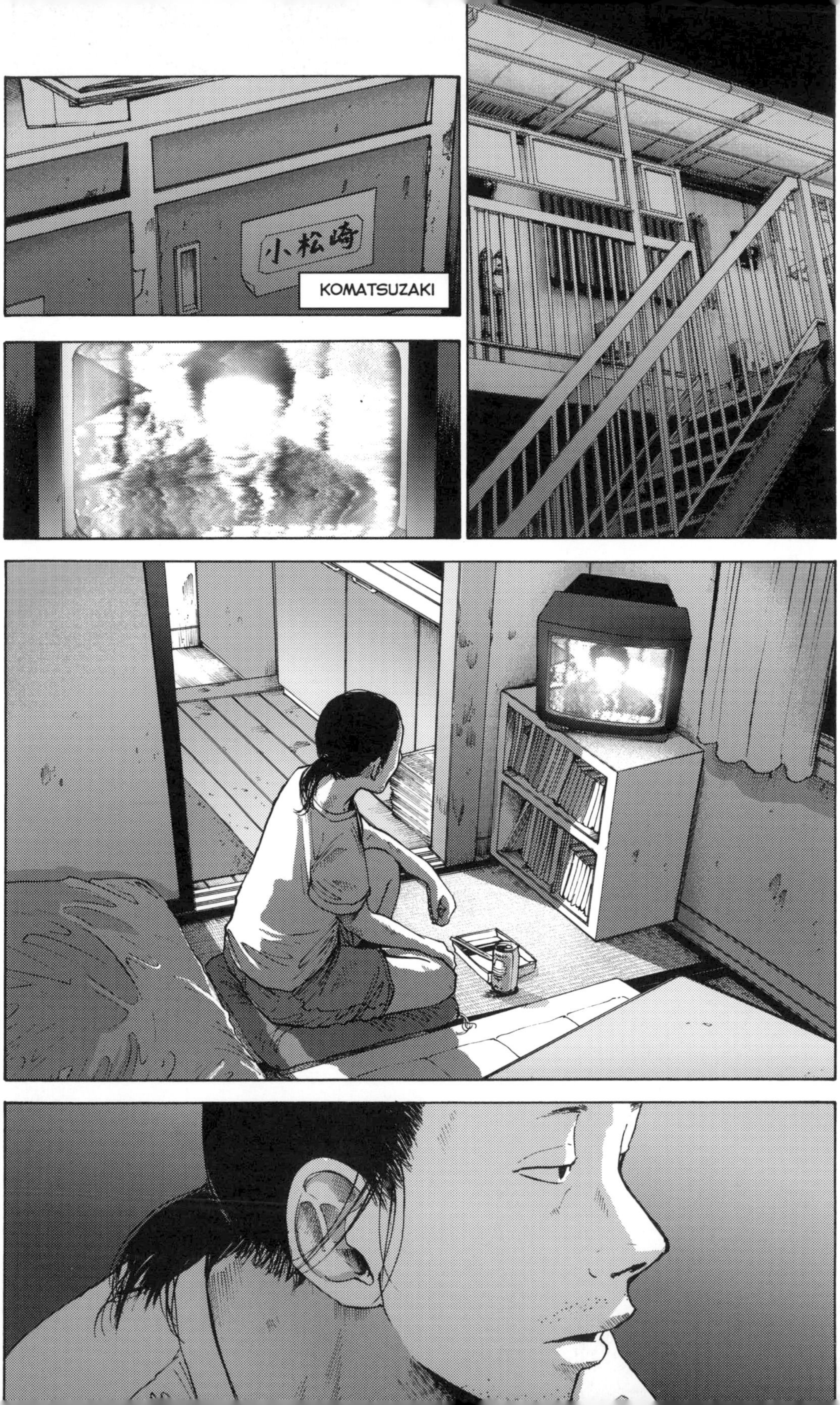
小松崎
KOMATSUZAKI

PRESCRIPTION
内用薬
UMF
病院
HOSPITAL
UMF

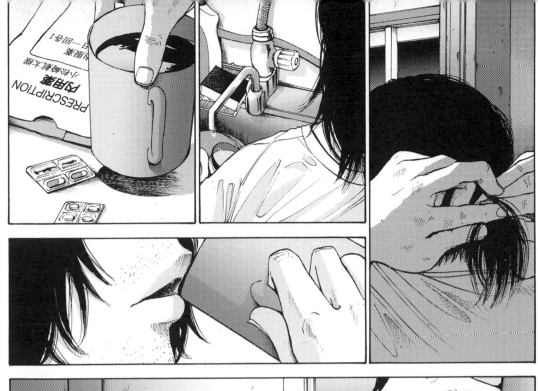

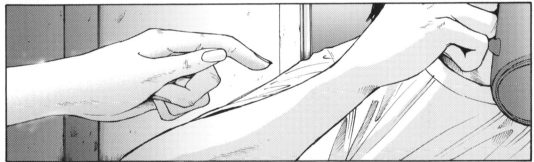

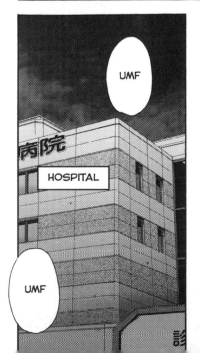

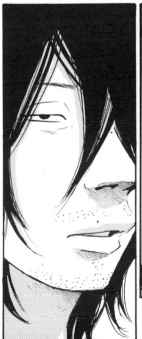

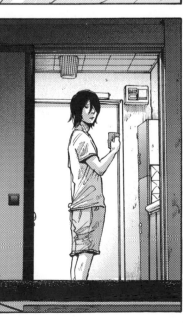

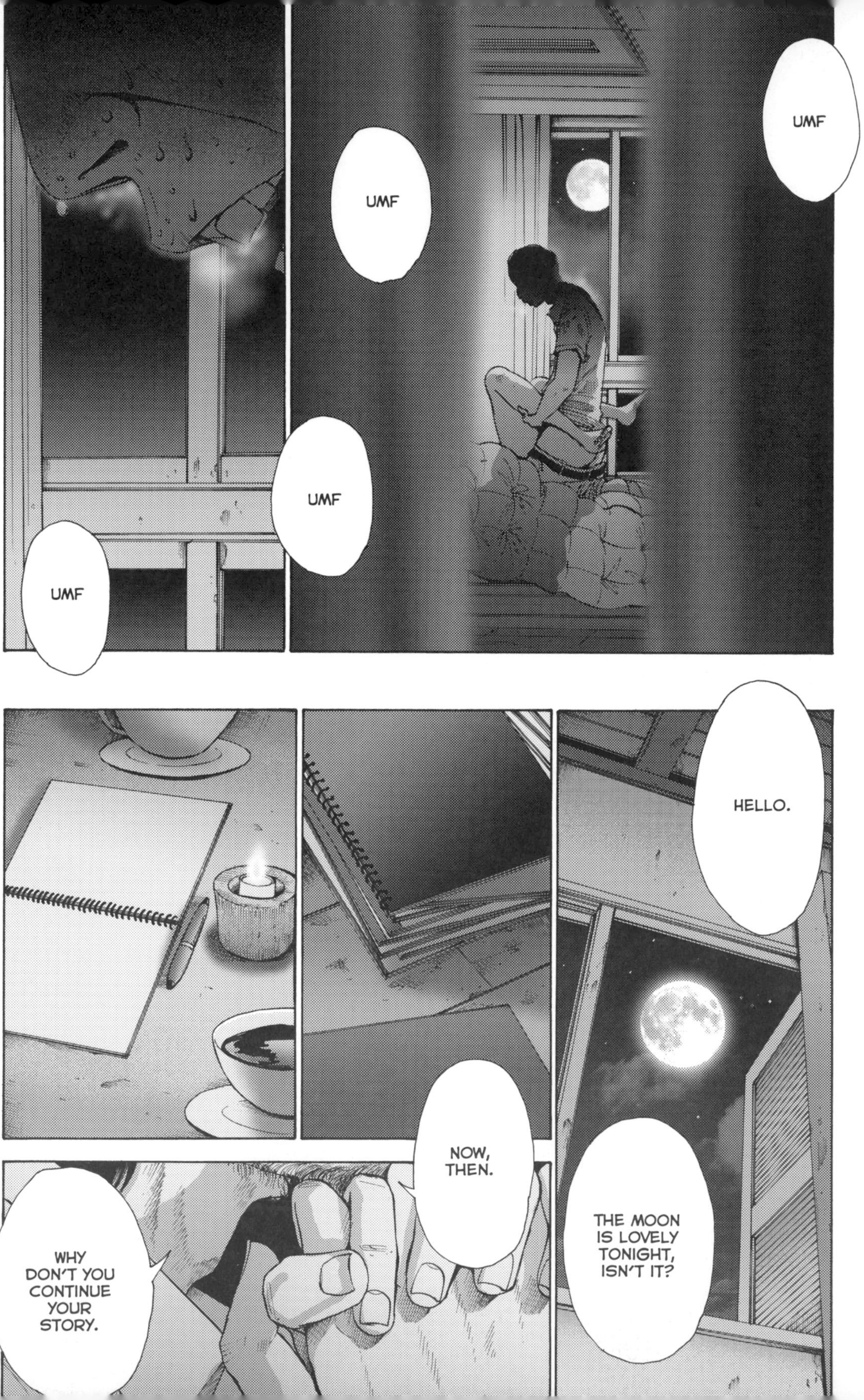
UMF
UMF
UMF
UMF
HELLO.
THE MOON IS LOVELY TONIGHT, ISN'T IT?
NOW, THEN.
WHY DON'T YOU CONTINUE YOUR STORY.

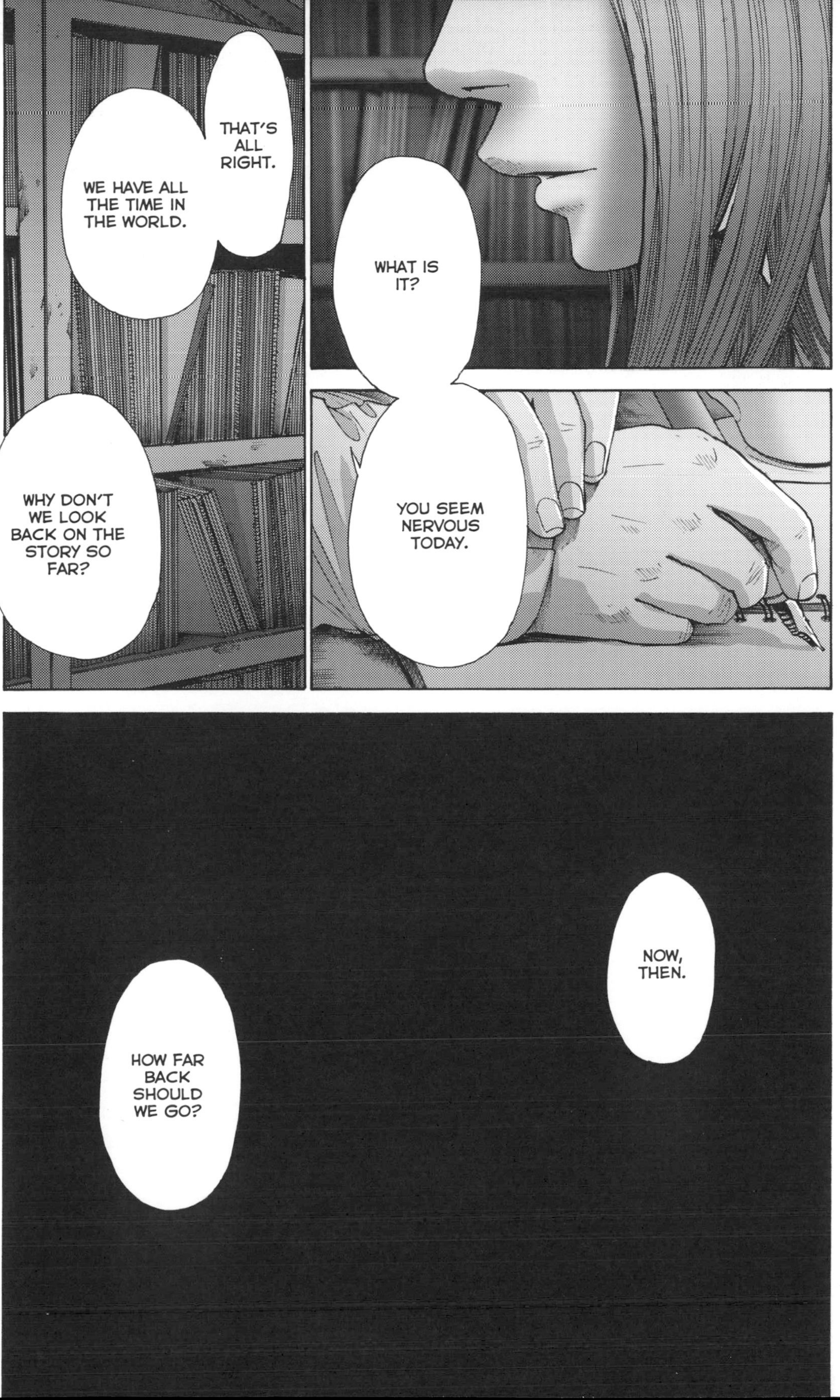
WHAT IS IT?
YOU SEEM NERVOUS TODAY.
THAT'S ALL RIGHT.
WE HAVE ALL THE TIME IN THE WORLD.
WHY DON'T WE LOOK BACK ON THE STORY SO FAR?
NOW, THEN.
HOW FAR BACK SHOULD WE GO?

CONTENTS

ELEVEN YEARS AGO

HELLO? HELLO?
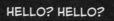

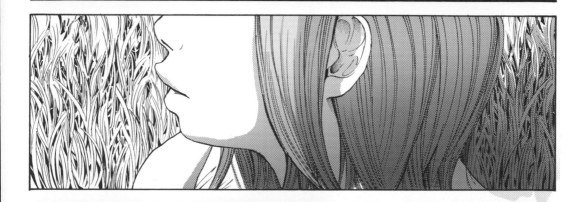

HELLO?

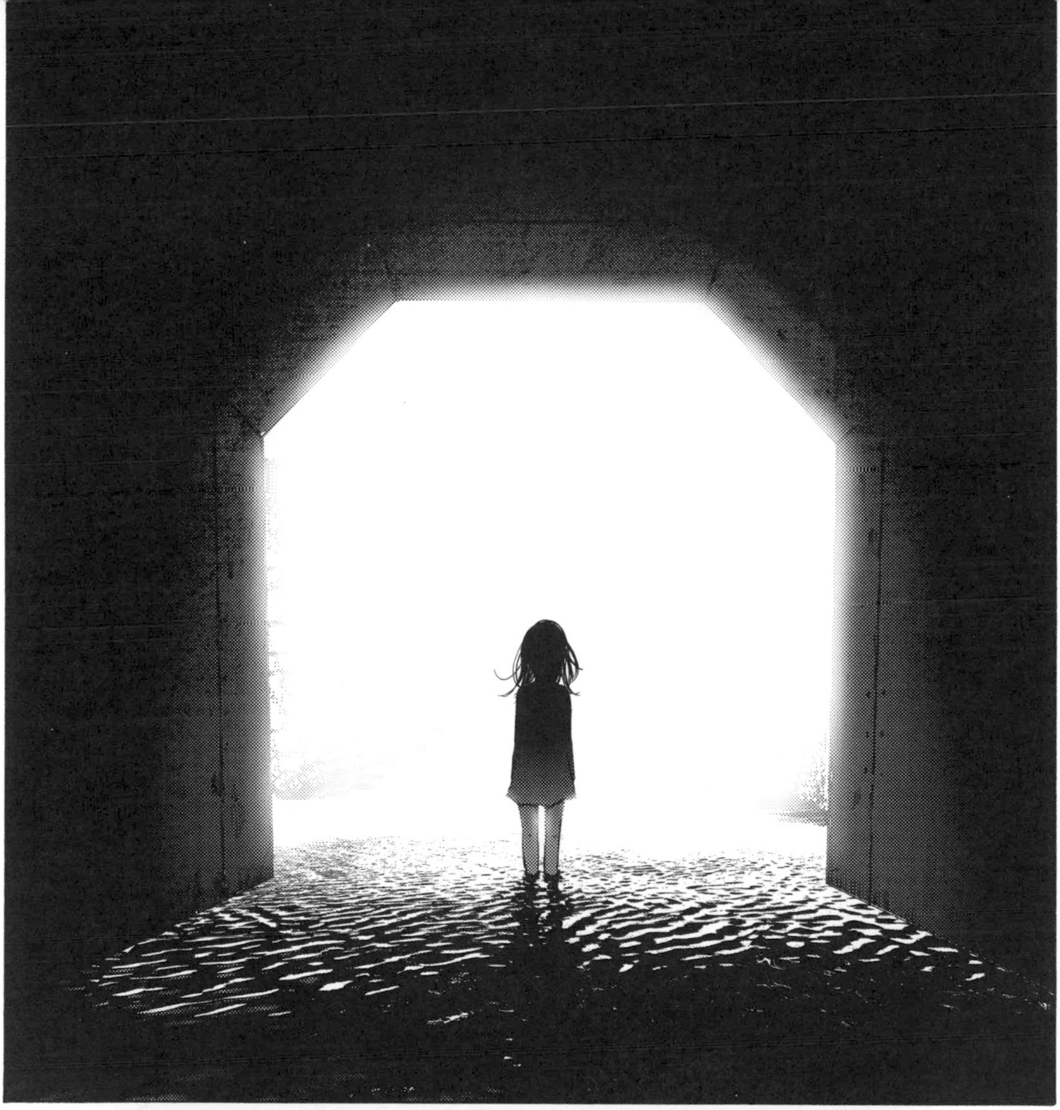
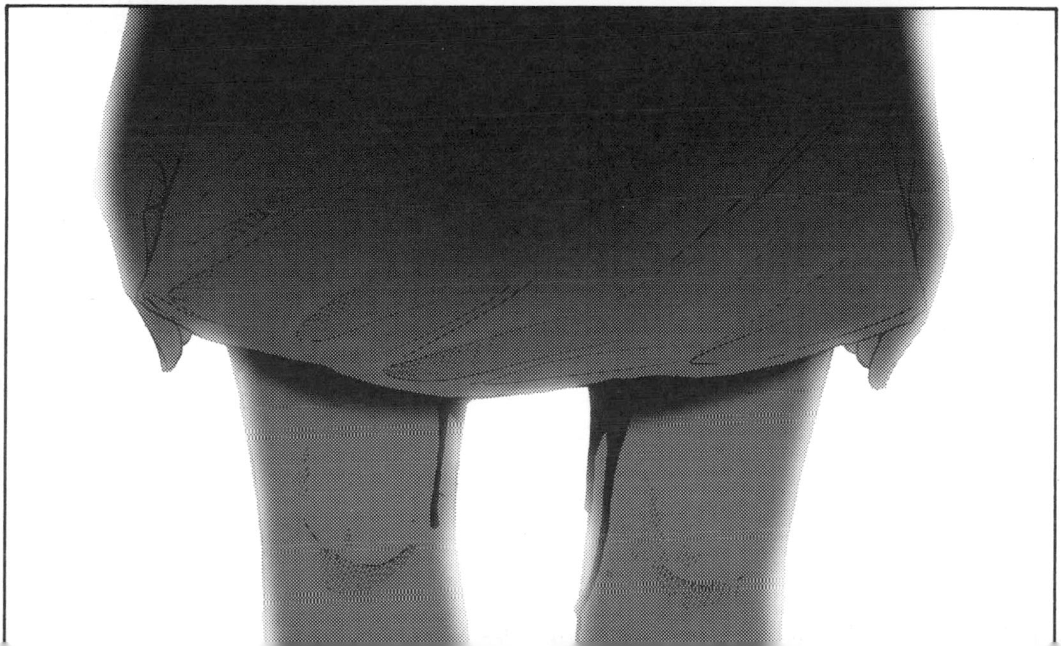

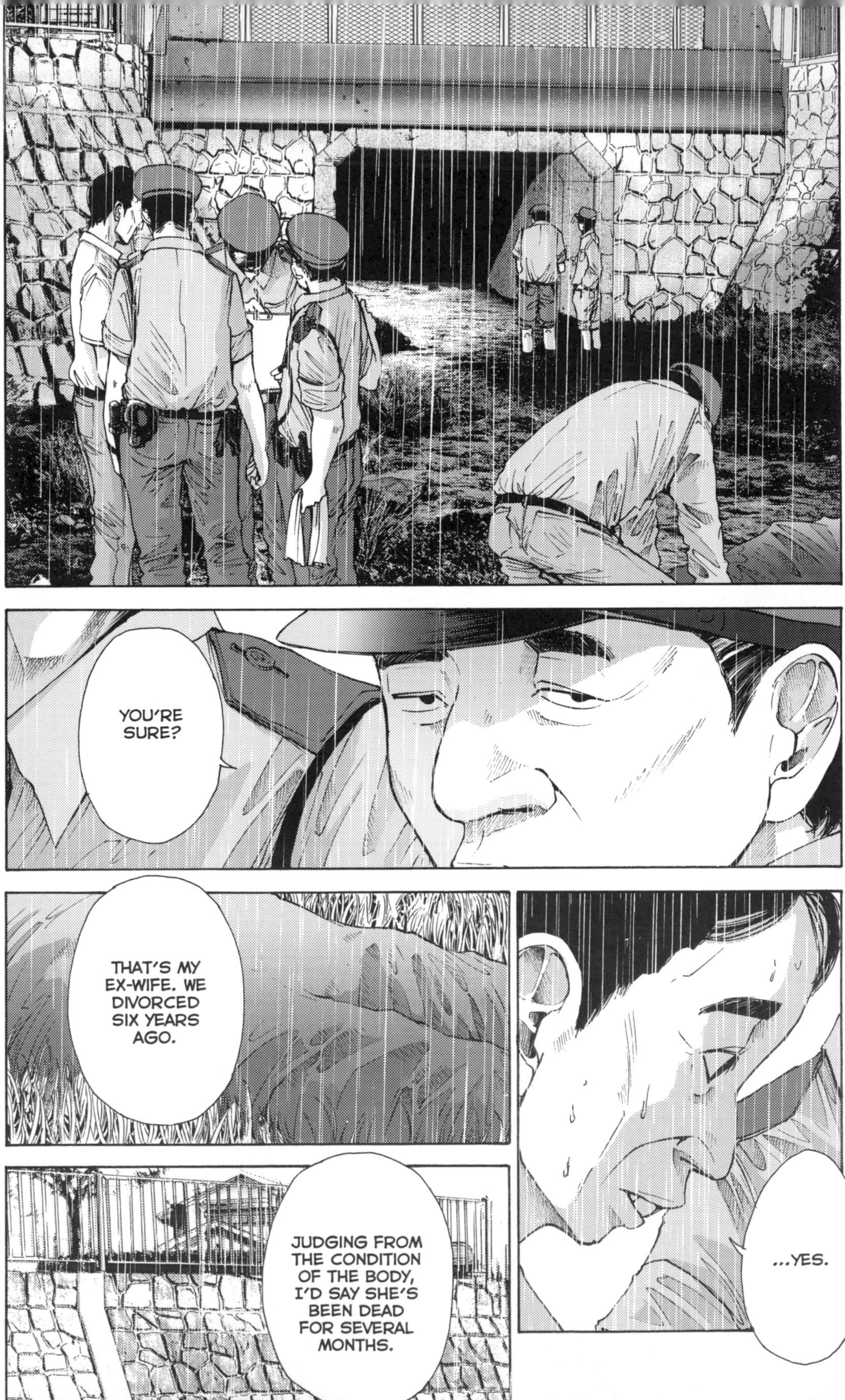
YOU'RE SURE?
...YES.
THAT'S MY EX-WIFE. WE DIVORCED SIX YEARS AGO.
JUDGING FROM THE CONDITION OF THE BODY, I'D SAY SHE'S BEEN DEAD FOR SEVERAL MONTHS.

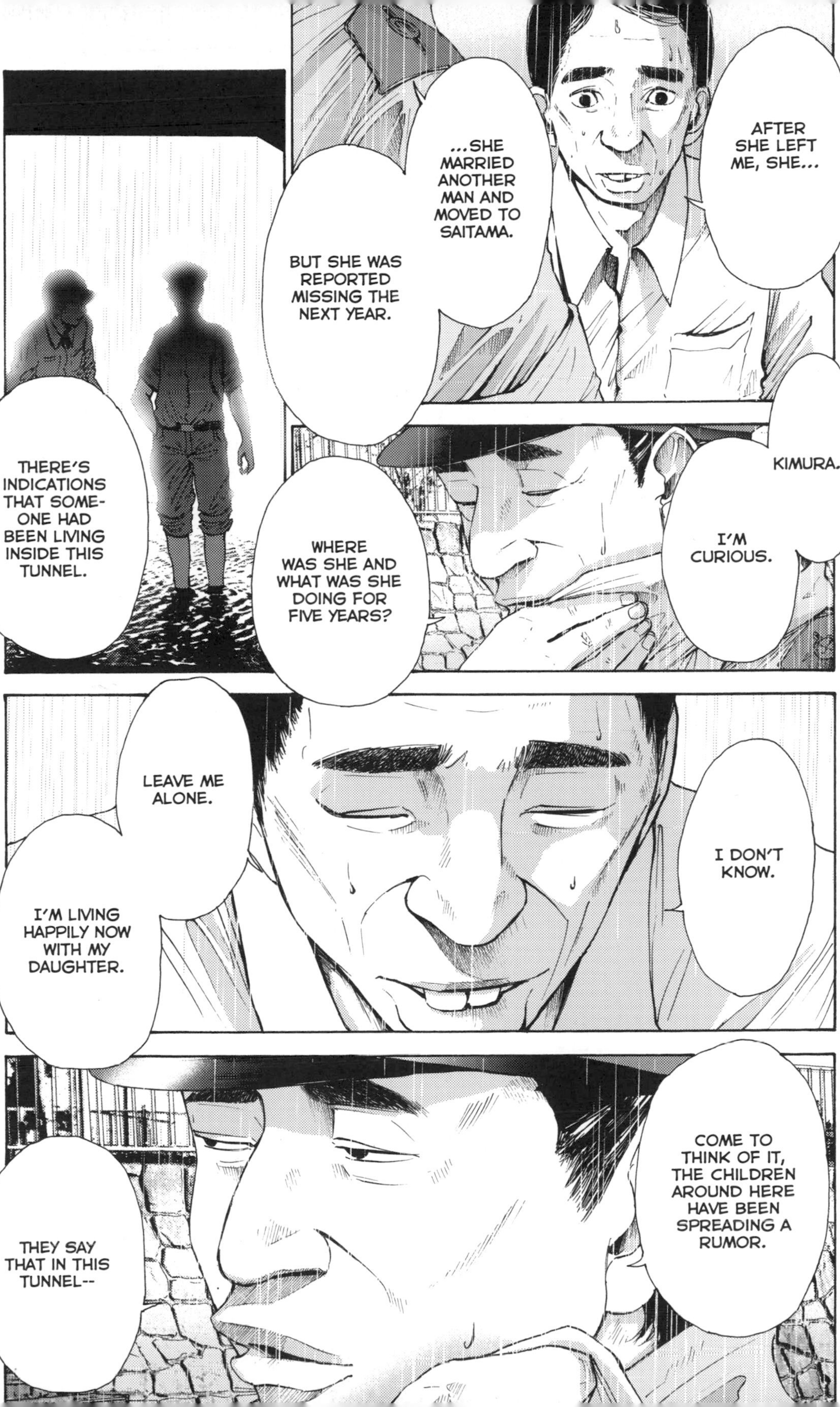
AFTER SHE LEFT ME, SHE...
...SHE MARRIED ANOTHER MAN AND MOVED TO SAITAMA.
BUT SHE WAS REPORTED MISSING THE NEXT YEAR.
KIMURA...
I'M CURIOUS.
WHERE WAS SHE AND WHAT WAS SHE DOING FOR FIVE YEARS?
THERE'S INDICATIONS THAT SOME-ONE HAD BEEN LIVING INSIDE THIS TUNNEL.
I DON'T KNOW.
LEAVE ME ALONE.
I'M LIVING HAPPILY NOW WITH MY DAUGHTER.
COME TO THINK OF IT, THE CHILDREN AROUND HERE HAVE BEEN SPREADING A RUMOR.
THEY SAY THAT IN THIS TUNNEL--

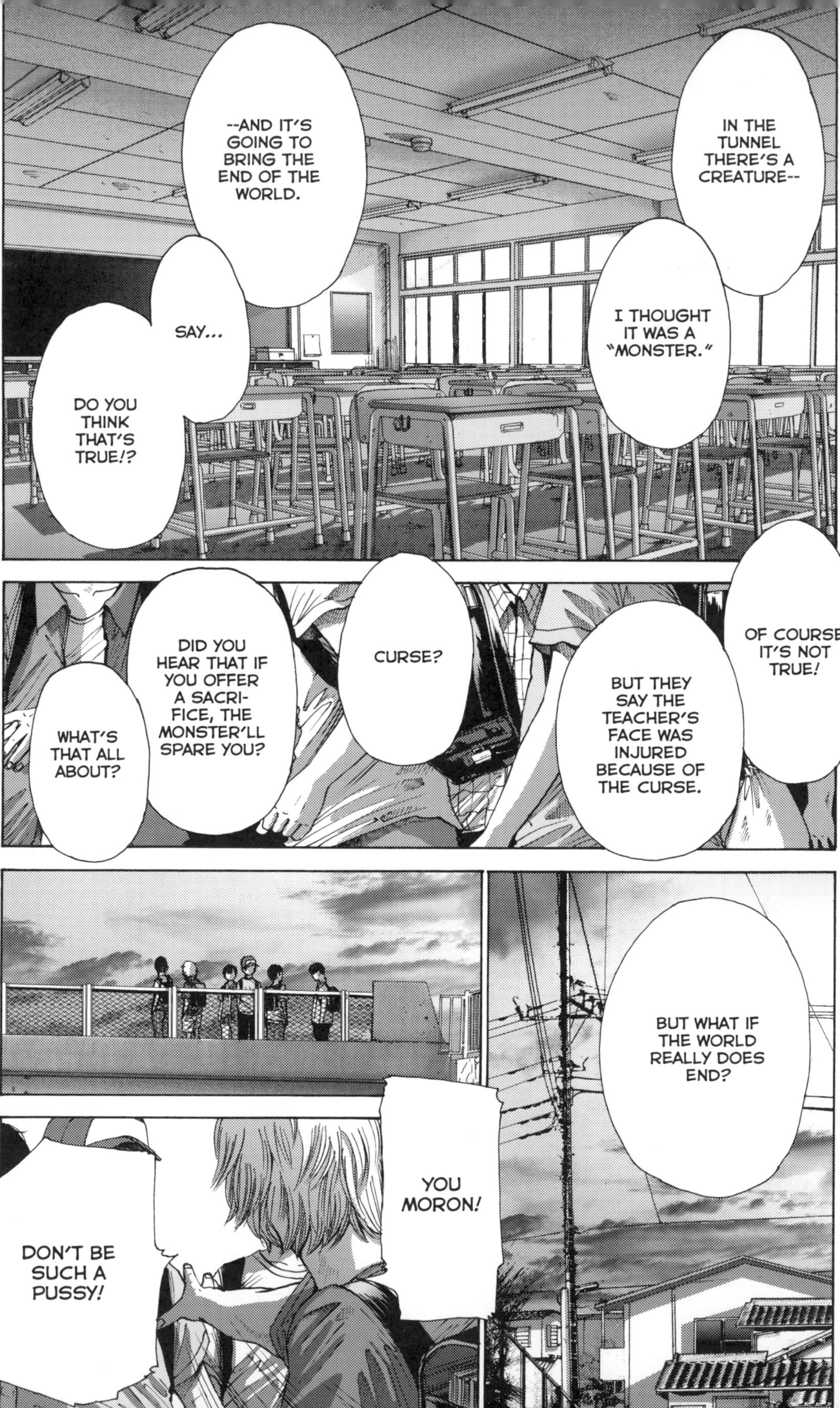
IN THE TUNNEL THERE'S A CREATURE--
--AND IT'S GOING TO BRING THE END OF THE WORLD.
I THOUGHT IT WAS A "MONSTER."
SAY...
DO YOU THINK THAT'S TRUE!?
OF COURSE IT'S NOT TRUE!
BUT THEY SAY THE TEACHER'S FACE WAS INJURED BECAUSE OF THE CURSE.
CURSE?
DID YOU HEAR THAT IF YOU OFFER A SACRI-FICE, THE MONSTER'LL SPARE YOU?
WHAT'S THAT ALL ABOUT?
BUT WHAT IF THE WORLD REALLY DOES END?
YOU MORON!
DON'T BE SUCH A PUSSY!

WHUMP

THAT'S JUST SOME BULLSHIT KIMURA MADE UP!

THAT CHICK'S CRA--

KOHTA...

K--

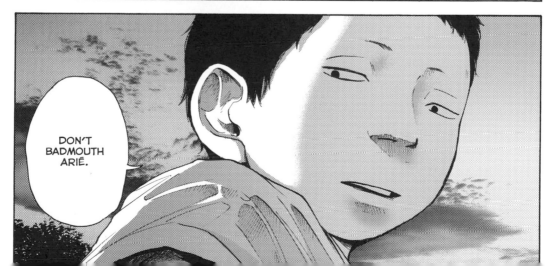

DON'T BADMOUTH ARIÉ.

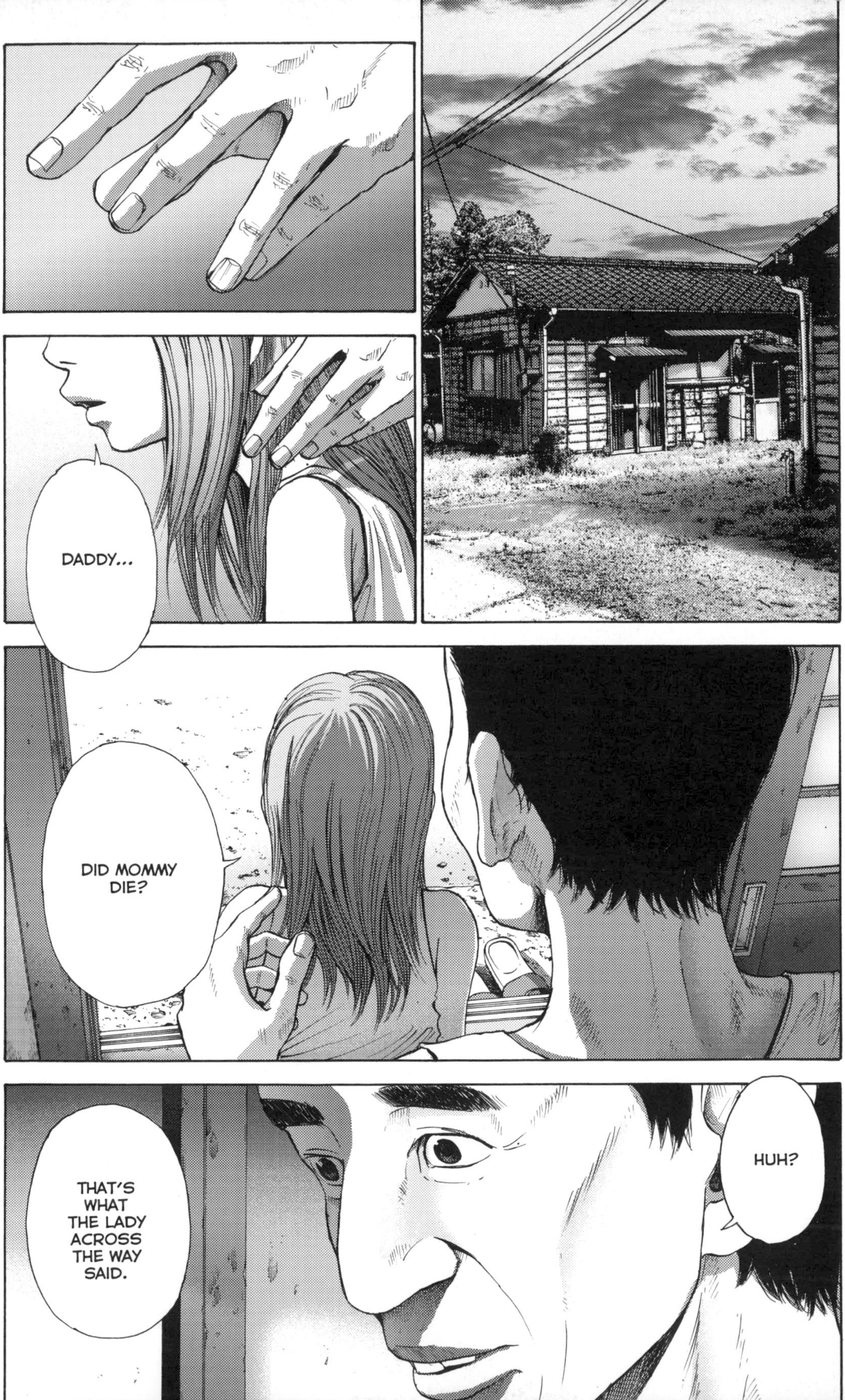
DADDY...
DID MOMMY DIE?
HUH?
THAT'S WHAT THE LADY ACROSS THE WAY SAID.

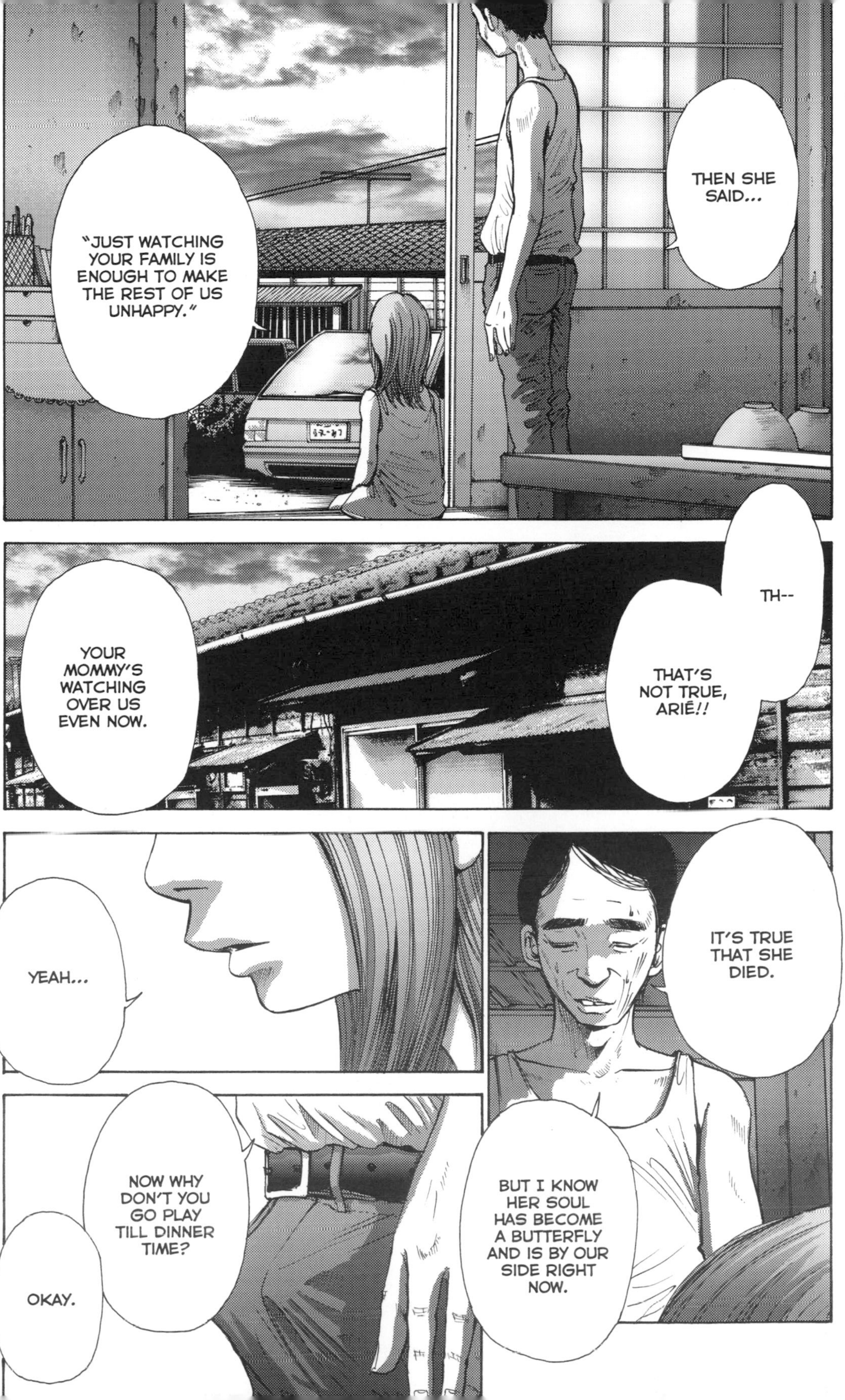
THEN SHE SAID...
"JUST WATCHING YOUR FAMILY IS ENOUGH TO MAKE THE REST OF US UNHAPPY."
TH--
THAT'S NOT TRUE, ARIÉ!!
YOUR MOMMY'S WATCHING OVER US EVEN NOW.
IT'S TRUE THAT SHE DIED.
BUT I KNOW HER SOUL HAS BECOME A BUTTERFLY AND IS BY OUR SIDE RIGHT NOW.
YEAH...
NOW WHY DON'T YOU GO PLAY TILL DINNER TIME?
OKAY.

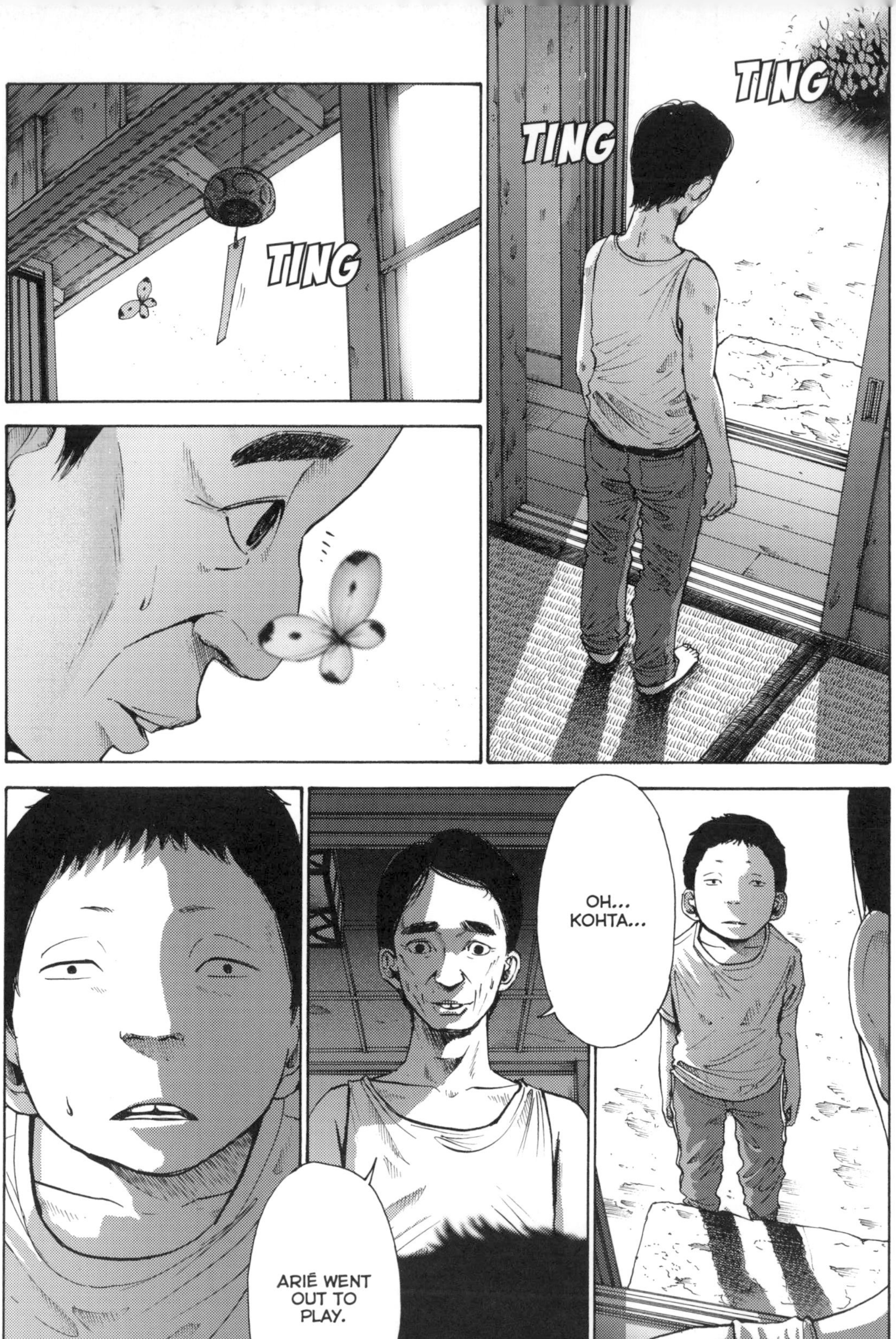
TING
TING
TING
OH... KOHTA...
ARIÉ WENT OUT TO PLAY.

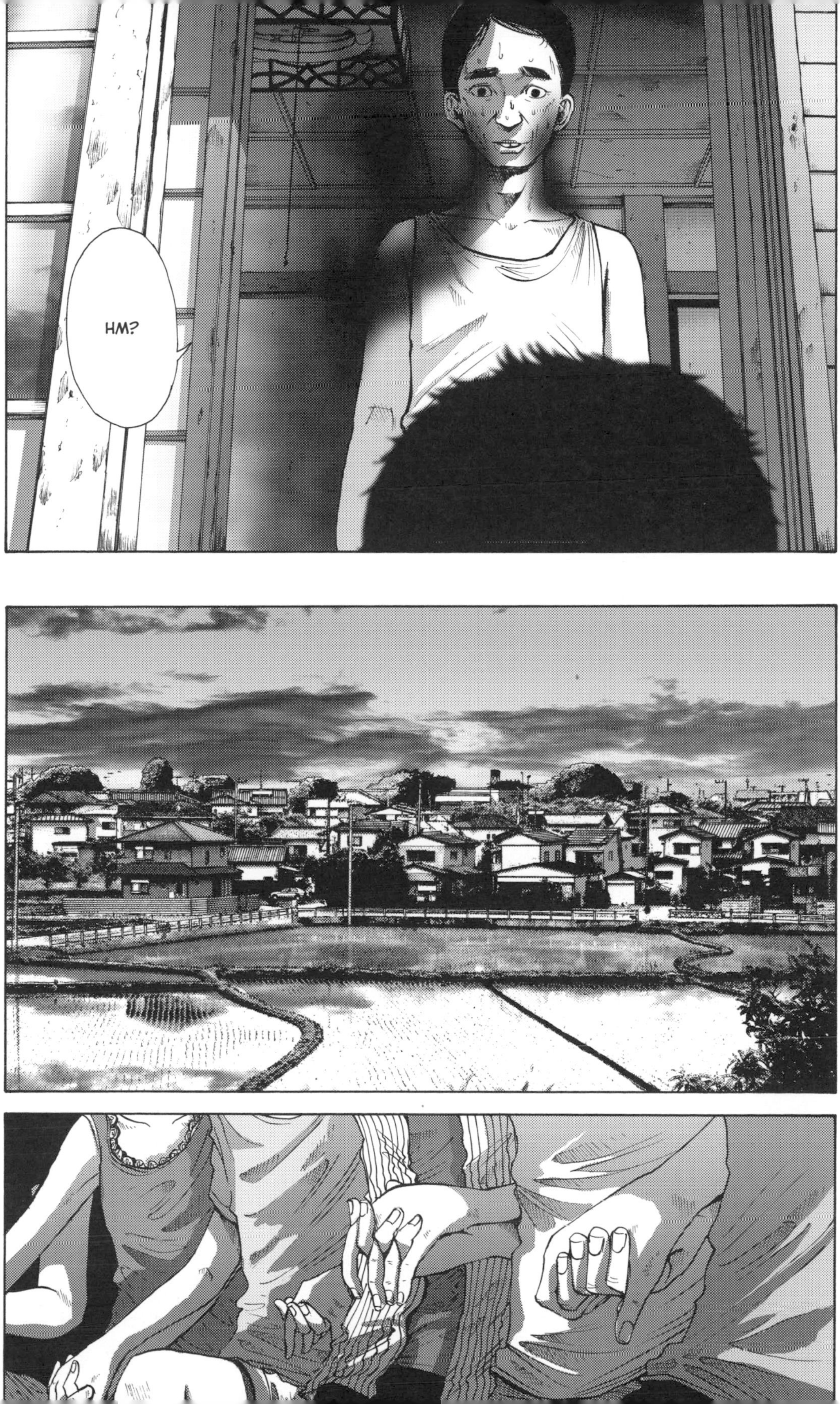
HM?

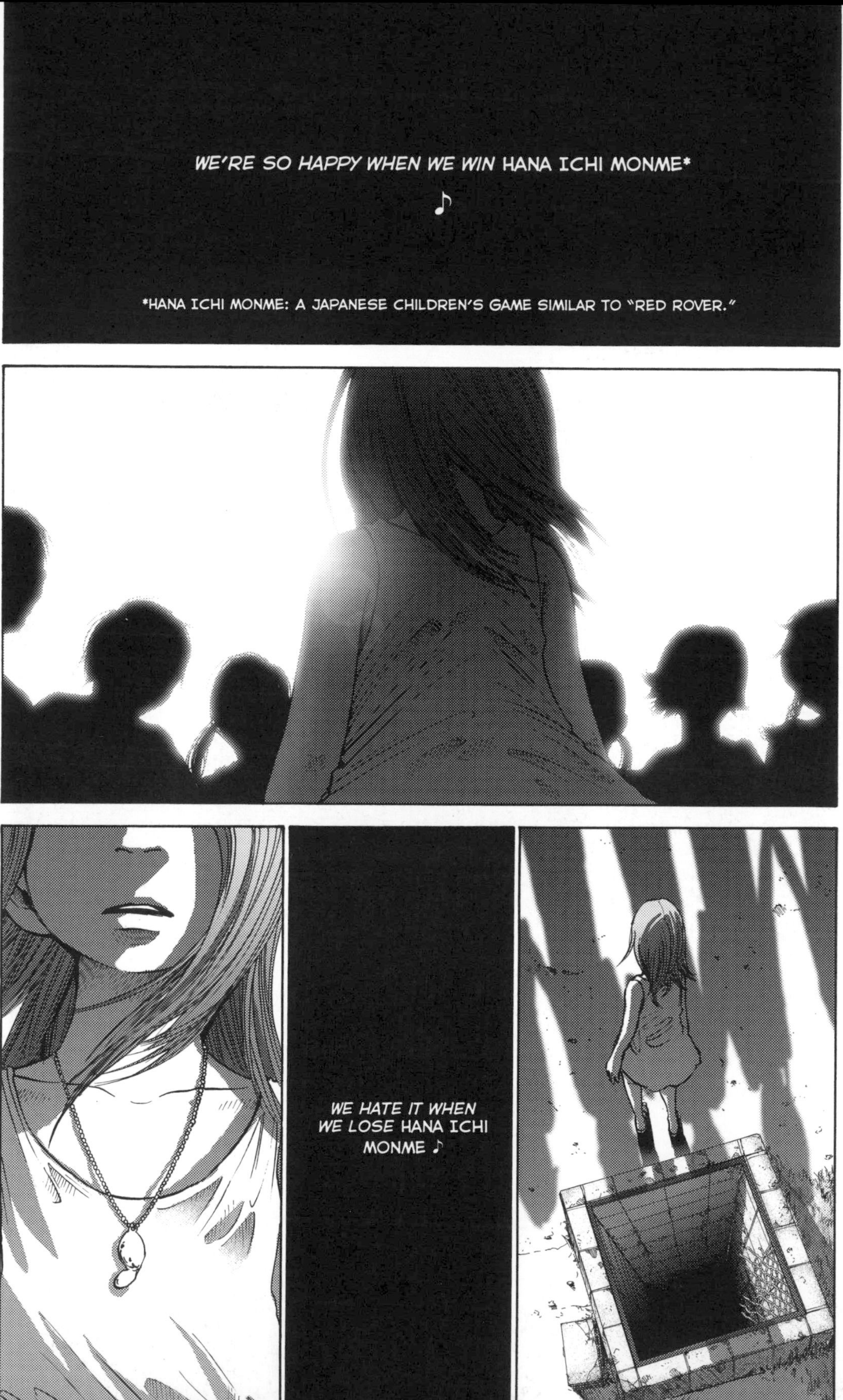
WE'RE SO HAPPY WHEN WE WIN HANA ICHI MONME* ♪
*HANA ICHI MONME: A JAPANESE CHILDREN'S GAME SIMILAR TO "RED ROVER."
WE HATE IT WHEN WE LOSE HANA ICHI MONME ♪

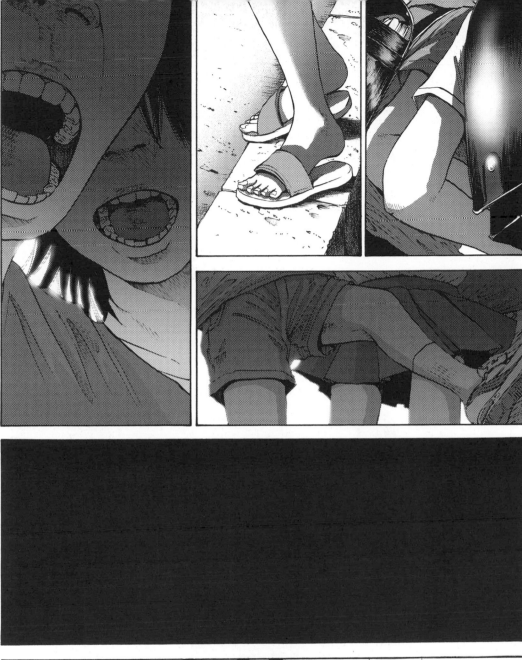

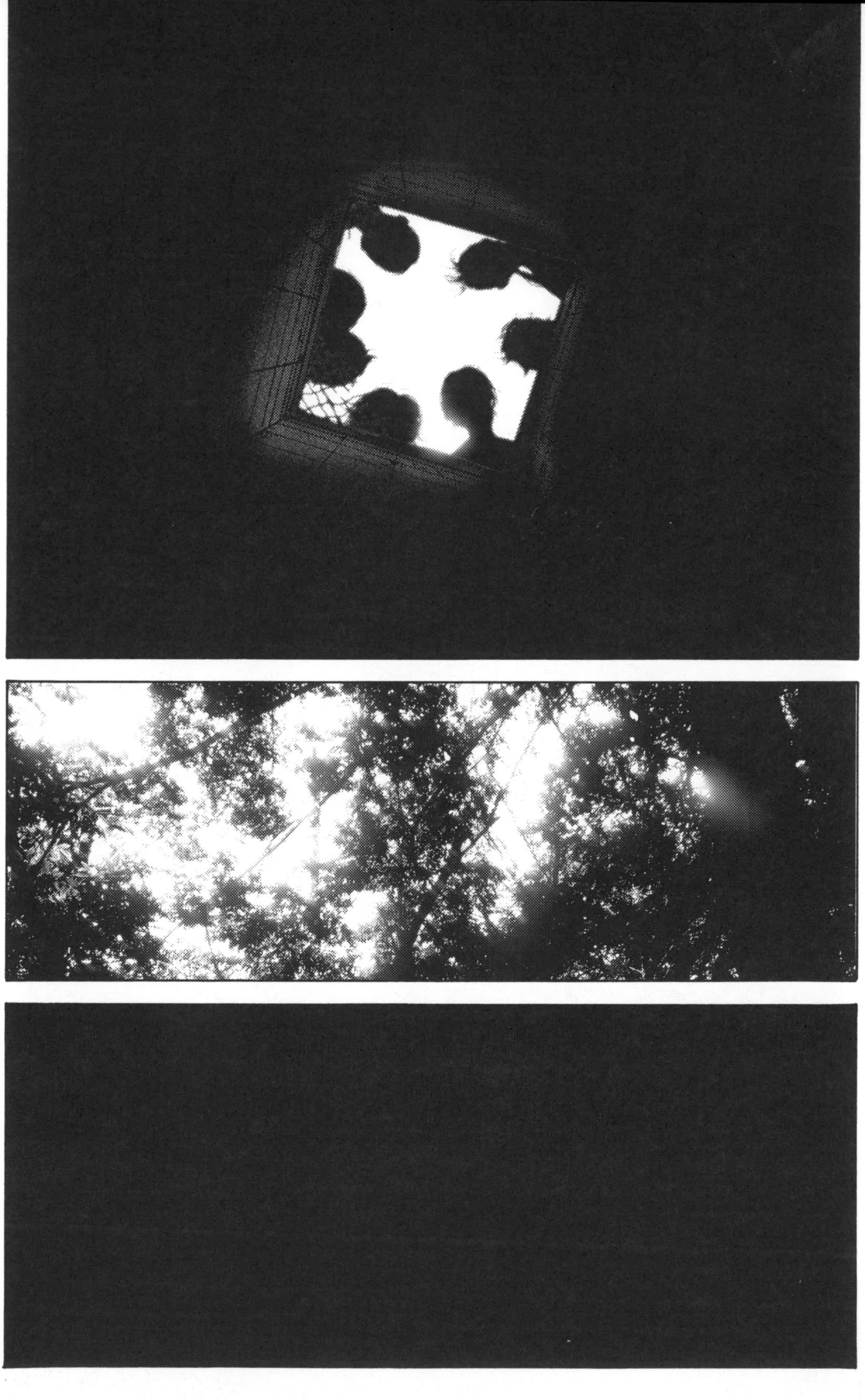

I CAN SEE IT. I CAN SEE IT ALL.

I CAN SEE EVERYTHING THERE IS IN THIS WORLD.

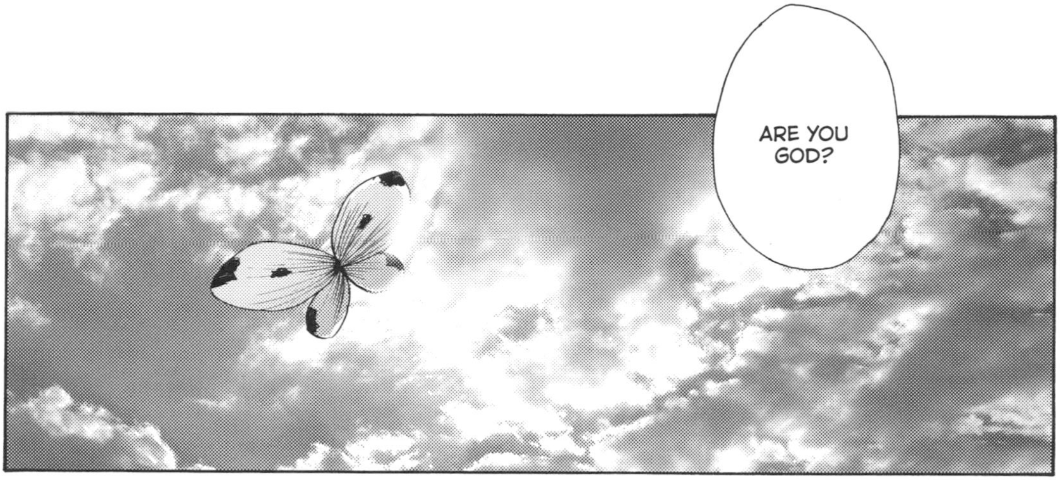
ARE YOU GOD?

NO. BUT I THINK I'VE MET GOD.

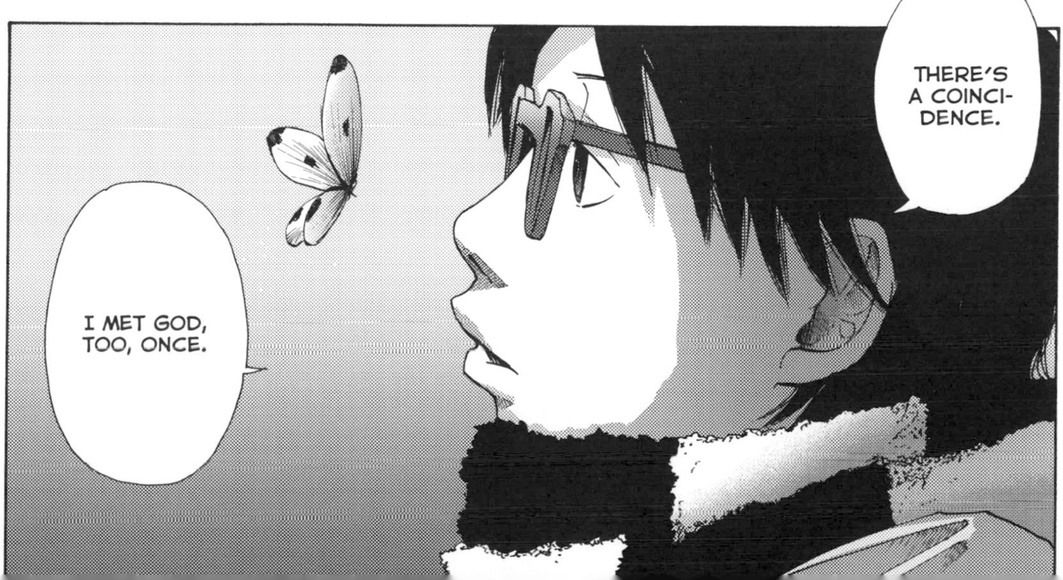
THERE'S A COINCI-DENCE.
I MET GOD, TOO, ONCE.

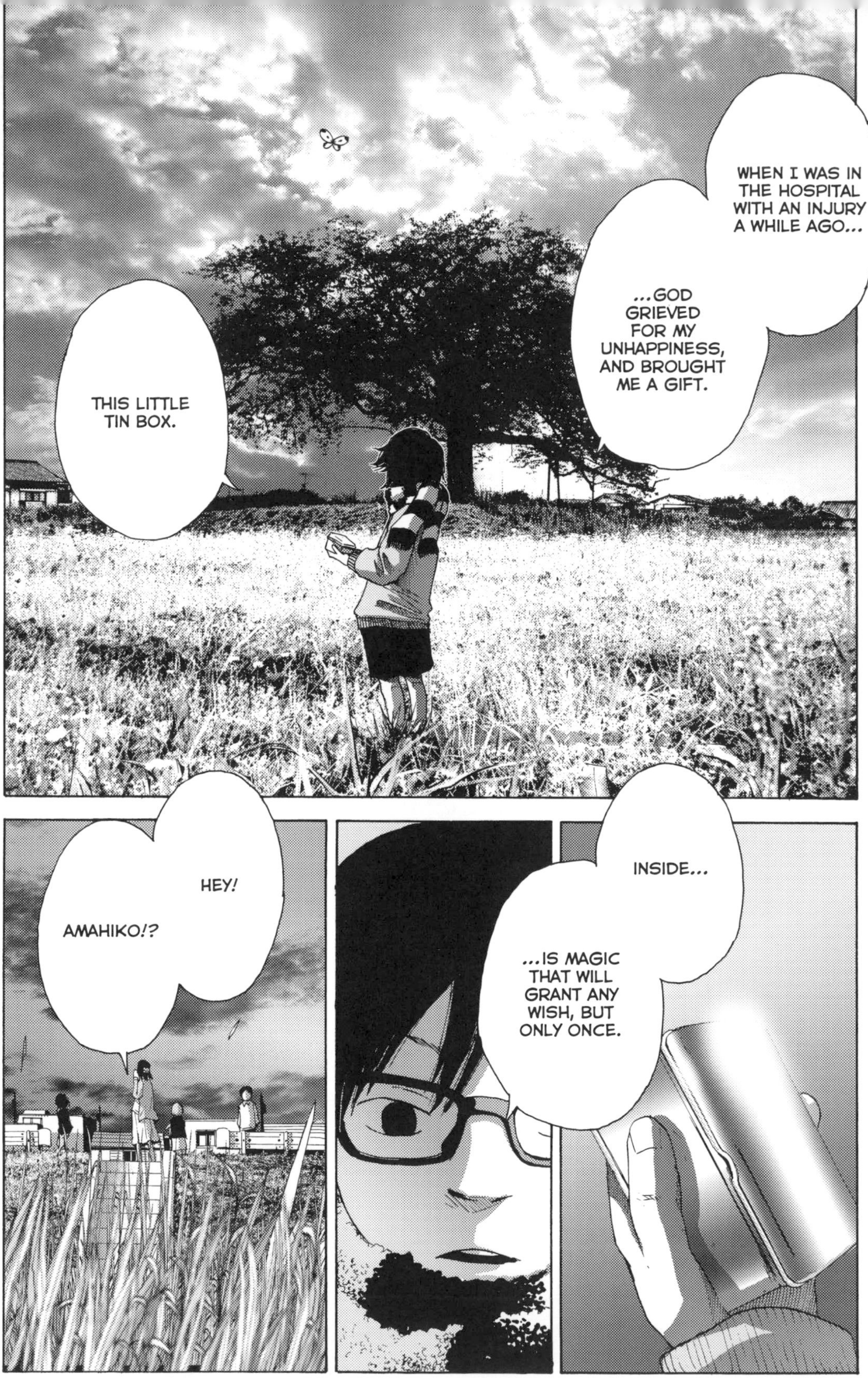
WHEN I WAS IN THE HOSPITAL WITH AN INJURY A WHILE AGO...
...GOD GRIEVED FOR MY UNHAPPINESS, AND BROUGHT ME A GIFT.
THIS LITTLE TIN BOX.
INSIDE...
...IS MAGIC THAT WILL GRANT ANY WISH, BUT ONLY ONCE.
HEY!
AMAHIKO!?

MY FIRST MOVE TO A NEW SCHOOL. A NEW TOWN.

WHAT OF IT?

THE SIGHTS AND PEOPLE ARE THE SAME WHEREVER YOU GO, RIGHT?

SPRING. THE FIFTH GRADE.

AND FOR WHATEVER REASON, TODAY I AM ONCE AGAIN MYSELF.

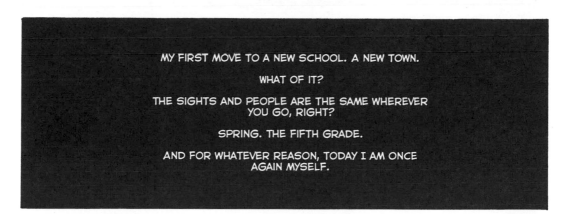

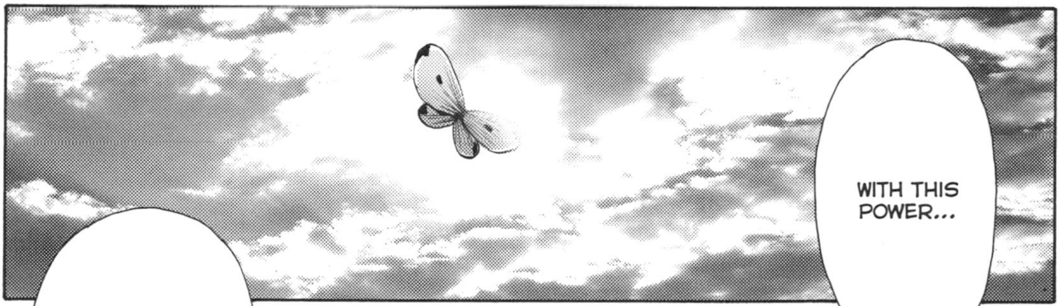
WITH THIS POWER...

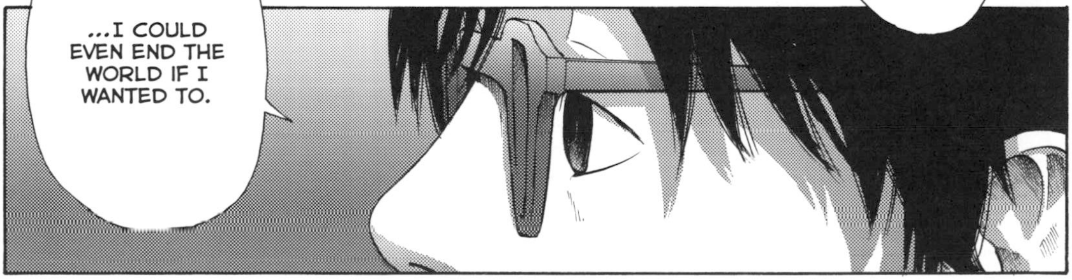
...I COULD EVEN END THE WORLD IF I WANTED TO.

CHAPTER 1

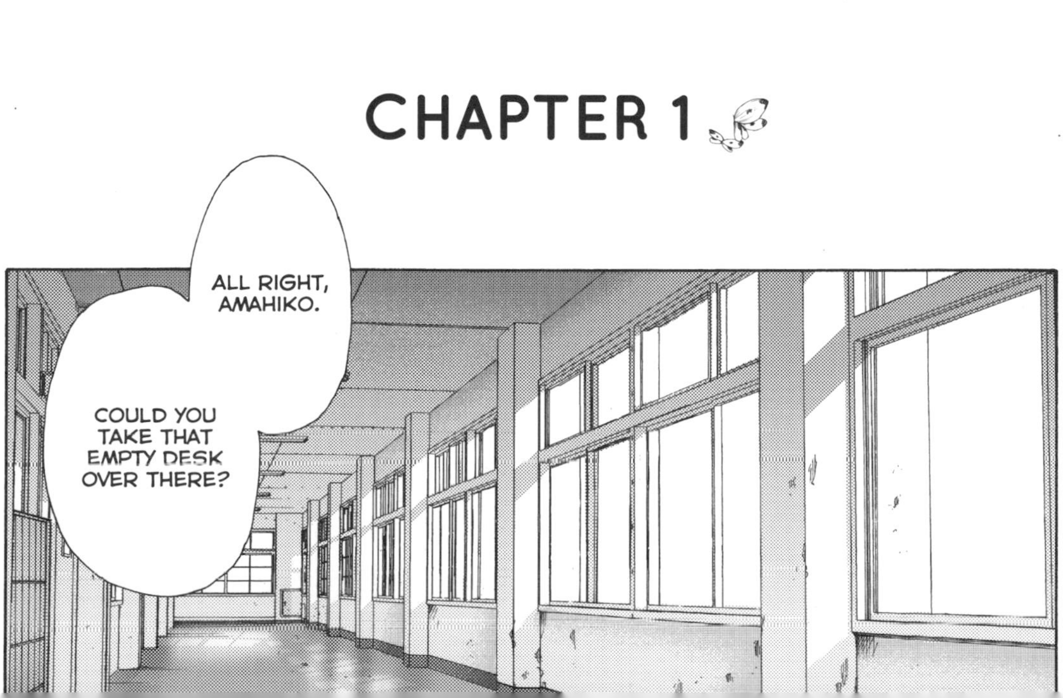
ALL RIGHT, AMAHIKO.
COULD YOU TAKE THAT EMPTY DESK OVER THERE?

THERE ARE TWO EMPTY DESKS.

OH, I'M SORRY.

YOURS IS THE BRAND NEW ONE.

HI.

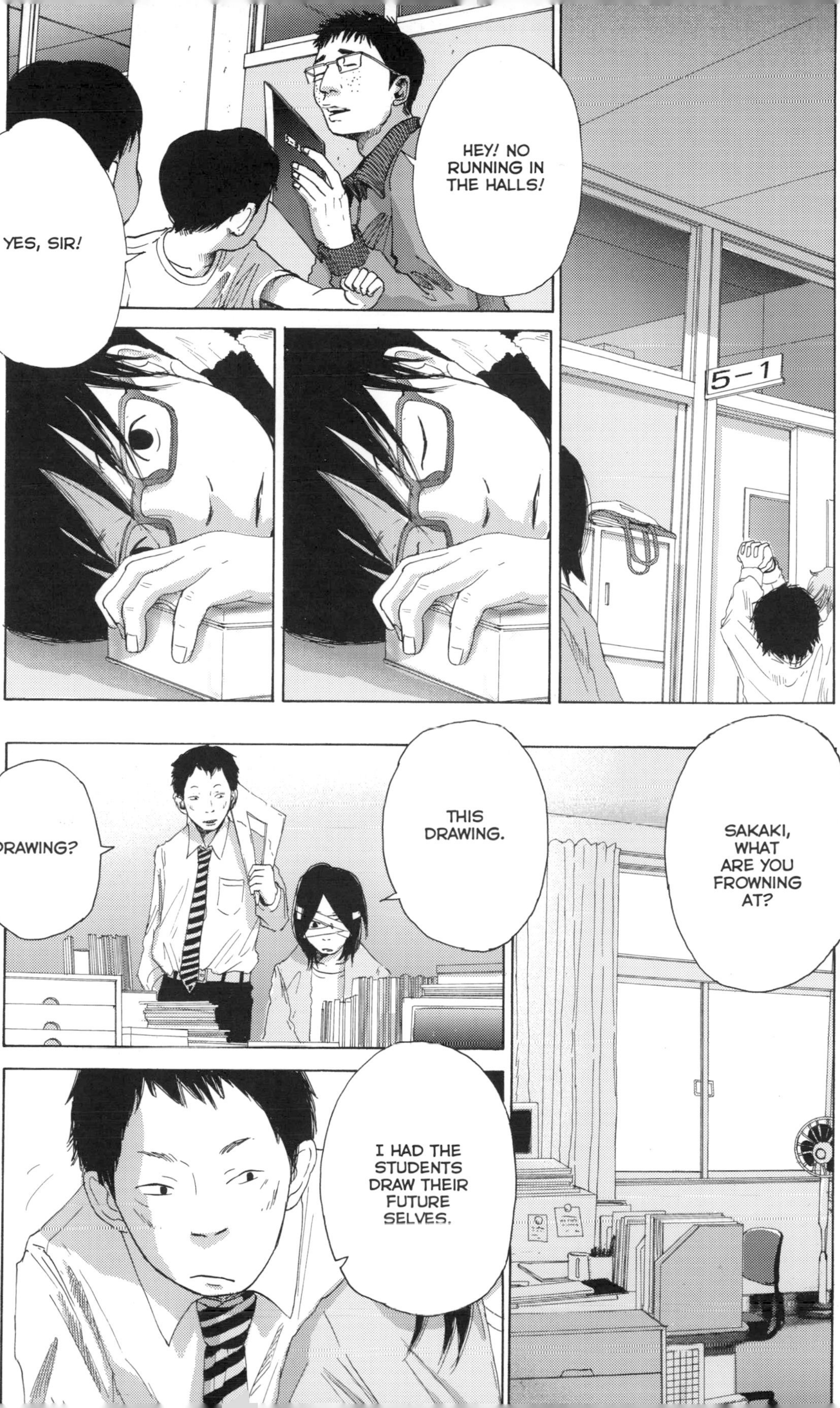
HEY! NO RUNNING IN THE HALLS!
YES, SIR!
5-1
SAKAKI, WHAT ARE YOU FROWNING AT?
THIS DRAWING.
DRAWING?
I HAD THE STUDENTS DRAW THEIR FUTURE SELVES.

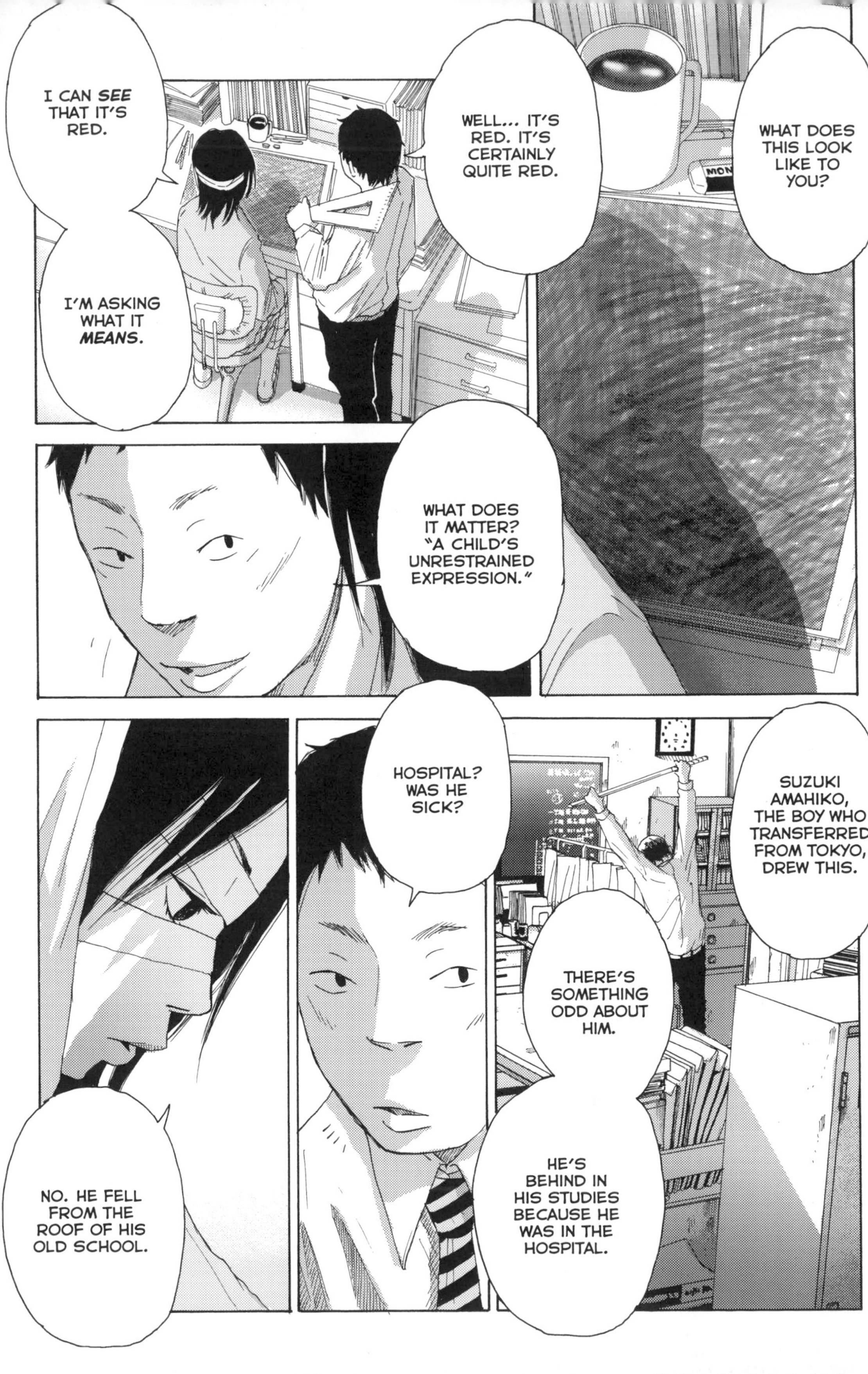
WHAT DOES THIS LOOK LIKE TO YOU?
WELL... IT'S RED. IT'S CERTAINLY QUITE RED.
I CAN *SEE* THAT IT'S RED.
I'M ASKING WHAT IT ***MEANS***.
WHAT DOES IT MATTER? "A CHILD'S UNRESTRAINED EXPRESSION."
SUZUKI AMAHIKO, THE BOY WHO TRANSFERRED FROM TOKYO, DREW THIS.
THERE'S SOMETHING ODD ABOUT HIM.
HE'S BEHIND IN HIS STUDIES BECAUSE HE WAS IN THE HOSPITAL.
HOSPITAL? WAS HE SICK?
NO. HE FELL FROM THE ROOF OF HIS OLD SCHOOL.

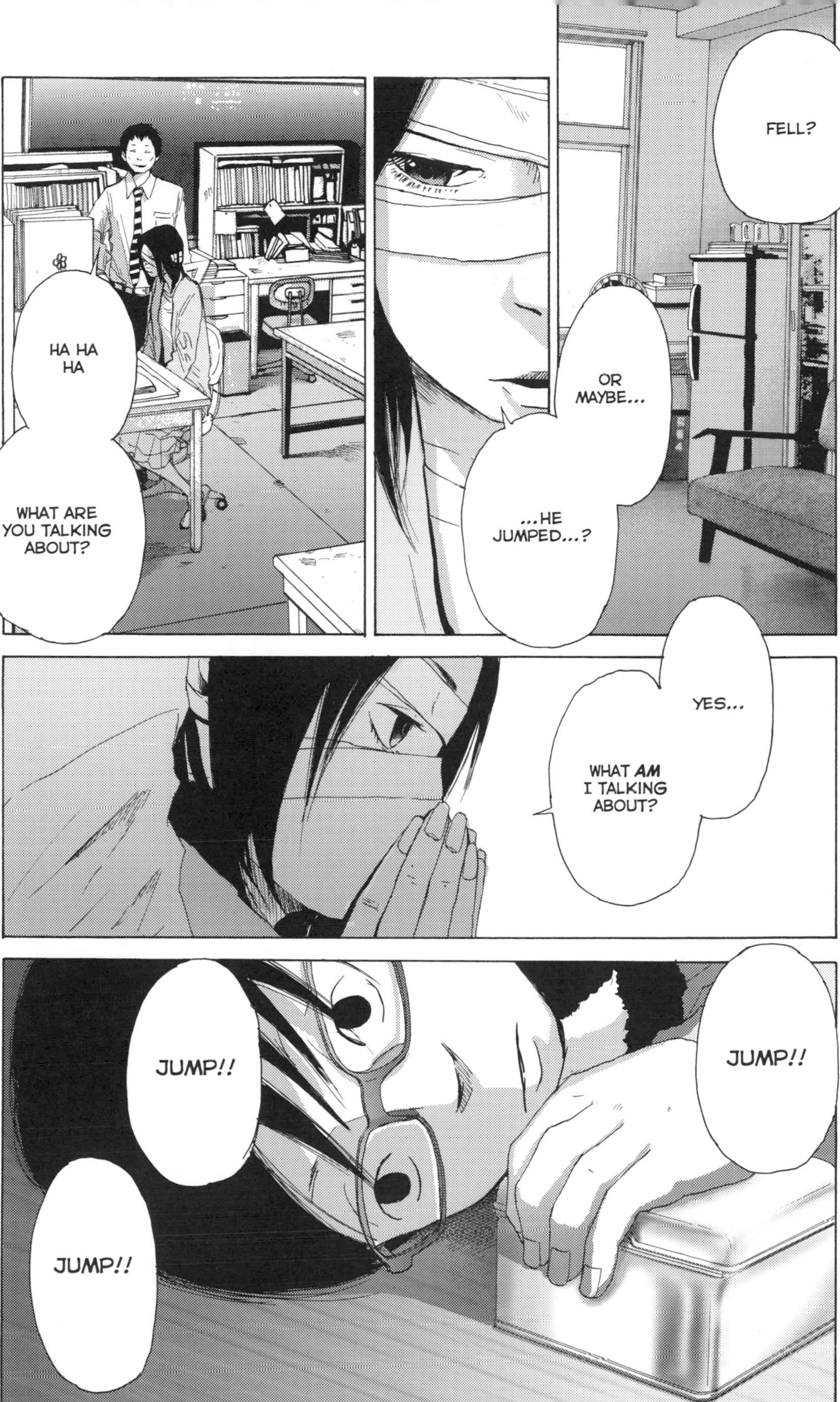
FELL?
OR MAYBE...
...HE JUMPED...?
HA HA HA
WHAT ARE YOU TALKING ABOUT?
YES...
WHAT *AM* I TALKING ABOUT?
JUMP!!
JUMP!!
JUMP!!

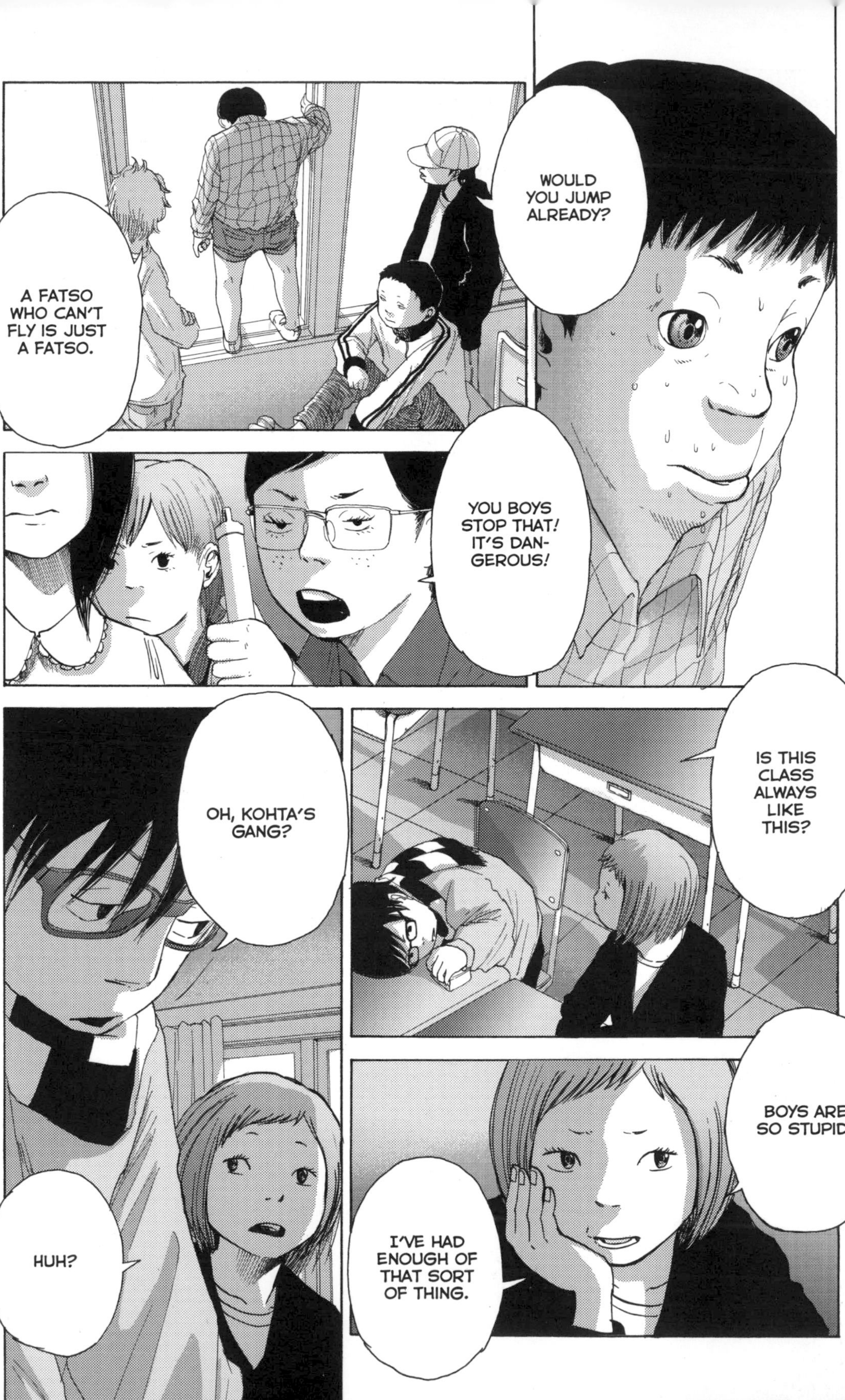
WOULD YOU JUMP ALREADY?
A FATSO WHO CAN'T FLY IS JUST A FATSO.
YOU BOYS STOP THAT! IT'S DAN-GEROUS!
IS THIS CLASS ALWAYS LIKE THIS?
BOYS ARE SO STUPID.
I'VE HAD ENOUGH OF THAT SORT OF THING.
OH, KOHTA'S GANG?
HUH?

THAT'S ENOUGH.

WHAT DO *YOU* WANT?

YOU REALLY WANT SOMEONE TO JUMP?

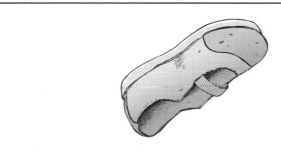

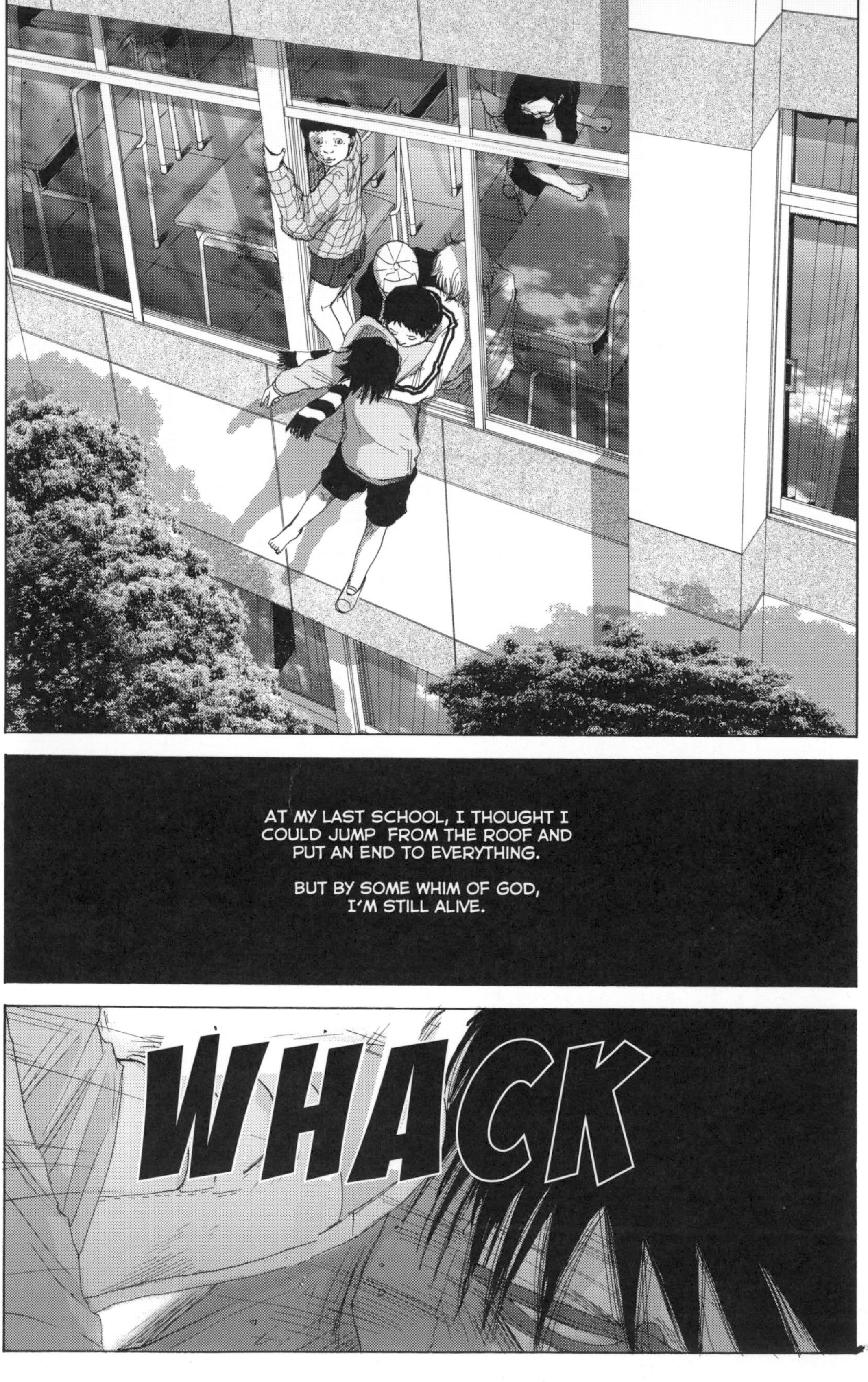
AT MY LAST SCHOOL, I THOUGHT I COULD JUMP FROM THE ROOF AND PUT AN END TO EVERYTHING.
BUT BY SOME WHIM OF GOD, I'M STILL ALIVE.
WHACK

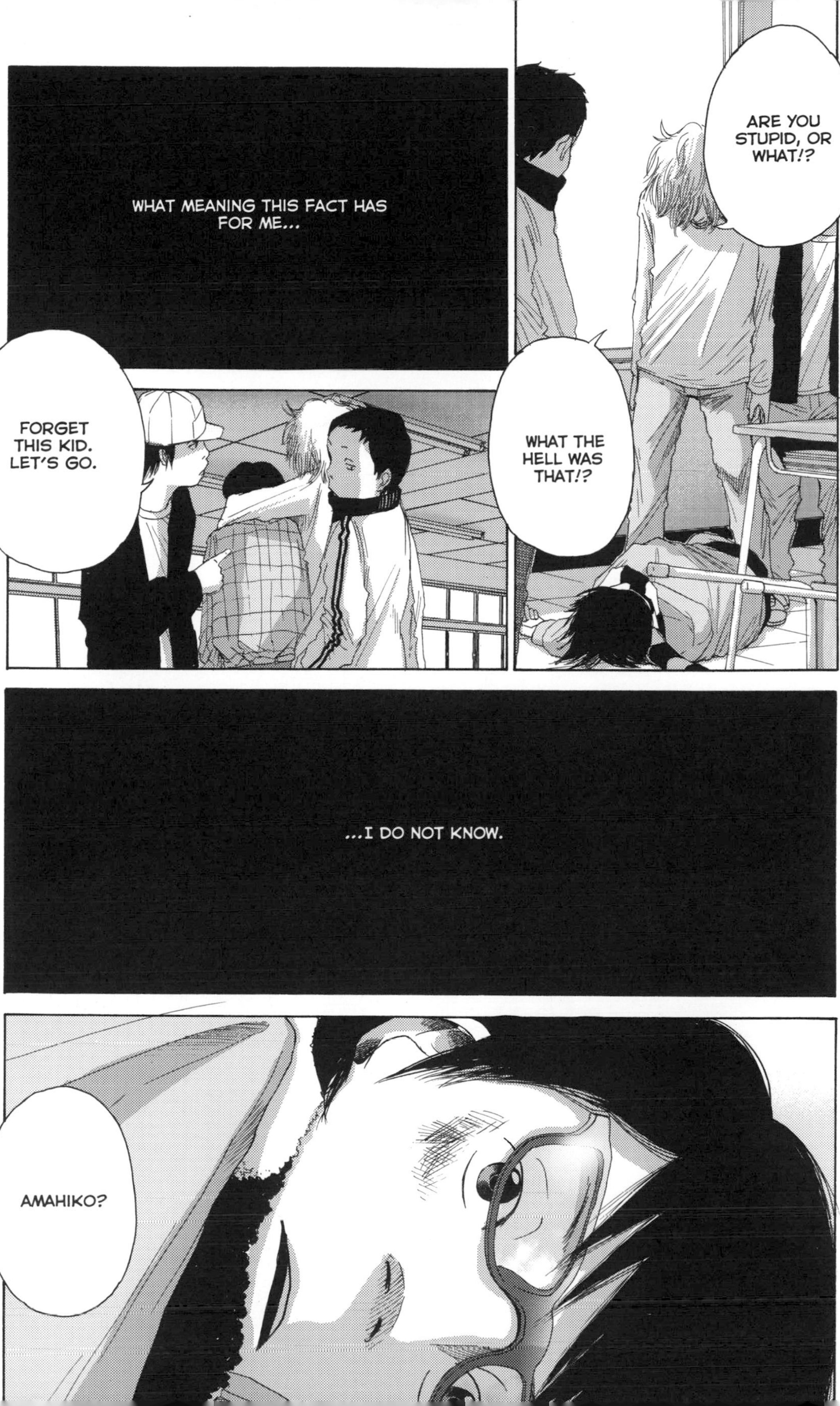
ARE YOU STUPID, OR WHAT!?
WHAT THE HELL WAS THAT!?
WHAT MEANING THIS FACT HAS FOR ME...
FORGET THIS KID. LET'S GO.
...I DO NOT KNOW.
AMAHIKO?

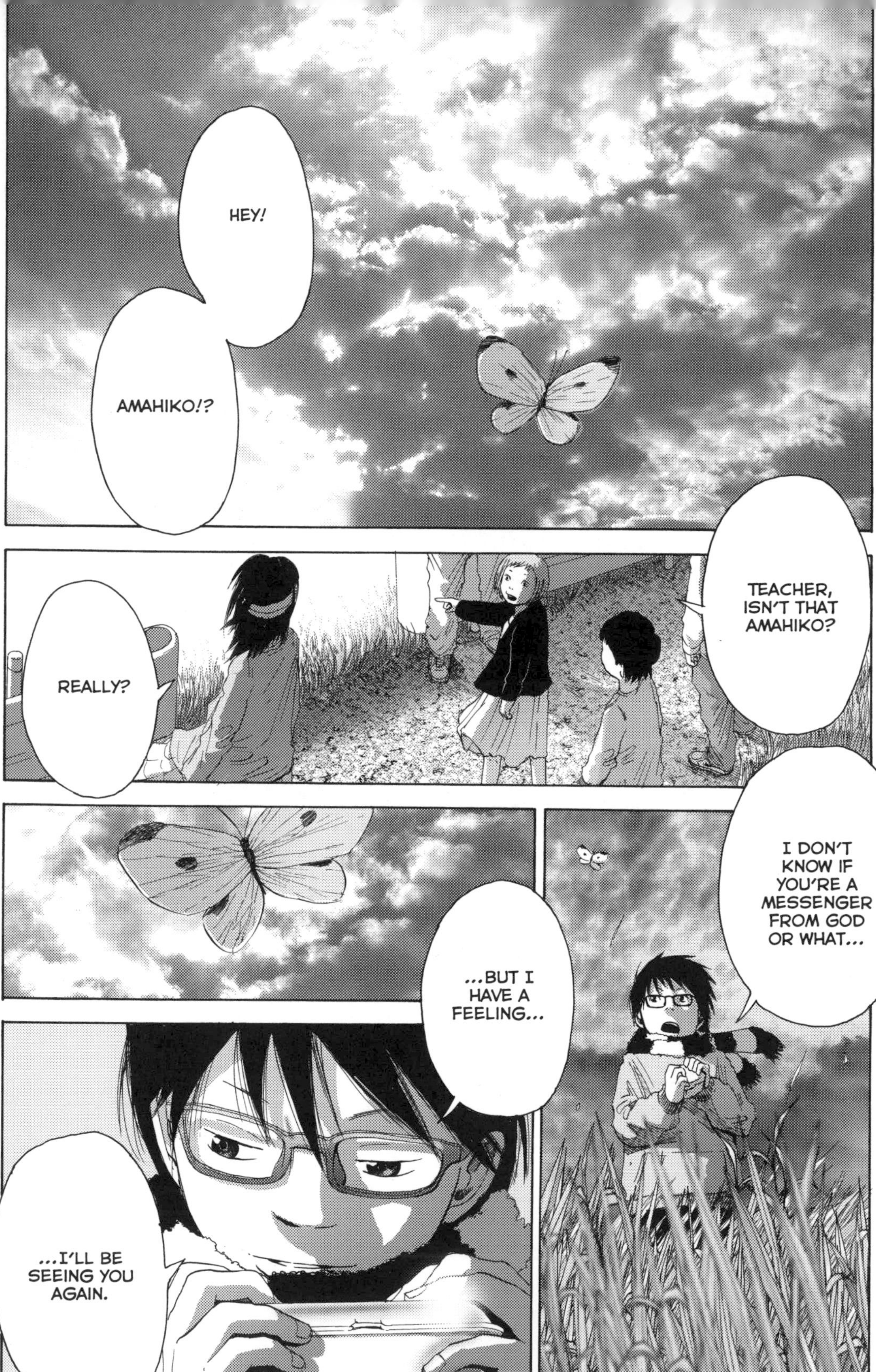
HEY!
AMAHIKO!?
TEACHER, ISN'T THAT AMAHIKO?
REALLY?
I DON'T KNOW IF YOU'RE A MESSENGER FROM GOD OR WHAT...
...BUT I HAVE A FEELING...
...I'LL BE SEEING YOU AGAIN.

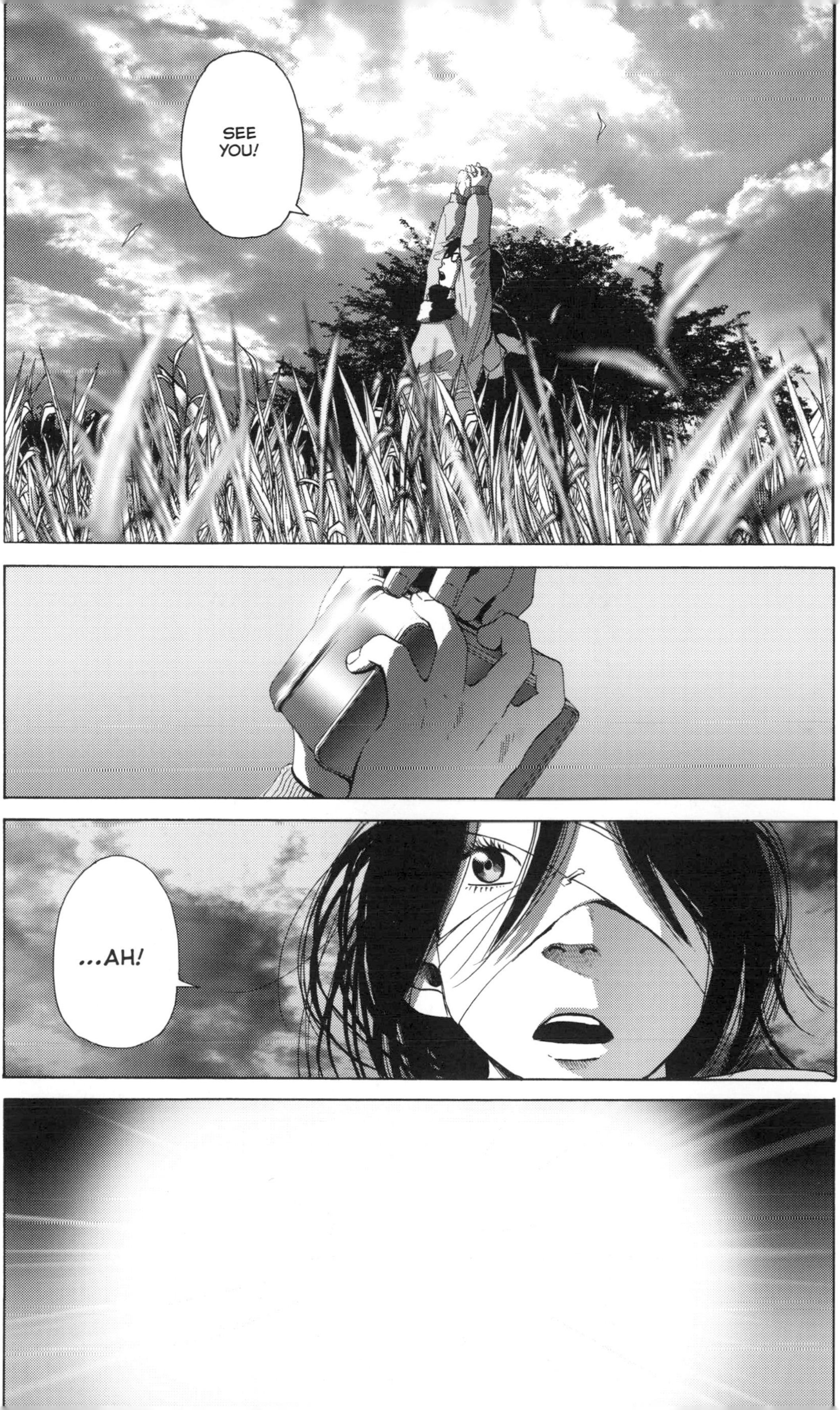
SEE YOU!
...AH!

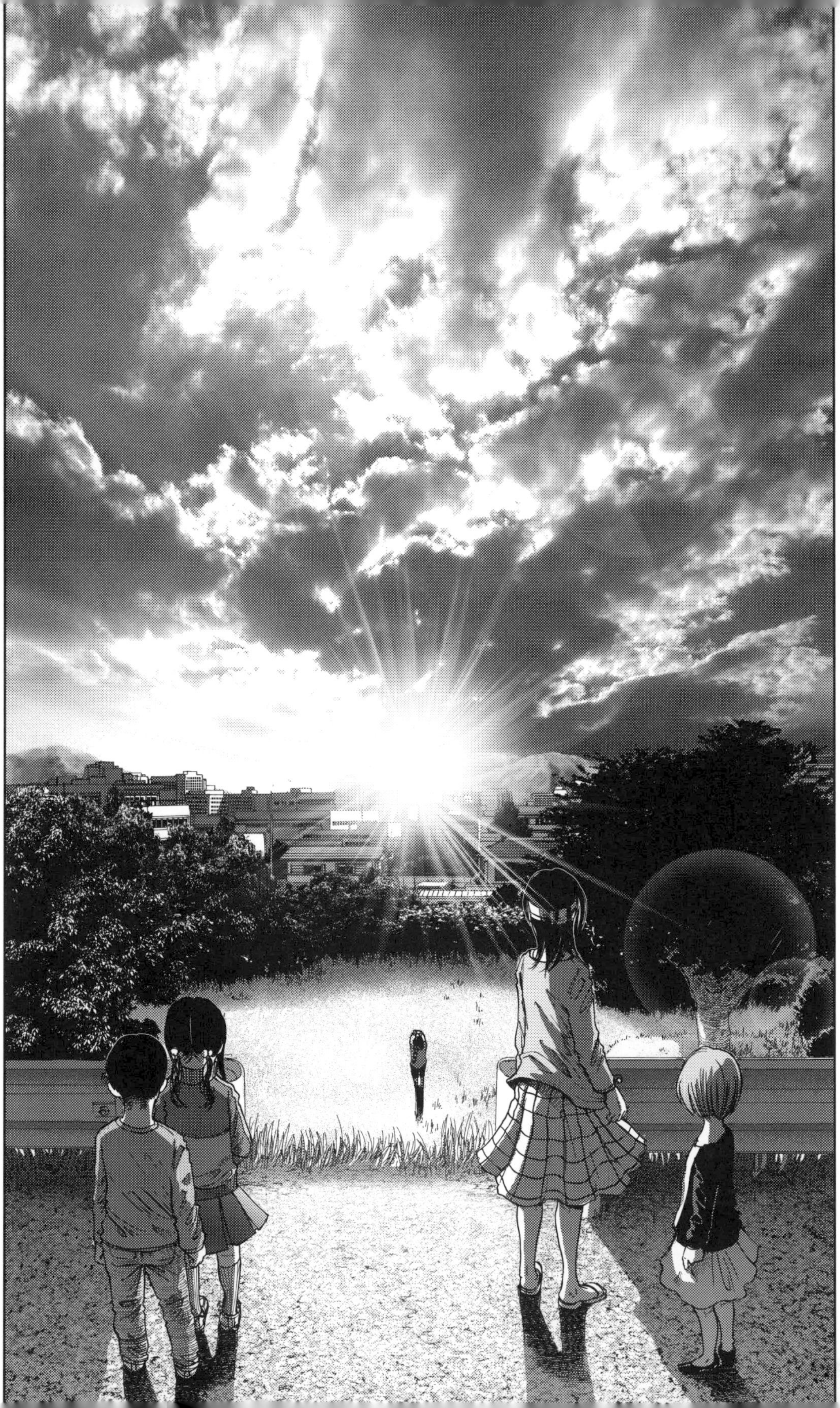

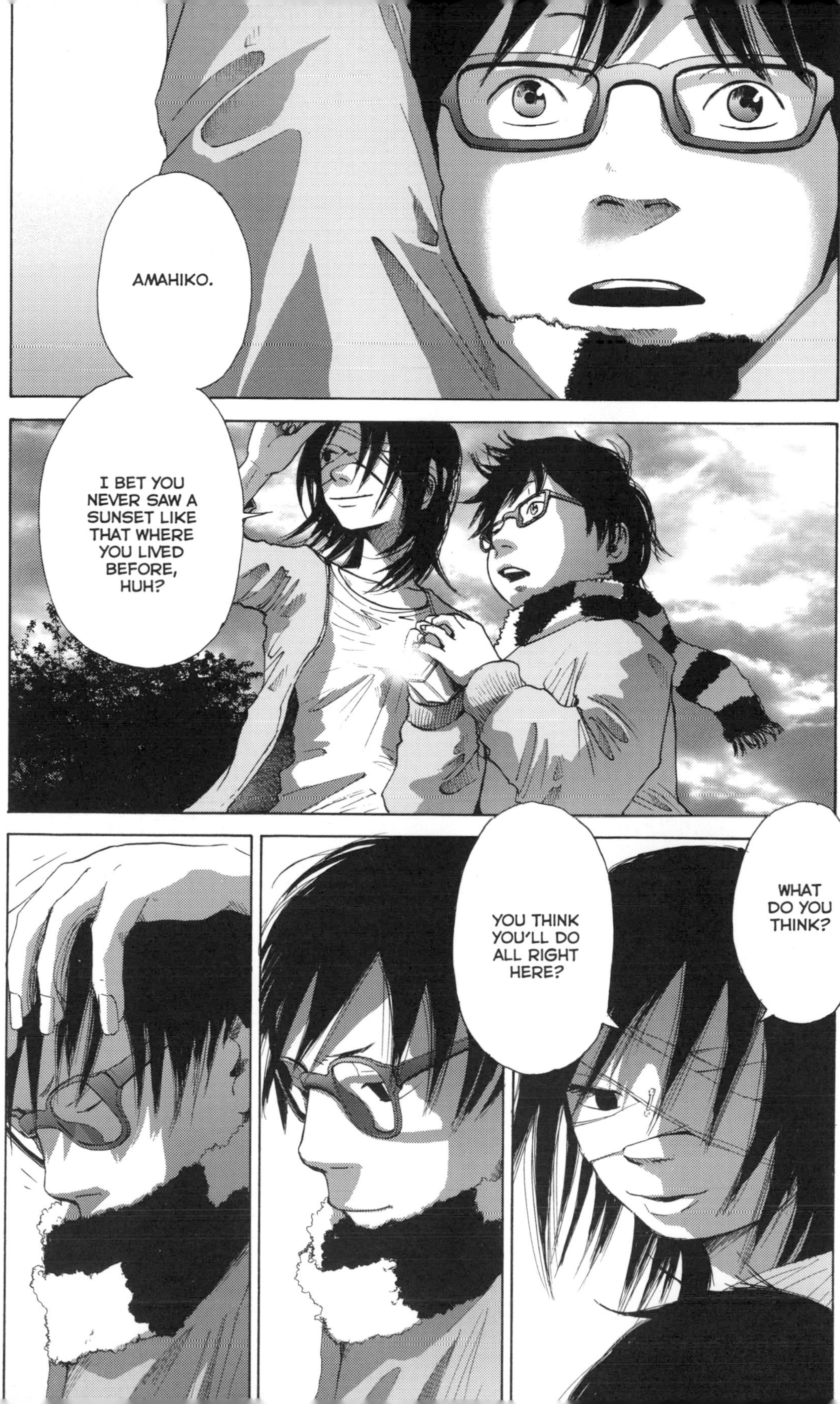
AMAHIKO.
I BET YOU NEVER SAW A SUNSET LIKE THAT WHERE YOU LIVED BEFORE, HUH?
WHAT DO YOU THINK?
YOU THINK YOU'LL DO ALL RIGHT HERE?

LET'S HANG IN THERE.

QUIETLY I RESPONDED, "YES."

I FELT LIKE I WAS TELLING A BIT OF A LIE.

BUT THAT SUNSET...

...WAS ENOUGH TO MAKE ME FEEL...

...I COULD FORGET ABOUT ALL THAT STUFF.

RIGHT.

SHALL WE GO BACK TO CLASS?

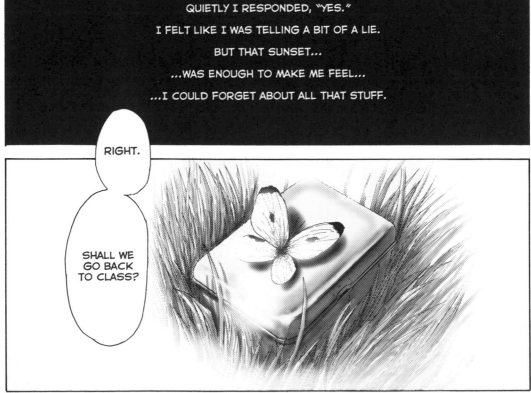

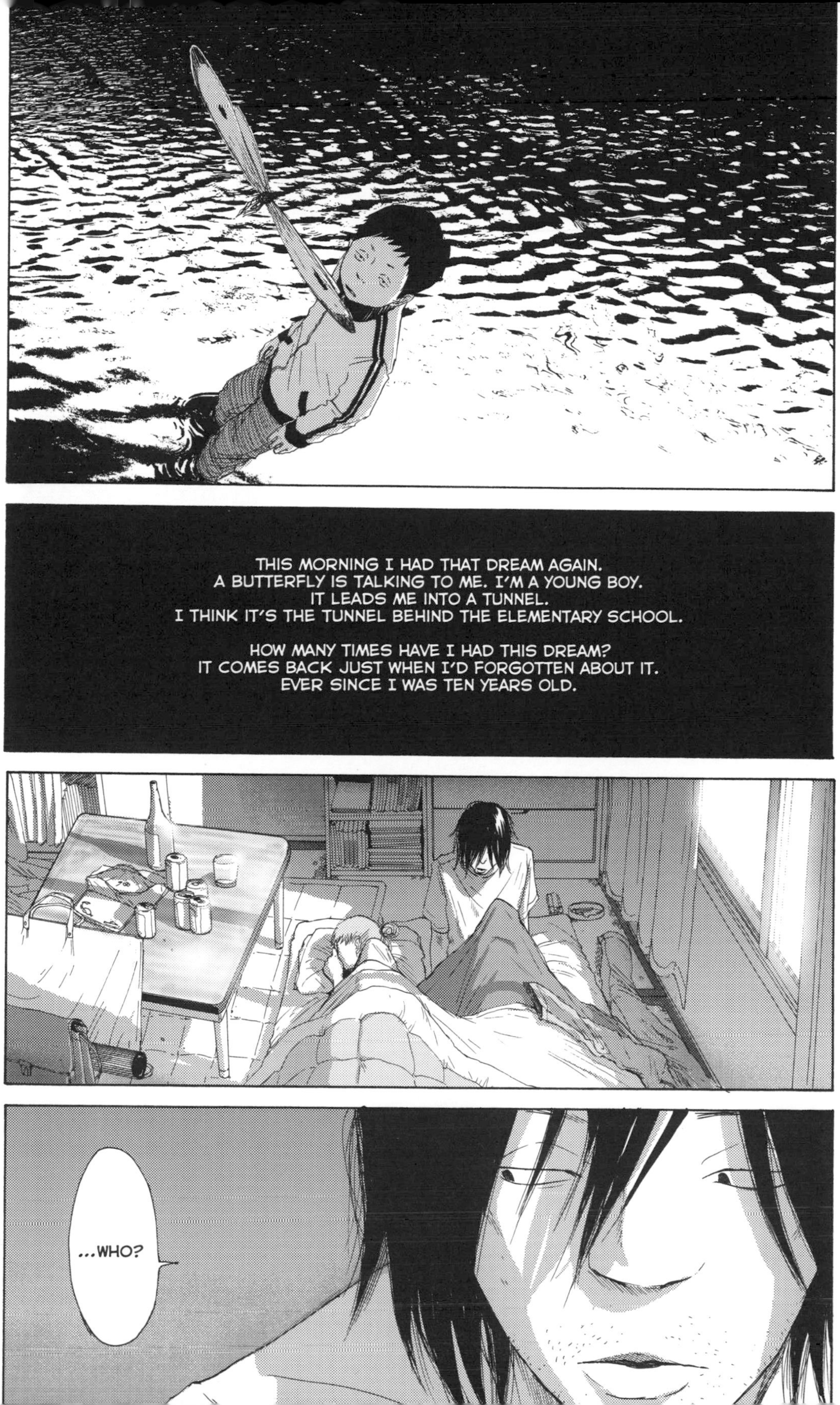
THIS MORNING I HAD THAT DREAM AGAIN.
A BUTTERFLY IS TALKING TO ME. I'M A YOUNG BOY.
IT LEADS ME INTO A TUNNEL.
I THINK IT'S THE TUNNEL BEHIND THE ELEMENTARY SCHOOL.
HOW MANY TIMES HAVE I HAD THIS DREAM?
IT COMES BACK JUST WHEN I'D FORGOTTEN ABOUT IT.
EVER SINCE I WAS TEN YEARS OLD.
...WHO?

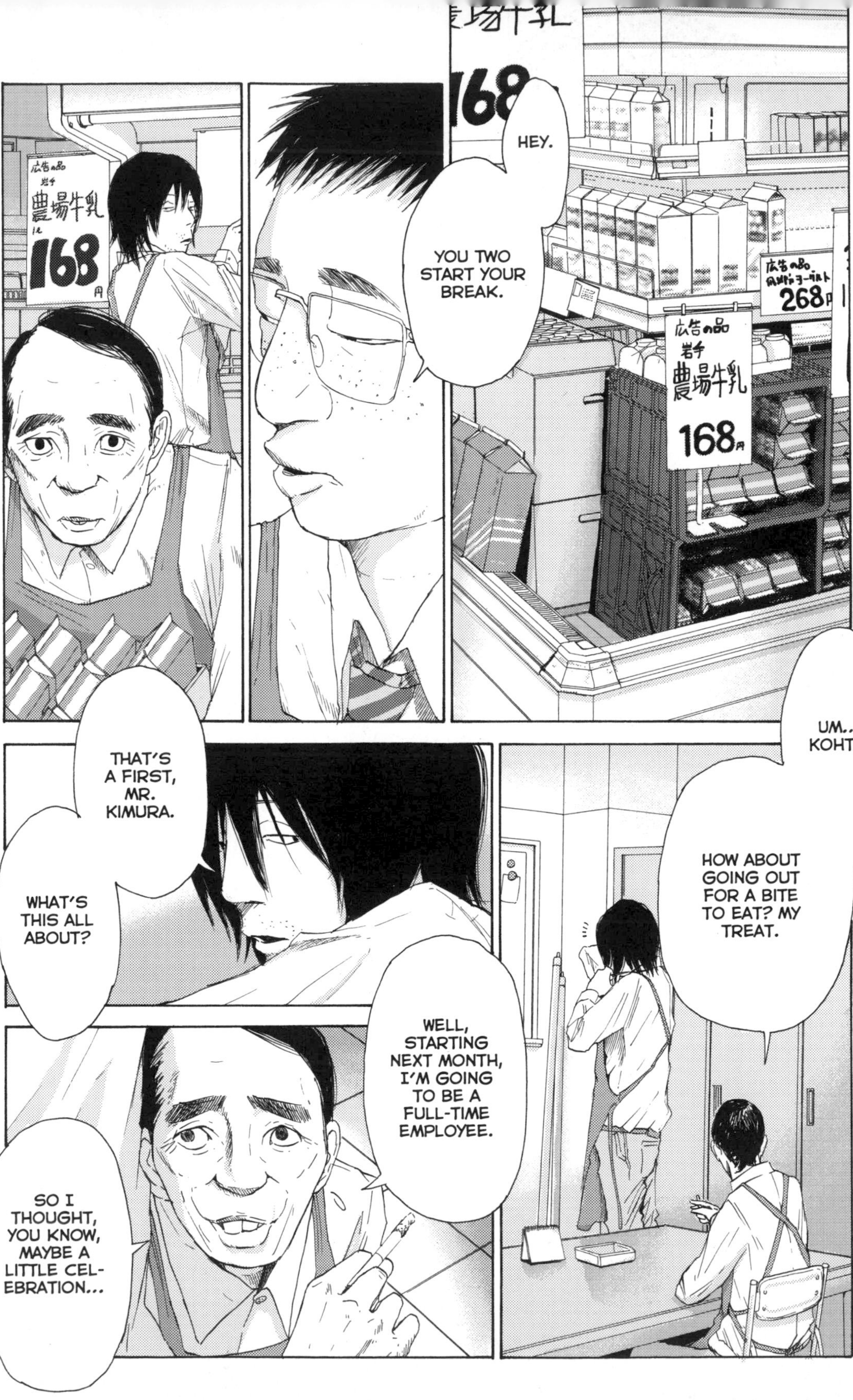

広告の品
岩手
農場牛乳
168円
268円
HEY.
YOU TWO START YOUR BREAK.
UM... KOHTA.
HOW ABOUT GOING OUT FOR A BITE TO EAT? MY TREAT.
THAT'S A FIRST, MR. KIMURA.
WHAT'S THIS ALL ABOUT?
WELL, STARTING NEXT MONTH, I'M GOING TO BE A FULL-TIME EMPLOYEE.
SO I THOUGHT, YOU KNOW, MAYBE A LITTLE CEL-EBRATION...

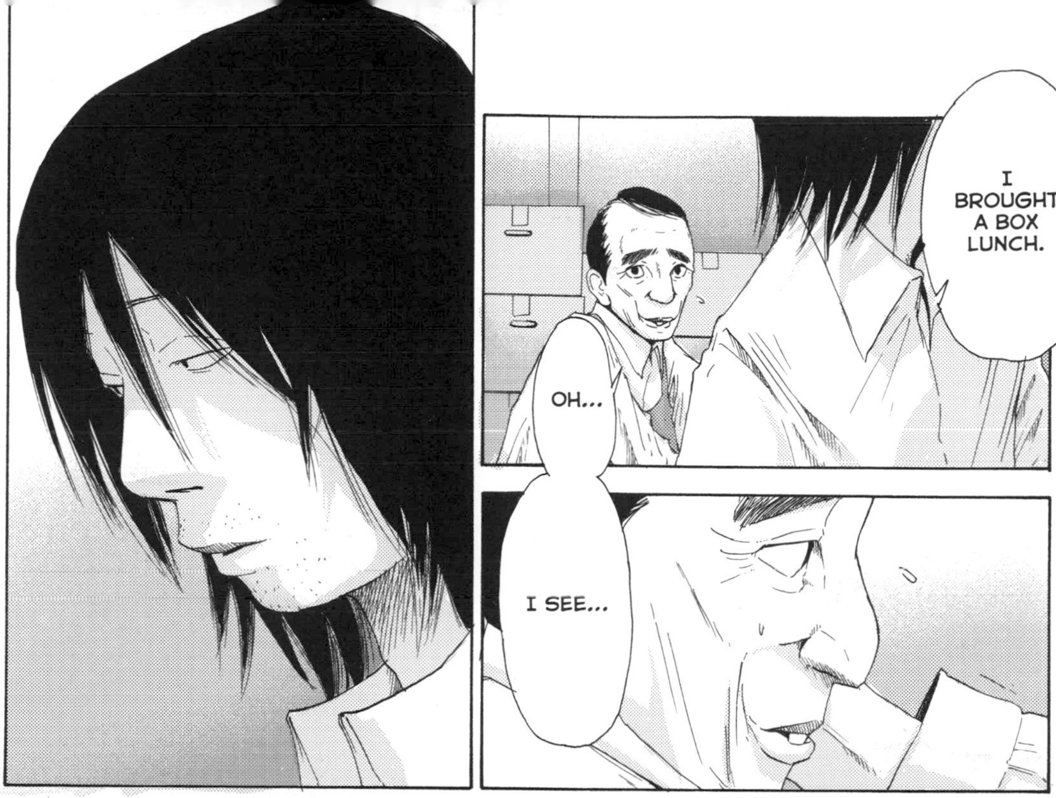
I BROUGHT A BOX LUNCH.
OH...
I SEE...

CHAPTER 2

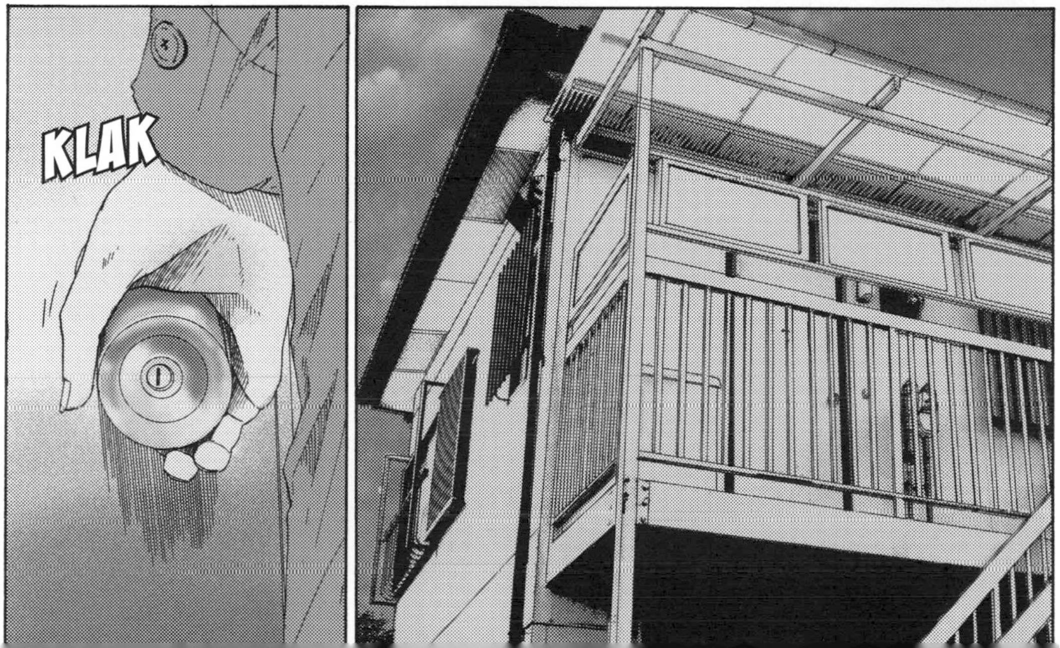
KLAK

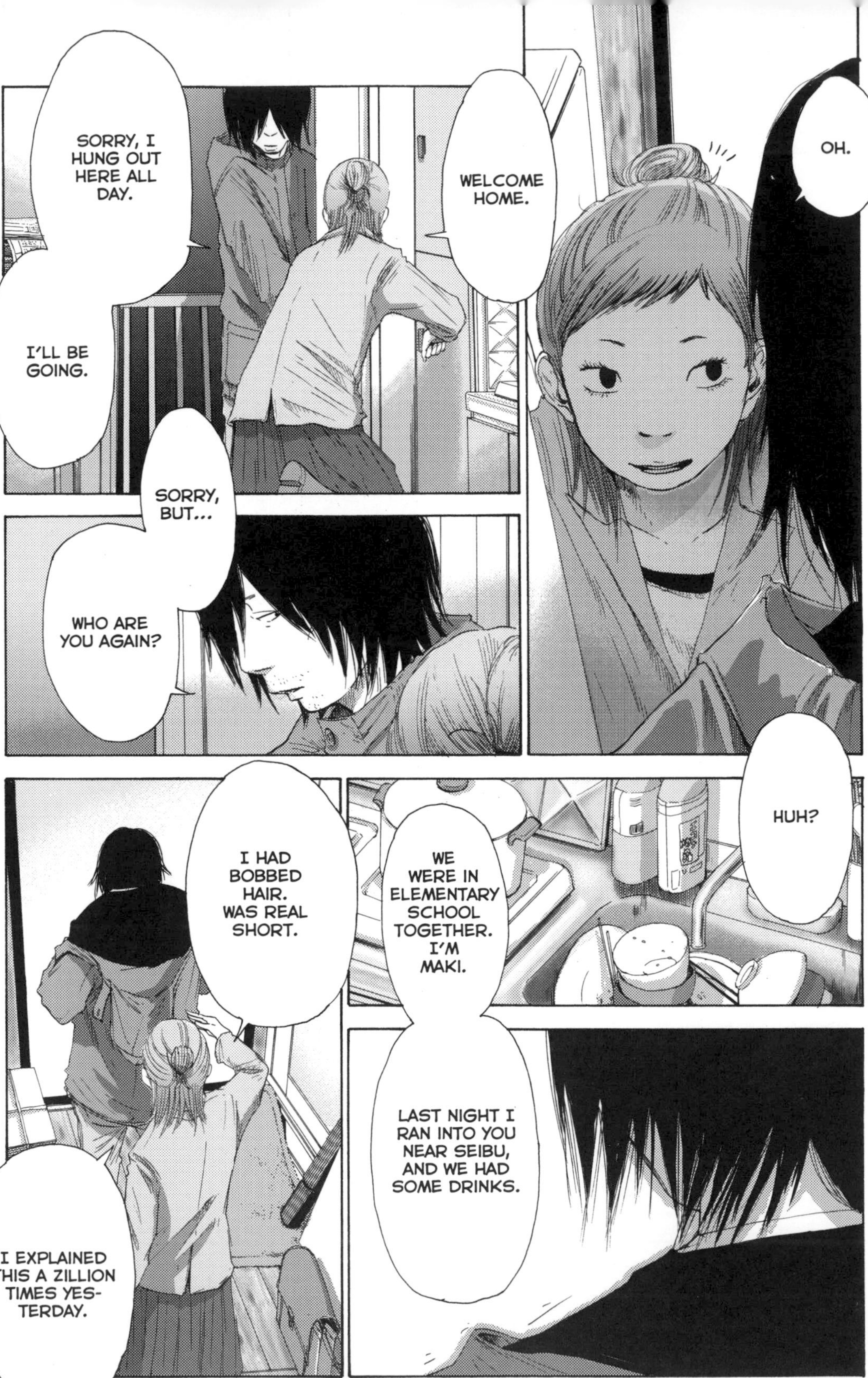
OH.
WELCOME HOME.
SORRY, I HUNG OUT HERE ALL DAY.
I'LL BE GOING.
SORRY, BUT...
WHO ARE YOU AGAIN?
HUH?
WE WERE IN ELEMENTARY SCHOOL TOGETHER. I'M MAKI.
LAST NIGHT I RAN INTO YOU NEAR SEIBU, AND WE HAD SOME DRINKS.
I HAD BOBBED HAIR. WAS REAL SHORT.
I EXPLAINED THIS A ZILLION TIMES YESTERDAY.

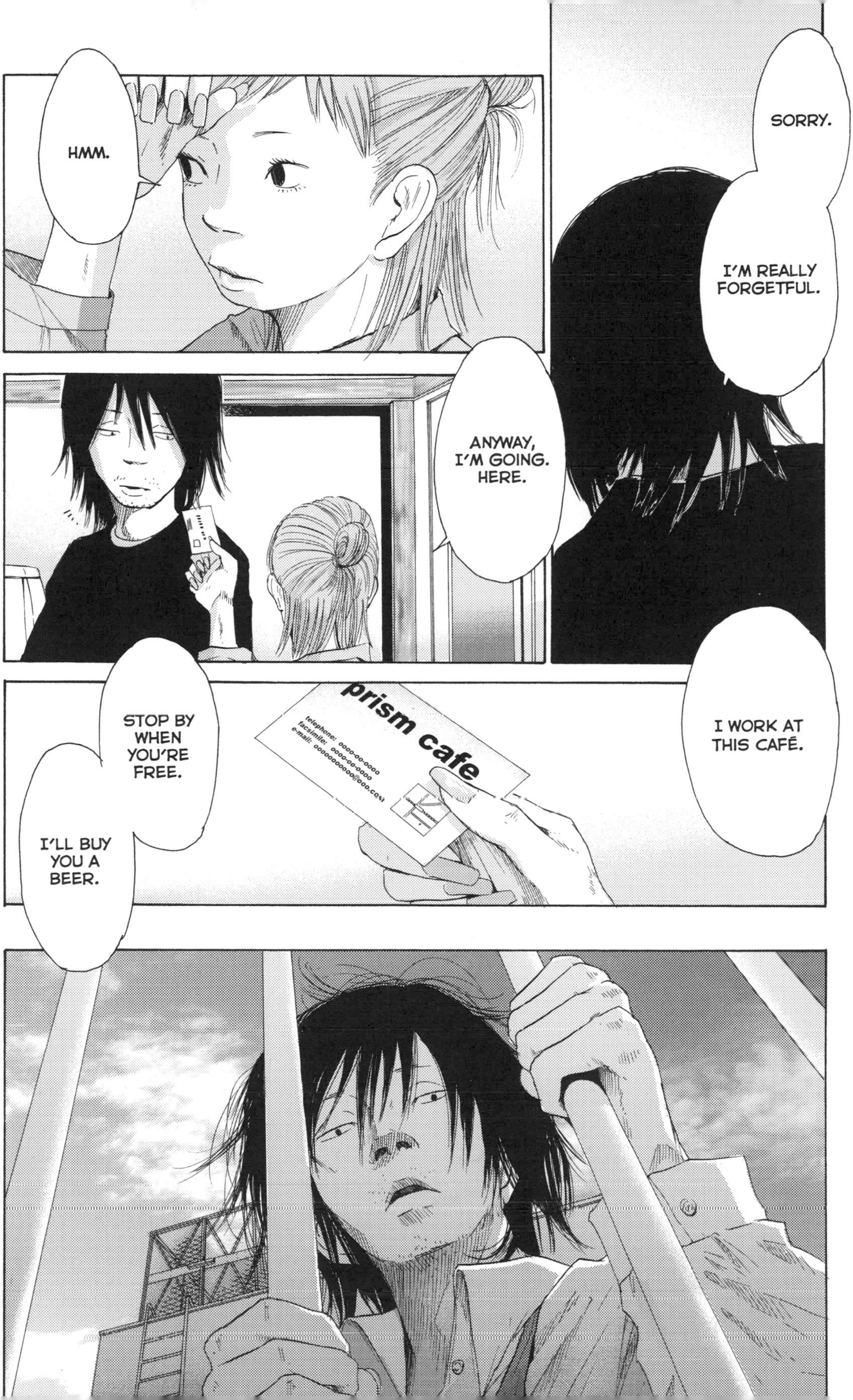

SORRY.
I'M REALLY FORGETFUL.
HMM.
ANYWAY, I'M GOING. HERE.
I WORK AT THIS CAFÉ.
prism cafe
telephone: 0000-00-0000
facsimile: 0000-00-0000
STOP BY WHEN YOU'RE FREE.
I'LL BUY YOU A BEER.

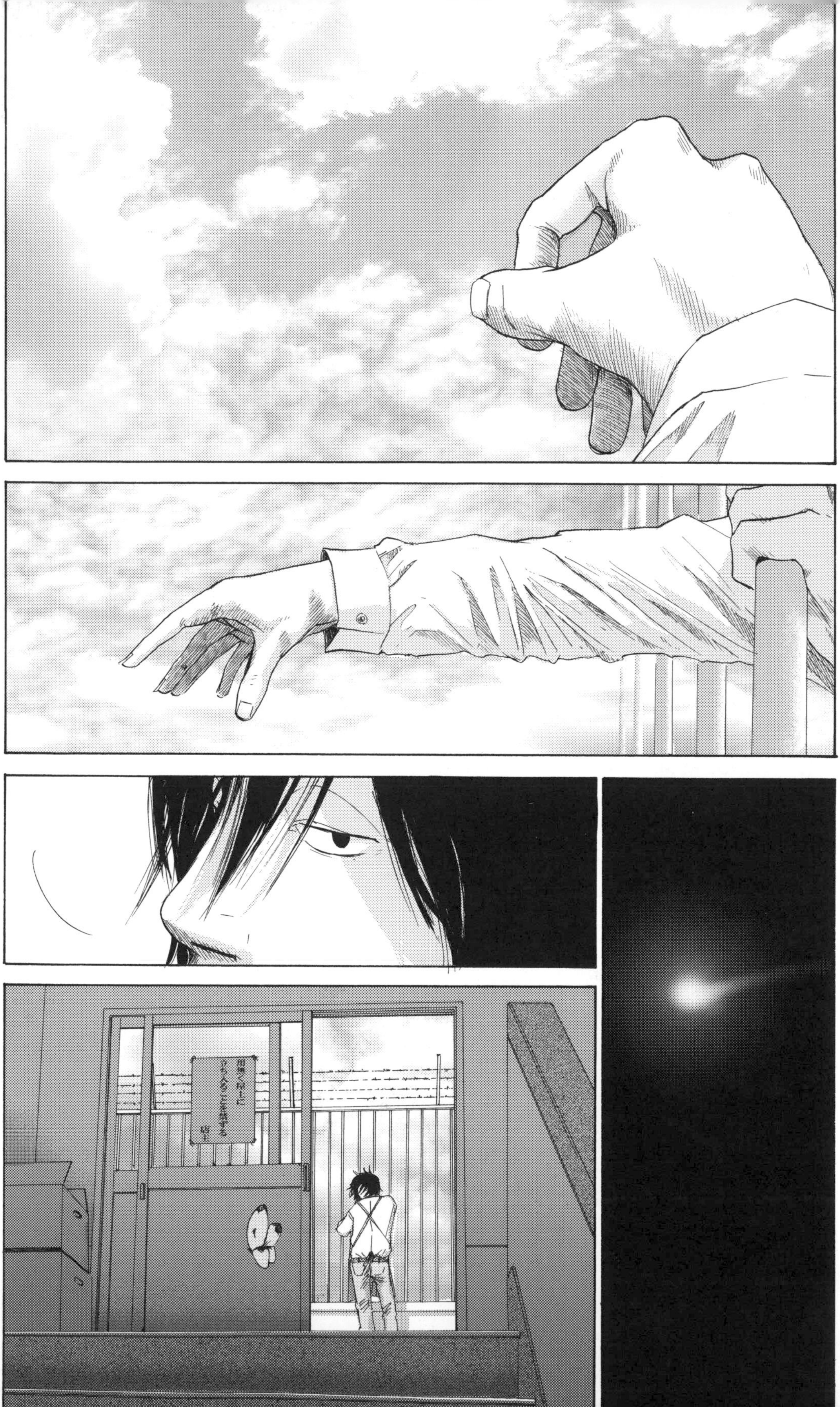
立ち入ることを禁止する
校長

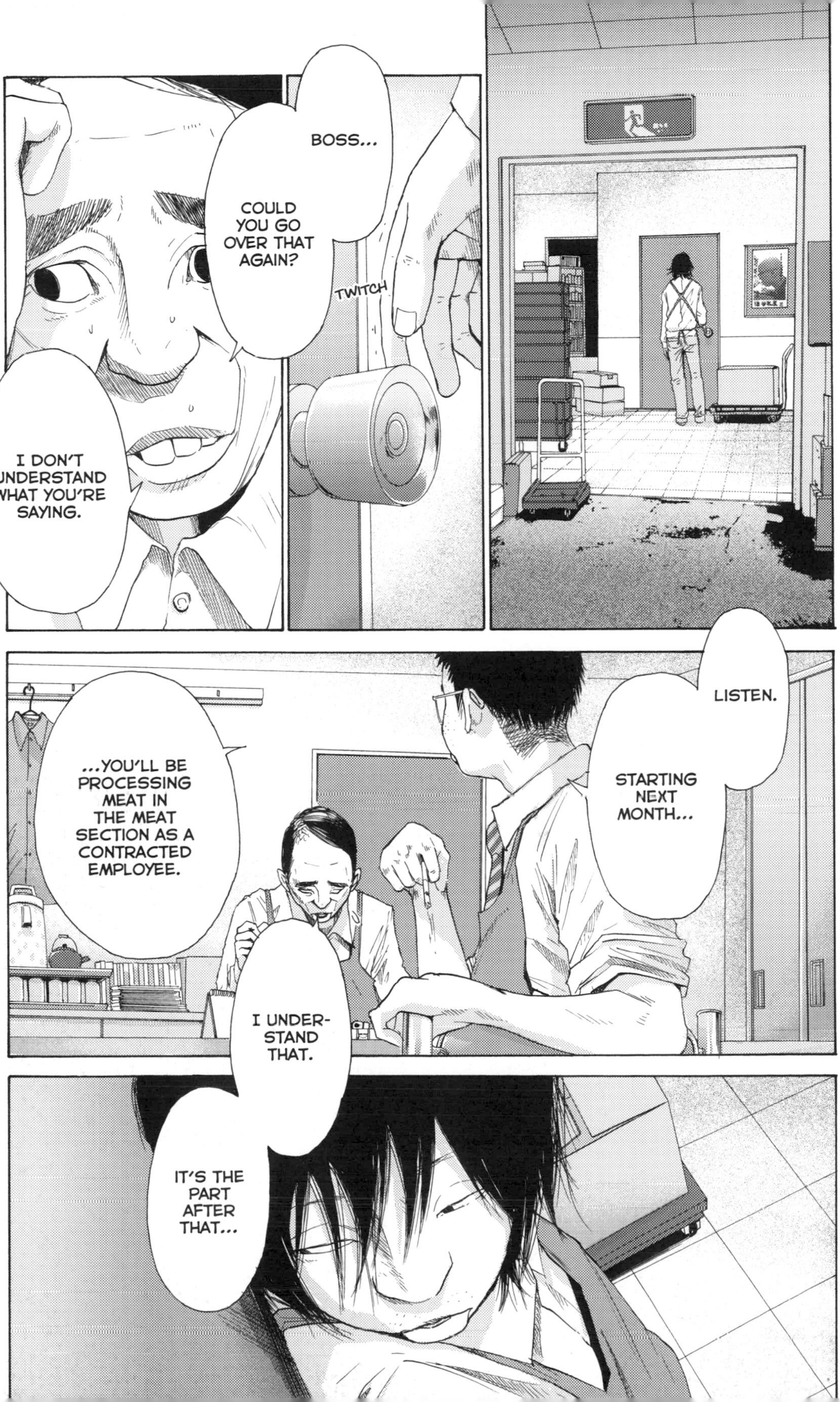
BOSS...
COULD YOU GO OVER THAT AGAIN?
TWITCH
I DON'T UNDERSTAND WHAT YOU'RE SAYING.
LISTEN.
STARTING NEXT MONTH...
...YOU'LL BE PROCESSING MEAT IN THE MEAT SECTION AS A CONTRACTED EMPLOYEE.
I UNDER-STAND THAT.
IT'S THE PART AFTER THAT...

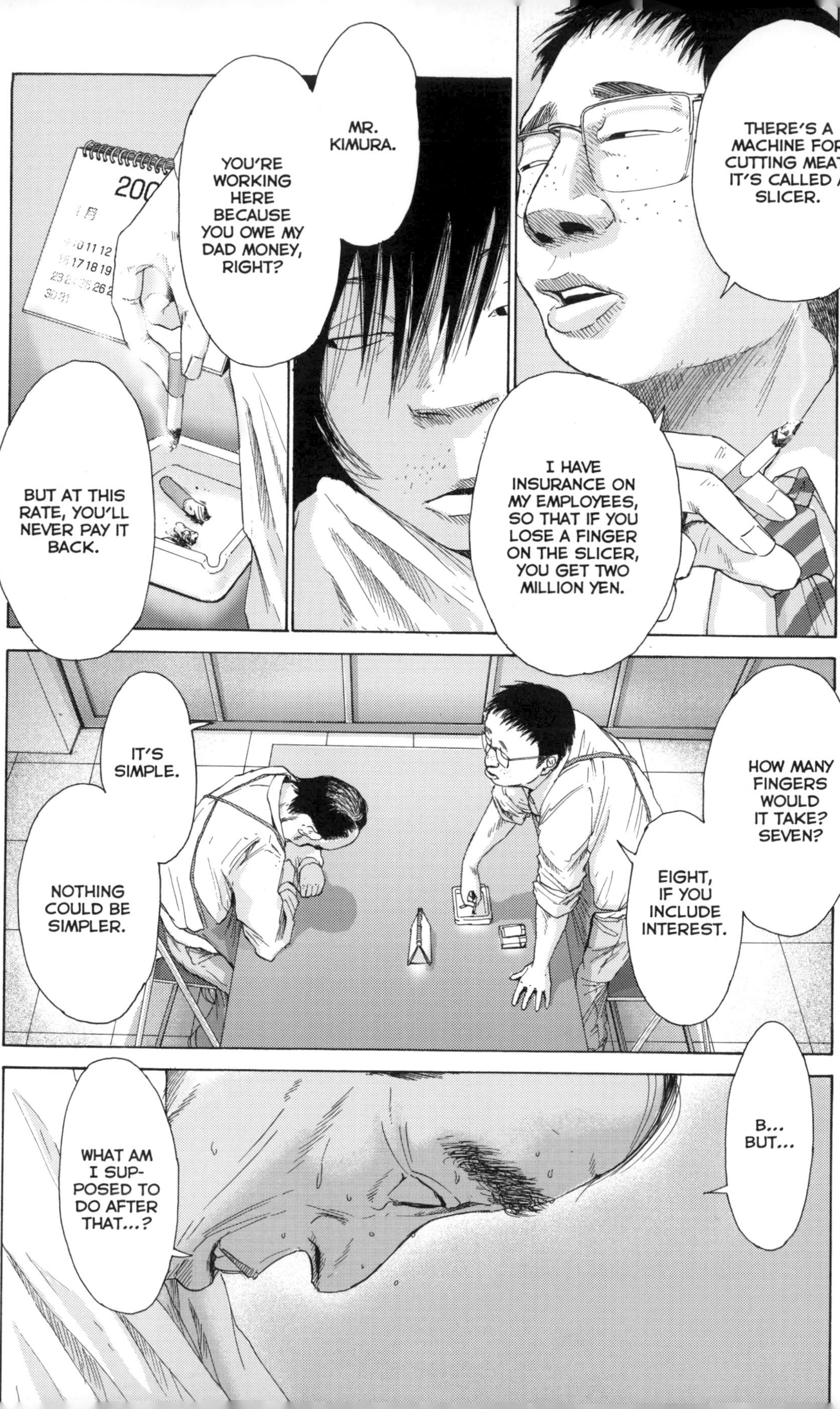
THERE'S A MACHINE FOR CUTTING MEAT. IT'S CALLED A SLICER.
I HAVE INSURANCE ON MY EMPLOYEES, SO THAT IF YOU LOSE A FINGER ON THE SLICER, YOU GET TWO MILLION YEN.
MR. KIMURA.
YOU'RE WORKING HERE BECAUSE YOU OWE MY DAD MONEY, RIGHT?
BUT AT THIS RATE, YOU'LL NEVER PAY IT BACK.
HOW MANY FINGERS WOULD IT TAKE? SEVEN?
EIGHT, IF YOU INCLUDE INTEREST.
IT'S SIMPLE.
NOTHING COULD BE SIMPLER.
B... BUT...
WHAT AM I SUP-POSED TO DO AFTER THAT...?

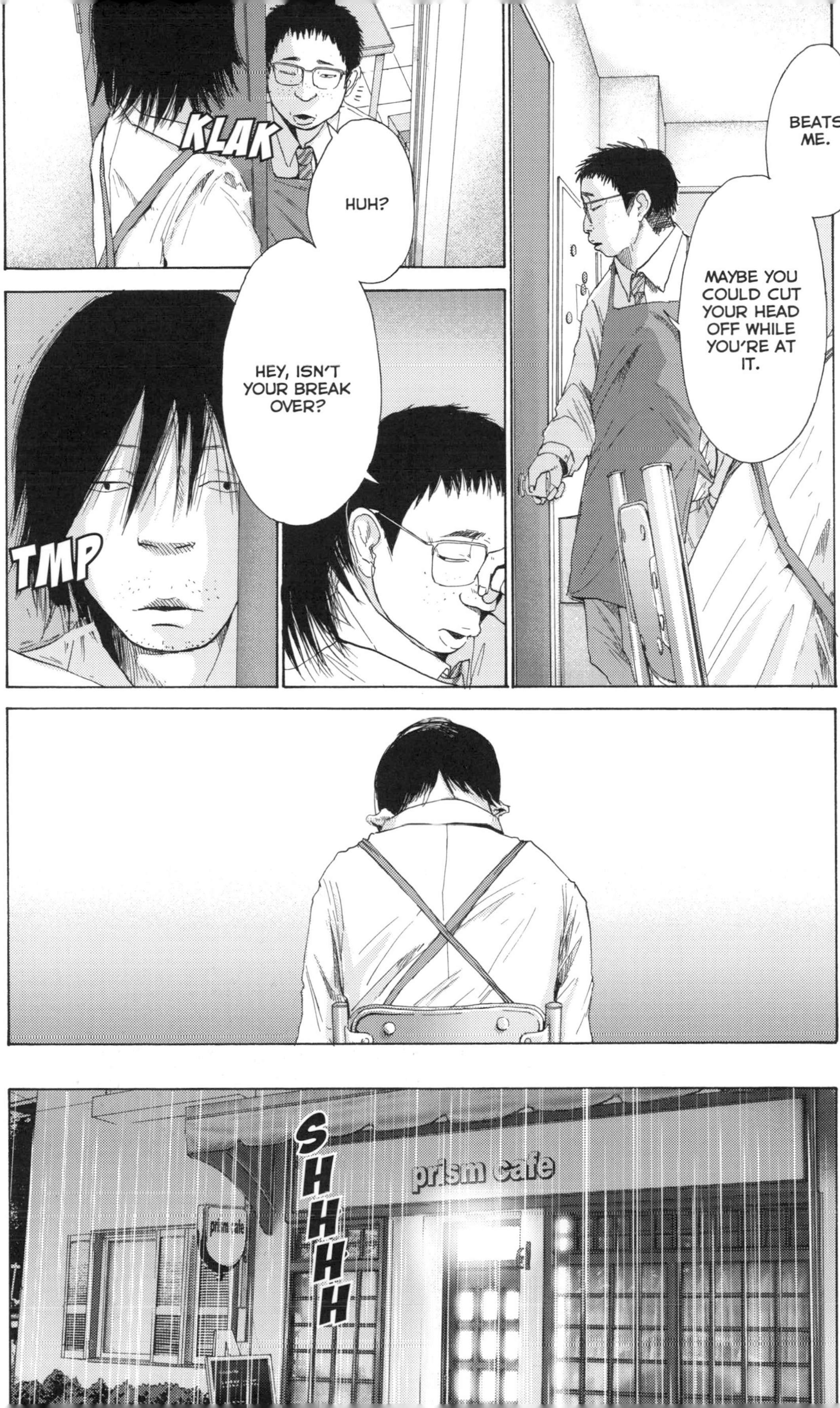
BEATS ME.
MAYBE YOU COULD CUT YOUR HEAD OFF WHILE YOU'RE AT IT.
KLAK
HUH?
HEY, ISN'T YOUR BREAK OVER?
TMP
SHHHHH
prism cafe
prism cafe

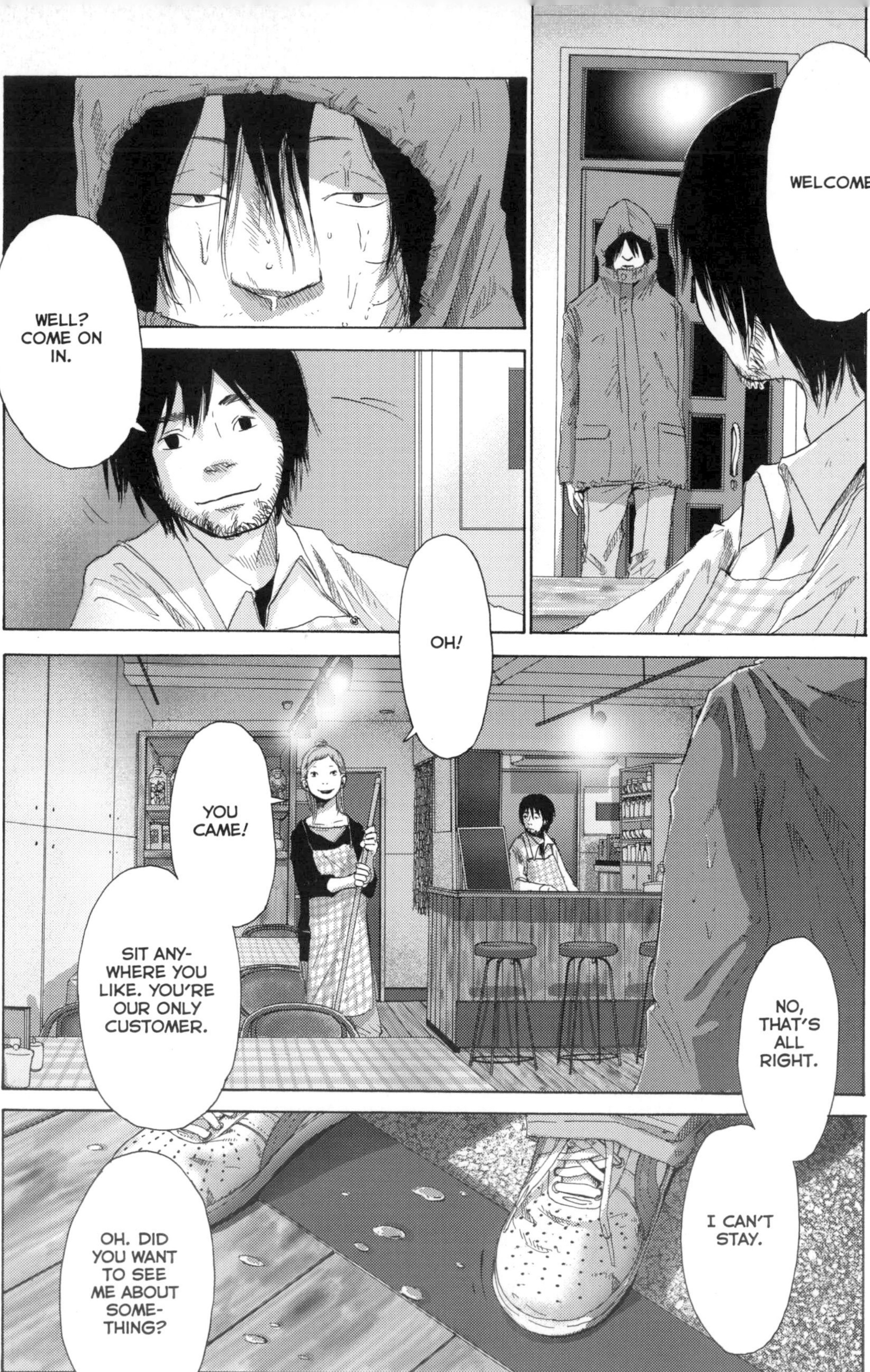
WELCOME.
WELL? COME ON IN.
OH!
YOU CAME!
SIT ANY-WHERE YOU LIKE. YOU'RE OUR ONLY CUSTOMER.
NO, THAT'S ALL RIGHT.
I CAN'T STAY.
OH. DID YOU WANT TO SEE ME ABOUT SOME-THING?

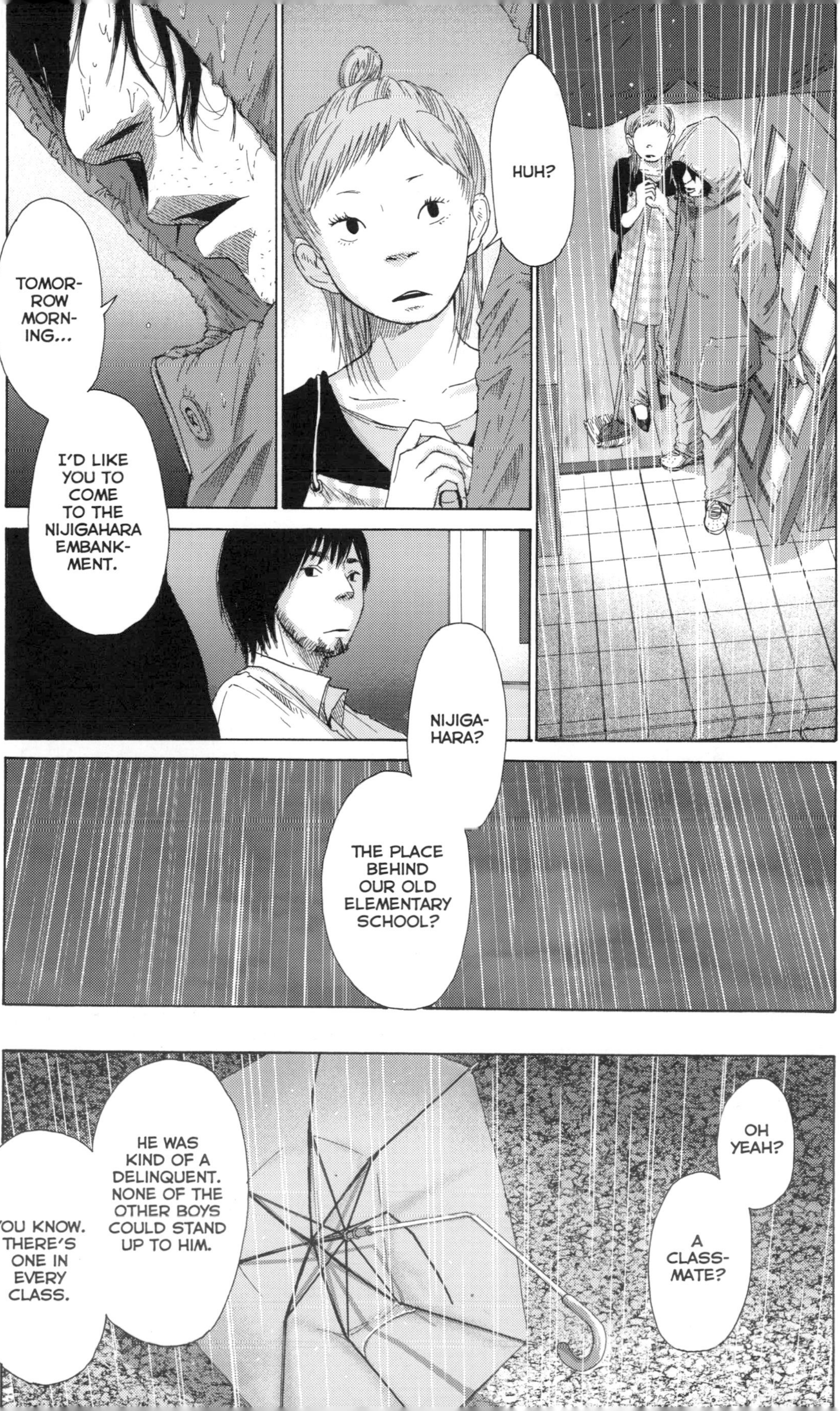
HUH?
TOMORROW MORNING...
I'D LIKE YOU TO COME TO THE NIJIGAHARA EMBANKMENT.
NIJIGAHARA?
THE PLACE BEHIND OUR OLD ELEMENTARY SCHOOL?
OH YEAH?
A CLASSMATE?
HE WAS KIND OF A DELINQUENT. NONE OF THE OTHER BOYS COULD STAND UP TO HIM.
YOU KNOW. THERE'S ONE IN EVERY CLASS.

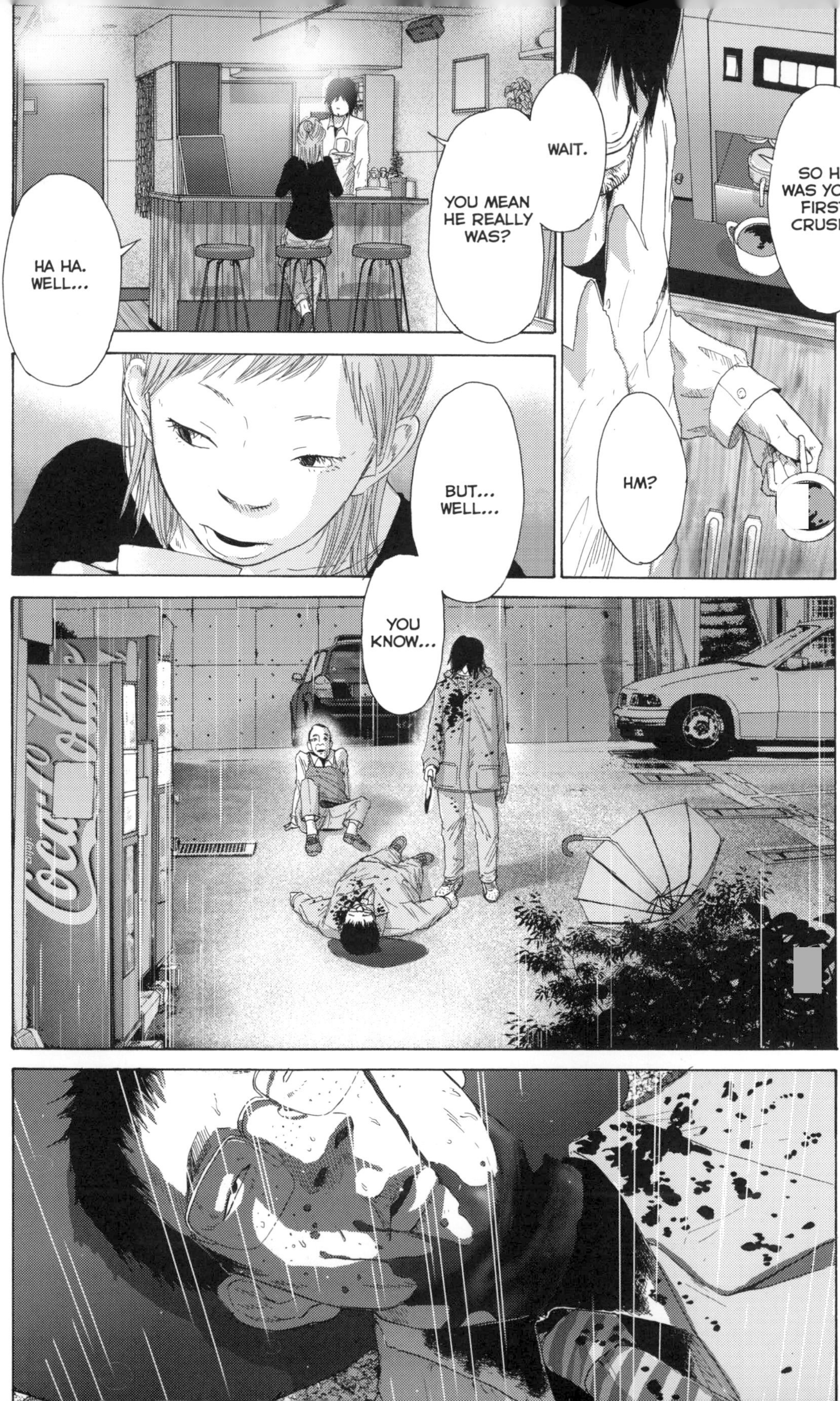
SO HE WAS YOUR FIRST CRUSH?
HA HA. WELL...
WAIT.
YOU MEAN HE REALLY WAS?
BUT... WELL...
HM?
YOU KNOW...

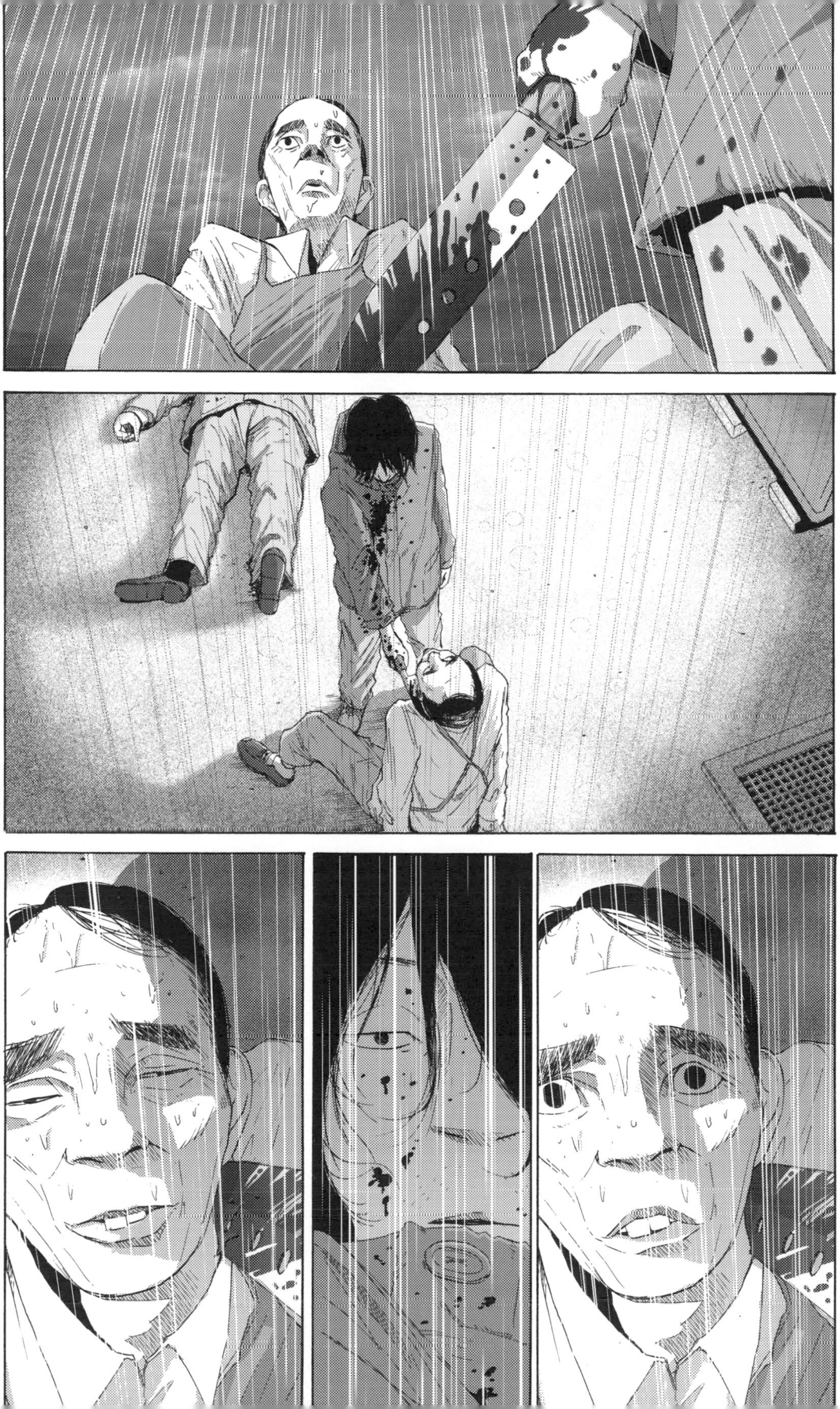

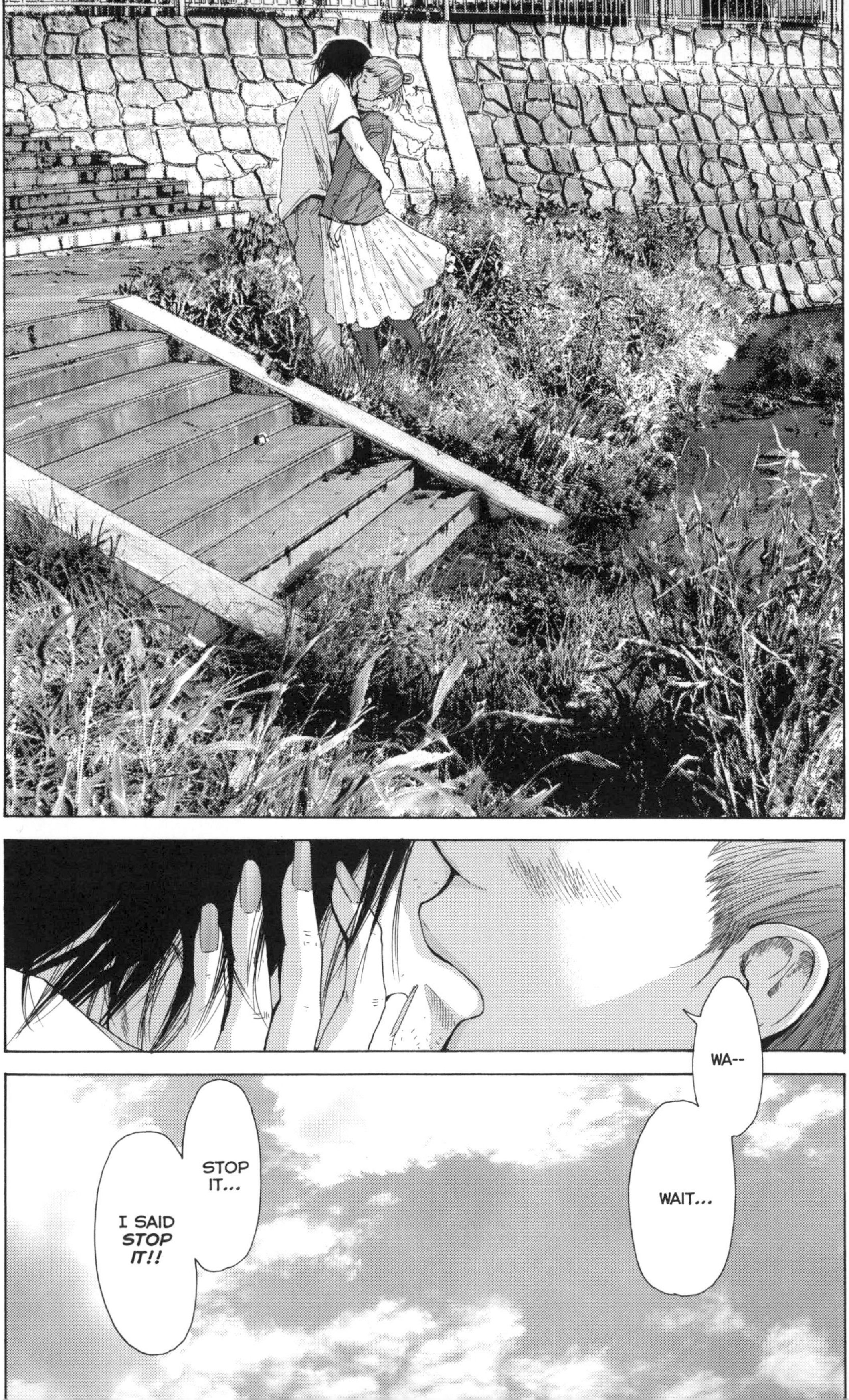
WA--
WAIT...
STOP IT...
I SAID *STOP IT!!*

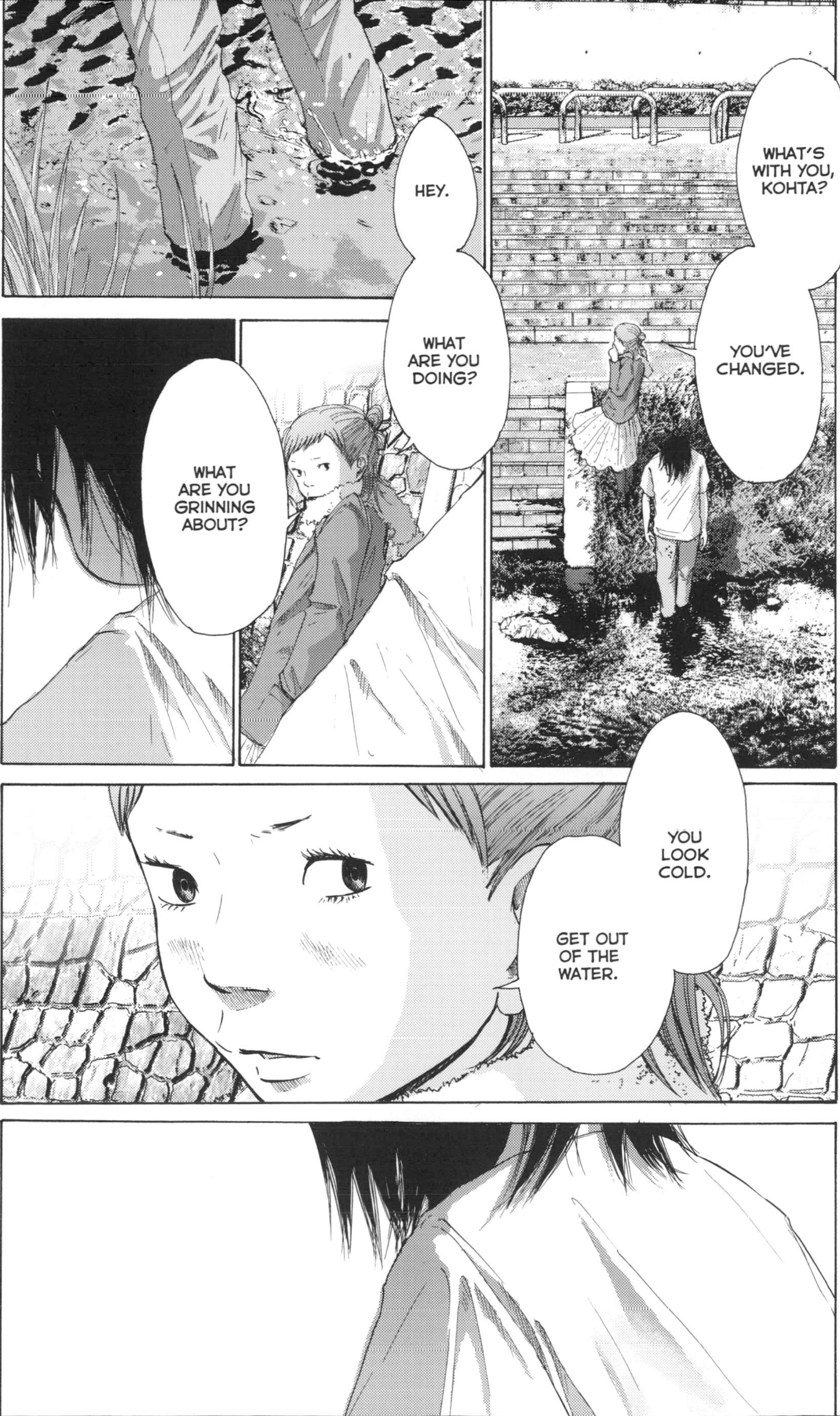
WHAT'S WITH YOU, KOHTA?
YOU'VE CHANGED.
HEY.
WHAT ARE YOU DOING?
WHAT ARE YOU GRINNING ABOUT?
YOU LOOK COLD.
GET OUT OF THE WATER.

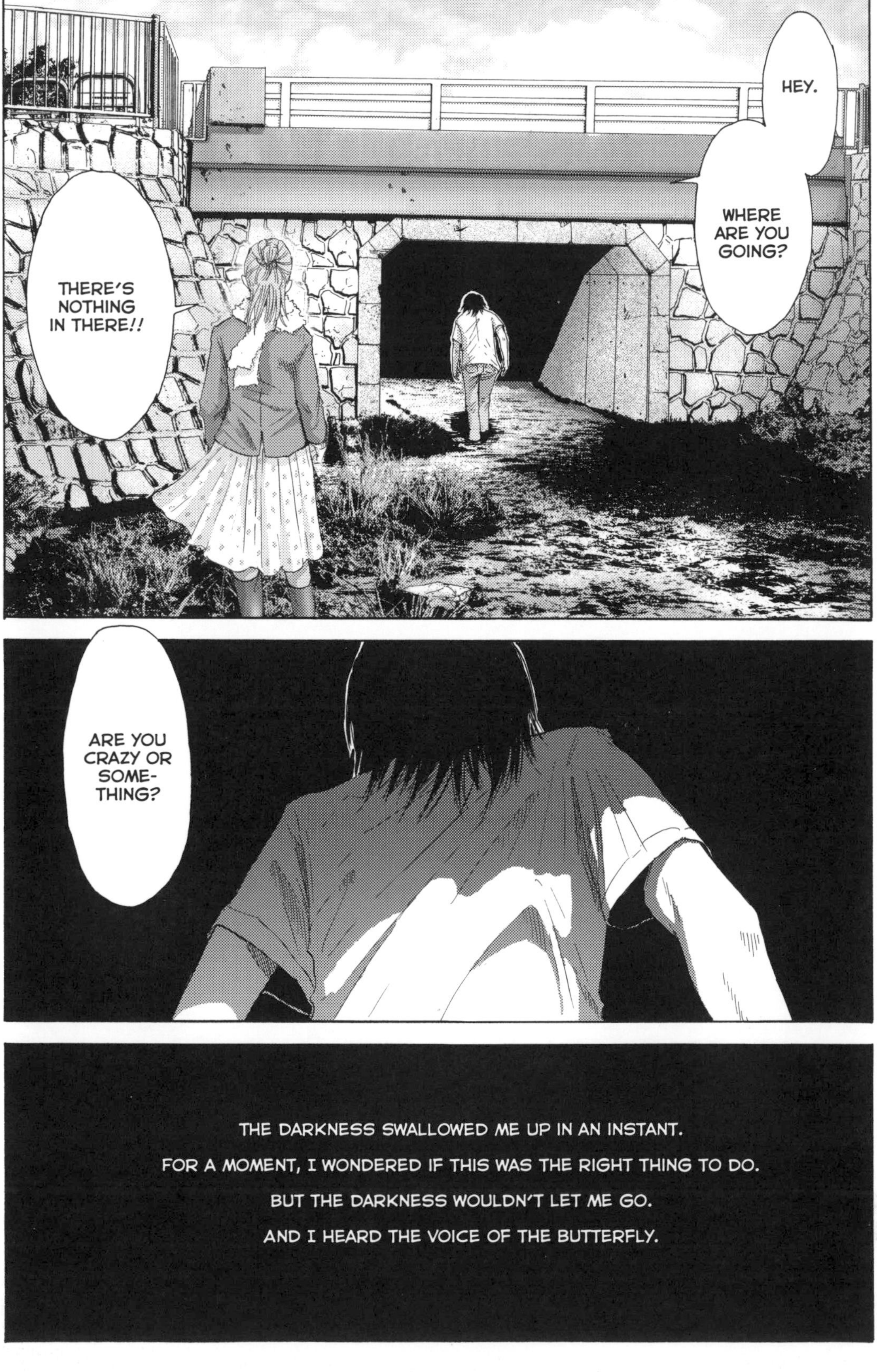
HEY.
WHERE ARE YOU GOING?
THERE'S NOTHING IN THERE!!
ARE YOU CRAZY OR SOME-THING?
THE DARKNESS SWALLOWED ME UP IN AN INSTANT.
FOR A MOMENT, I WONDERED IF THIS WAS THE RIGHT THING TO DO.
BUT THE DARKNESS WOULDN'T LET ME GO.
AND I HEARD THE VOICE OF THE BUTTERFLY.

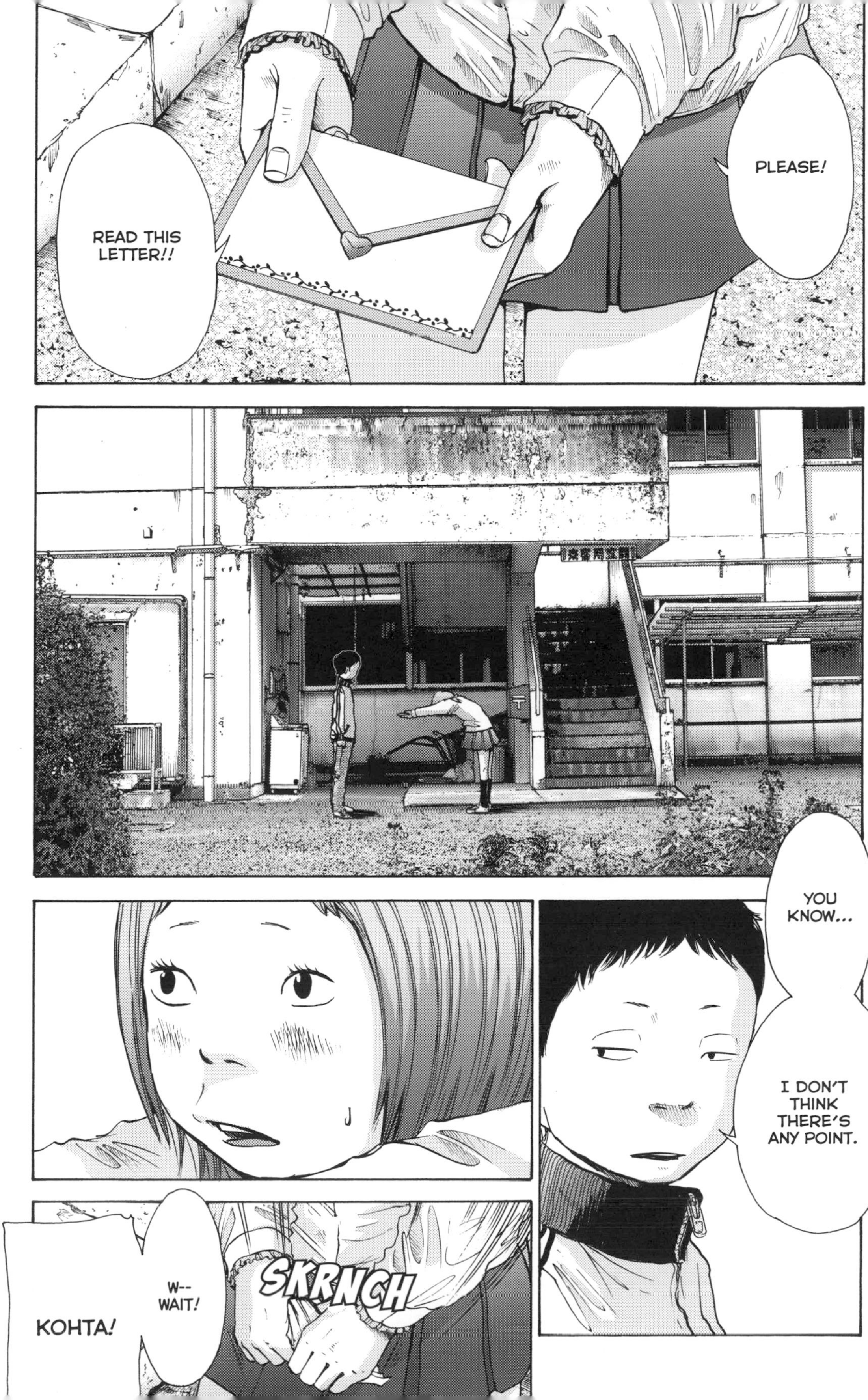
PLEASE!
READ THIS LETTER!!
YOU KNOW...
I DON'T THINK THERE'S ANY POINT.
W-- WAIT!
SKRNCH
KOHTA!

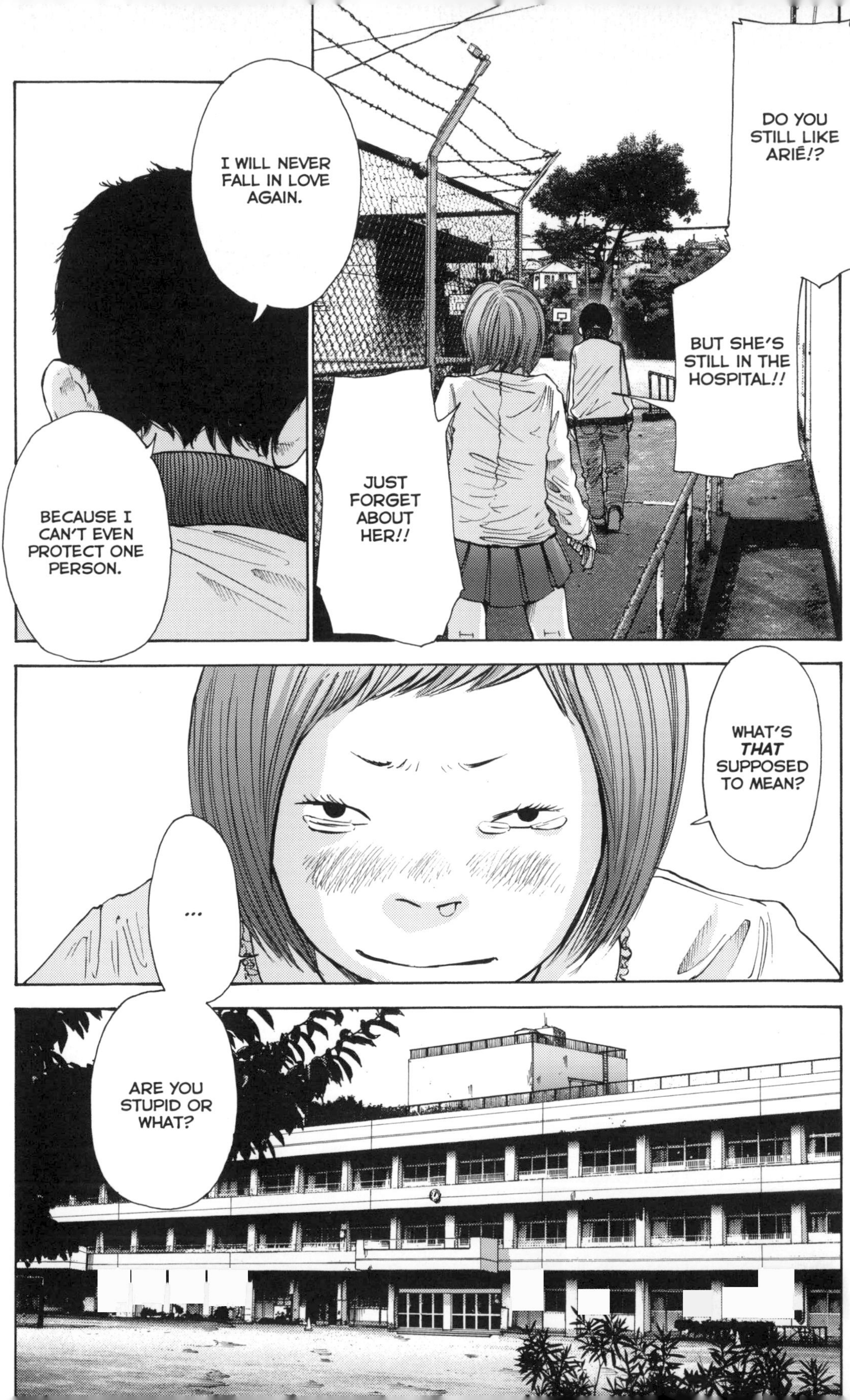
DO YOU STILL LIKE ARIÉ!?
BUT SHE'S STILL IN THE HOSPITAL!!
JUST FORGET ABOUT HER!!
I WILL NEVER FALL IN LOVE AGAIN.
BECAUSE I CAN'T EVEN PROTECT ONE PERSON.
WHAT'S ***THAT*** SUPPOSED TO MEAN?
...
ARE YOU STUPID OR WHAT?

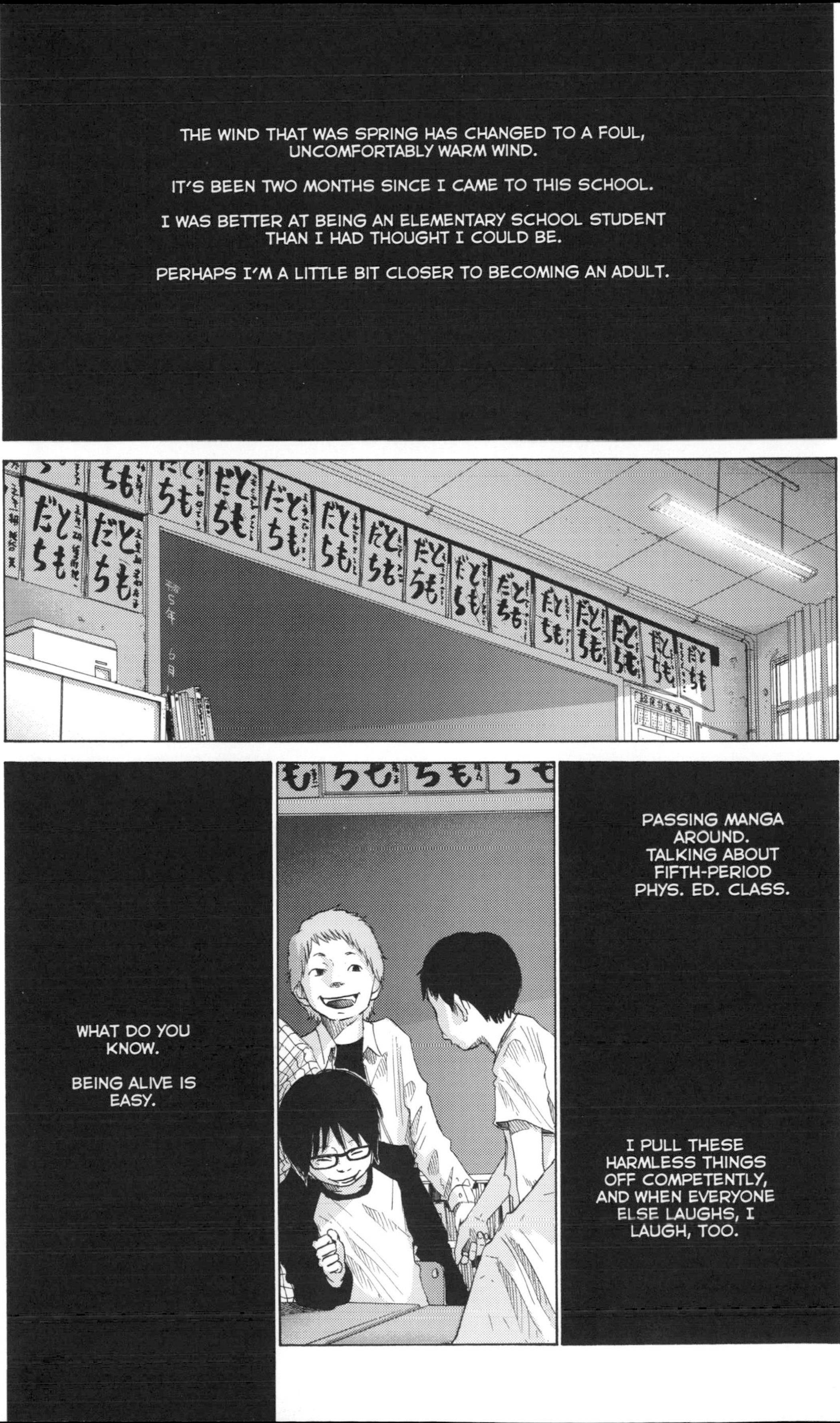
THE WIND THAT WAS SPRING HAS CHANGED TO A FOUL, UNCOMFORTABLY WARM WIND.
IT'S BEEN TWO MONTHS SINCE I CAME TO THIS SCHOOL.
I WAS BETTER AT BEING AN ELEMENTARY SCHOOL STUDENT THAN I HAD THOUGHT I COULD BE.
PERHAPS I'M A LITTLE BIT CLOSER TO BECOMING AN ADULT.
PASSING MANGA AROUND. TALKING ABOUT FIFTH-PERIOD PHYS. ED. CLASS.
I PULL THESE HARMLESS THINGS OFF COMPETENTLY, AND WHEN EVERYONE ELSE LAUGHS, I LAUGH, TOO.
WHAT DO YOU KNOW.
BEING ALIVE IS EASY.

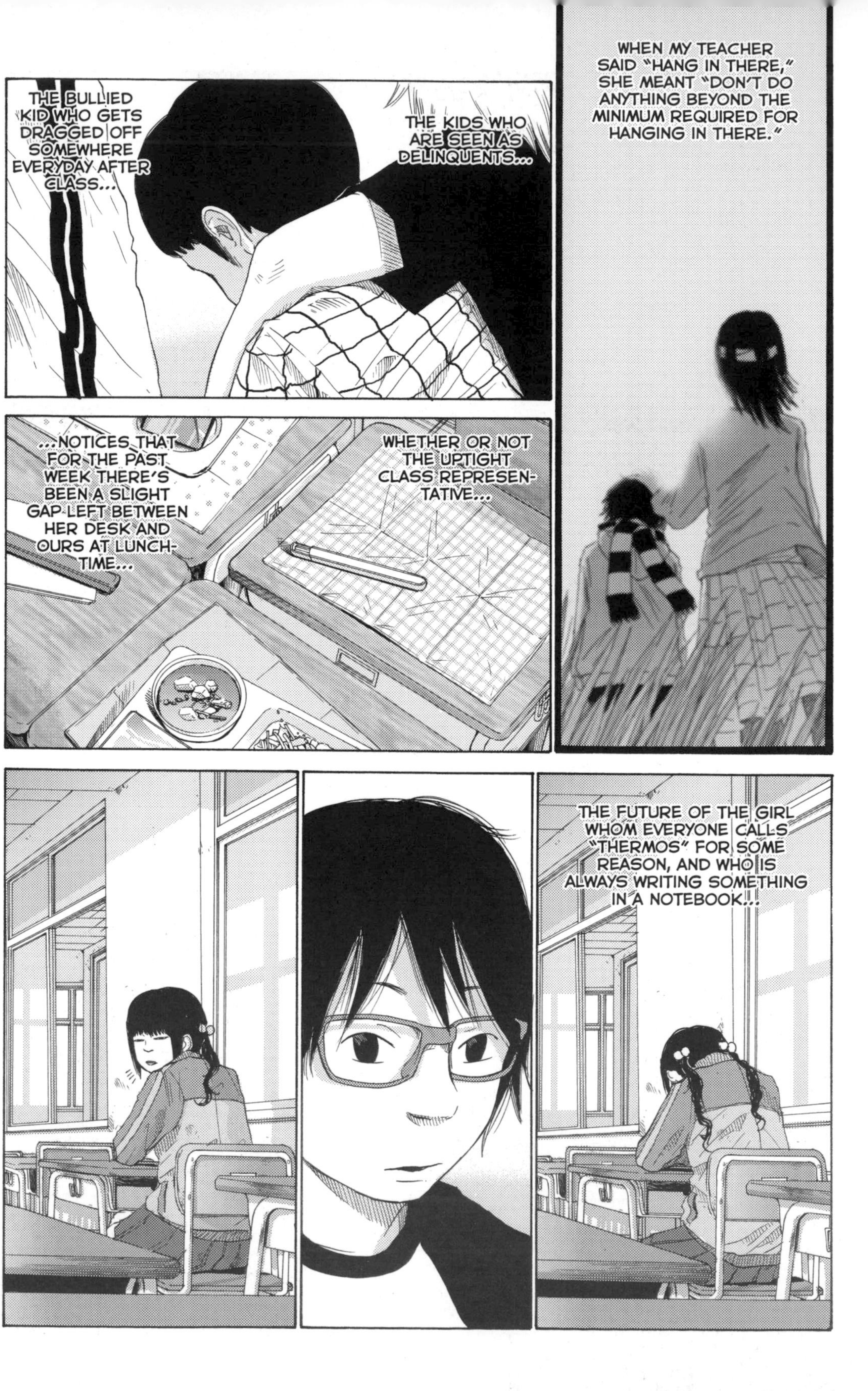
WHEN MY TEACHER SAID "HANG IN THERE," SHE MEANT "DON'T DO ANYTHING BEYOND THE MINIMUM REQUIRED FOR HANGING IN THERE."
THE KIDS WHO ARE SEEN AS DELINQUENTS...
THE BULLIED KID WHO GETS DRAGGED OFF SOMEWHERE EVERYDAY AFTER CLASS...
WHETHER OR NOT THE UPTIGHT CLASS REPRESEN-TATIVE...
...NOTICES THAT FOR THE PAST WEEK THERE'S BEEN A SLIGHT GAP LEFT BETWEEN HER DESK AND OURS AT LUNCH-TIME...
THE FUTURE OF THE GIRL WHOM EVERYONE CALLS "THERMOS" FOR SOME REASON, AND WHO IS ALWAYS WRITING SOMETHING IN A NOTEBOOK...

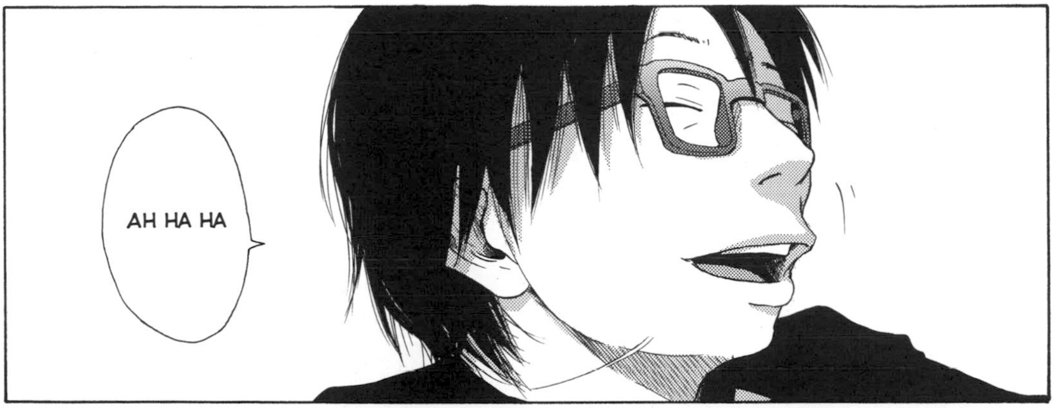
AH HA HA

THERE'S NO NEED TO THINK ABOUT THESE THINGS.

CHAPTER 3

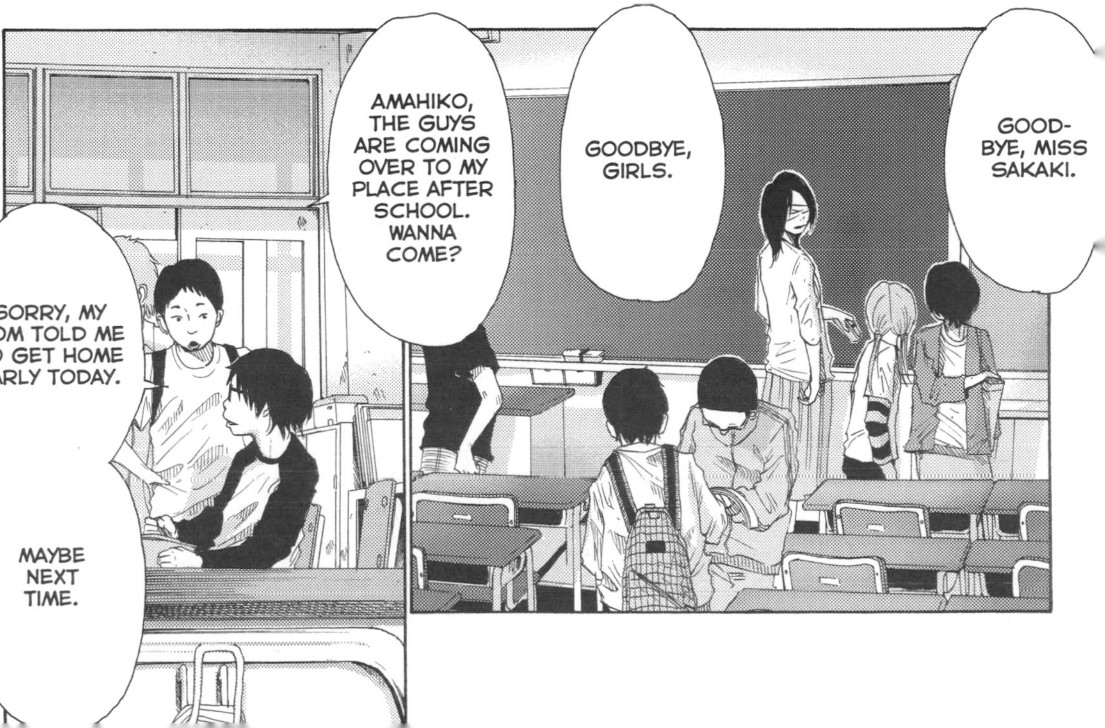
GOOD-BYE, MISS SAKAKI.
GOODBYE, GIRLS.
AMAHIKO, THE GUYS ARE COMING OVER TO MY PLACE AFTER SCHOOL. WANNA COME?
SORRY, MY MOM TOLD ME TO GET HOME EARLY TODAY.
MAYBE NEXT TIME.

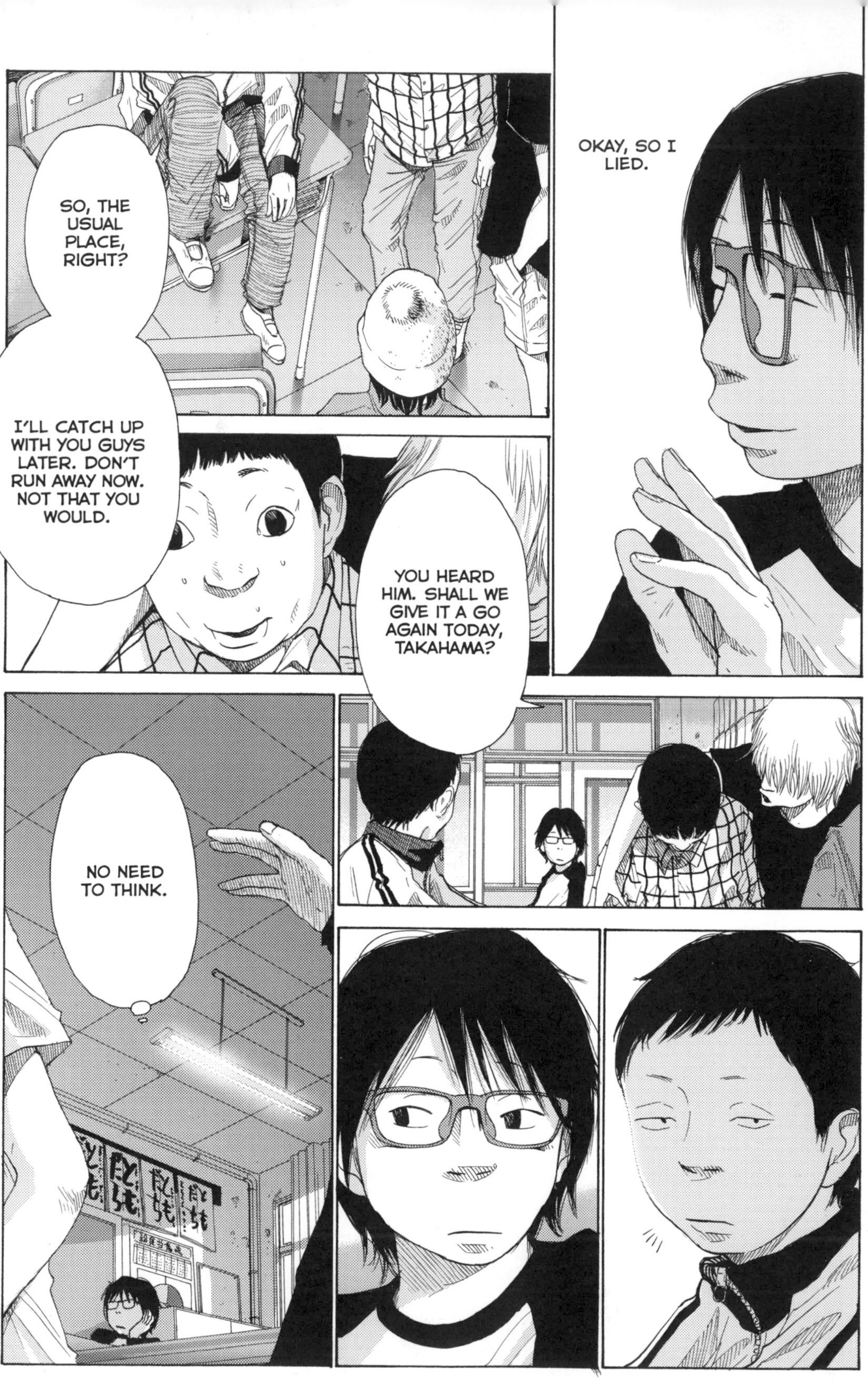
OKAY, SO I LIED.
SO, THE USUAL PLACE, RIGHT?
I'LL CATCH UP WITH YOU GUYS LATER. DON'T RUN AWAY NOW. NOT THAT YOU WOULD.
YOU HEARD HIM. SHALL WE GIVE IT A GO AGAIN TODAY, TAKAHAMA?
NO NEED TO THINK.

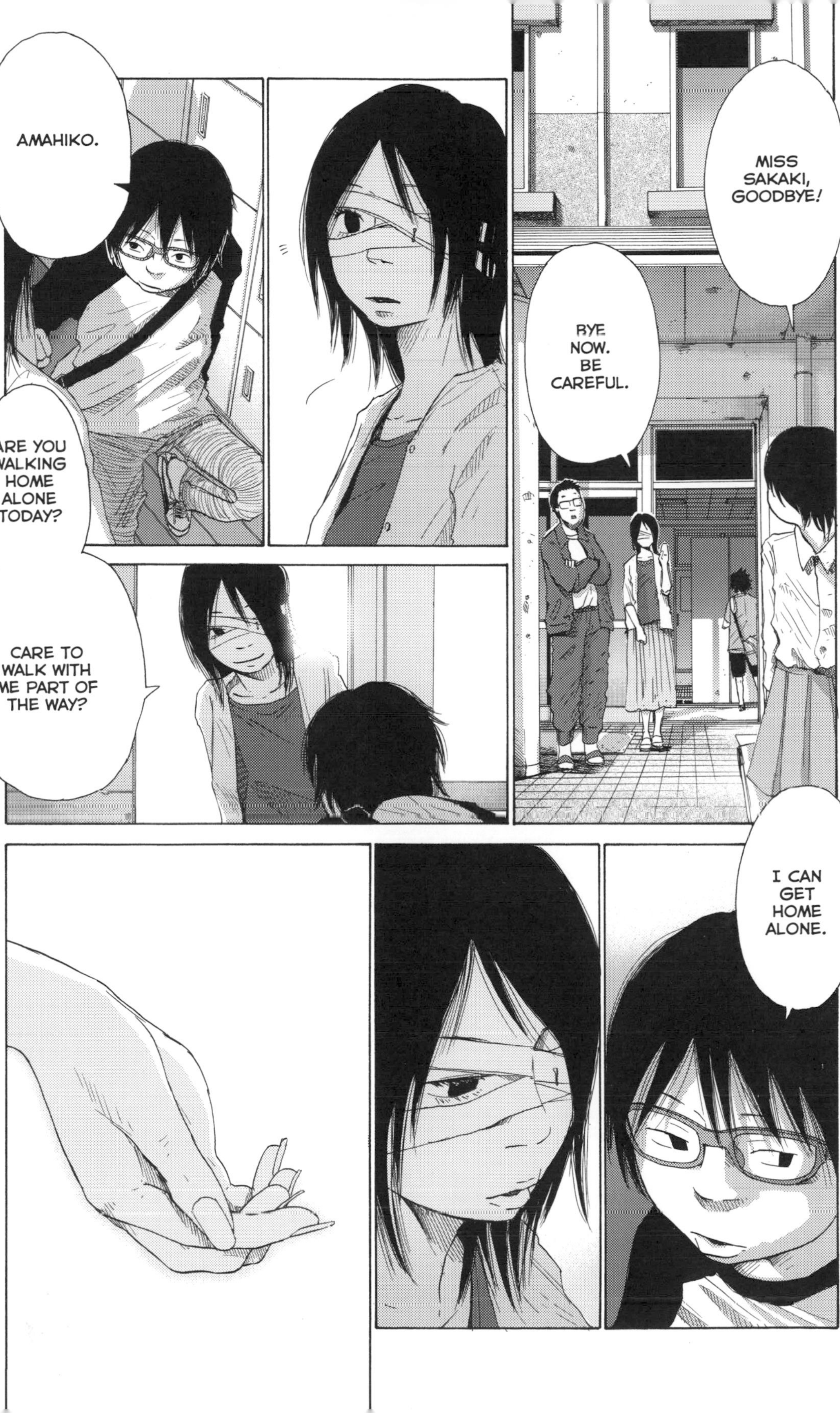
MISS SAKAKI, GOODBYE!
BYE NOW. BE CAREFUL.
AMAHIKO.
ARE YOU WALKING HOME ALONE TODAY?
CARE TO WALK WITH ME PART OF THE WAY?
I CAN GET HOME ALONE.

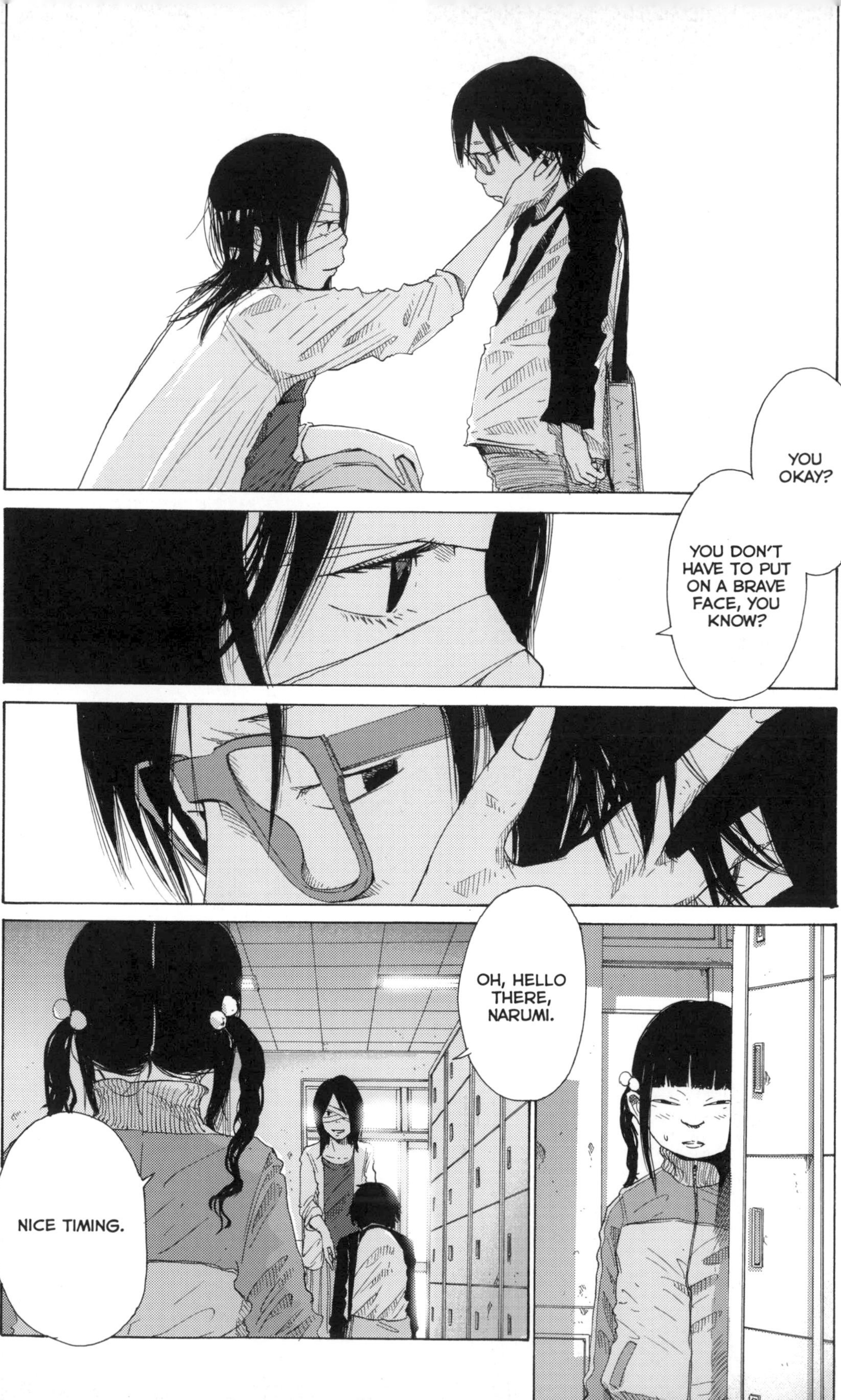
YOU OKAY?
YOU DON'T HAVE TO PUT ON A BRAVE FACE, YOU KNOW?
OH, HELLO THERE, NARUMI.
NICE TIMING.

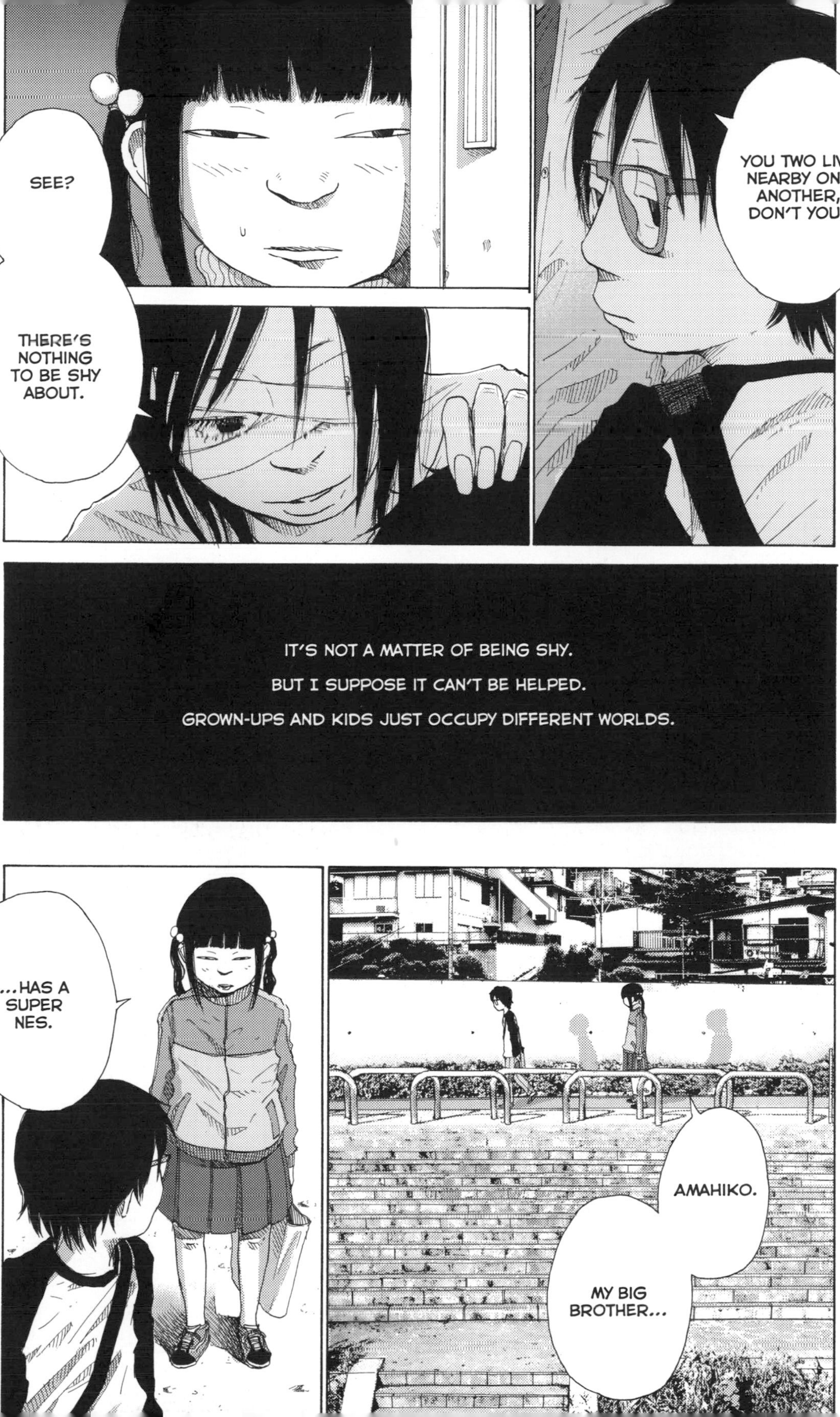
YOU TWO LIVE NEARBY ONE ANOTHER, DON'T YOU?
SEE?
THERE'S NOTHING TO BE SHY ABOUT.
IT'S NOT A MATTER OF BEING SHY.
BUT I SUPPOSE IT CAN'T BE HELPED.
GROWN-UPS AND KIDS JUST OCCUPY DIFFERENT WORLDS.
AMAHIKO.
MY BIG BROTHER...
...HAS A SUPER NES.

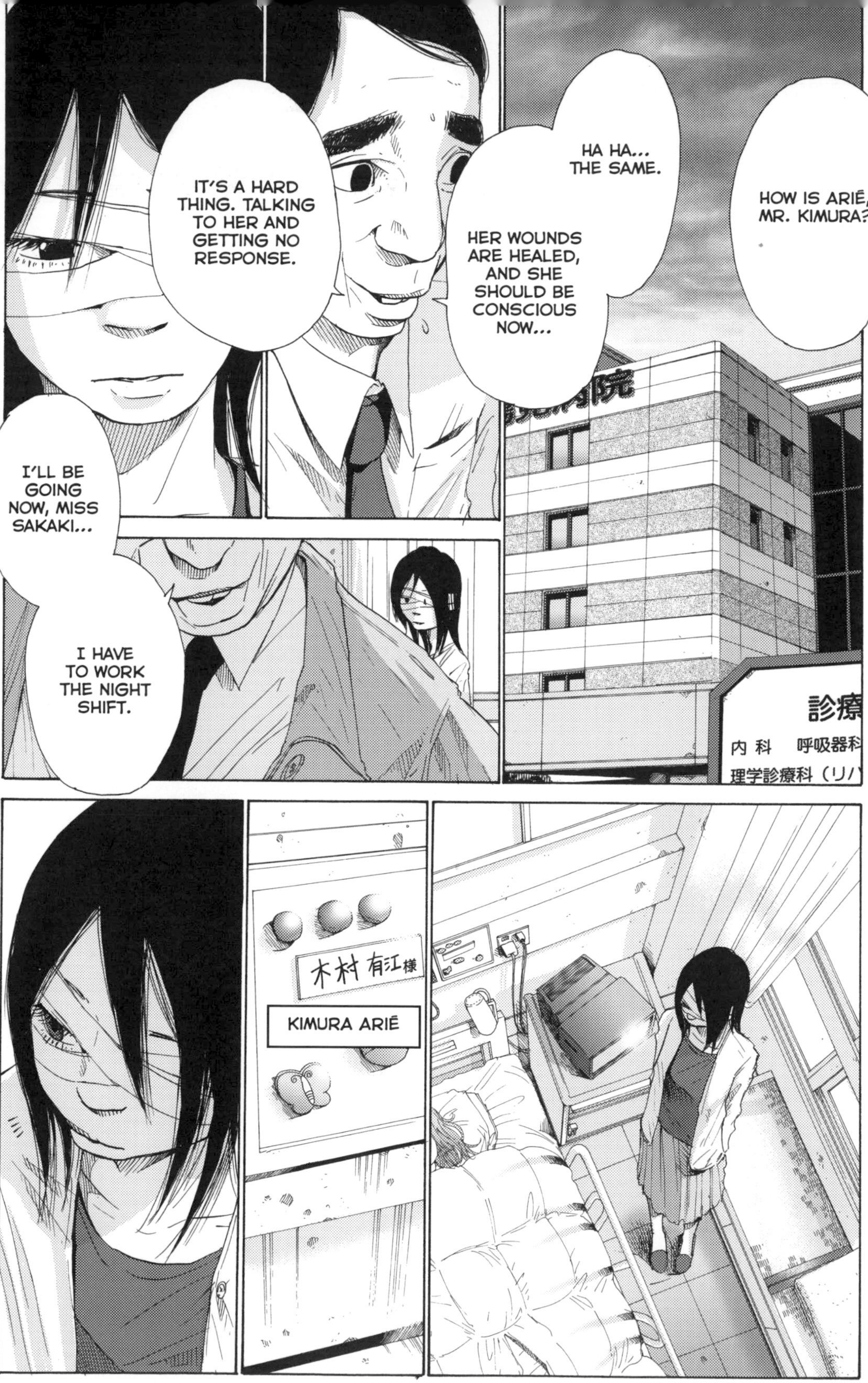
HOW IS ARIÉ, MR. KIMURA?
HA HA... THE SAME.
HER WOUNDS ARE HEALED, AND SHE SHOULD BE CONSCIOUS NOW...
診療
内科 呼吸器科
理学診療科（リハ
IT'S A HARD THING. TALKING TO HER AND GETTING NO RESPONSE.
I'LL BE GOING NOW, MISS SAKAKI...
I HAVE TO WORK THE NIGHT SHIFT.
木村有江様
KIMURA ARIÉ

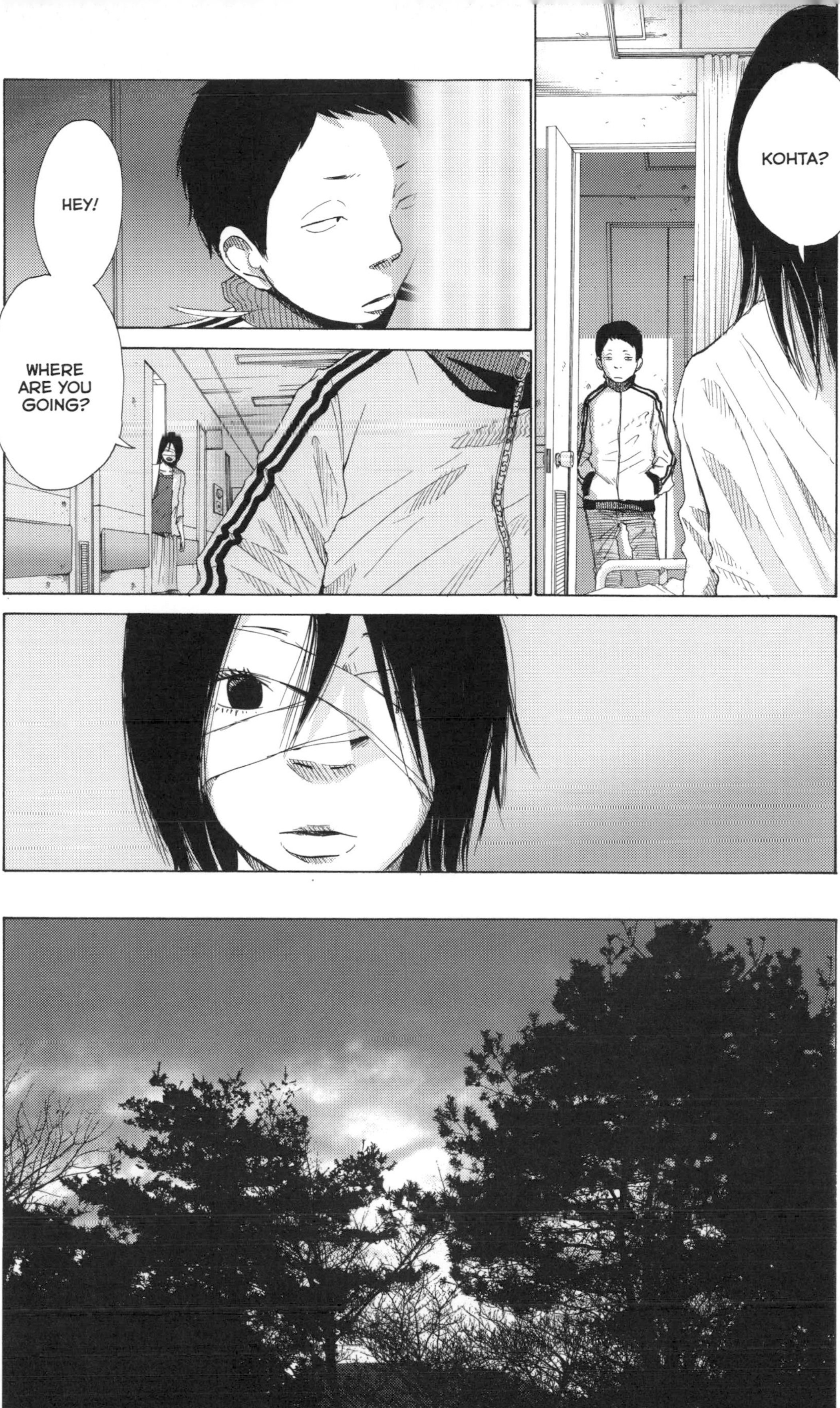
KOHTA?
HEY!
WHERE ARE YOU GOING?

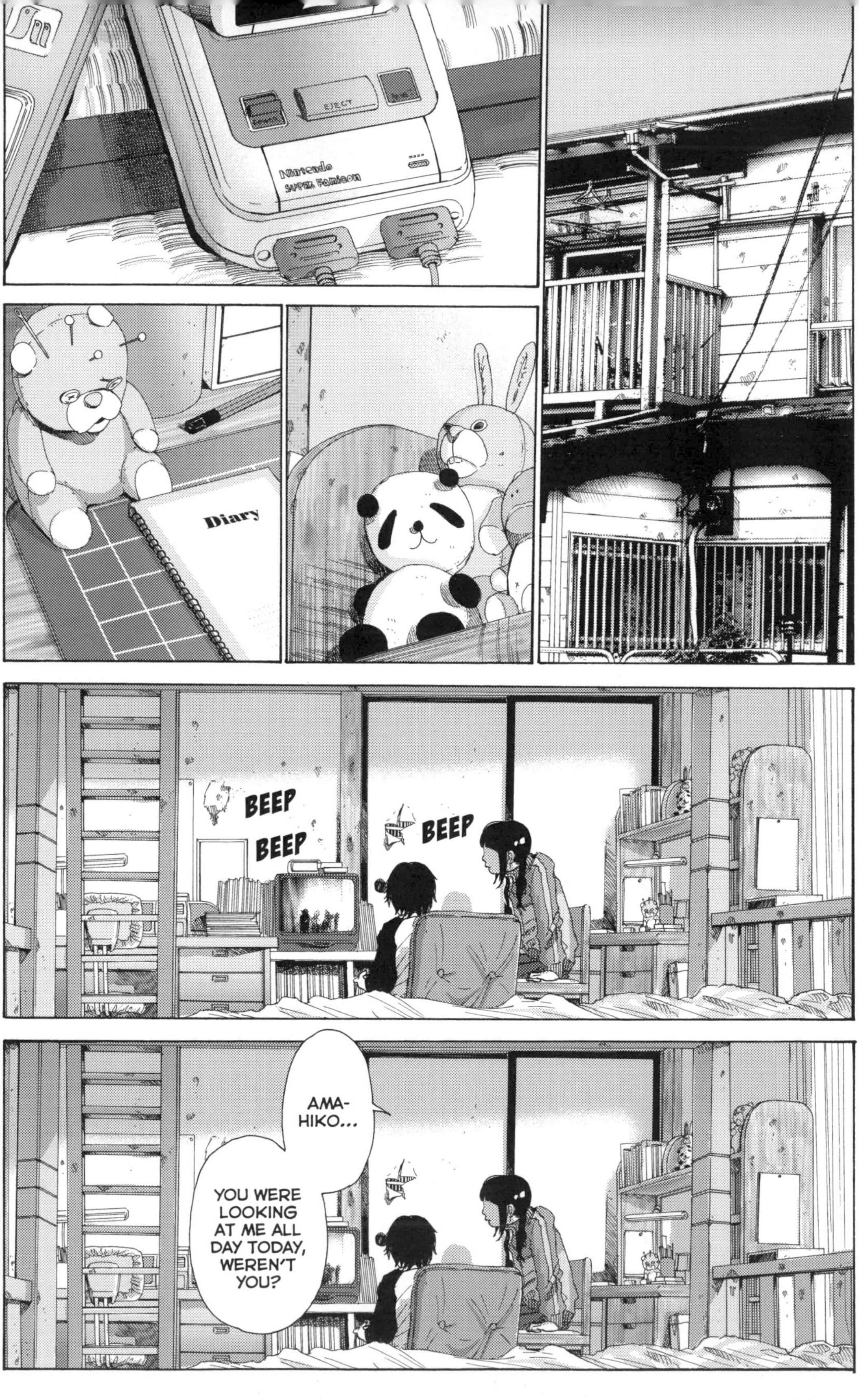
EJECT
Nintendo
SUPER Famicom
Diary
BEEP
BEEP
BEEP
AMA-HIKO...
YOU WERE LOOKING AT ME ALL DAY TODAY, WEREN'T YOU?

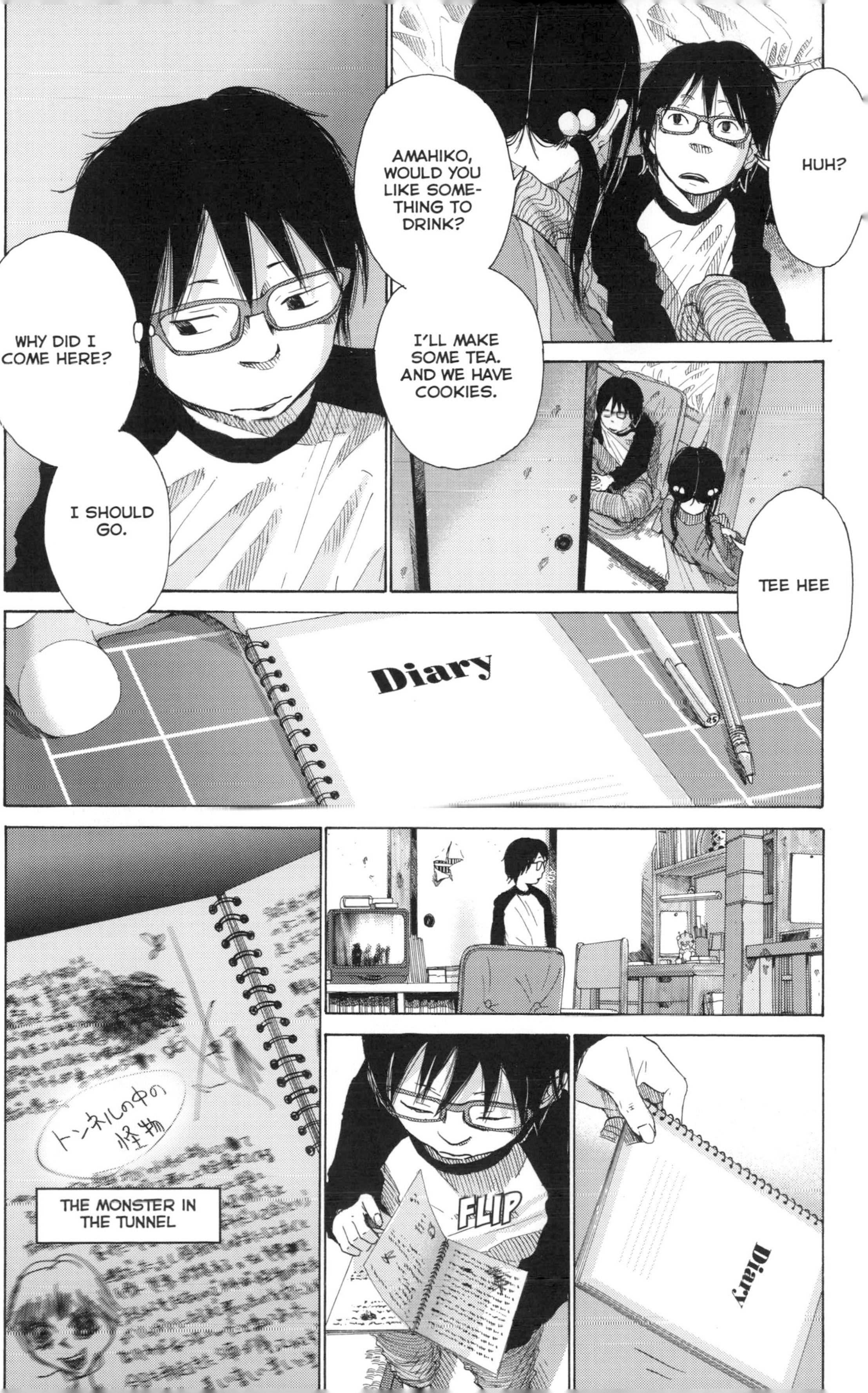
AMAHIKO, WOULD YOU LIKE SOME-THING TO DRINK?
HUH?
I'LL MAKE SOME TEA. AND WE HAVE COOKIES.
TEE HEE
WHY DID I COME HERE?
I SHOULD GO.
Diary
Diary
FLIP
トンネルの中の怪物
THE MONSTER IN THE TUNNEL

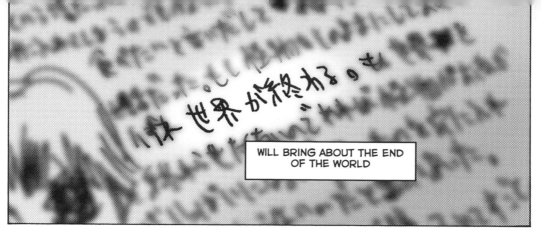

世界が終わるのな

WILL BRING ABOUT THE END
OF THE WORLD

HEY.

YOU
GUYS ARE
PUSSIES.
GIVE HIM
TO ME.

HUH?...
OKAY.

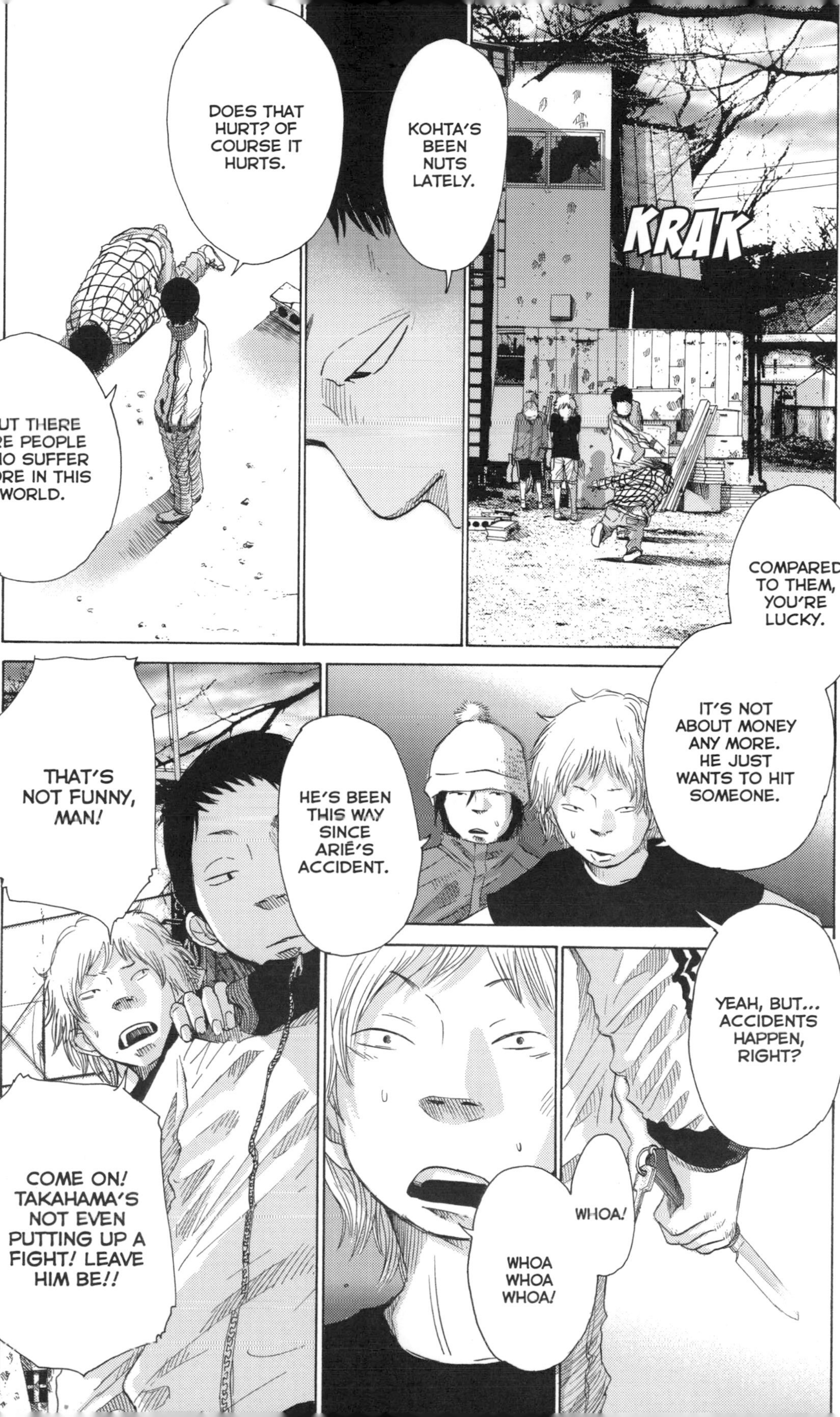
KRAK
COMPARED TO THEM, YOU'RE LUCKY.
KOHTA'S BEEN NUTS LATELY.
DOES THAT HURT? OF COURSE IT HURTS.
BUT THERE ARE PEOPLE WHO SUFFER MORE IN THIS WORLD.
IT'S NOT ABOUT MONEY ANY MORE. HE JUST WANTS TO HIT SOMEONE.
HE'S BEEN THIS WAY SINCE ARIÉ'S ACCIDENT.
THAT'S NOT FUNNY, MAN!
YEAH, BUT... ACCIDENTS HAPPEN, RIGHT?
WHOA!
WHOA WHOA WHOA!
COME ON! TAKAHAMA'S NOT EVEN PUTTING UP A FIGHT! LEAVE HIM BE!!

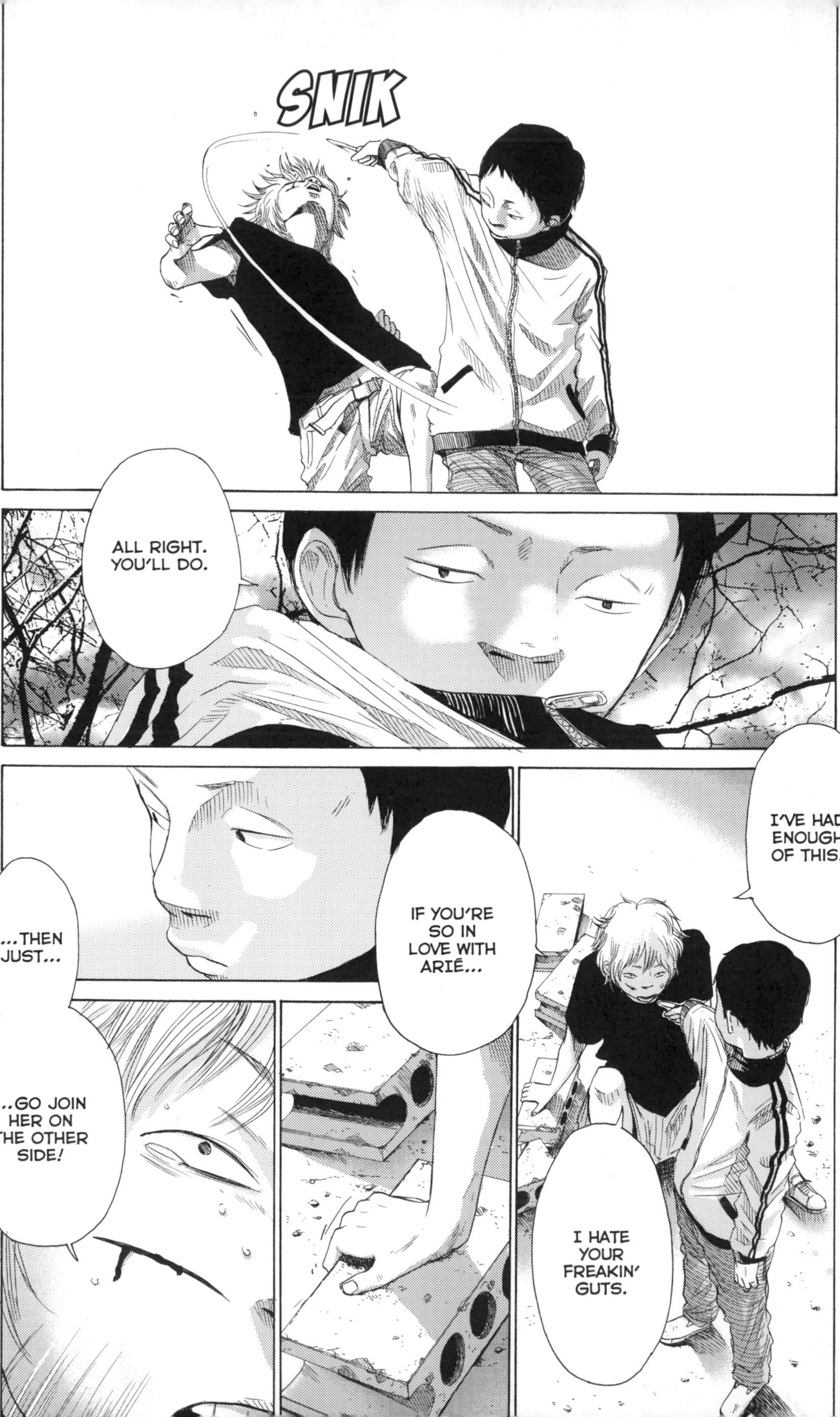
SNIK
ALL RIGHT. YOU'LL DO.
I'VE HAD ENOUGH OF THIS.
I HATE YOUR FREAKIN' GUTS.
IF YOU'RE SO IN LOVE WITH ARIÉ...
...THEN JUST...
...GO JOIN HER ON THE OTHER SIDE!

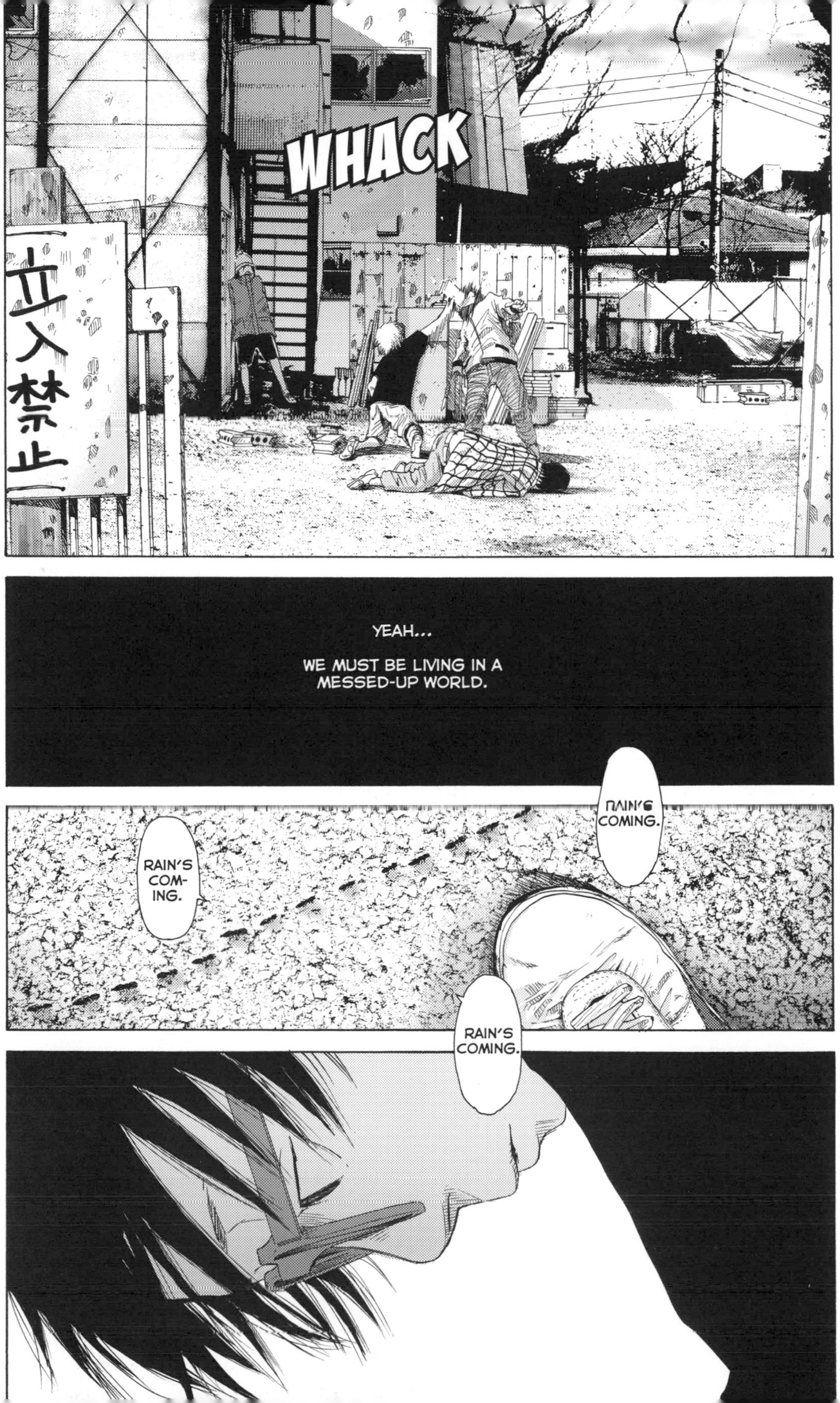
WHACK
立入禁止
YEAH...
WE MUST BE LIVING IN A MESSED-UP WORLD.
RAIN'S COMING.
RAIN'S COM-ING.
RAIN'S COMING.

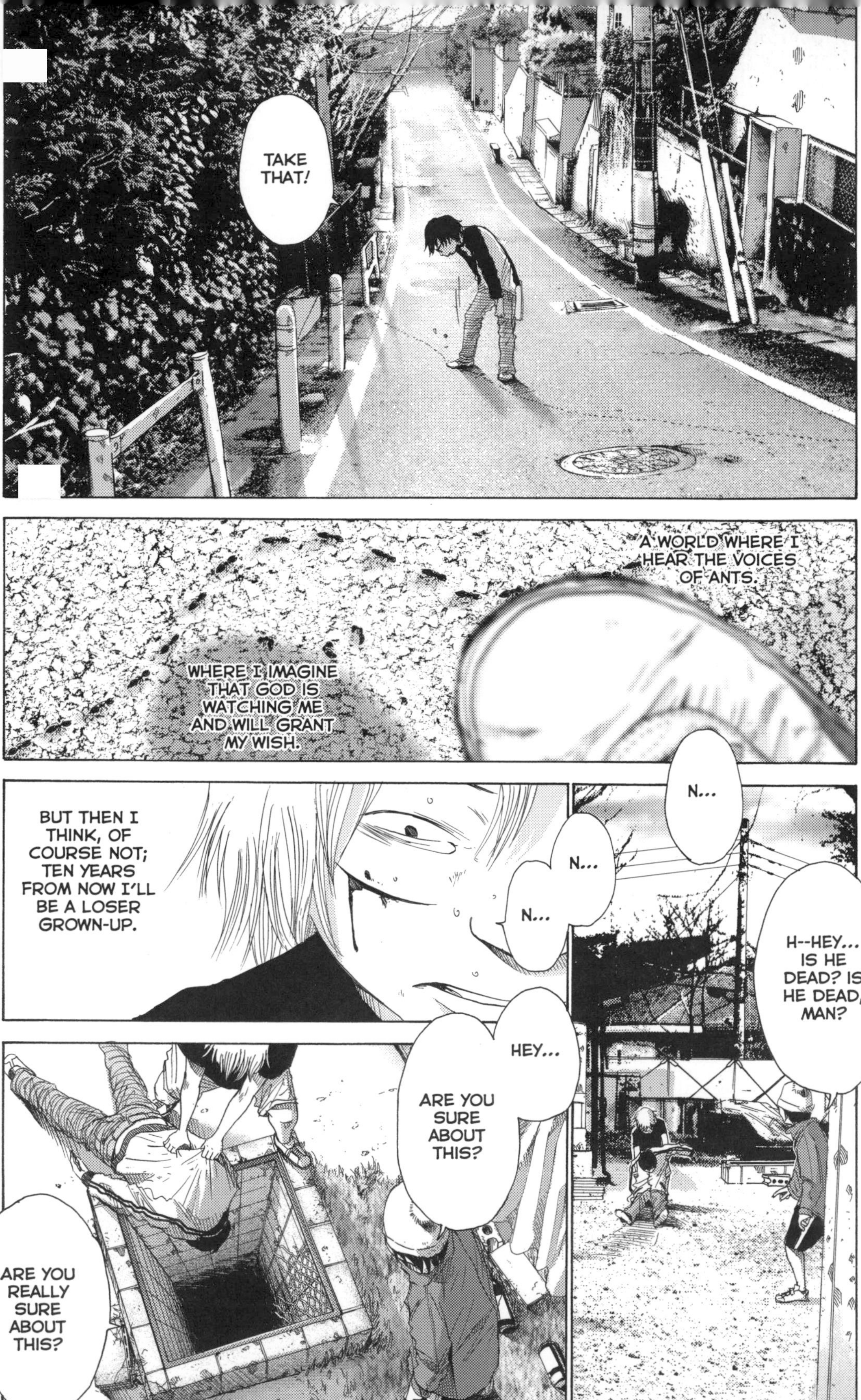

TAKE THAT!
A WORLD WHERE I HEAR THE VOICES OF ANTS.
WHERE I IMAGINE THAT GOD IS WATCHING ME AND WILL GRANT MY WISH.
N...
N...
N...
H--HEY... IS HE DEAD? IS HE DEAD, MAN?
HEY...
ARE YOU SURE ABOUT THIS?
BUT THEN I THINK, OF COURSE NOT; TEN YEARS FROM NOW I'LL BE A LOSER GROWN-UP.
ARE YOU REALLY SURE ABOUT THIS?

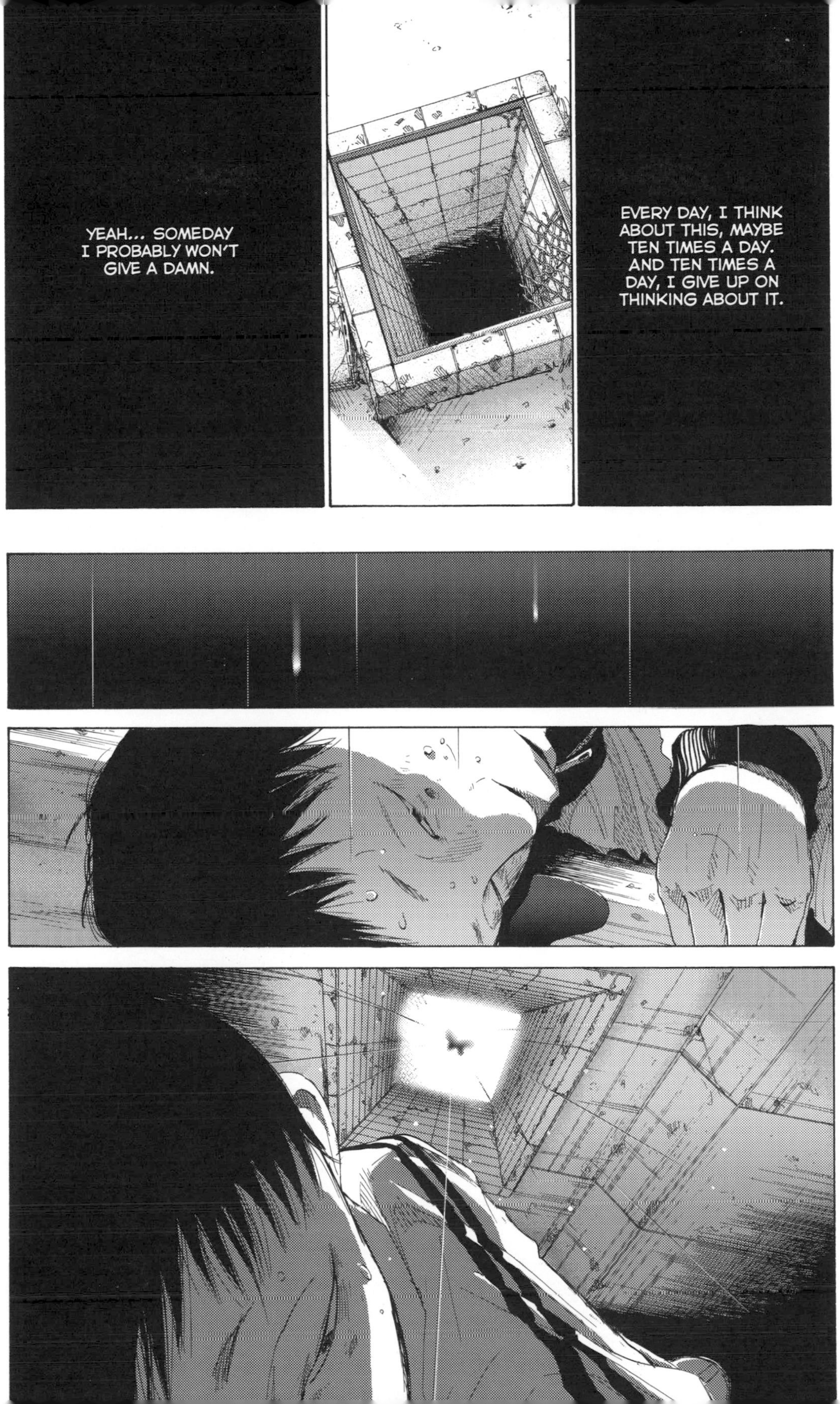
EVERY DAY, I THINK ABOUT THIS, MAYBE TEN TIMES A DAY. AND TEN TIMES A DAY, I GIVE UP ON THINKING ABOUT IT.
YEAH... SOMEDAY I PROBABLY WON'T GIVE A DAMN.

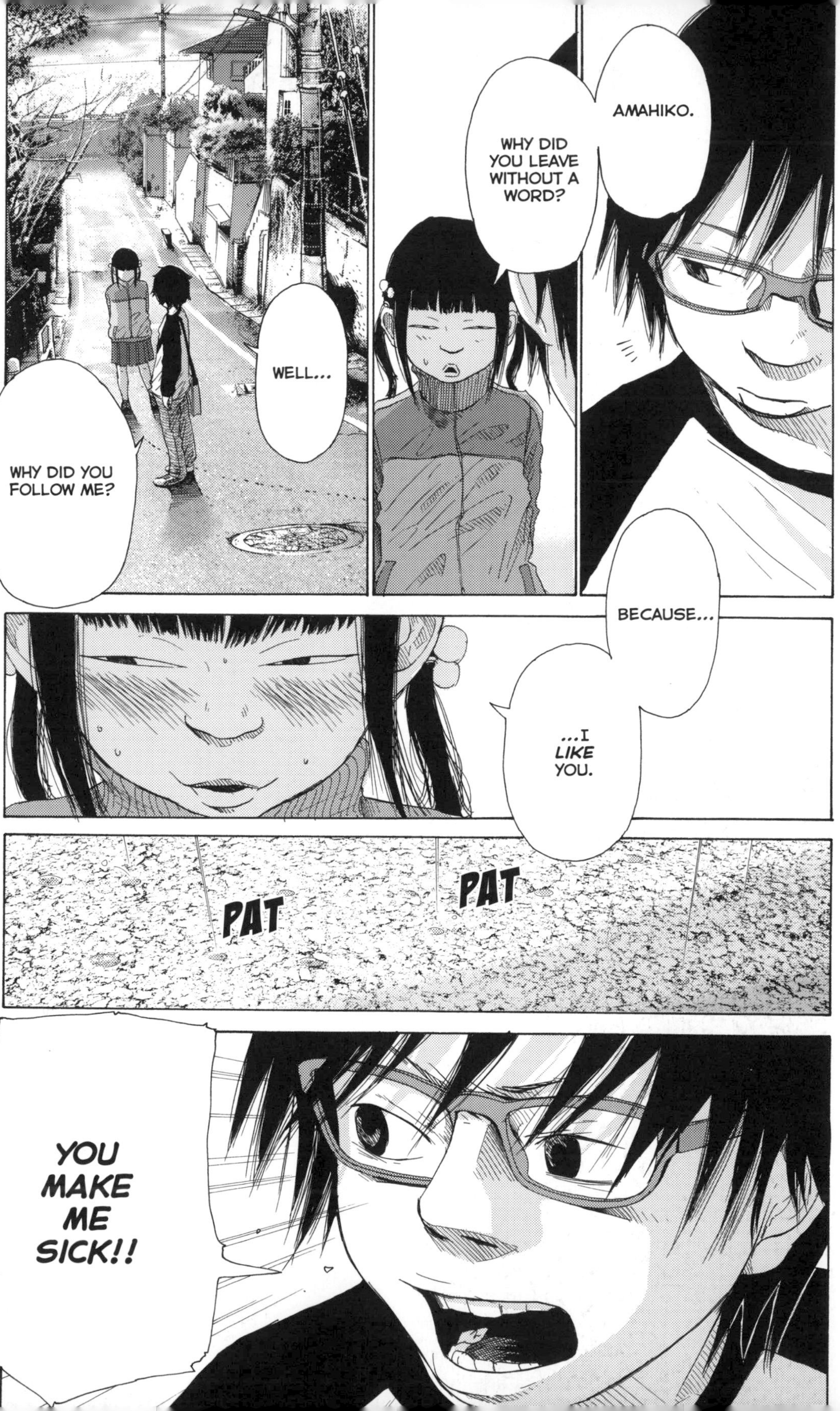
AMAHIKO.
WHY DID YOU LEAVE WITHOUT A WORD?
WELL...
WHY DID YOU FOLLOW ME?
BECAUSE...
...I *LIKE* YOU.
PAT
PAT
YOU MAKE ME SICK!!

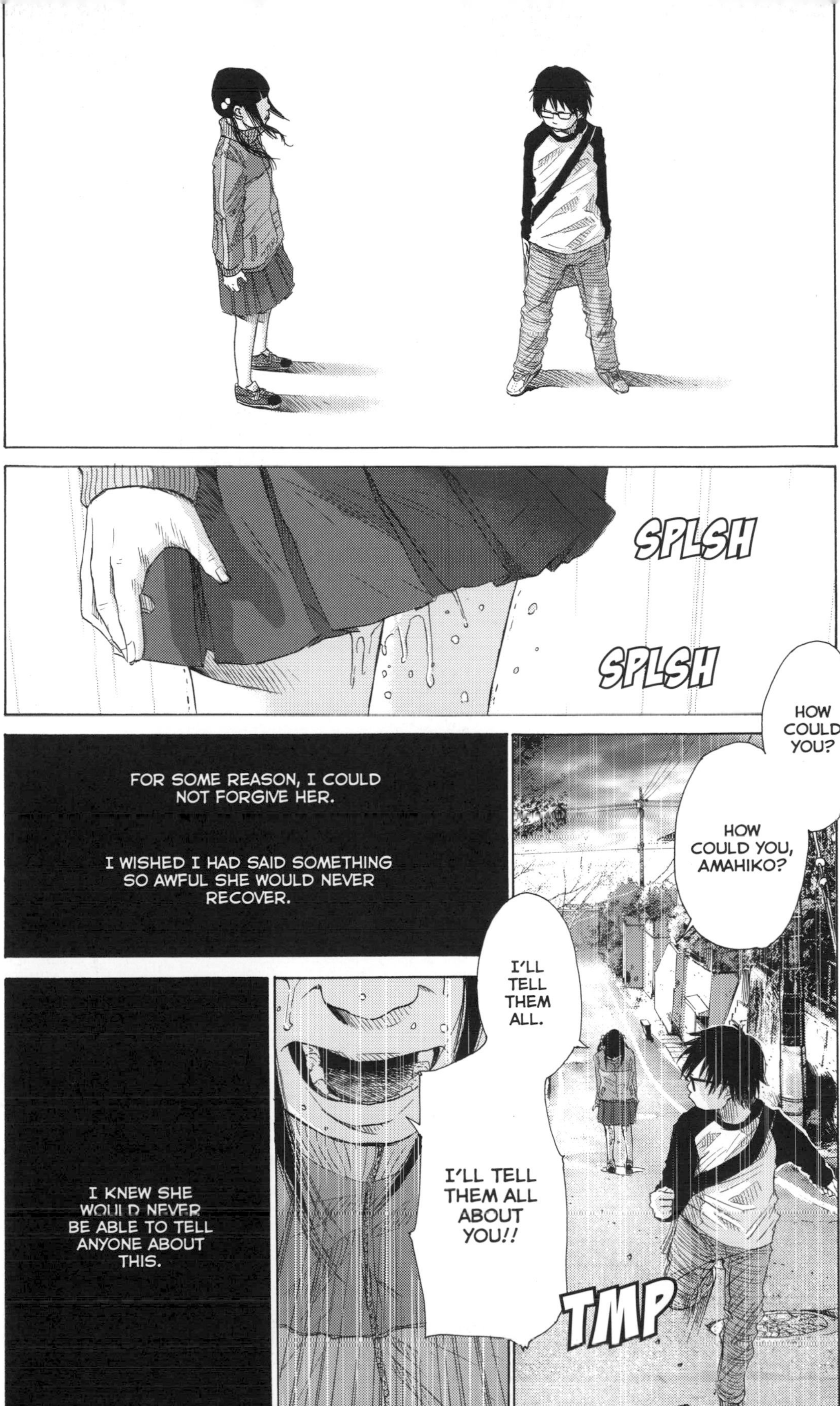
SPLSH
SPLSH
HOW COULD YOU?
HOW COULD YOU, AMAHIKO?
I'LL TELL THEM ALL.
I'LL TELL THEM ALL ABOUT YOU!!
TMP
FOR SOME REASON, I COULD NOT FORGIVE HER.
I WISHED I HAD SAID SOMETHING SO AWFUL SHE WOULD NEVER RECOVER.
I KNEW SHE WOULD NEVER BE ABLE TO TELL ANYONE ABOUT THIS.

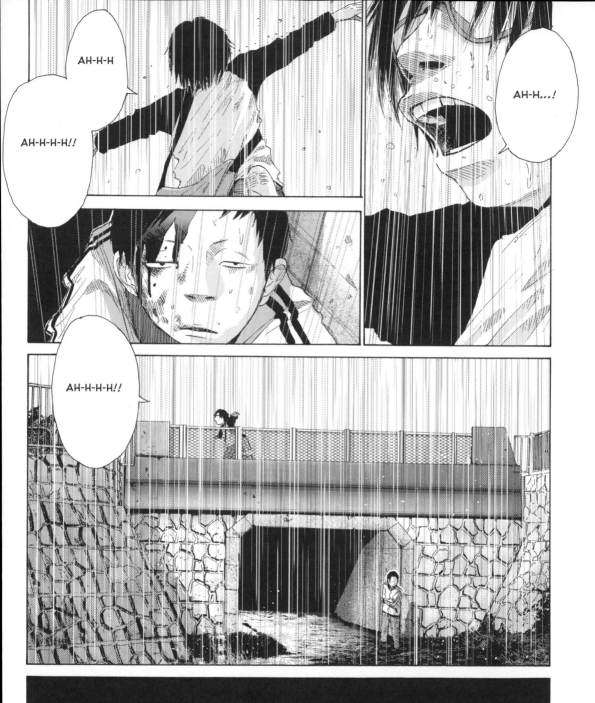

SUDDENLY THE RAIN CAME DOWN WITH VIOLENCE.

RAIN SO HARD IT HURT WHEN IT HIT YOU.

I WISHED THE RAIN WOULD WASH AWAY MY FILTH, HER
FILTH, EVERYONE'S FILTH.

BUT THE RAIN STOPPED SOON, AND ALL THAT WAS
LEFT IN THE TOWN WAS A FOUL, HUMID HEAT.

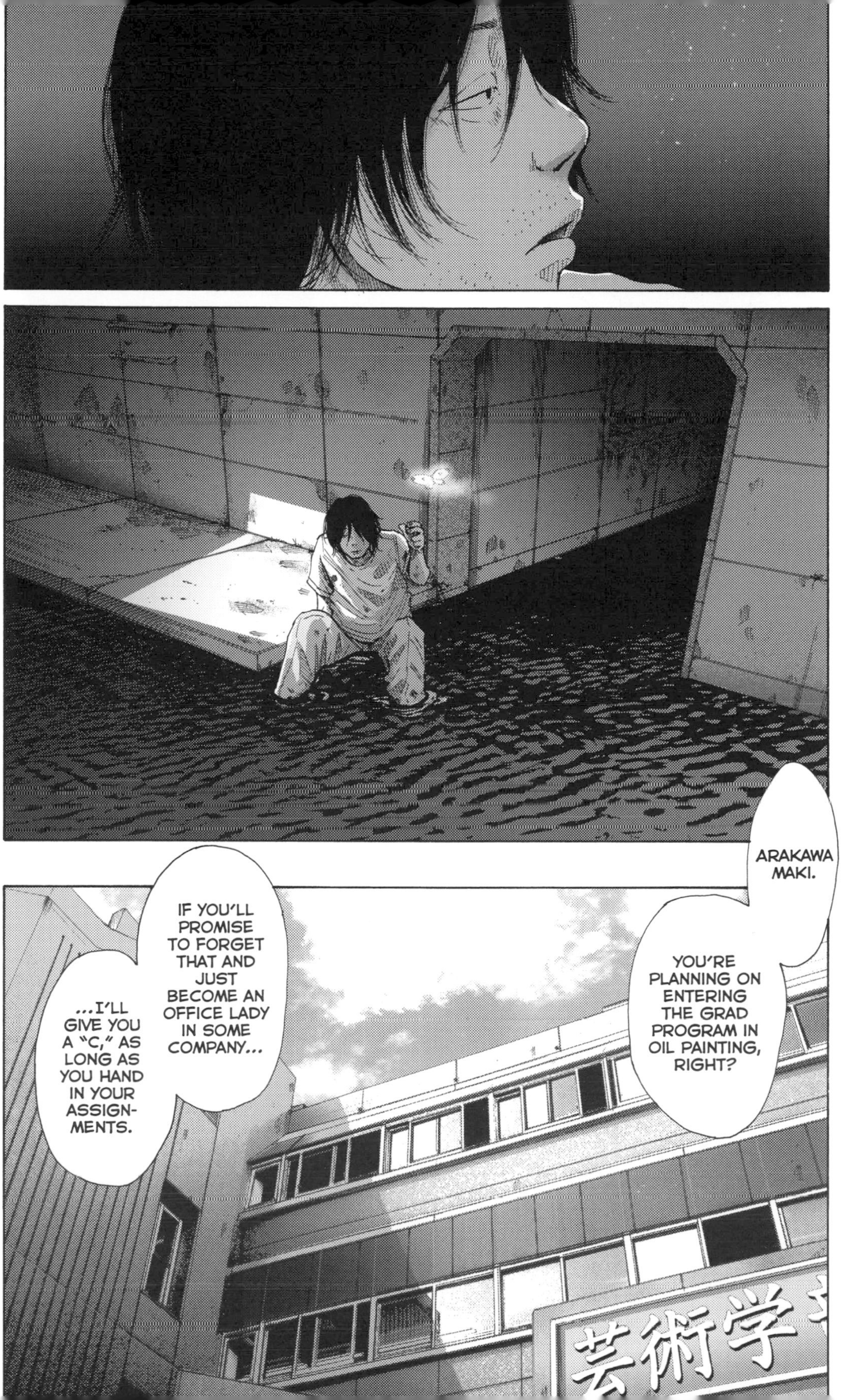
ARAKAWA MAKI.
YOU'RE PLANNING ON ENTERING THE GRAD PROGRAM IN OIL PAINTING, RIGHT?
IF YOU'LL PROMISE TO FORGET THAT AND JUST BECOME AN OFFICE LADY IN SOME COMPANY...
...I'LL GIVE YOU A "C," AS LONG AS YOU HAND IN YOUR ASSIGN-MENTS.
芸術学

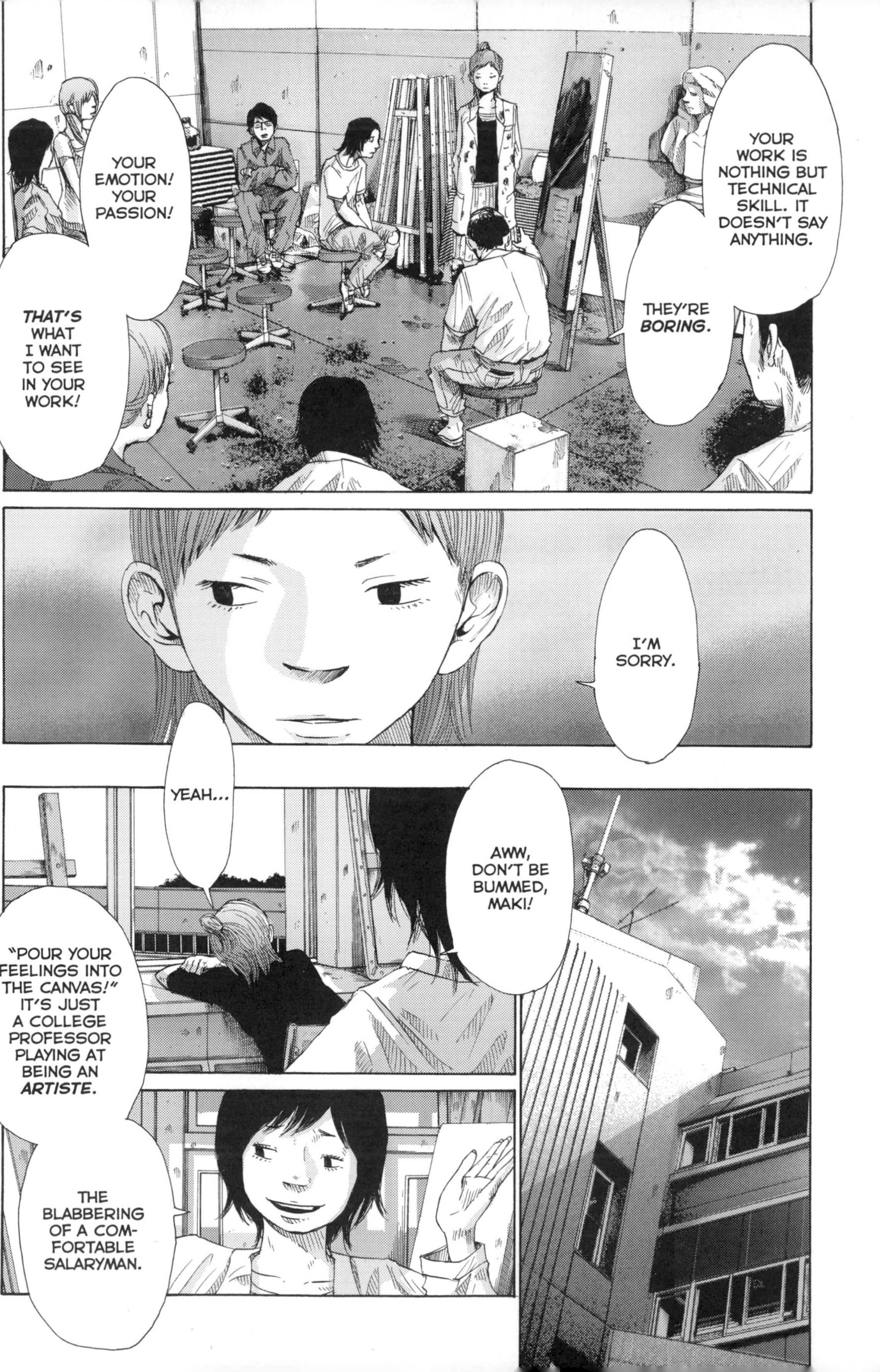
YOUR WORK IS NOTHING BUT TECHNICAL SKILL. IT DOESN'T SAY ANYTHING.
THEY'RE *BORING*.
YOUR EMOTION! YOUR PASSION!
THAT'S WHAT I WANT TO SEE IN YOUR WORK!
I'M SORRY.
YEAH...
AWW, DON'T BE BUMMED, MAKI!
"POUR YOUR FEELINGS INTO THE CANVAS!" IT'S JUST A COLLEGE PROFESSOR PLAYING AT BEING AN *ARTISTE*.
THE BLABBERING OF A COM-FORTABLE SALARYMAN.

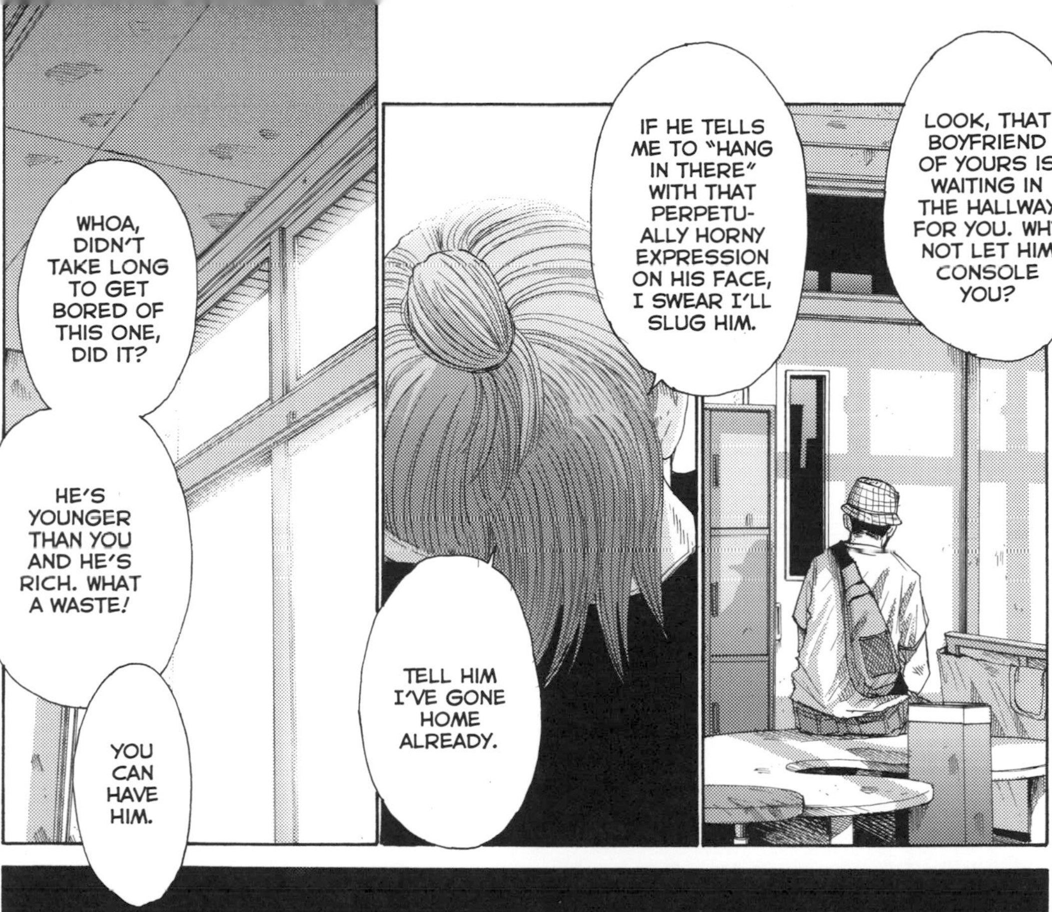
LOOK, THAT BOYFRIEND OF YOURS IS WAITING IN THE HALLWAY FOR YOU. WHY NOT LET HIM CONSOLE YOU?
IF HE TELLS ME TO "HANG IN THERE" WITH THAT PERPETU-ALLY HORNY EXPRESSION ON HIS FACE, I SWEAR I'LL SLUG HIM.
TELL HIM I'VE GONE HOME ALREADY.
WHOA, DIDN'T TAKE LONG TO GET BORED OF THIS ONE, DID IT?
HE'S YOUNGER THAN YOU AND HE'S RICH. WHAT A WASTE!
YOU CAN HAVE HIM.

CHAPTER 4

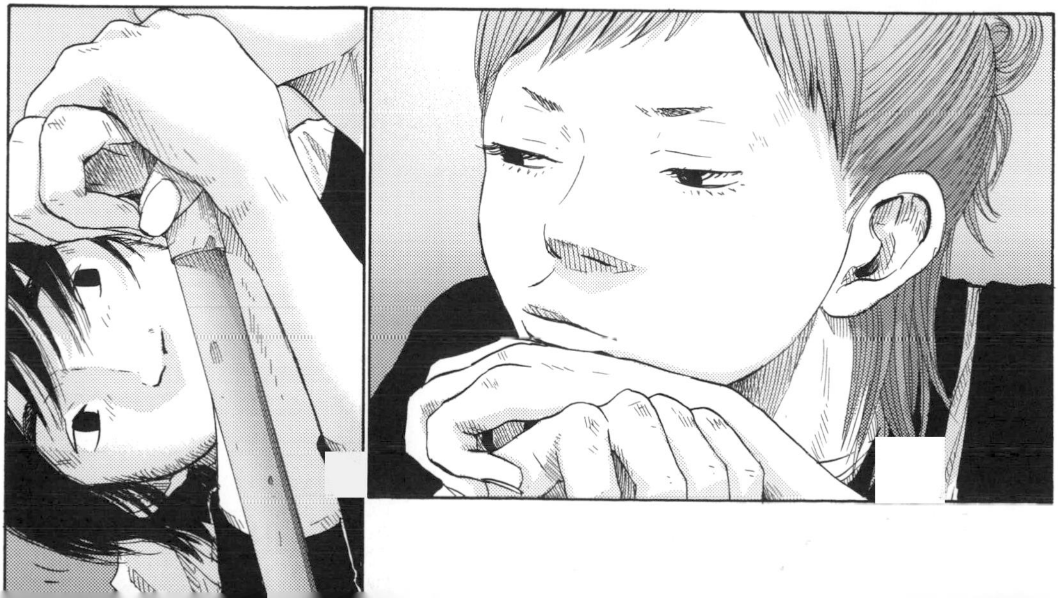

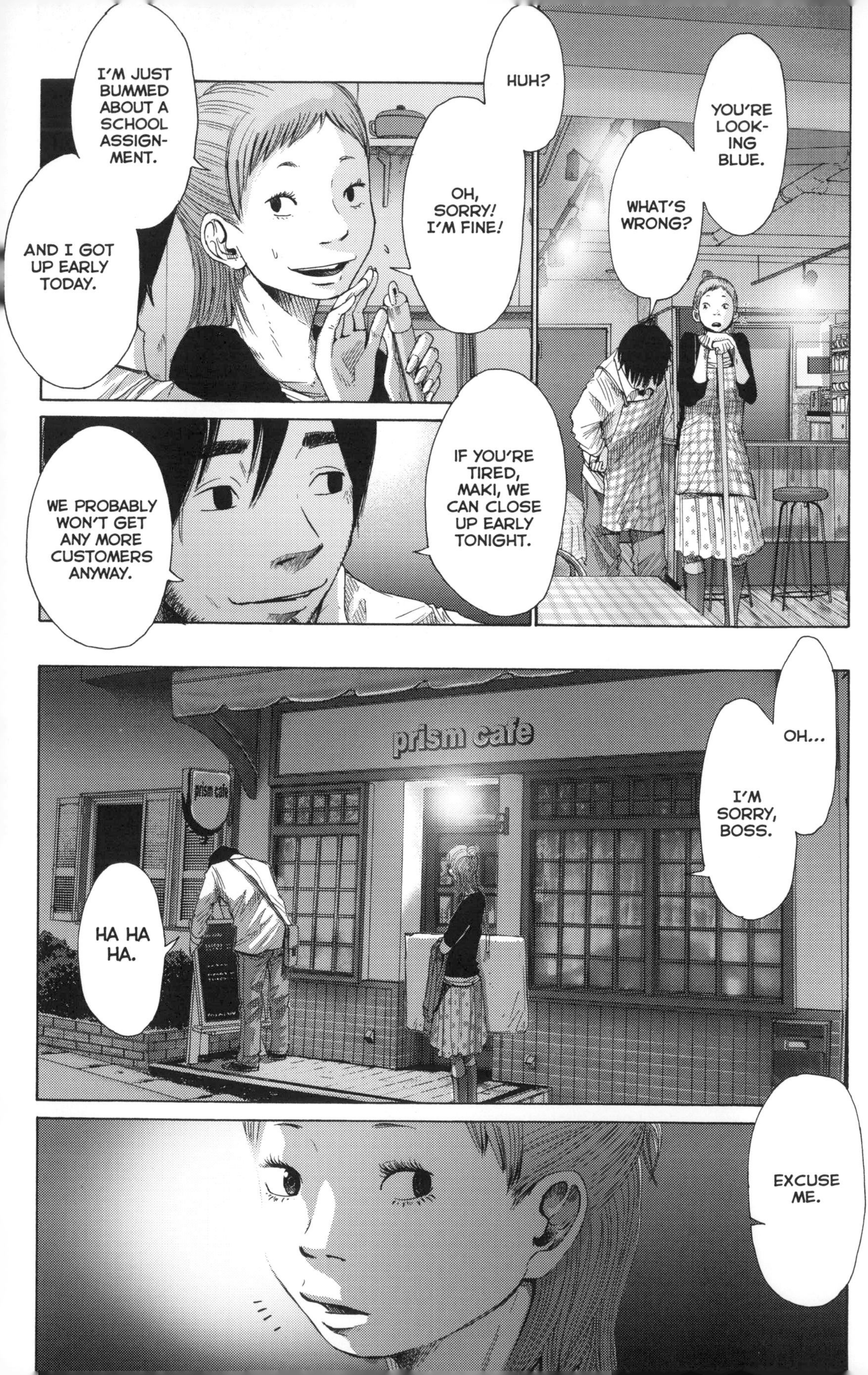
YOU'RE LOOKING BLUE.
WHAT'S WRONG?
HUH?
OH, SORRY! I'M FINE!
I'M JUST BUMMED ABOUT A SCHOOL ASSIGNMENT.
AND I GOT UP EARLY TODAY.
IF YOU'RE TIRED, MAKI, WE CAN CLOSE UP EARLY TONIGHT.
WE PROBABLY WON'T GET ANY MORE CUSTOMERS ANYWAY.
prism cafe
prism cafe
OH...
I'M SORRY, BOSS.
HA HA HA.
EXCUSE ME.

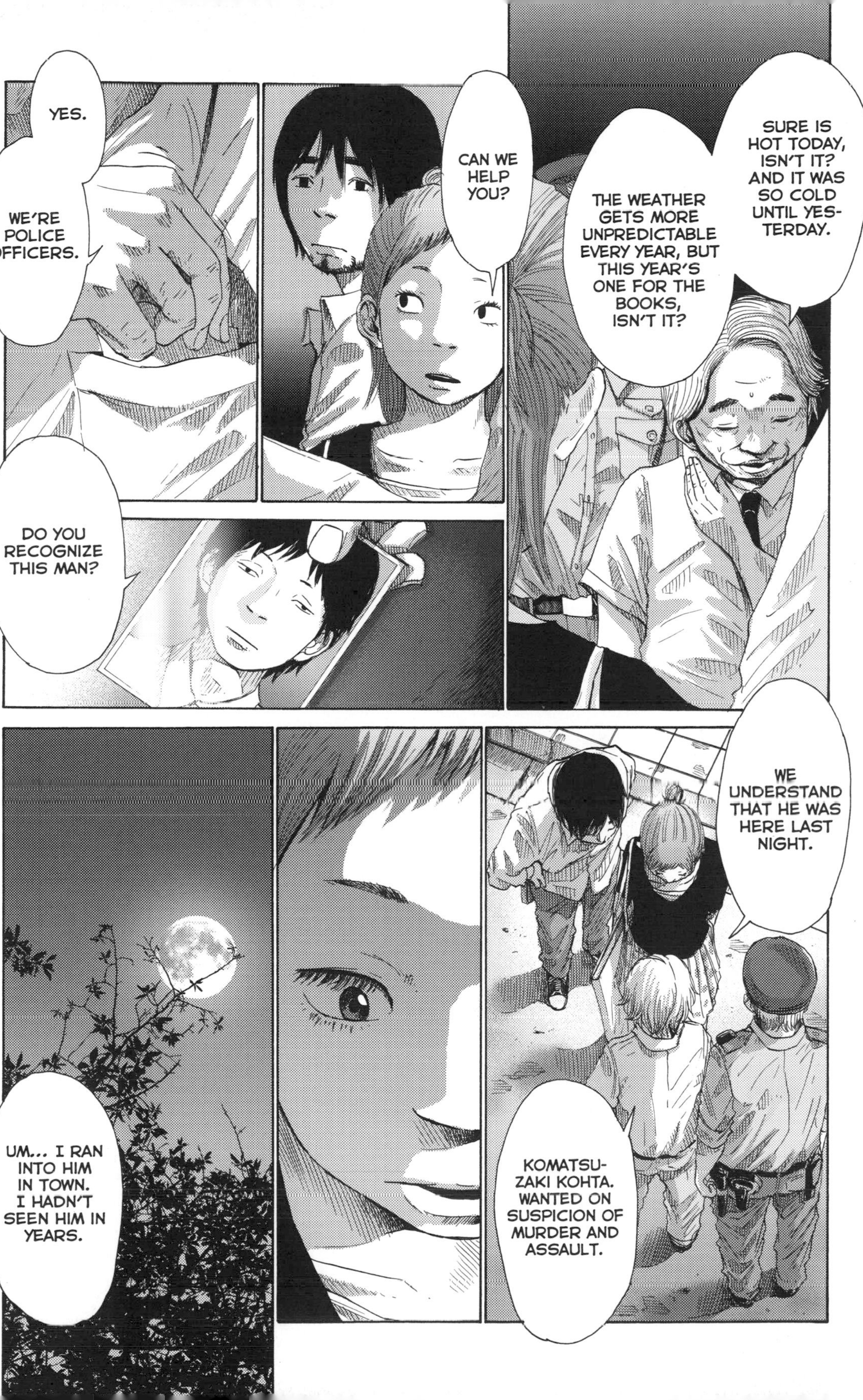
SURE IS HOT TODAY, ISN'T IT? AND IT WAS SO COLD UNTIL YESTERDAY.
THE WEATHER GETS MORE UNPREDICTABLE EVERY YEAR, BUT THIS YEAR'S ONE FOR THE BOOKS, ISN'T IT?
CAN WE HELP YOU?
YES.
WE'RE POLICE OFFICERS.
DO YOU RECOGNIZE THIS MAN?
WE UNDERSTAND THAT HE WAS HERE LAST NIGHT.
KOMATSUZAKI KOHTA. WANTED ON SUSPICION OF MURDER AND ASSAULT.
UM... I RAN INTO HIM IN TOWN. I HADN'T SEEN HIM IN YEARS.

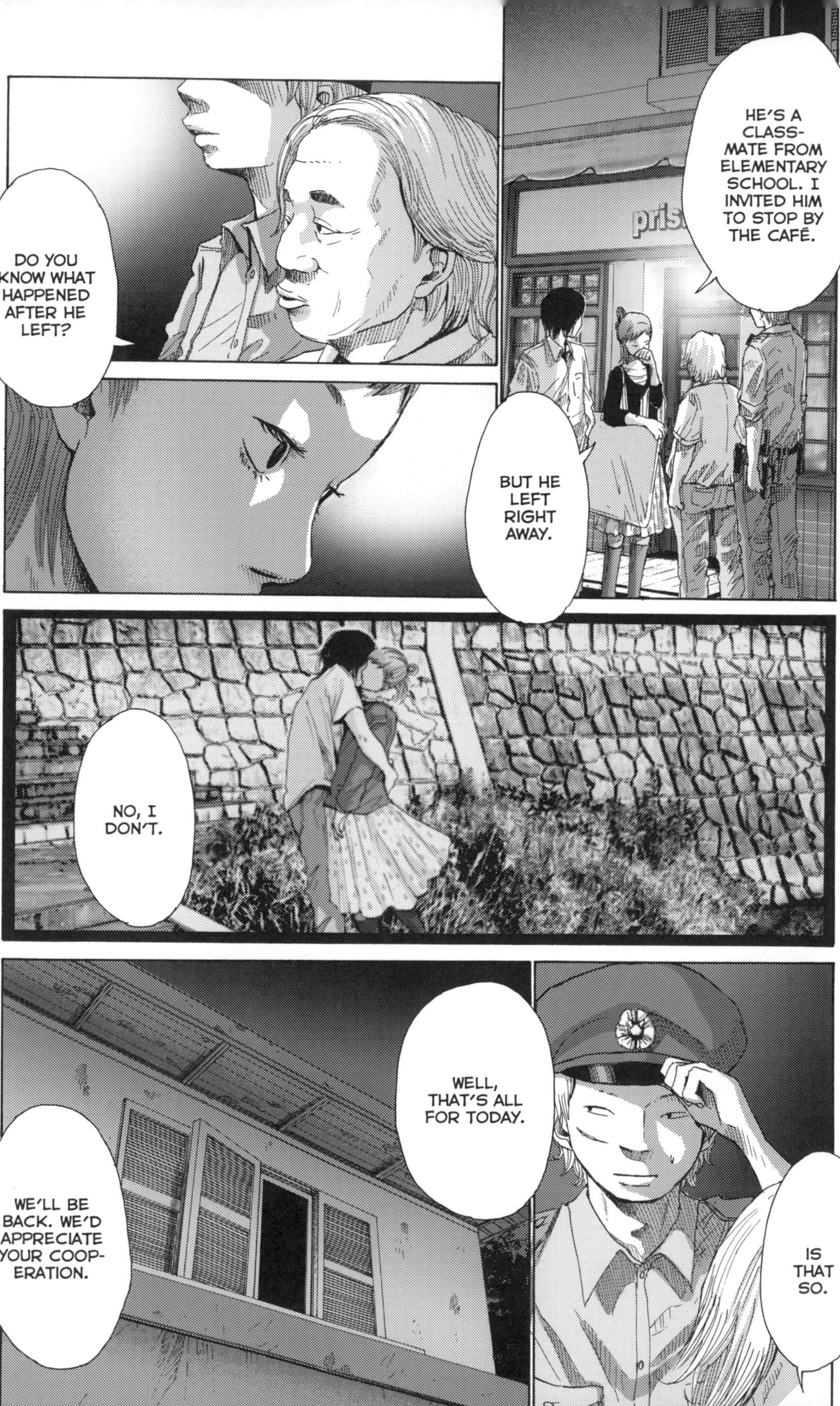
HE'S A CLASS-MATE FROM ELEMENTARY SCHOOL. I INVITED HIM TO STOP BY THE CAFÉ.
BUT HE LEFT RIGHT AWAY.
DO YOU KNOW WHAT HAPPENED AFTER HE LEFT?
NO, I DON'T.
WELL, THAT'S ALL FOR TODAY.
IS THAT SO.
WE'LL BE BACK. WE'D APPRECIATE YOUR COOP-ERATION.

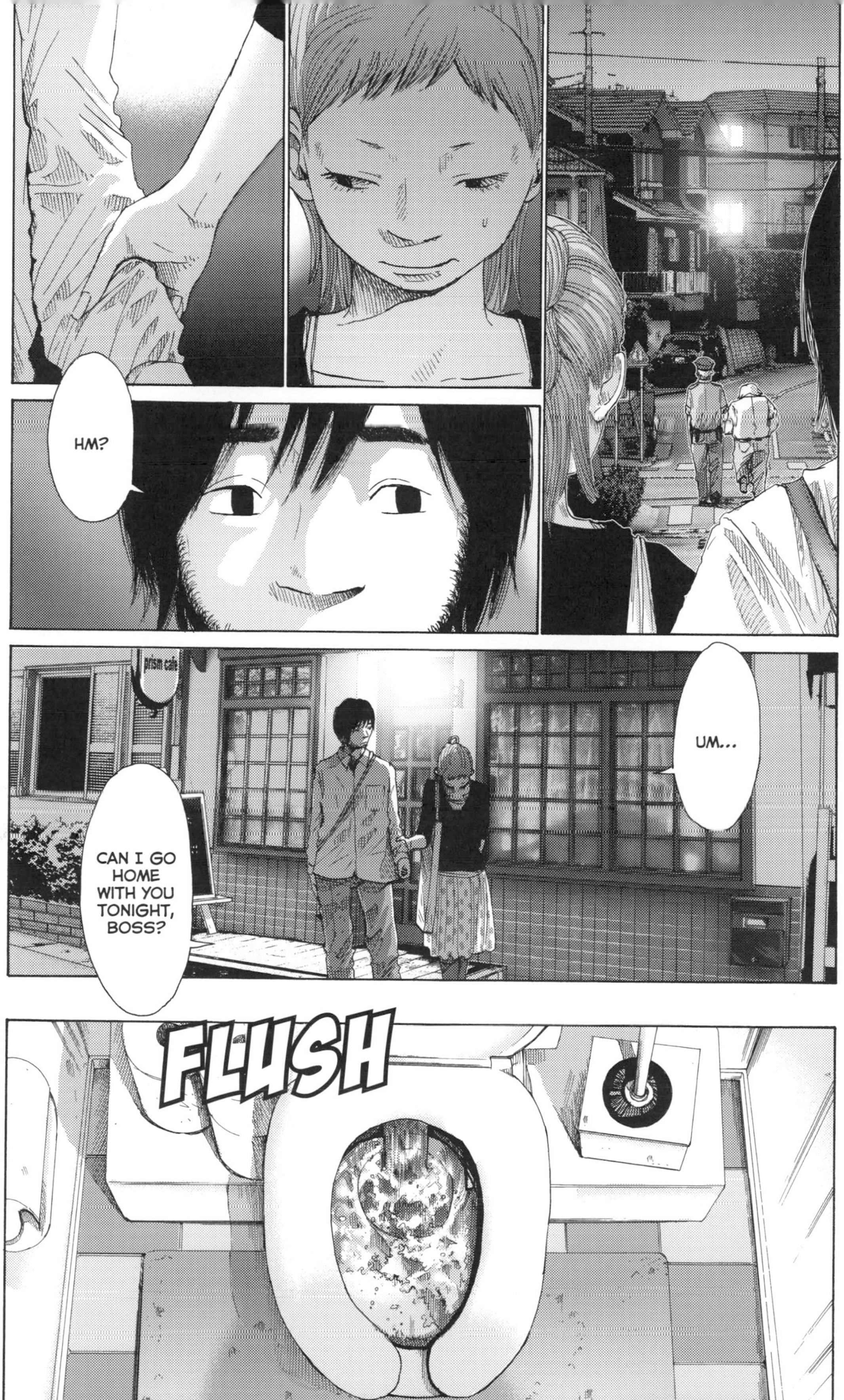
HM?
UM...
CAN I GO HOME WITH YOU TONIGHT, BOSS?
FLUSH

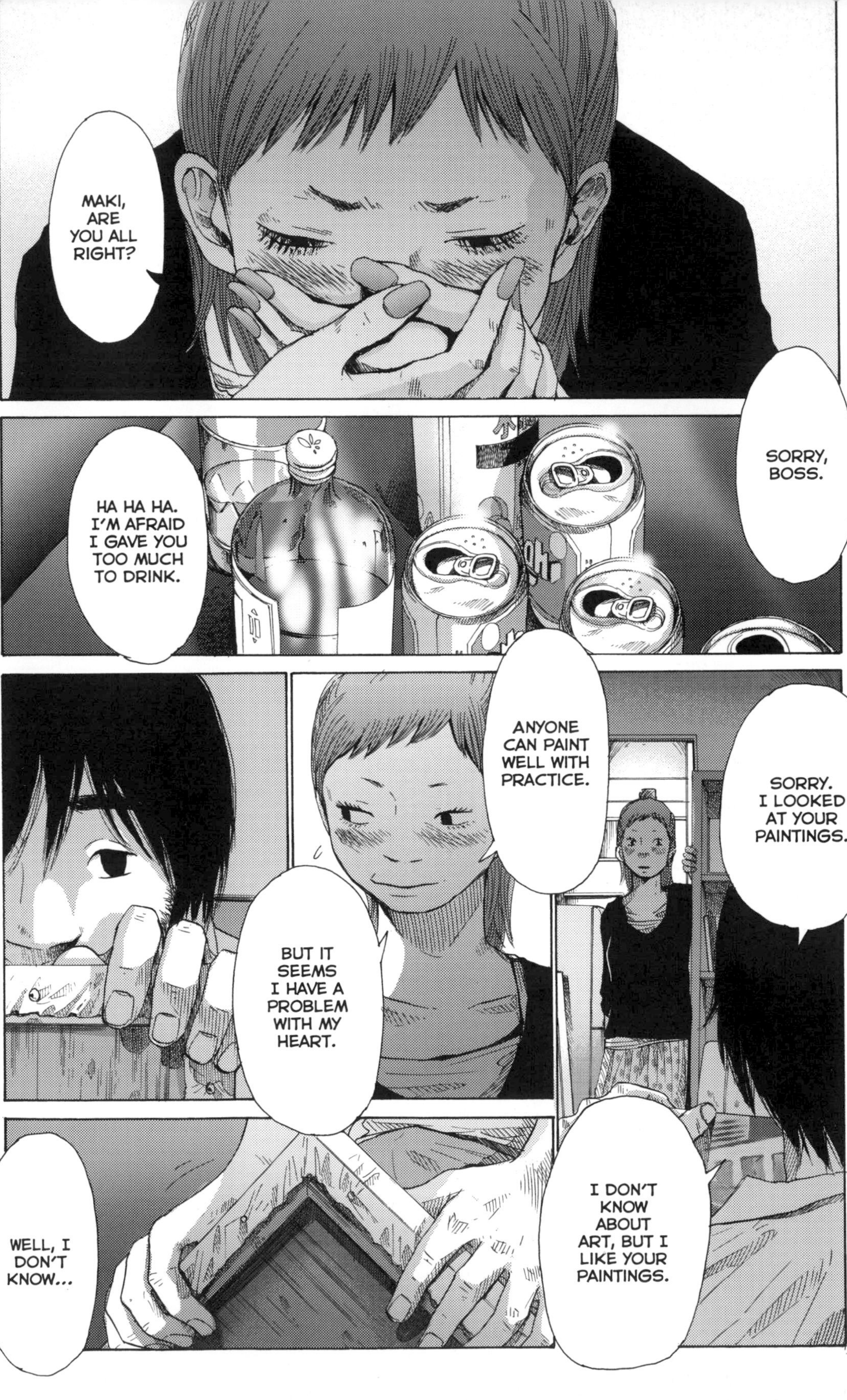
MAKI, ARE YOU ALL RIGHT?
SORRY, BOSS.
HA HA HA. I'M AFRAID I GAVE YOU TOO MUCH TO DRINK.
SORRY. I LOOKED AT YOUR PAINTINGS.
ANYONE CAN PAINT WELL WITH PRACTICE.
BUT IT SEEMS I HAVE A PROBLEM WITH MY HEART.
I DON'T KNOW ABOUT ART, BUT I LIKE YOUR PAINTINGS.
WELL, I DON'T KNOW...

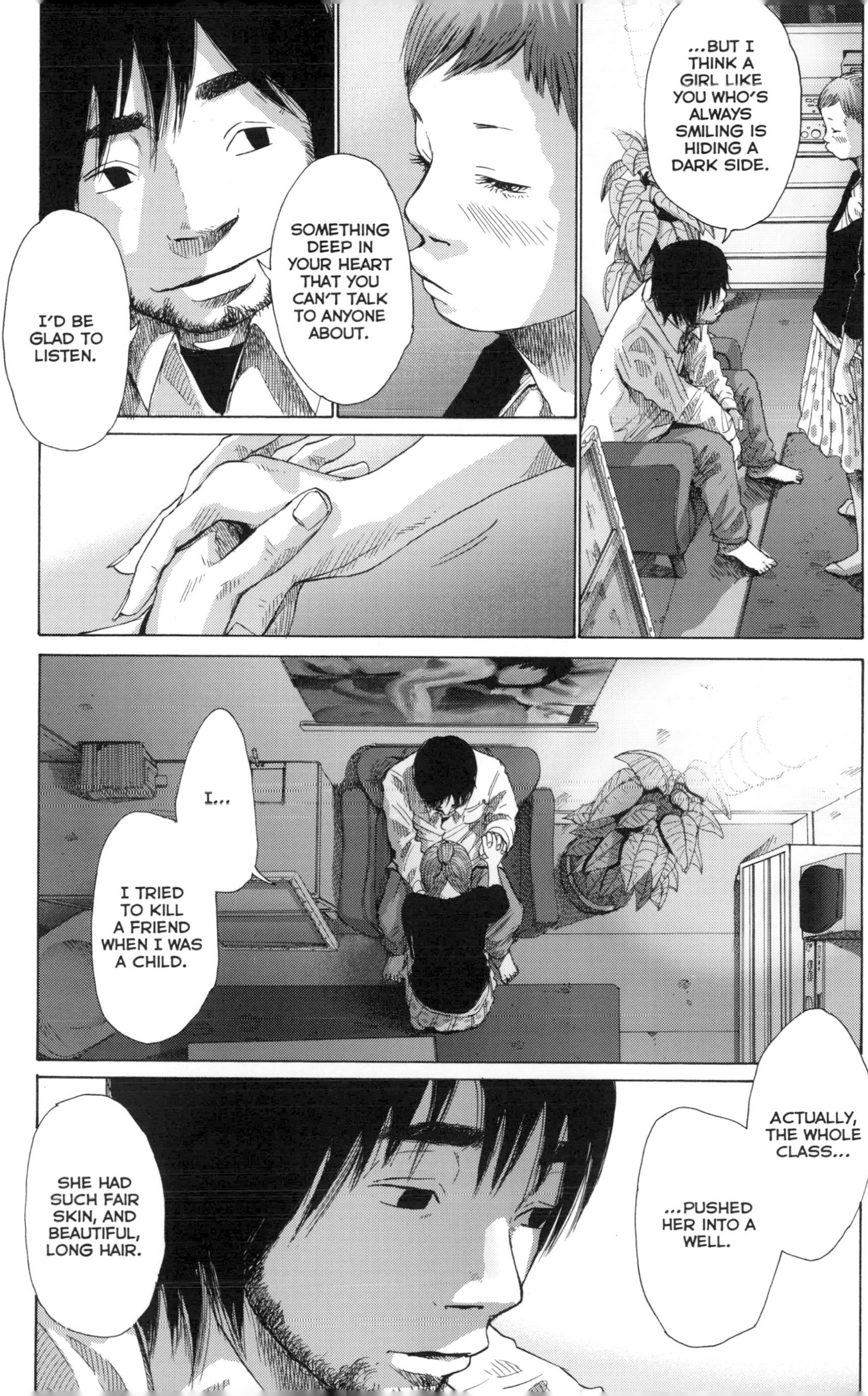
...BUT I THINK A GIRL LIKE YOU WHO'S ALWAYS SMILING IS HIDING A DARK SIDE.
SOMETHING DEEP IN YOUR HEART THAT YOU CAN'T TALK TO ANYONE ABOUT.
I'D BE GLAD TO LISTEN.
I...
I TRIED TO KILL A FRIEND WHEN I WAS A CHILD.
ACTUALLY, THE WHOLE CLASS...
...PUSHED HER INTO A WELL.
SHE HAD SUCH FAIR SKIN, AND BEAUTIFUL, LONG HAIR.

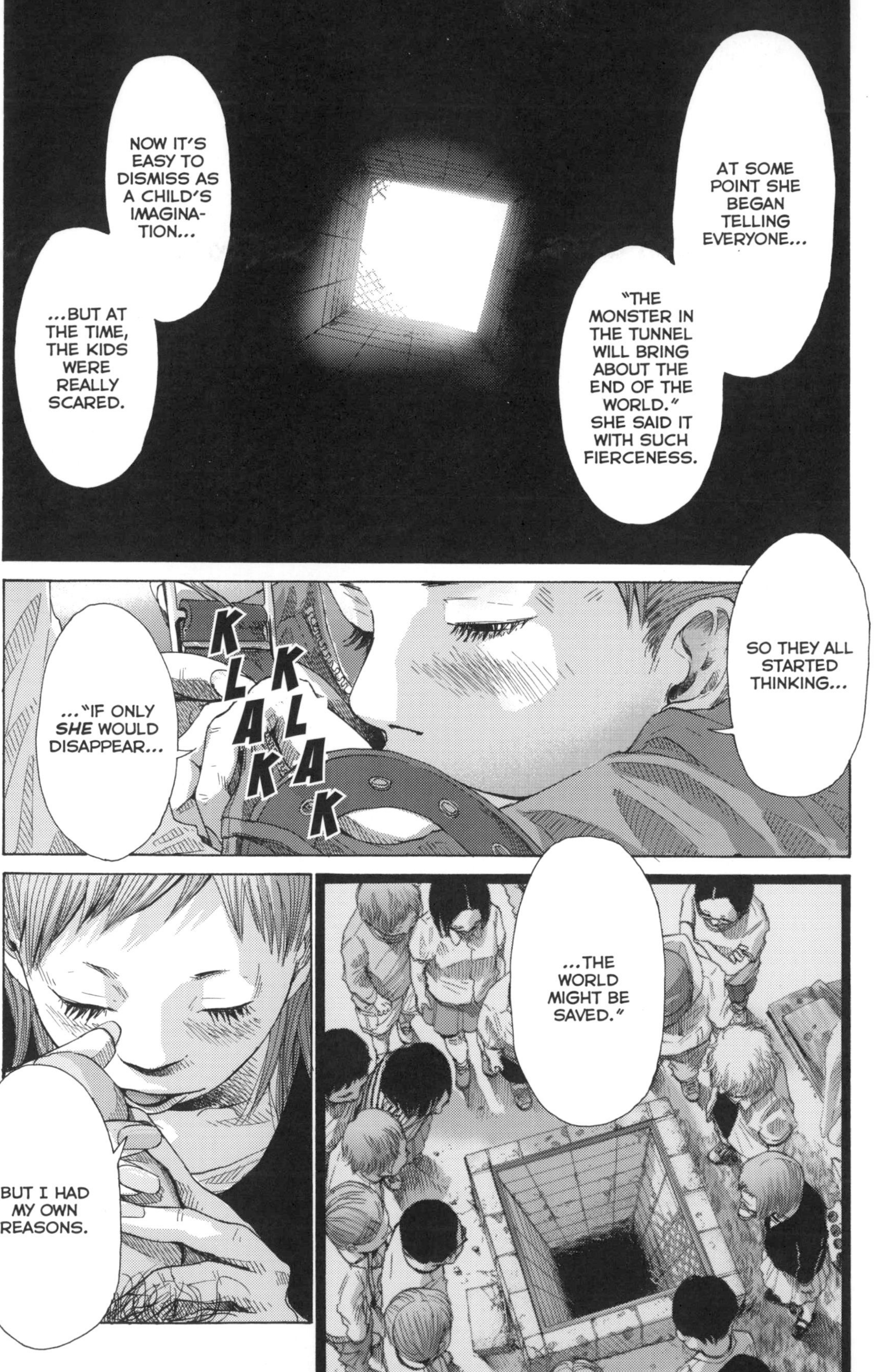
AT SOME POINT SHE BEGAN TELLING EVERYONE...
"THE MONSTER IN THE TUNNEL WILL BRING ABOUT THE END OF THE WORLD." SHE SAID IT WITH SUCH FIERCENESS.
NOW IT'S EASY TO DISMISS AS A CHILD'S IMAGINATION...
...BUT AT THE TIME, THE KIDS WERE REALLY SCARED.
SO THEY ALL STARTED THINKING...
KLAK KLAK
..."IF ONLY *SHE* WOULD DISAPPEAR...
...THE WORLD MIGHT BE SAVED."
BUT I HAD MY OWN REASONS.

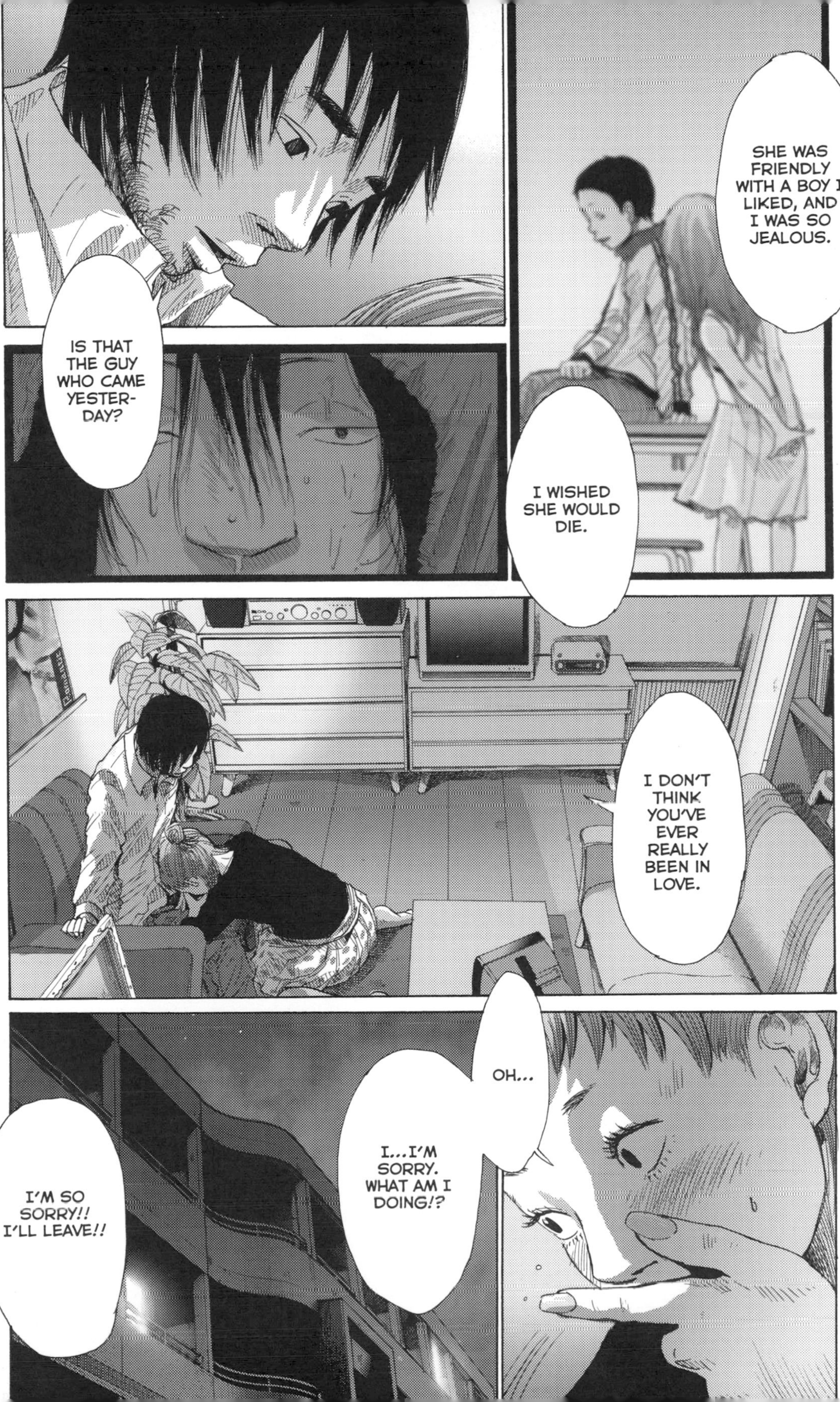
SHE WAS FRIENDLY WITH A BOY I LIKED, AND I WAS SO JEALOUS.
I WISHED SHE WOULD DIE.
IS THAT THE GUY WHO CAME YESTER-DAY?
I DON'T THINK YOU'VE EVER REALLY BEEN IN LOVE.
OH...
I...I'M SORRY. WHAT AM I DOING!?
I'M SO SORRY!! I'LL LEAVE!!

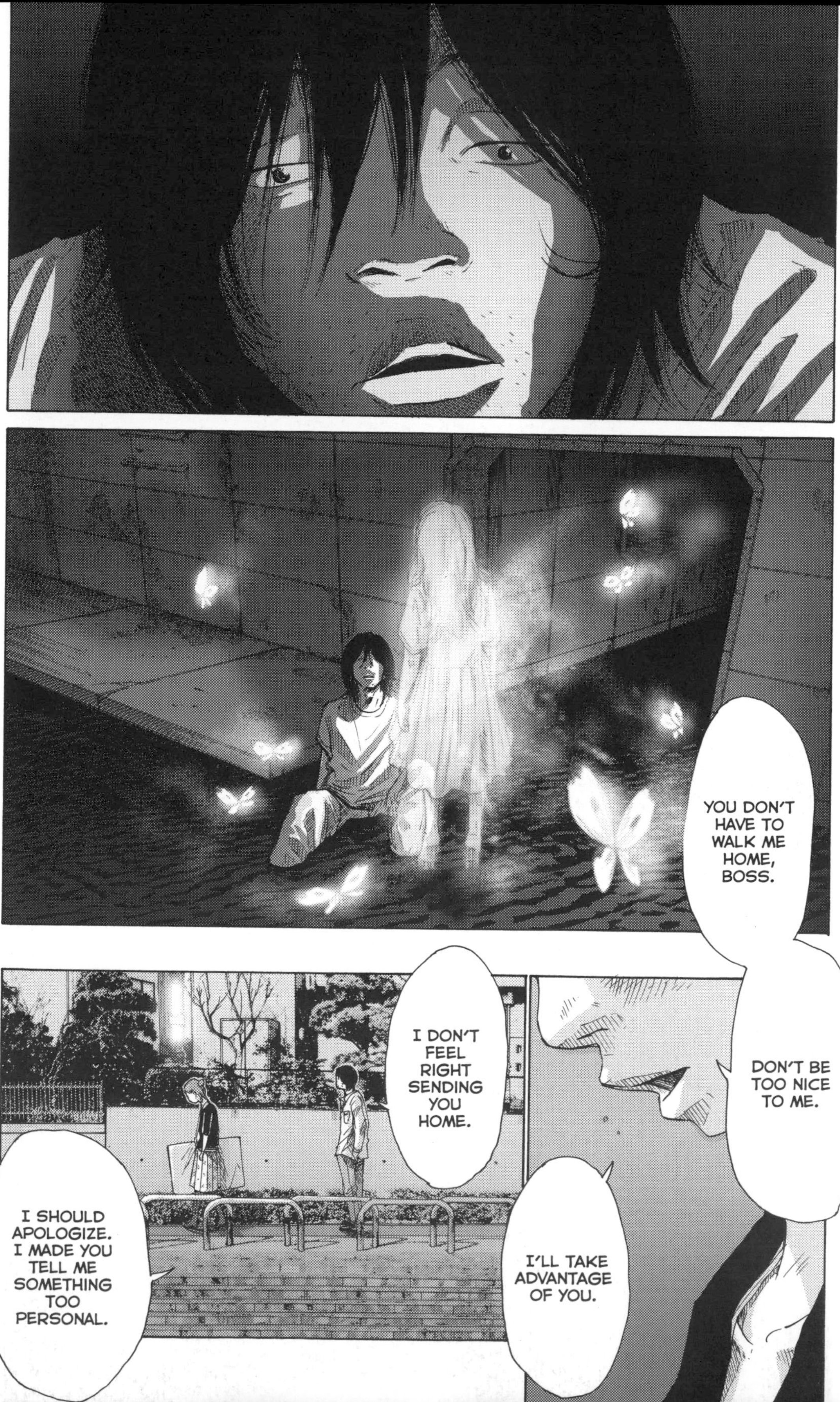
YOU DON'T HAVE TO WALK ME HOME, BOSS.
DON'T BE TOO NICE TO ME.
I'LL TAKE ADVANTAGE OF YOU.
I DON'T FEEL RIGHT SENDING YOU HOME.
I SHOULD APOLOGIZE. I MADE YOU TELL ME SOMETHING TOO PERSONAL.

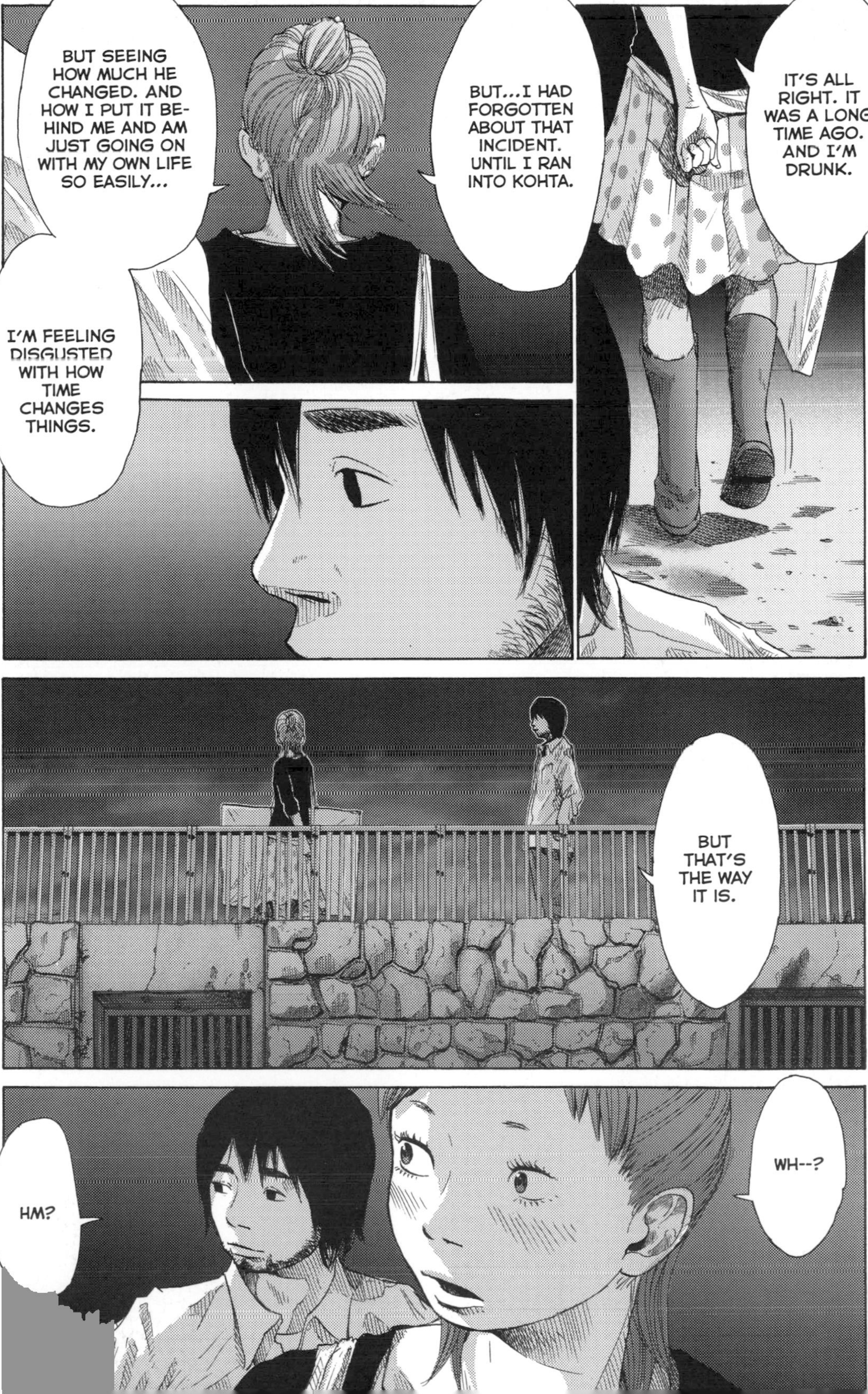
IT'S ALL RIGHT. IT WAS A LONG TIME AGO. AND I'M DRUNK.
BUT...I HAD FORGOTTEN ABOUT THAT INCIDENT. UNTIL I RAN INTO KOHTA.
BUT SEEING HOW MUCH HE CHANGED. AND HOW I PUT IT BE-HIND ME AND AM JUST GOING ON WITH MY OWN LIFE SO EASILY...
I'M FEELING DISGUSTED WITH HOW TIME CHANGES THINGS.
BUT THAT'S THE WAY IT IS.
WH--?
HM?

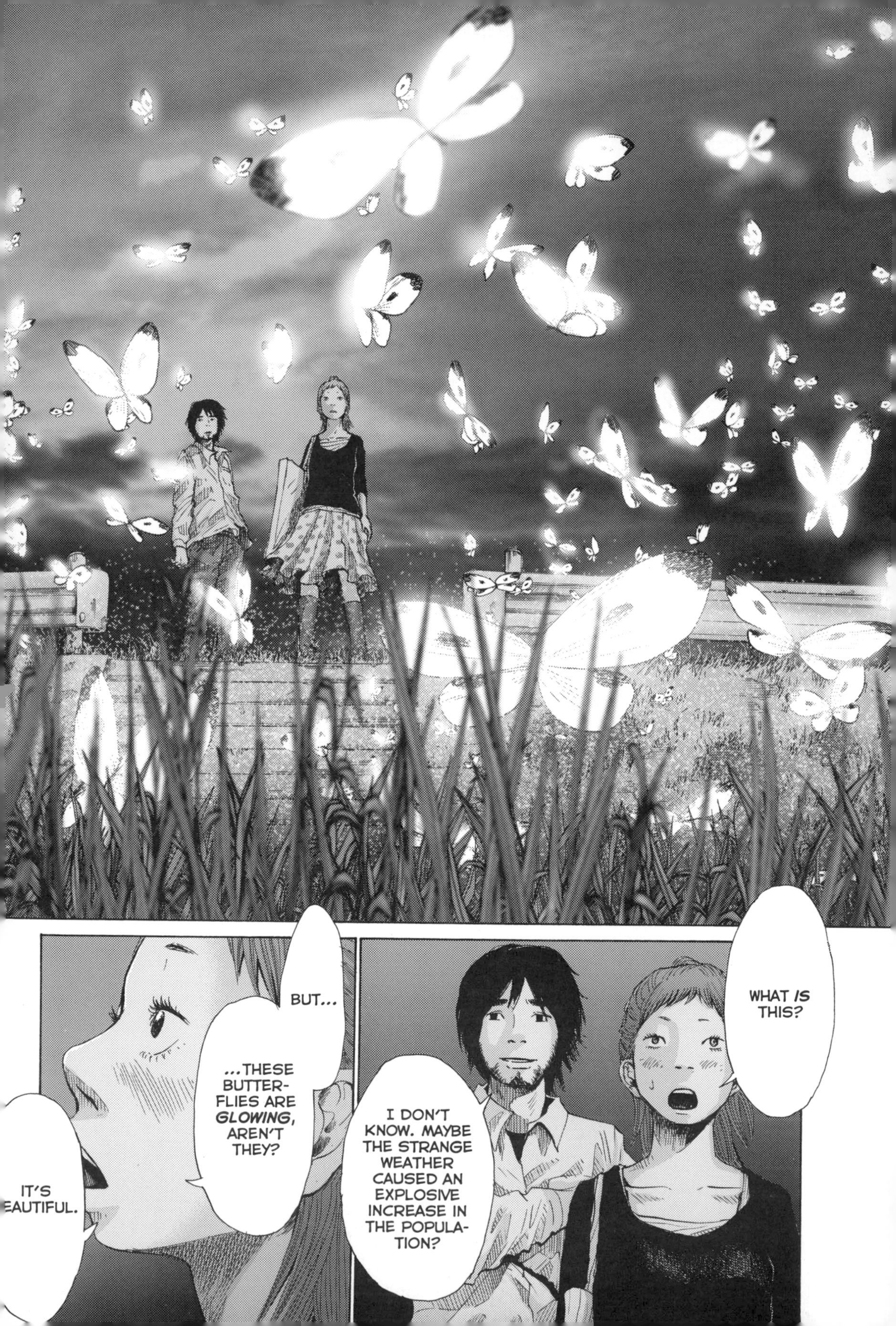
WHAT *IS* THIS?
I DON'T KNOW. MAYBE THE STRANGE WEATHER CAUSED AN EXPLOSIVE INCREASE IN THE POPULATION?
BUT...
...THESE BUTTER-FLIES ARE ***GLOWING***, AREN'T THEY?
IT'S EAUTIFUL.

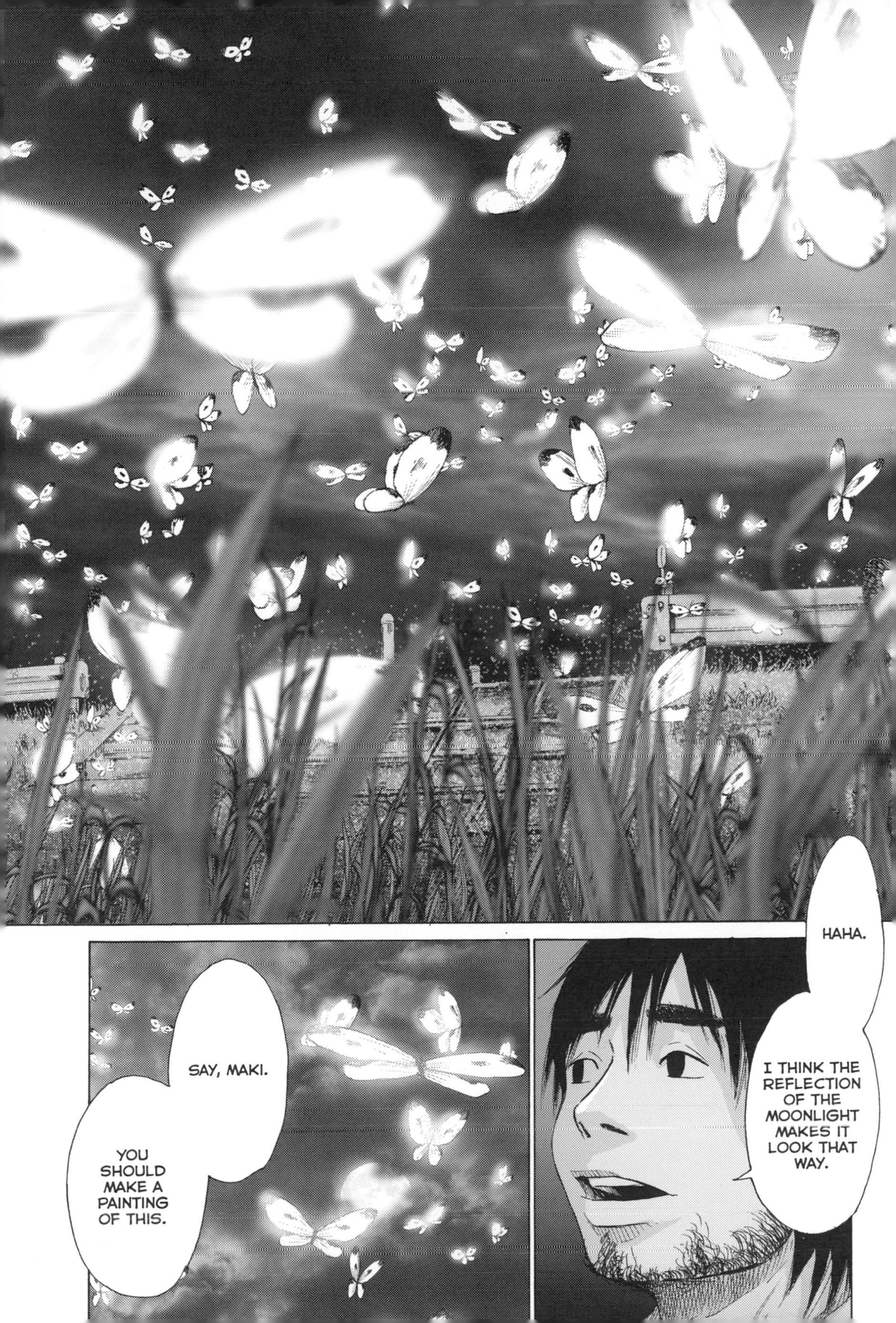
HAHA.
I THINK THE REFLECTION OF THE MOONLIGHT MAKES IT LOOK THAT WAY.
SAY, MAKI.
YOU SHOULD MAKE A PAINTING OF THIS.

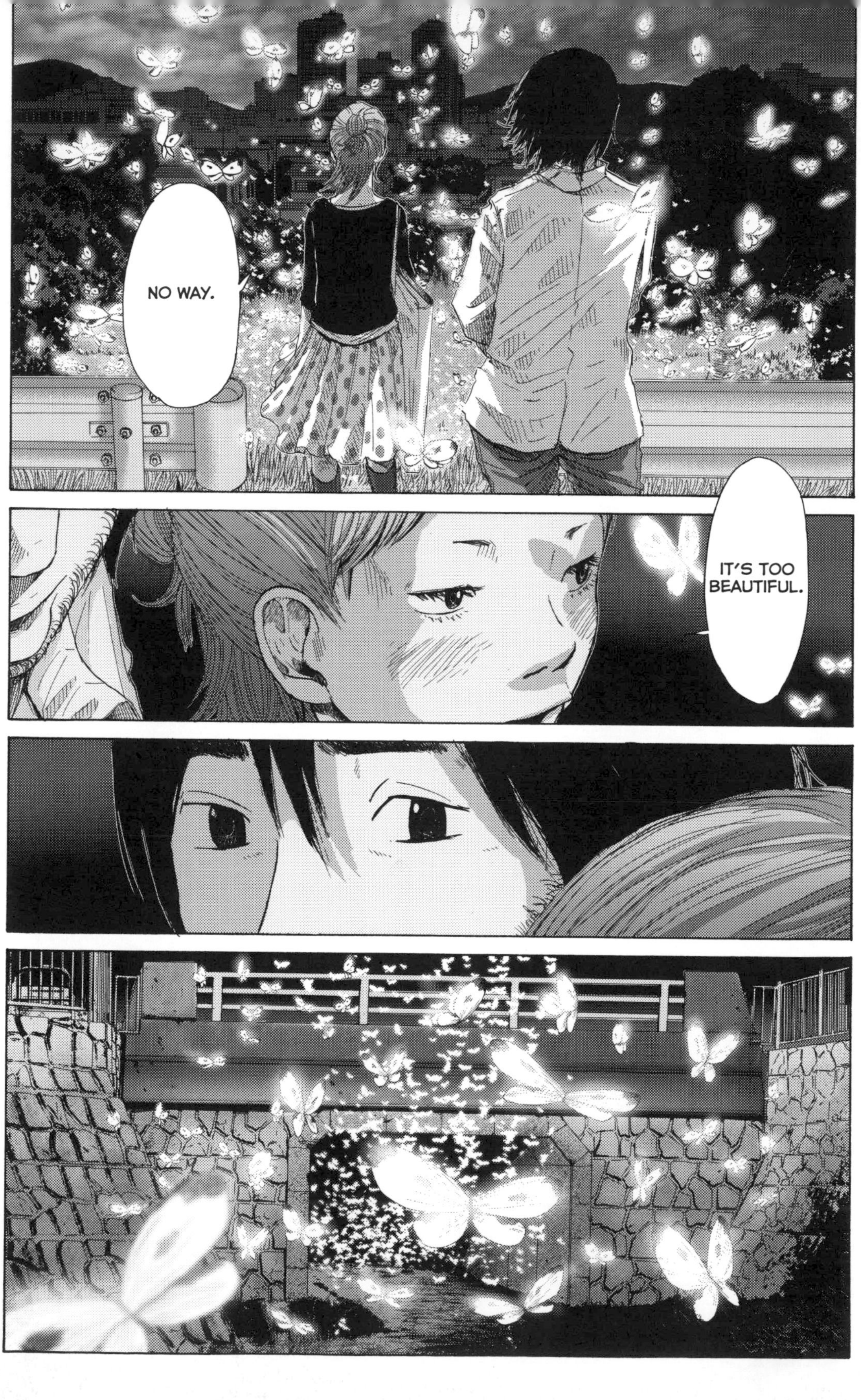
NO WAY.
IT'S TOO BEAUTIFUL.

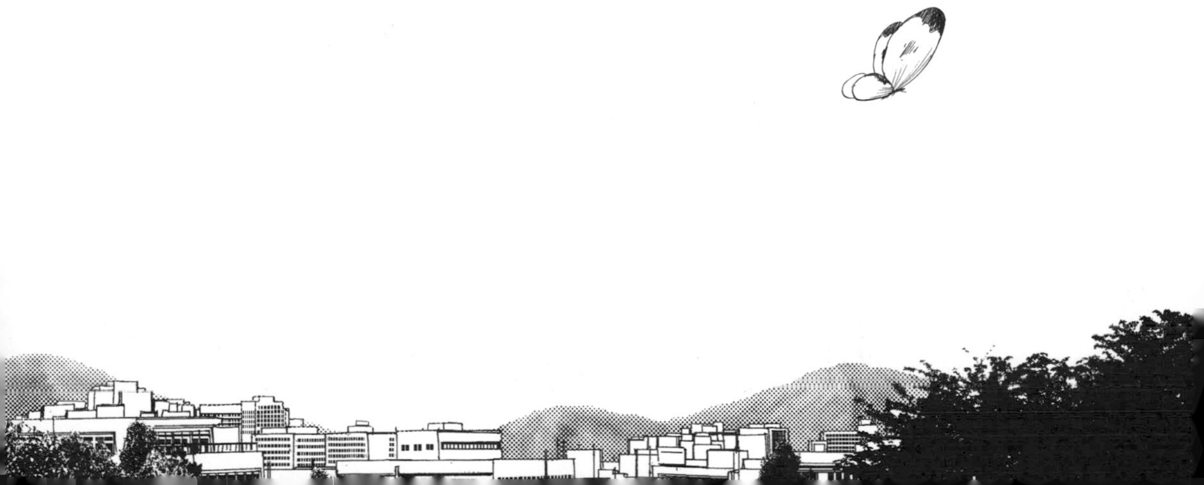

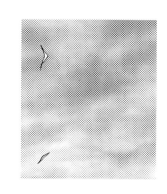

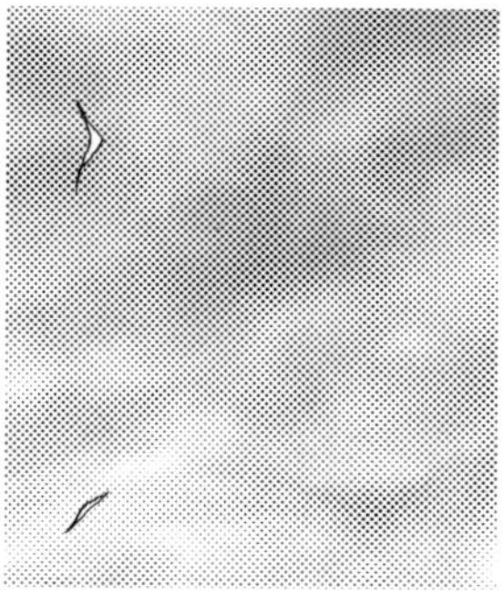

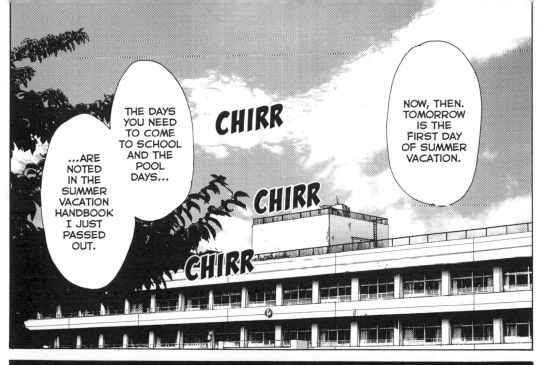

NOW, THEN. TOMORROW IS THE FIRST DAY OF SUMMER VACATION.

THE DAYS YOU NEED TO COME TO SCHOOL AND THE POOL DAYS...

...ARE NOTED IN THE SUMMER VACATION HANDBOOK I JUST PASSED OUT.

CHIRR

CHIRR

CHIRR

I FEEL LIKE THE ATMOSPHERE IN OUR CLASS HAS IMPROVED EVER SINCE KOHTA FELL AND WAS INJURED.

I CAME FROM OUTSIDE, SO I DON'T KNOW THE DETAILS OF HOW THINGS WERE BEFORE...

...BUT IT'S NICE HAVING PEACE IN THE CLASSROOM.

I KNOW IT'S HOT, BUT DON'T USE THAT AS AN EXCUSE TO PUT OFF YOUR SUMMER HOMEWORK TILL THE LAST MINUTE.

RIGHT. GOODBYE, CHILDREN.

AMAHIKO! LET'S GO HANG OUT AT THE VIDEO ARCADE.

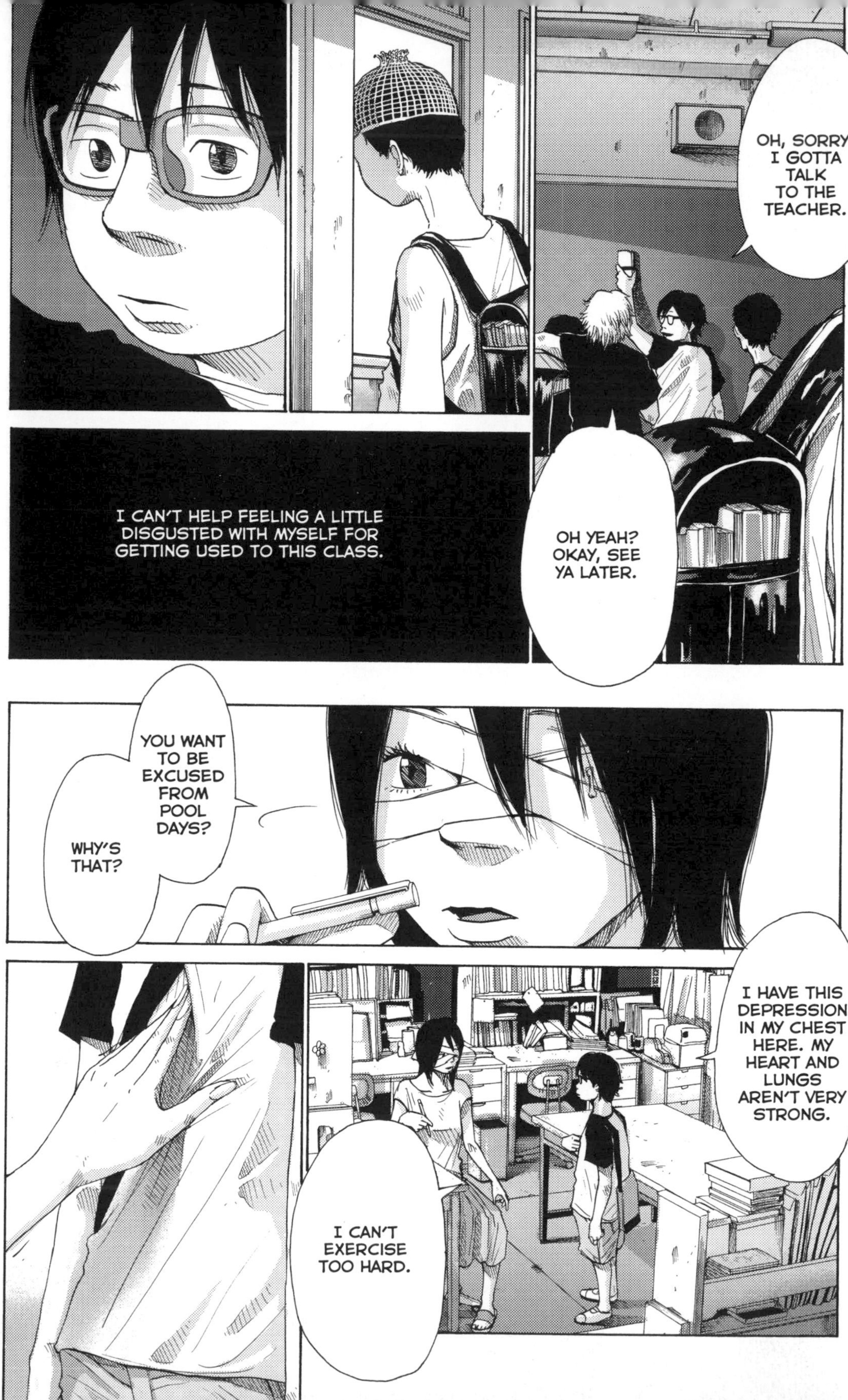
OH, SORRY. I GOTTA TALK TO THE TEACHER.
OH YEAH? OKAY, SEE YA LATER.
I CAN'T HELP FEELING A LITTLE DISGUSTED WITH MYSELF FOR GETTING USED TO THIS CLASS.
YOU WANT TO BE EXCUSED FROM POOL DAYS?
WHY'S THAT?
I HAVE THIS DEPRESSION IN MY CHEST HERE. MY HEART AND LUNGS AREN'T VERY STRONG.
I CAN'T EXERCISE TOO HARD.

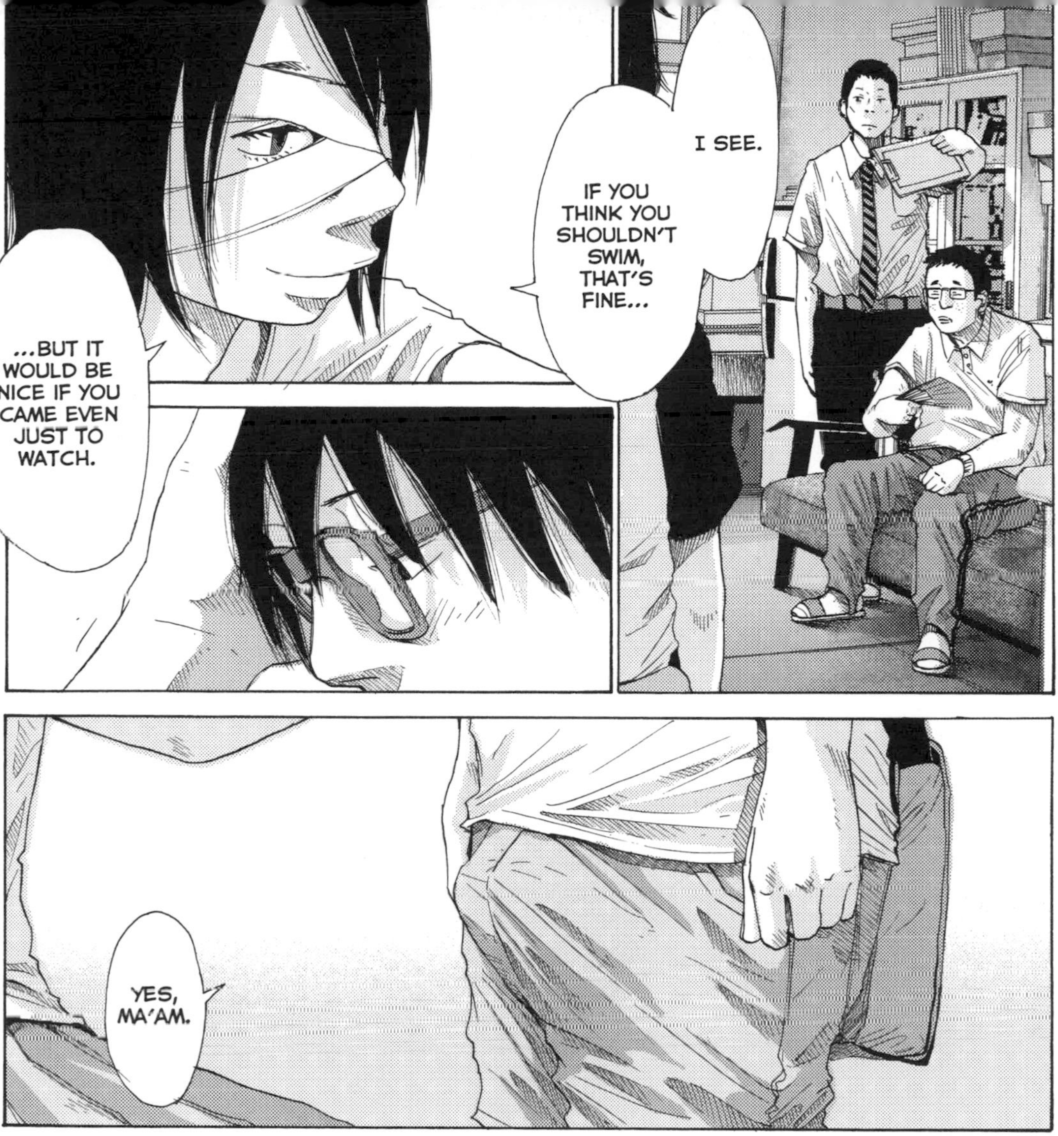
I SEE.
IF YOU THINK YOU SHOULDN'T SWIM, THAT'S FINE...
...BUT IT WOULD BE NICE IF YOU CAME EVEN JUST TO WATCH.
YES, MA'AM.

CHAPTER 5

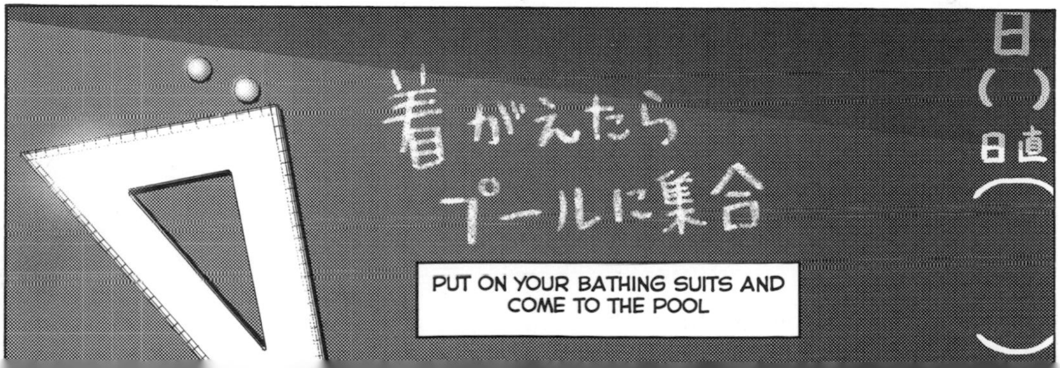
日
( )
日直
着がえたら
プールに集合
PUT ON YOUR BATHING SUITS AND COME TO THE POOL

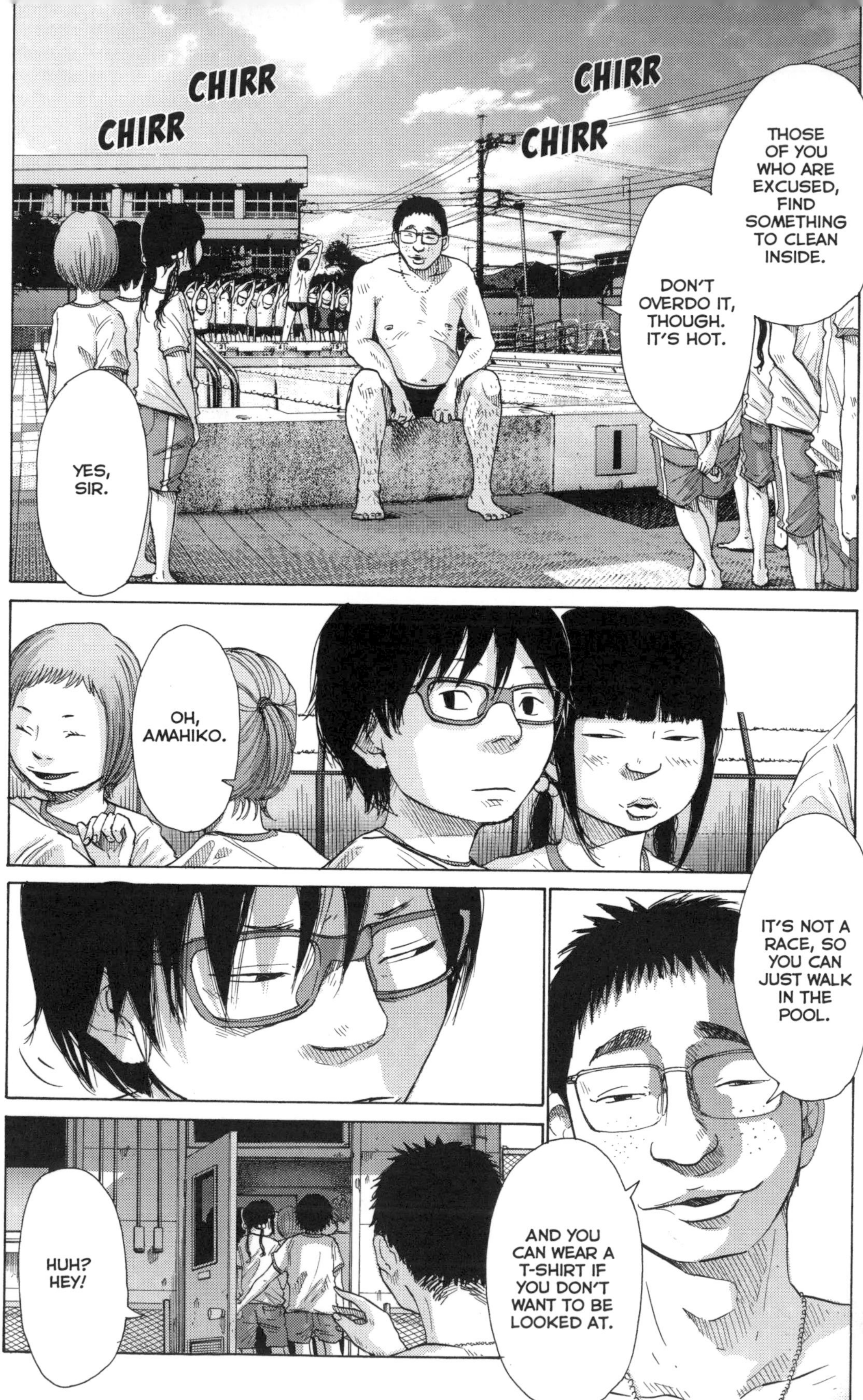
CHIRR
CHIRR
CHIRR
CHIRR
THOSE OF YOU WHO ARE EXCUSED, FIND SOMETHING TO CLEAN INSIDE.
DON'T OVERDO IT, THOUGH. IT'S HOT.
YES, SIR.
OH, AMAHIKO.
IT'S NOT A RACE, SO YOU CAN JUST WALK IN THE POOL.
AND YOU CAN WEAR A T-SHIRT IF YOU DON'T WANT TO BE LOOKED AT.
HUH? HEY!

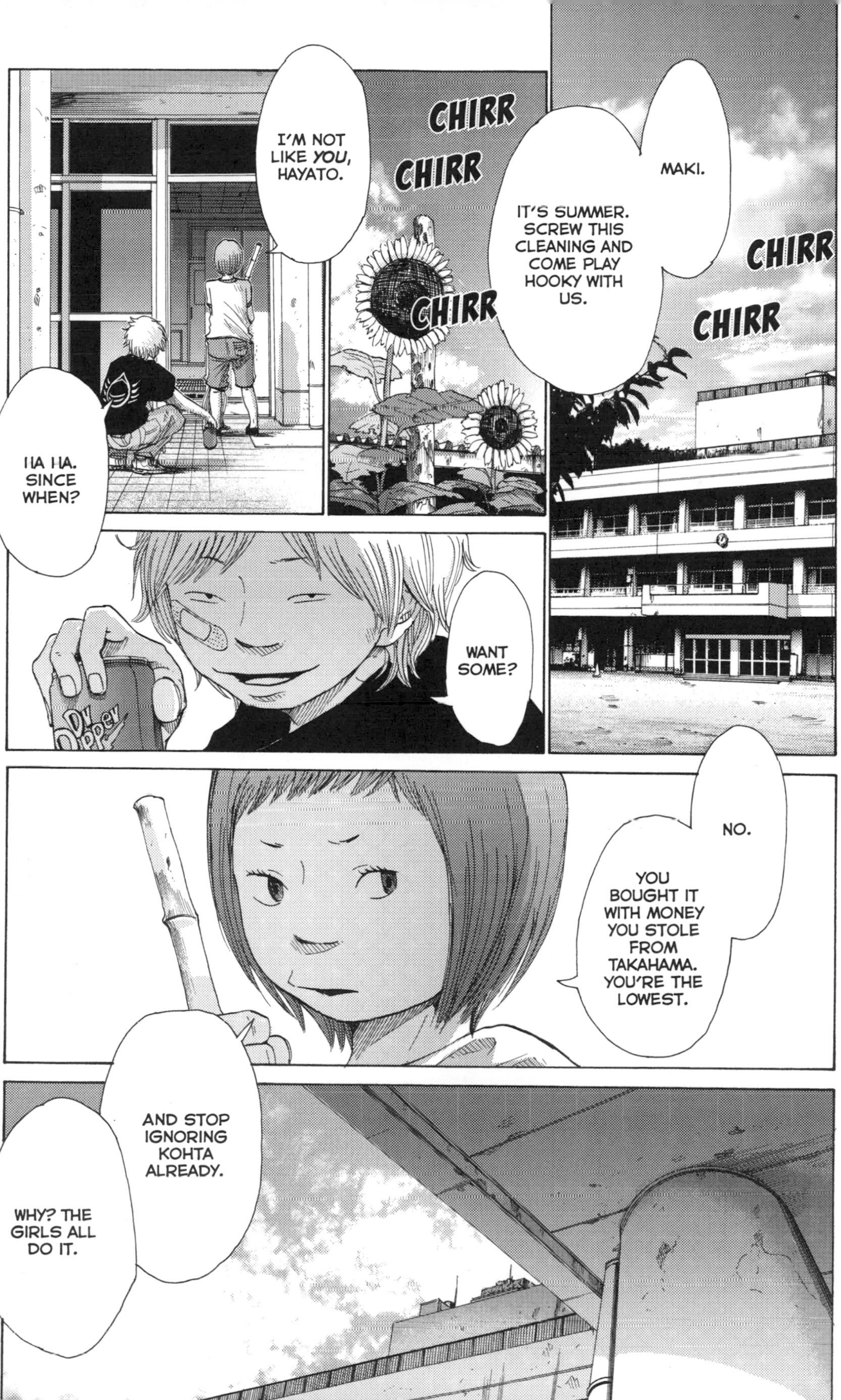

CHIRR
CHIRR
MAKI.
IT'S SUMMER. SCREW THIS CLEANING AND COME PLAY HOOKY WITH US.
CHIRR
CHIRR
CHIRR
I'M NOT LIKE *YOU*, HAYATO.
HA HA. SINCE WHEN?
WANT SOME?
Dr Pepper
NO.
YOU BOUGHT IT WITH MONEY YOU STOLE FROM TAKAHAMA. YOU'RE THE LOWEST.
AND STOP IGNORING KOHTA ALREADY.
WHY? THE GIRLS ALL DO IT.

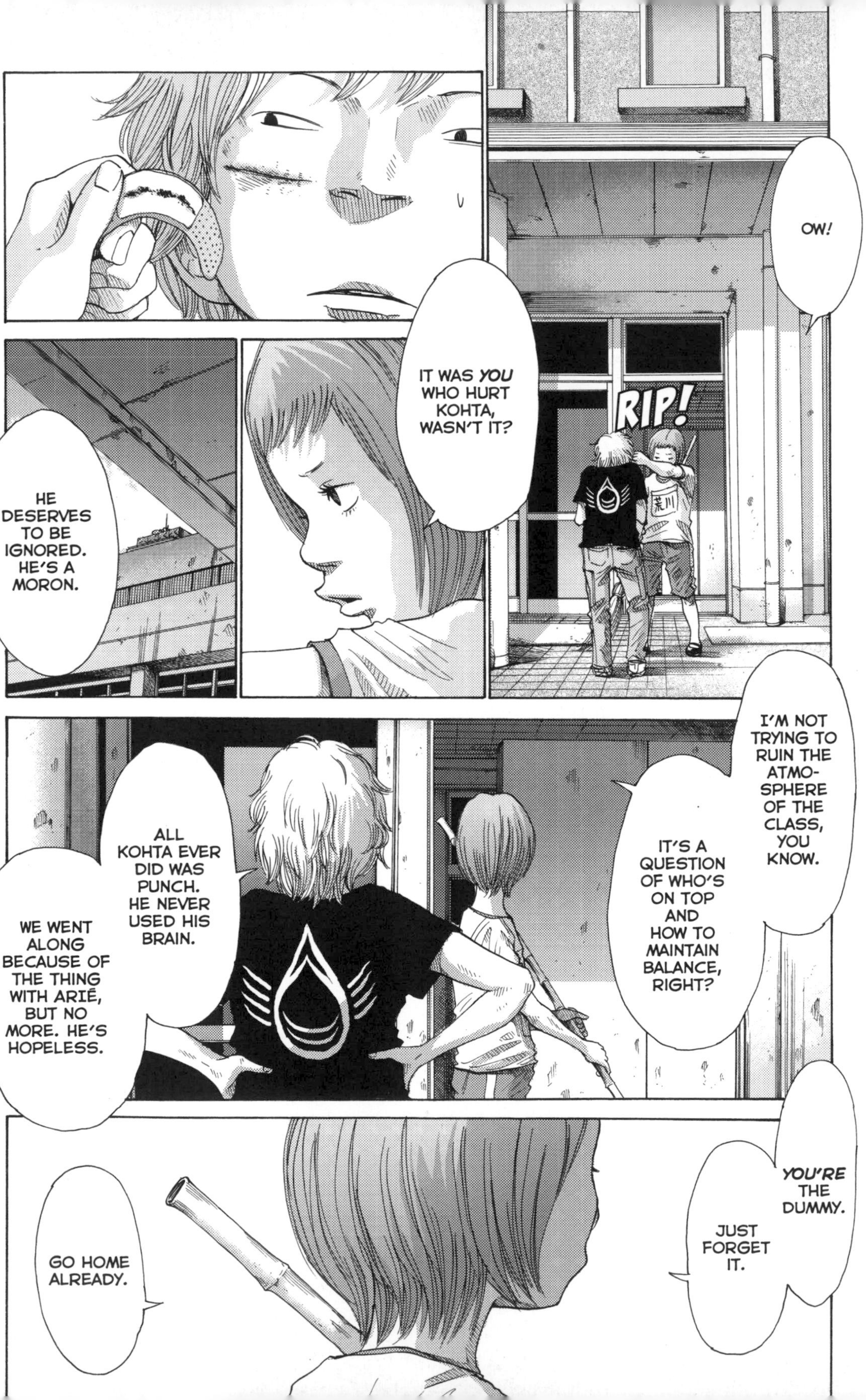
OW!
RIP!
荒川
IT WAS *YOU* WHO HURT KOHTA, WASN'T IT?
HE DESERVES TO BE IGNORED. HE'S A MORON.
I'M NOT TRYING TO RUIN THE ATMO-SPHERE OF THE CLASS, YOU KNOW.
IT'S A QUESTION OF WHO'S ON TOP AND HOW TO MAINTAIN BALANCE, RIGHT?
ALL KOHTA EVER DID WAS PUNCH. HE NEVER USED HIS BRAIN.
WE WENT ALONG BECAUSE OF THE THING WITH ARIÉ, BUT NO MORE. HE'S HOPELESS.
YOU'RE THE DUMMY.
JUST FORGET IT.
GO HOME ALREADY.

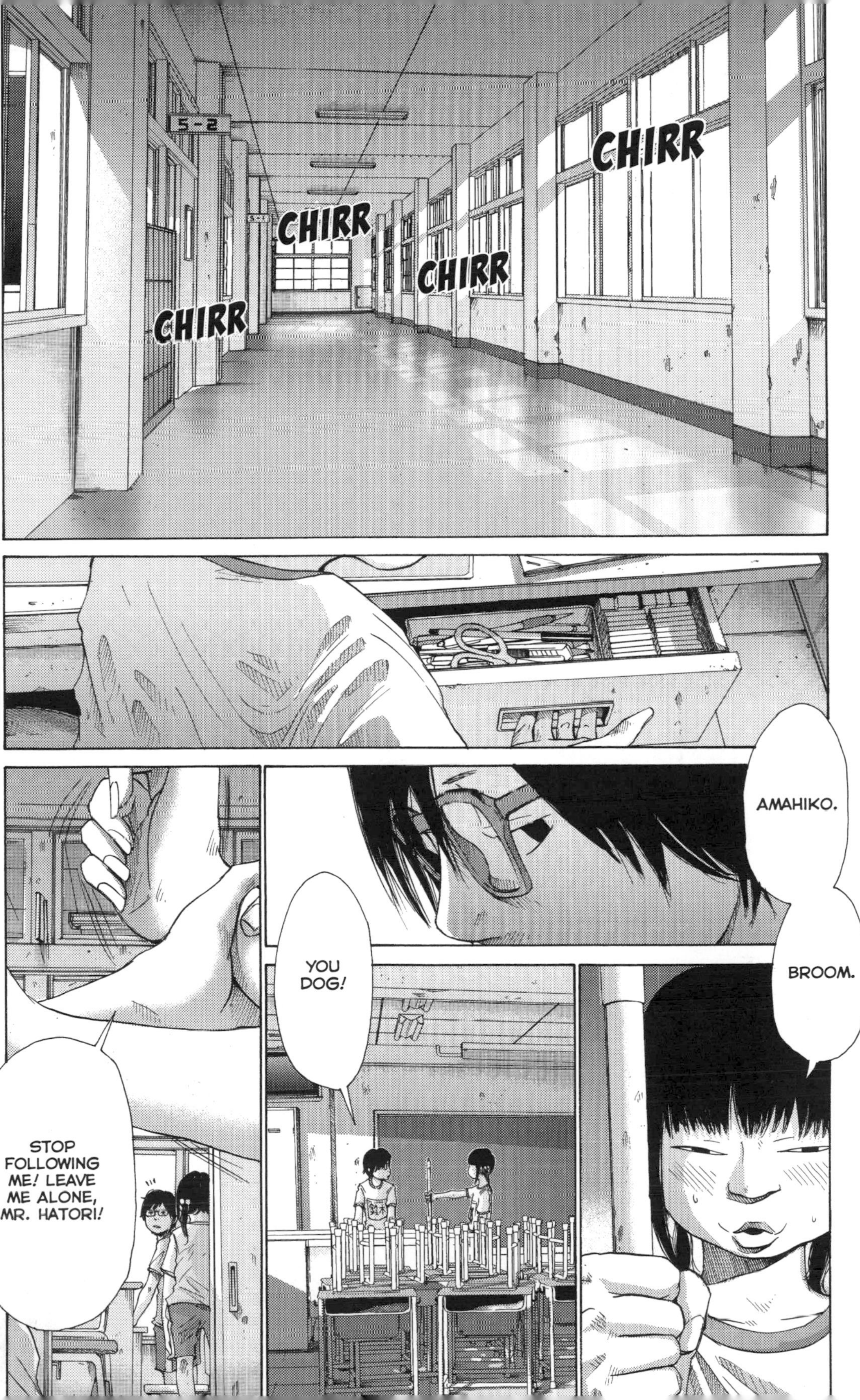
CHIRR
CHIRR
CHIRR
CHIRR
AMAHIKO.
BROOM.
YOU DOG!
STOP FOLLOWING ME! LEAVE ME ALONE, MR. HATORI!

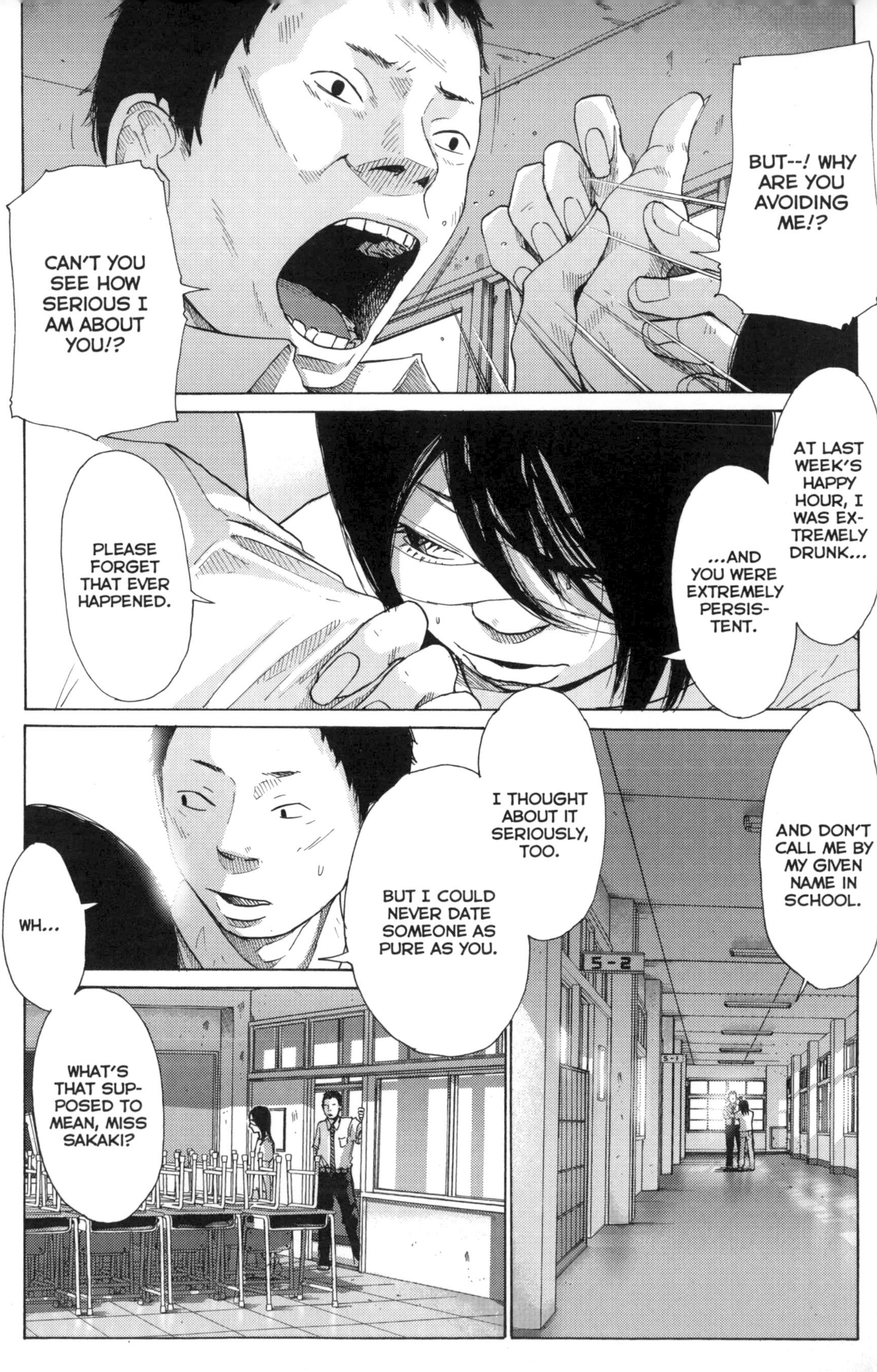
BUT--! WHY ARE YOU AVOIDING ME!?
CAN'T YOU SEE HOW SERIOUS I AM ABOUT YOU!?
AT LAST WEEK'S HAPPY HOUR, I WAS EXTREMELY DRUNK...
...AND YOU WERE EXTREMELY PERSISTENT.
PLEASE FORGET THAT EVER HAPPENED.
AND DON'T CALL ME BY MY GIVEN NAME IN SCHOOL.
5-2
I THOUGHT ABOUT IT SERIOUSLY, TOO.
BUT I COULD NEVER DATE SOMEONE AS PURE AS YOU.
WH...
WHAT'S THAT SUPPOSED TO MEAN, MISS SAKAKI?

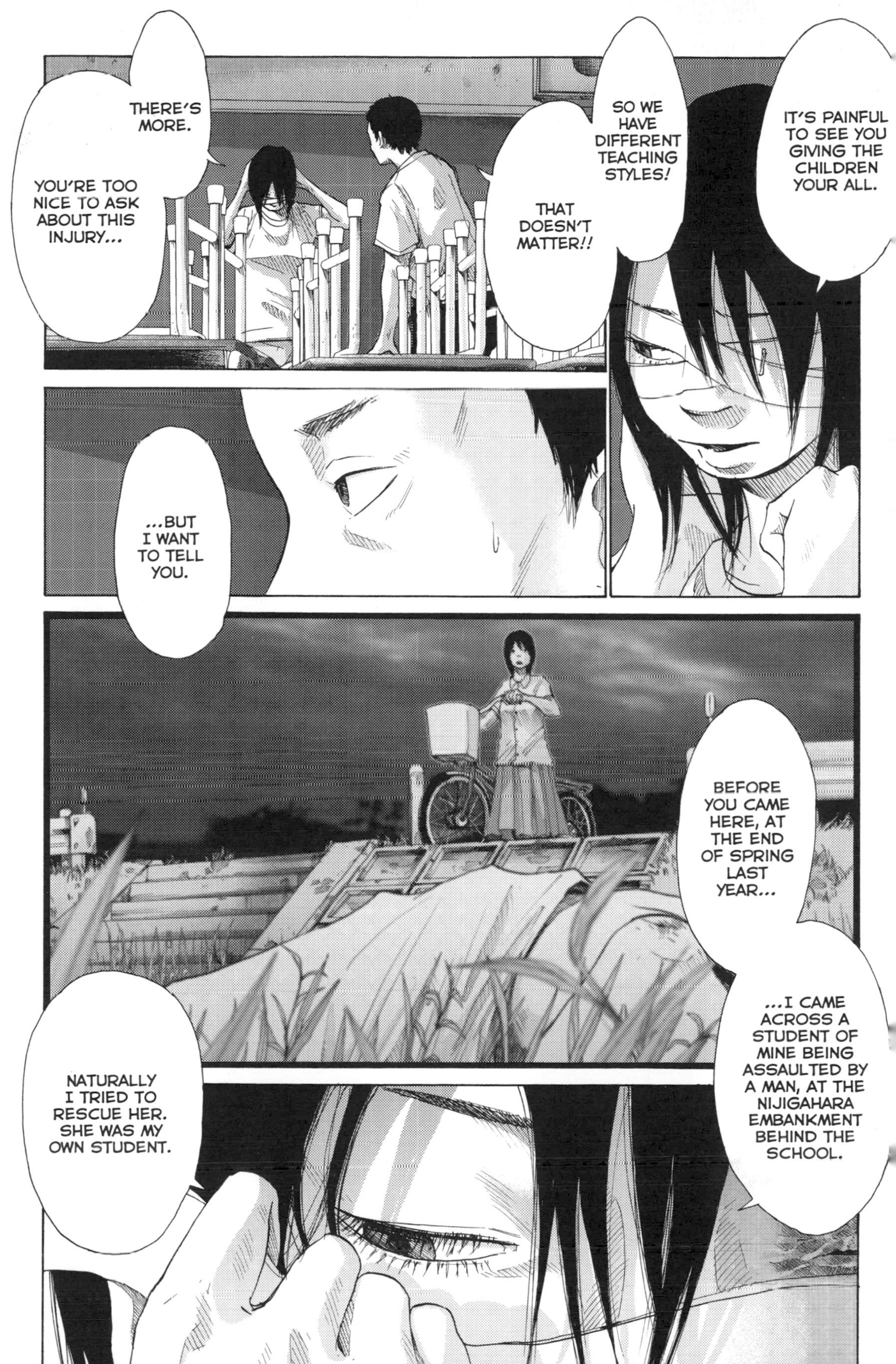
IT'S PAINFUL TO SEE YOU GIVING THE CHILDREN YOUR ALL.
SO WE HAVE DIFFERENT TEACHING STYLES!
THAT DOESN'T MATTER!!
THERE'S MORE.
YOU'RE TOO NICE TO ASK ABOUT THIS INJURY...
...BUT I WANT TO TELL YOU.
BEFORE YOU CAME HERE, AT THE END OF SPRING LAST YEAR...
...I CAME ACROSS A STUDENT OF MINE BEING ASSAULTED BY A MAN, AT THE NIJIGAHARA EMBANKMENT BEHIND THE SCHOOL.
NATURALLY I TRIED TO RESCUE HER. SHE WAS MY OWN STUDENT.

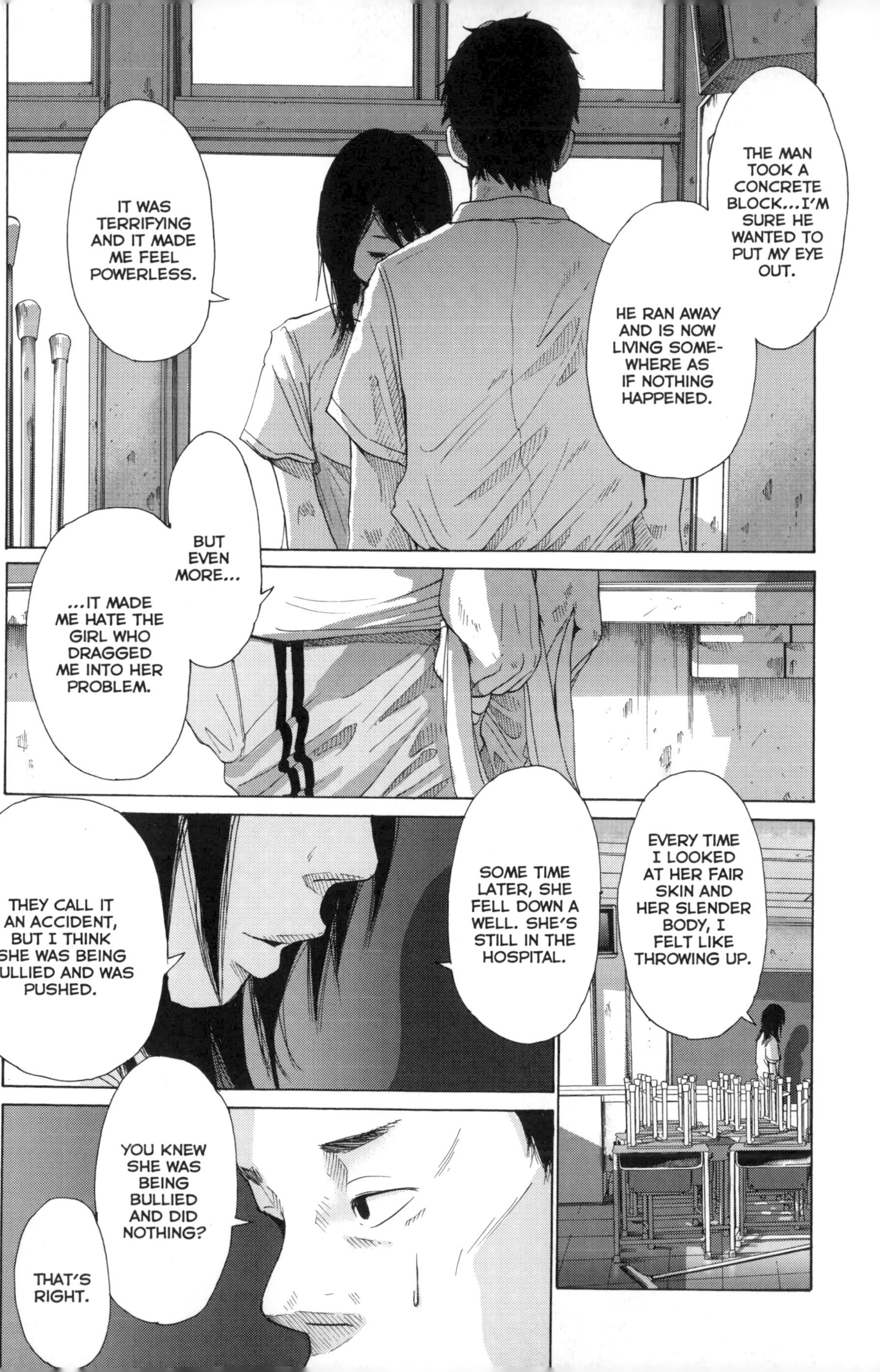
THE MAN TOOK A CONCRETE BLOCK...I'M SURE HE WANTED TO PUT MY EYE OUT.
HE RAN AWAY AND IS NOW LIVING SOME-WHERE AS IF NOTHING HAPPENED.
IT WAS TERRIFYING AND IT MADE ME FEEL POWERLESS.
BUT EVEN MORE...
...IT MADE ME HATE THE GIRL WHO DRAGGED ME INTO HER PROBLEM.
EVERY TIME I LOOKED AT HER FAIR SKIN AND HER SLENDER BODY, I FELT LIKE THROWING UP.
SOME TIME LATER, SHE FELL DOWN A WELL. SHE'S STILL IN THE HOSPITAL.
THEY CALL IT AN ACCIDENT, BUT I THINK SHE WAS BEING BULLIED AND WAS PUSHED.
YOU KNEW SHE WAS BEING BULLIED AND DID NOTHING?
THAT'S RIGHT.

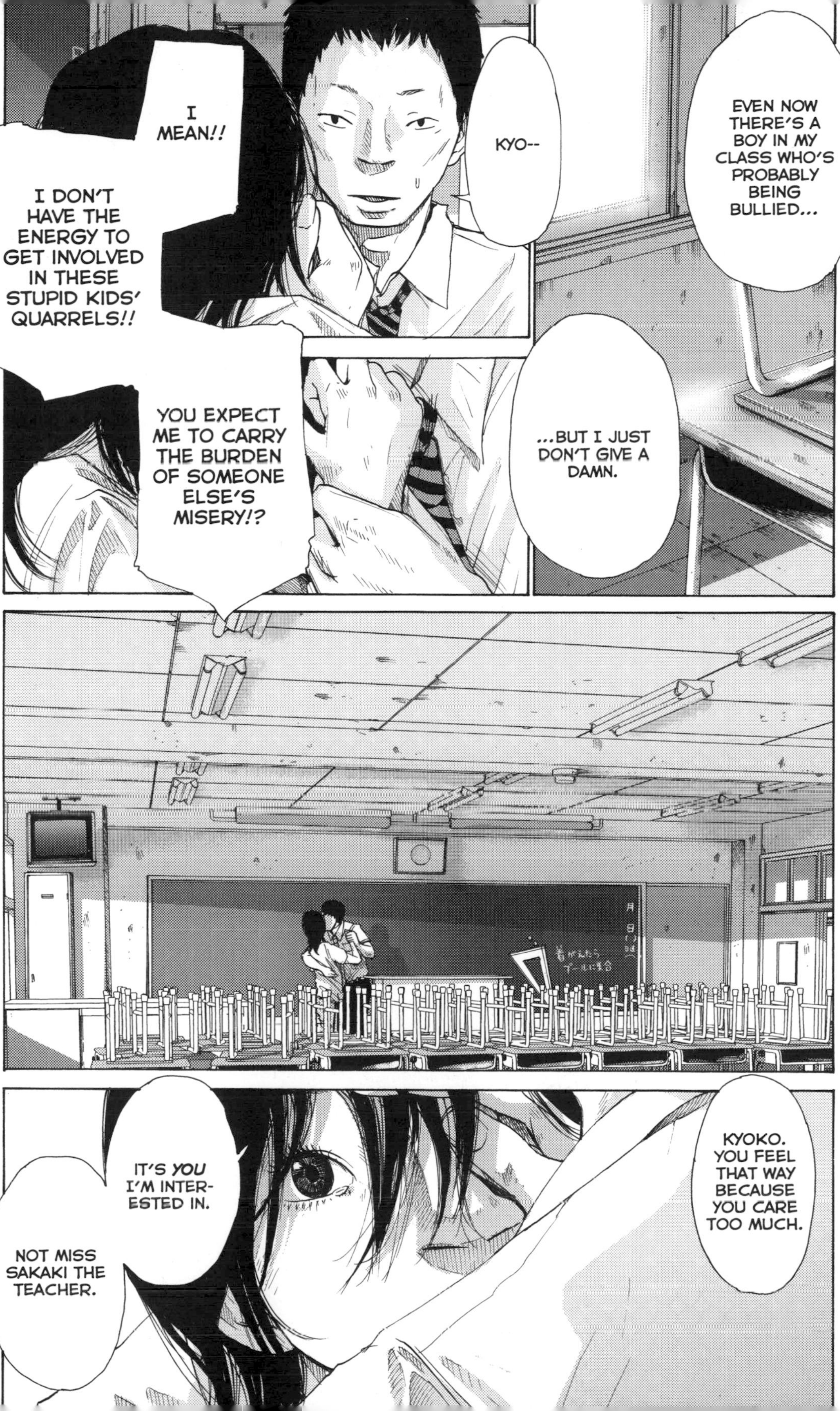
EVEN NOW THERE'S A BOY IN MY CLASS WHO'S PROBABLY BEING BULLIED...
...BUT I JUST DON'T GIVE A DAMN.
KYO--
I MEAN!!
I DON'T HAVE THE ENERGY TO GET INVOLVED IN THESE STUPID KIDS' QUARRELS!!
YOU EXPECT ME TO CARRY THE BURDEN OF SOMEONE ELSE'S MISERY!?
KYOKO. YOU FEEL THAT WAY BECAUSE YOU CARE TOO MUCH.
IT'S *YOU* I'M INTER-ESTED IN.
NOT MISS SAKAKI THE TEACHER.

I LOVE YOU!!

STOP.

...AH...

KYOKO...

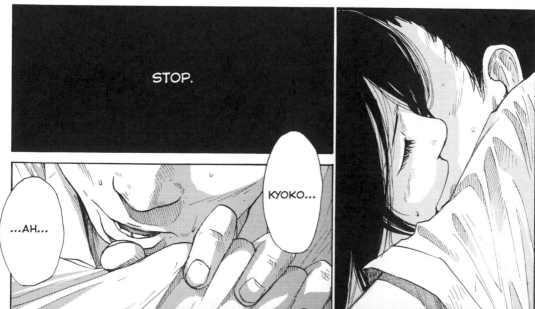

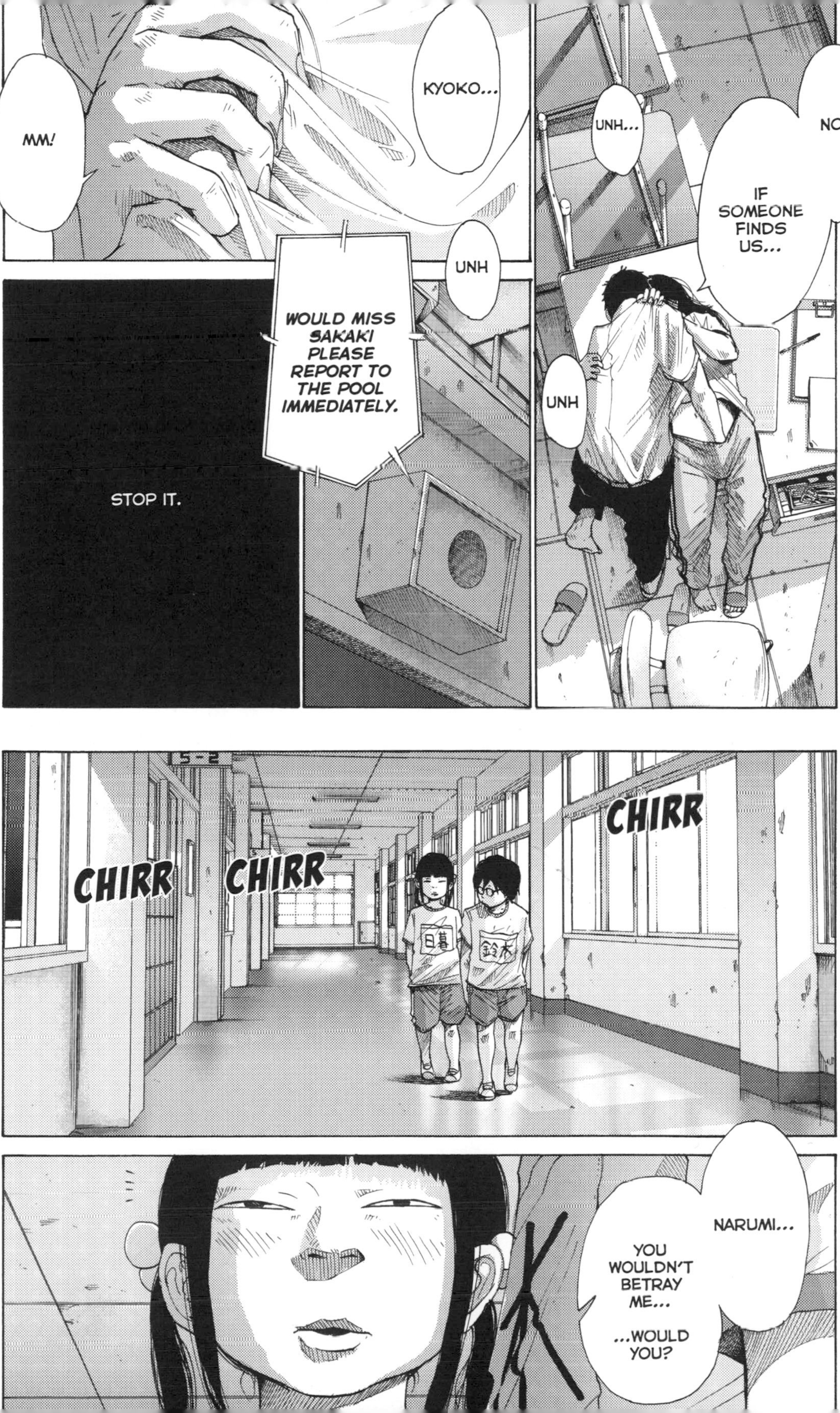
NO.
IF SOMEONE FINDS US...
UNH...
UNH
KYOKO...
MM!
UNH
WOULD MISS SAKAKI PLEASE REPORT TO THE POOL IMMEDIATELY.
STOP IT.
CHIRR
CHIRR
CHIRR
日暮
鈴木
NARUMI...
YOU WOULDN'T BETRAY ME...
...WOULD YOU?

WHACK

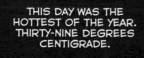
THIS DAY WAS THE HOTTEST OF THE YEAR. THIRTY-NINE DEGREES CENTIGRADE.

AS IF!!

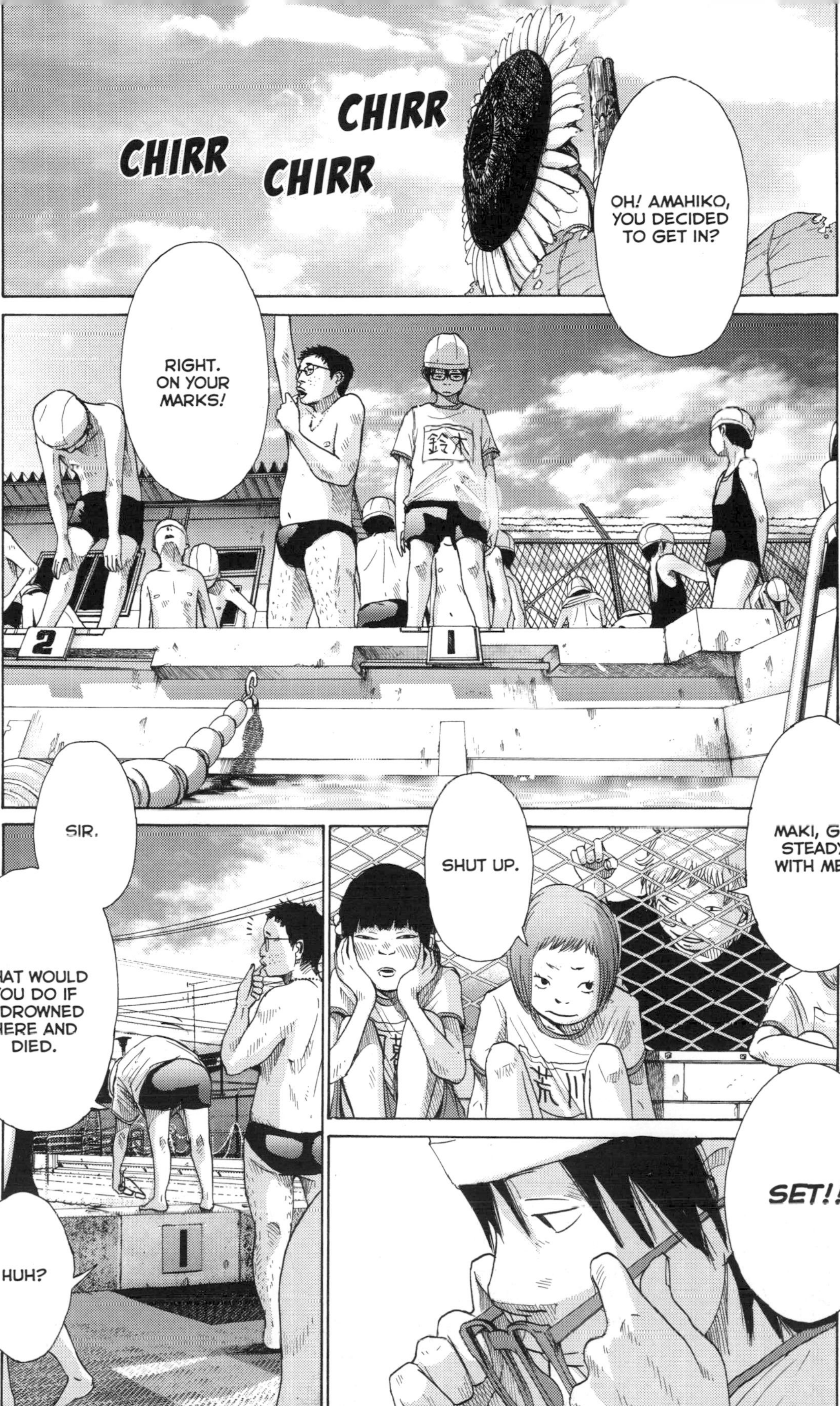
OH! AMAHIKO, YOU DECIDED TO GET IN?
CHIRR
CHIRR
CHIRR
RIGHT. ON YOUR MARKS!
MAKI, GO STEADY WITH ME.
SHUT UP.
SET!!
SIR.
WHAT WOULD YOU DO IF I DROWNED HERE AND DIED.
HUH?

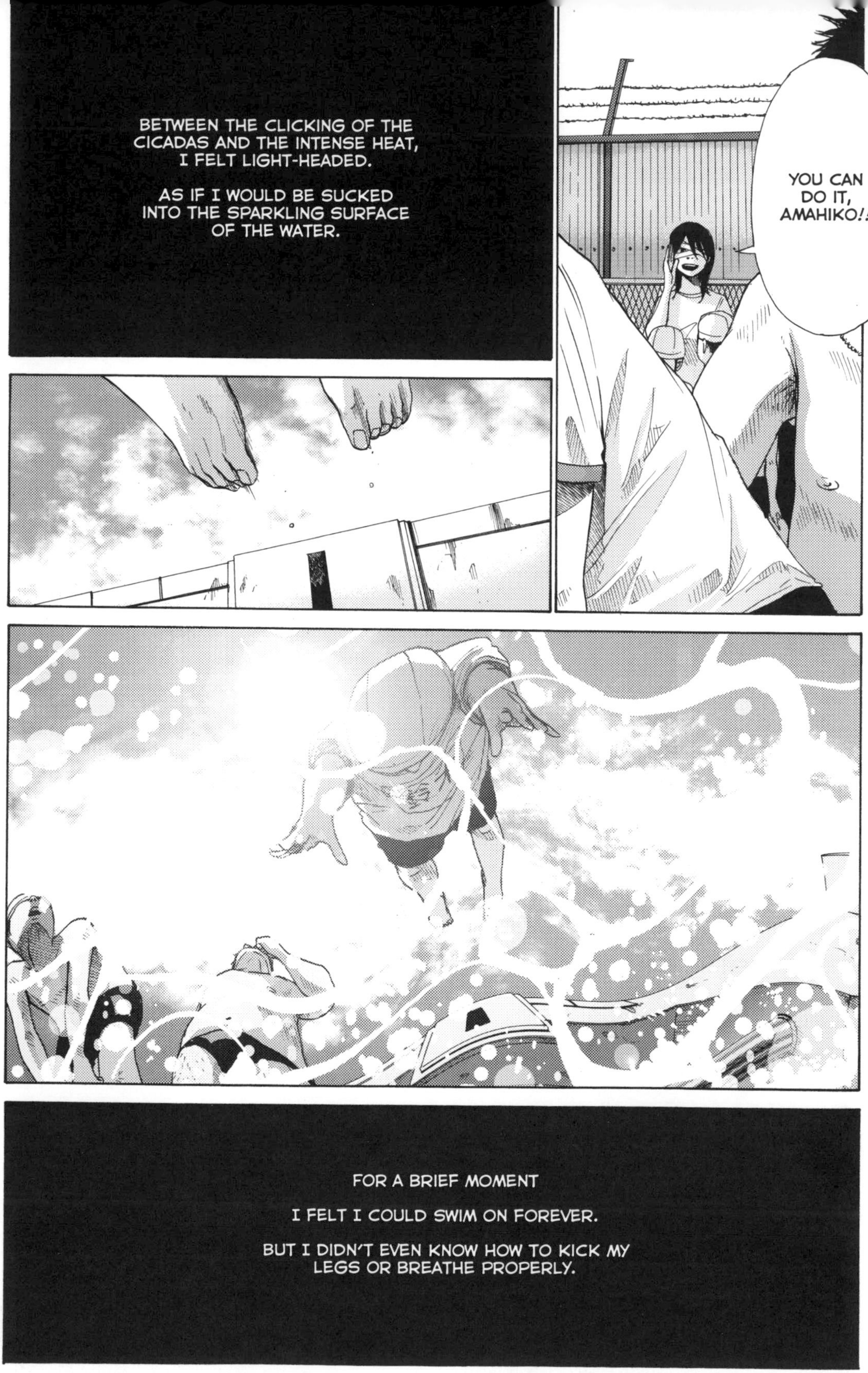
YOU CAN DO IT, AMAHIKO!!
BETWEEN THE CLICKING OF THE CICADAS AND THE INTENSE HEAT, I FELT LIGHT-HEADED.
AS IF I WOULD BE SUCKED INTO THE SPARKLING SURFACE OF THE WATER.
FOR A BRIEF MOMENT
I FELT I COULD SWIM ON FOREVER.
BUT I DIDN'T EVEN KNOW HOW TO KICK MY LEGS OR BREATHE PROPERLY.

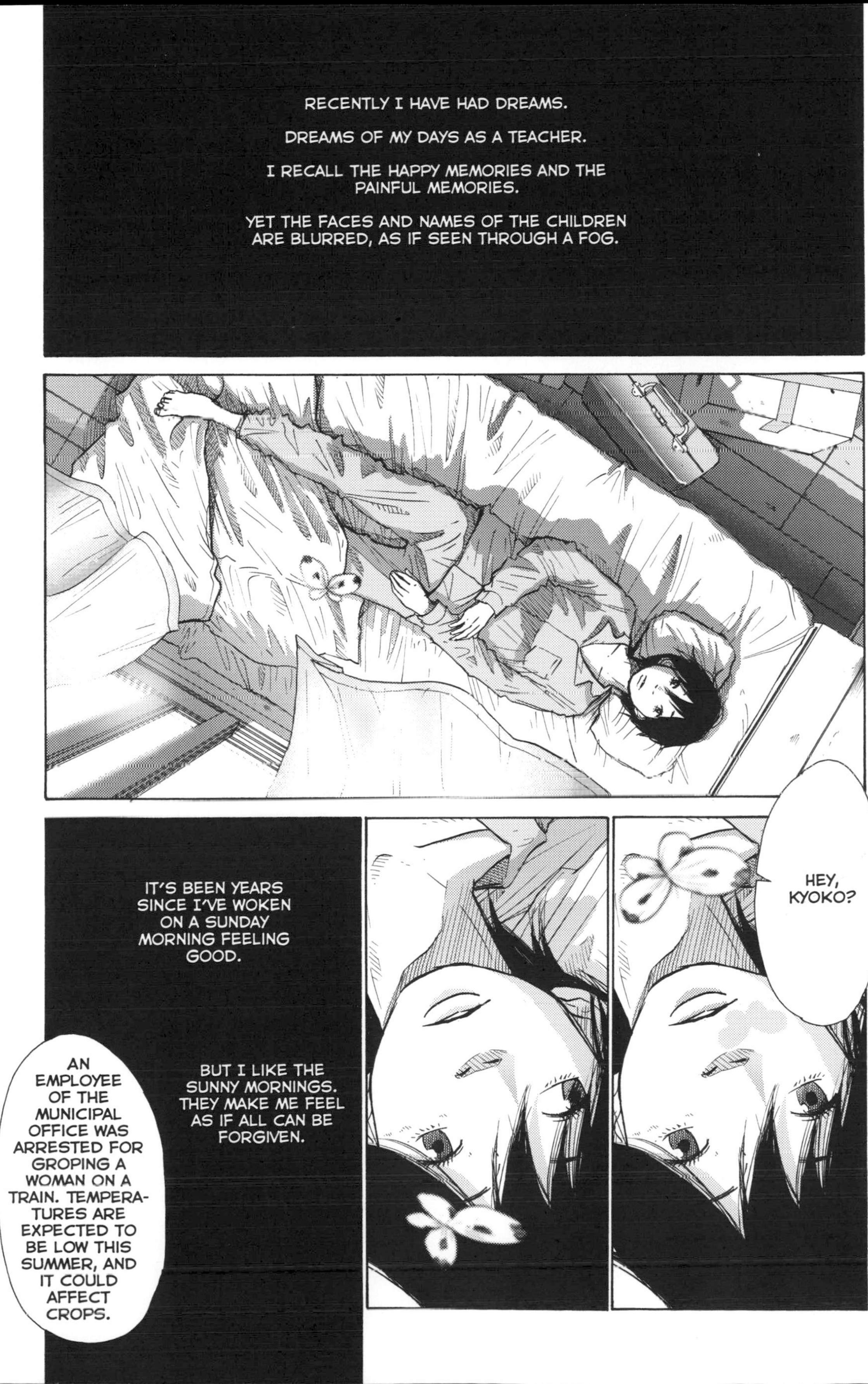
RECENTLY I HAVE HAD DREAMS.
DREAMS OF MY DAYS AS A TEACHER.
I RECALL THE HAPPY MEMORIES AND THE PAINFUL MEMORIES.
YET THE FACES AND NAMES OF THE CHILDREN ARE BLURRED, AS IF SEEN THROUGH A FOG.
HEY, KYOKO?
IT'S BEEN YEARS SINCE I'VE WOKEN ON A SUNDAY MORNING FEELING GOOD.
BUT I LIKE THE SUNNY MORNINGS. THEY MAKE ME FEEL AS IF ALL CAN BE FORGIVEN.
AN EMPLOYEE OF THE MUNICIPAL OFFICE WAS ARRESTED FOR GROPING A WOMAN ON A TRAIN. TEMPERATURES ARE EXPECTED TO BE LOW THIS SUMMER, AND IT COULD AFFECT CROPS.

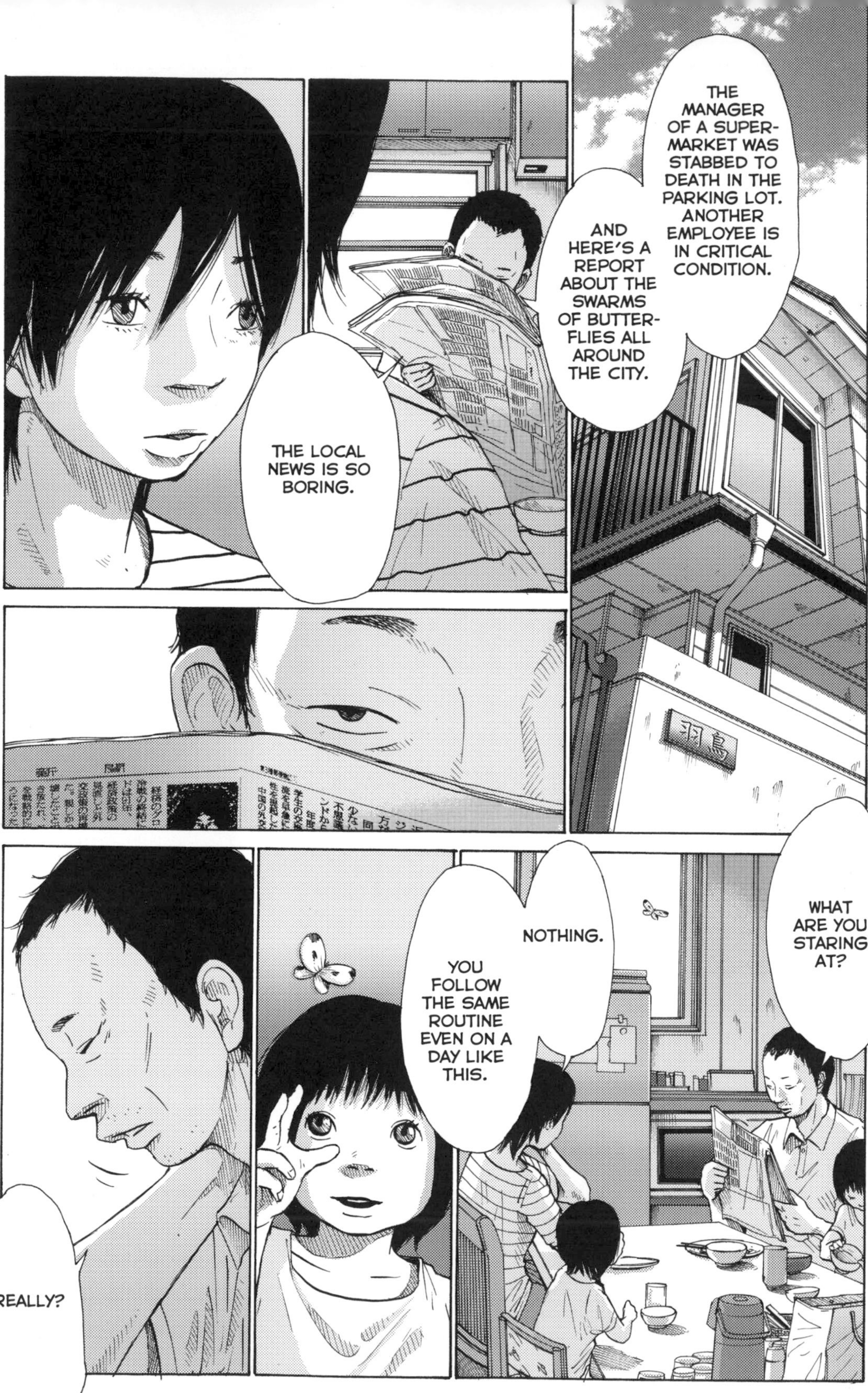
THE MANAGER OF A SUPER-MARKET WAS STABBED TO DEATH IN THE PARKING LOT. ANOTHER EMPLOYEE IS IN CRITICAL CONDITION.
AND HERE'S A REPORT ABOUT THE SWARMS OF BUTTER-FLIES ALL AROUND THE CITY.
羽鳥
THE LOCAL NEWS IS SO BORING.
WHAT ARE YOU STARING AT?
NOTHING.
YOU FOLLOW THE SAME ROUTINE EVEN ON A DAY LIKE THIS.
REALLY?

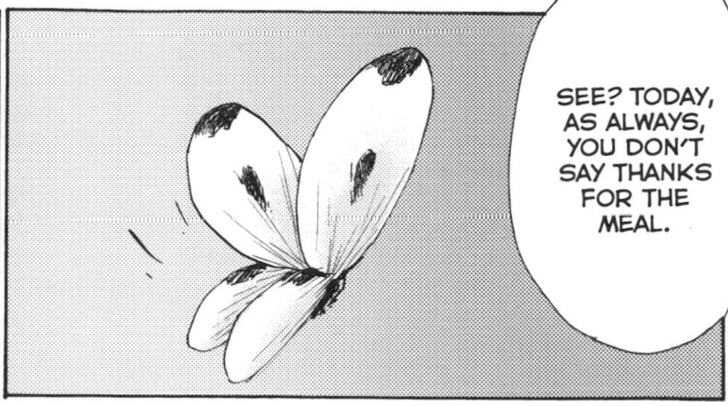
SEE? TODAY, AS ALWAYS, YOU DON'T SAY THANKS FOR THE MEAL.

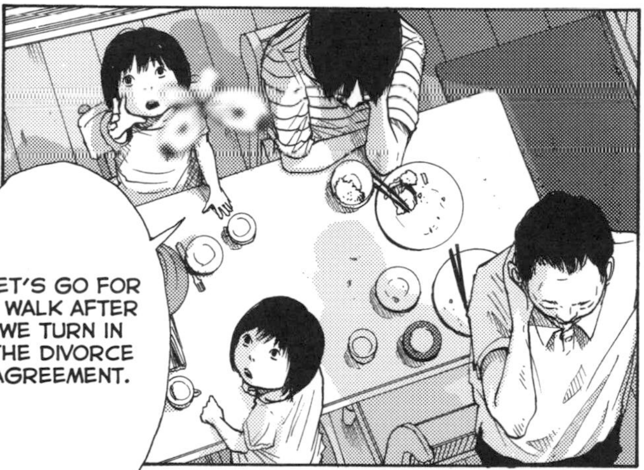
LET'S GO FOR A WALK AFTER WE TURN IN THE DIVORCE AGREEMENT.

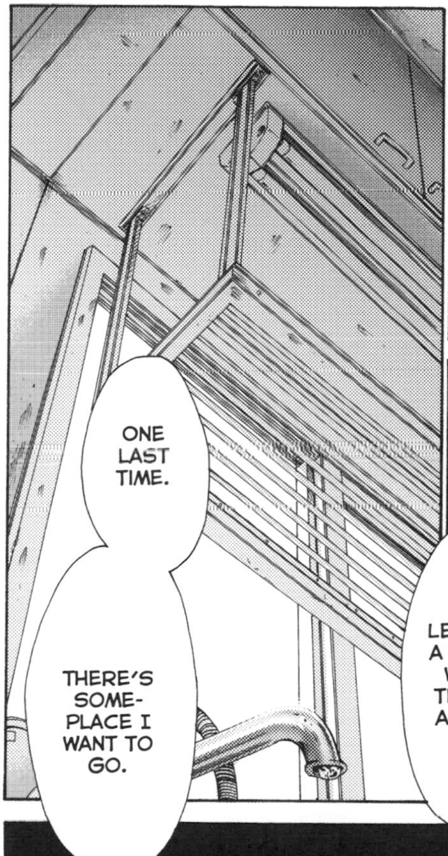
ONE LAST TIME.
THERE'S SOME-PLACE I WANT TO GO.

CHAPTER 6

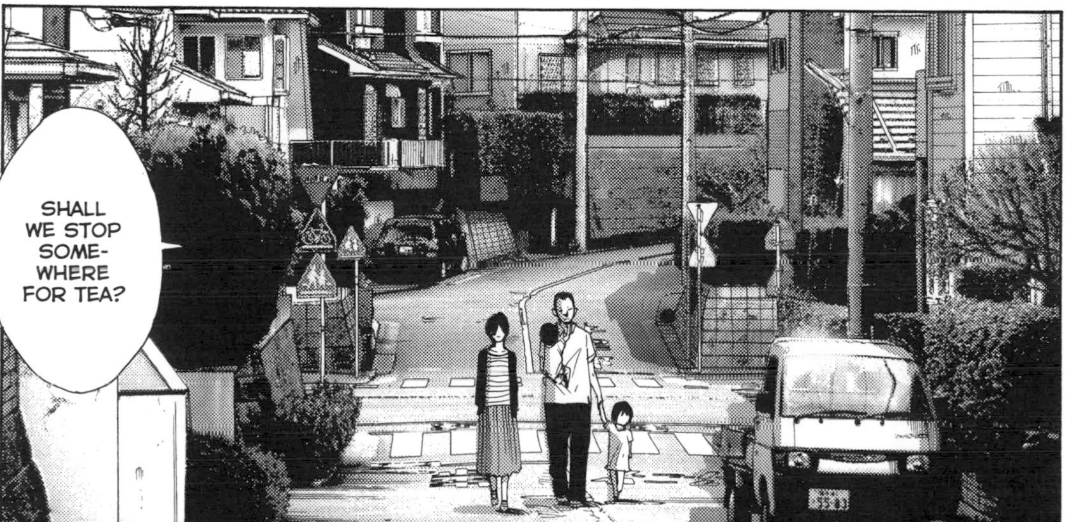
SHALL WE STOP SOME-WHERE FOR TEA?

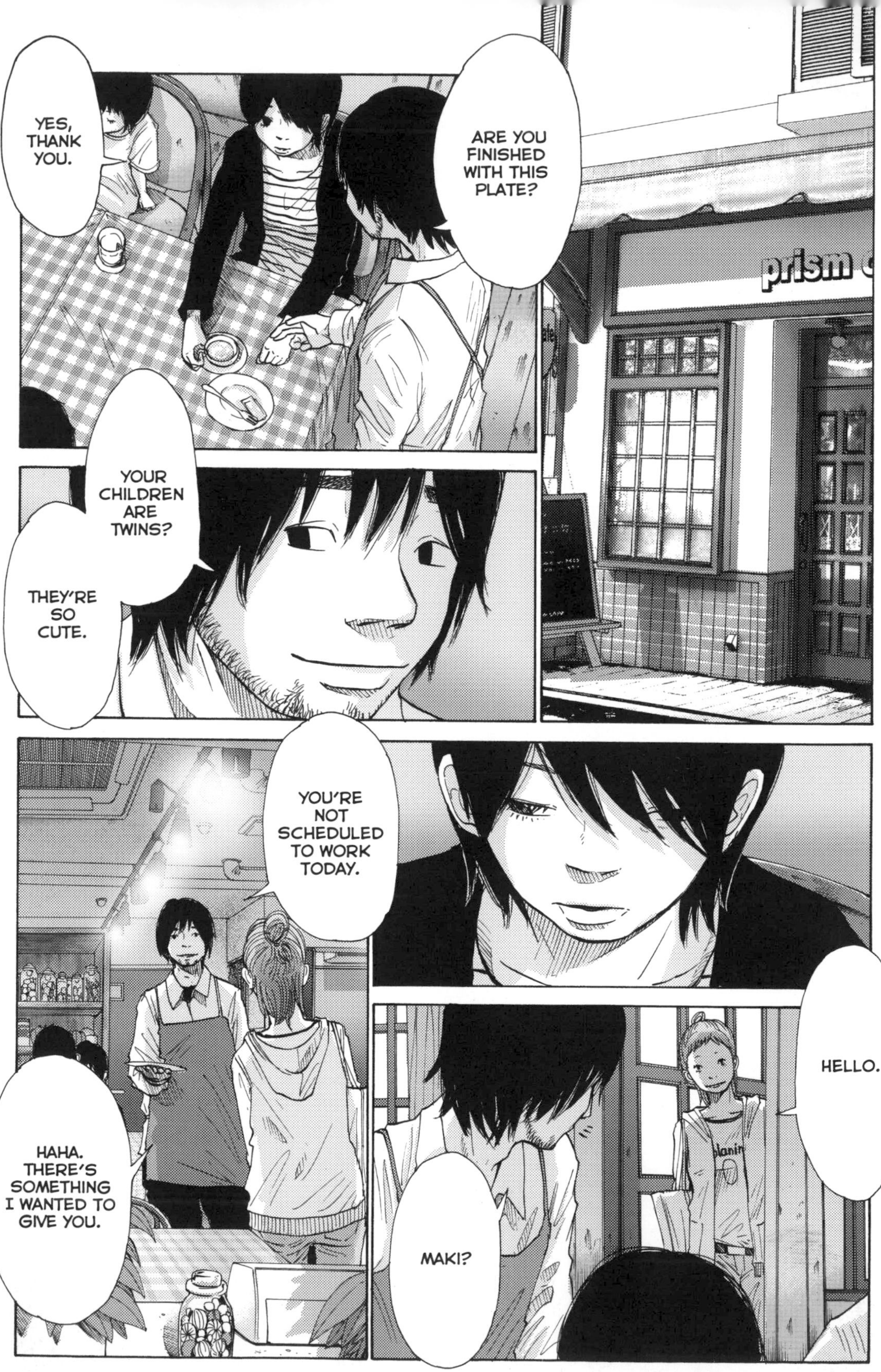
prism
ARE YOU FINISHED WITH THIS PLATE?
YES, THANK YOU.
YOUR CHILDREN ARE TWINS?
THEY'RE SO CUTE.
HELLO.
MAKI?
YOU'RE NOT SCHEDULED TO WORK TODAY.
HAHA. THERE'S SOMETHING I WANTED TO GIVE YOU.

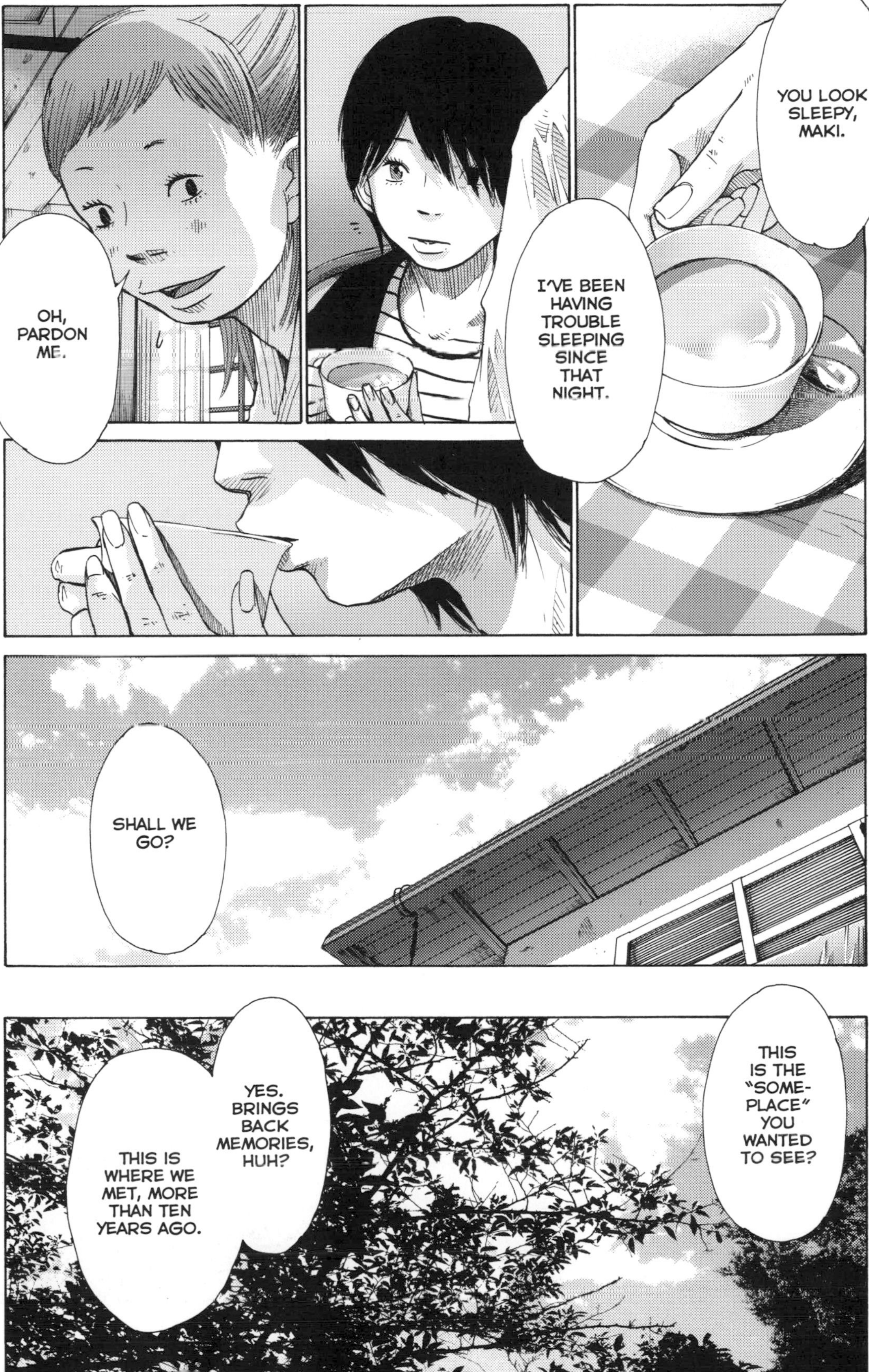
YOU LOOK SLEEPY, MAKI.
I'VE BEEN HAVING TROUBLE SLEEPING SINCE THAT NIGHT.
OH, PARDON ME.
SHALL WE GO?
THIS IS THE "SOME-PLACE" YOU WANTED TO SEE?
YES. BRINGS BACK MEMORIES, HUH?
THIS IS WHERE WE MET, MORE THAN TEN YEARS AGO.

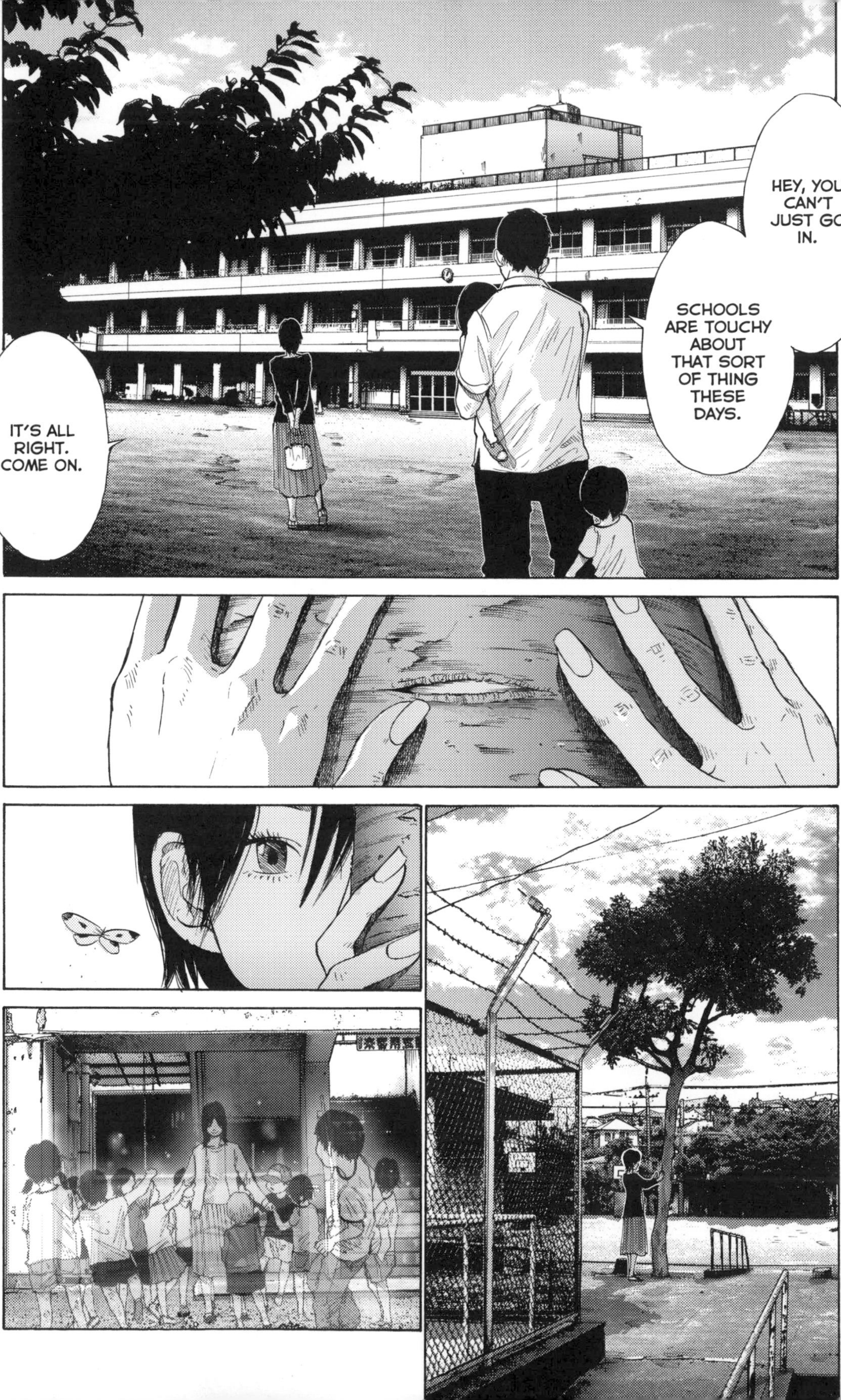
HEY, YOU CAN'T JUST GO IN.
SCHOOLS ARE TOUCHY ABOUT THAT SORT OF THING THESE DAYS.
IT'S ALL RIGHT. COME ON.

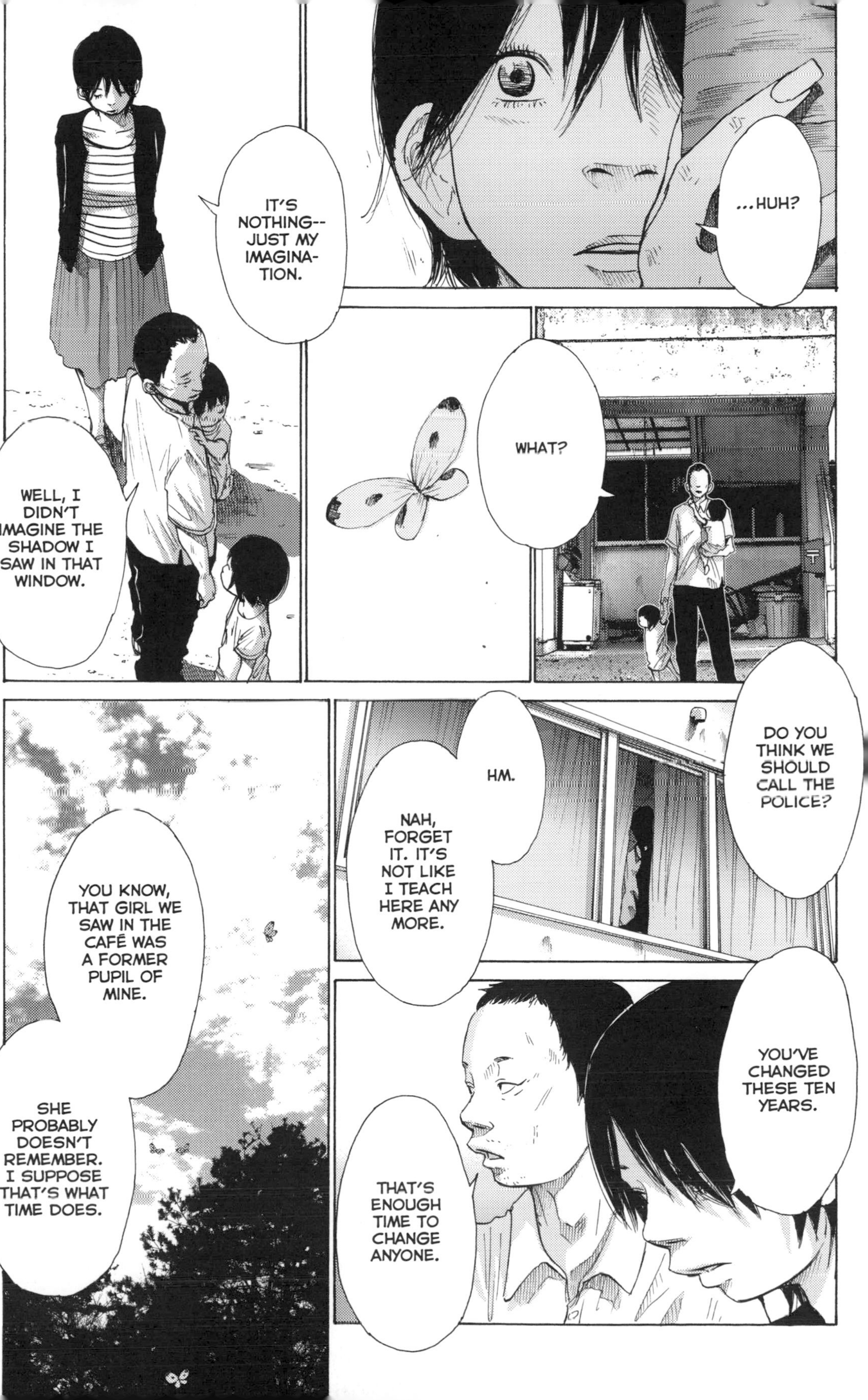
...HUH?
WHAT?
IT'S NOTHING--JUST MY IMAGINATION.
WELL, I DIDN'T IMAGINE THE SHADOW I SAW IN THAT WINDOW.
DO YOU THINK WE SHOULD CALL THE POLICE?
HM.
NAH, FORGET IT. IT'S NOT LIKE I TEACH HERE ANY MORE.
YOU'VE CHANGED THESE TEN YEARS.
THAT'S ENOUGH TIME TO CHANGE ANYONE.
YOU KNOW, THAT GIRL WE SAW IN THE CAFÉ WAS A FORMER PUPIL OF MINE.
SHE PROBABLY DOESN'T REMEMBER. I SUPPOSE THAT'S WHAT TIME DOES.

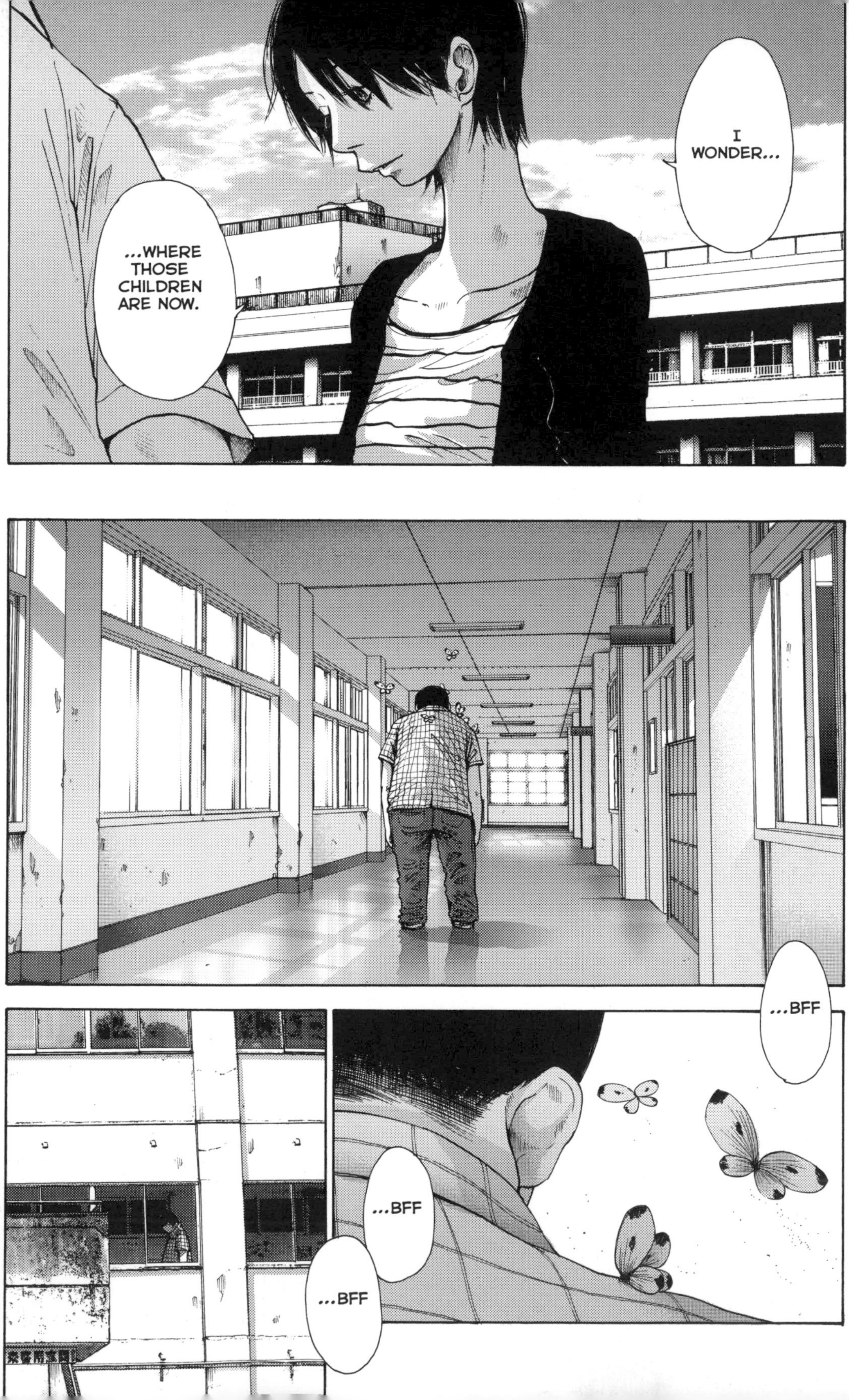
I WONDER...
...WHERE THOSE CHILDREN ARE NOW.
...BFF
...BFF
...BFF

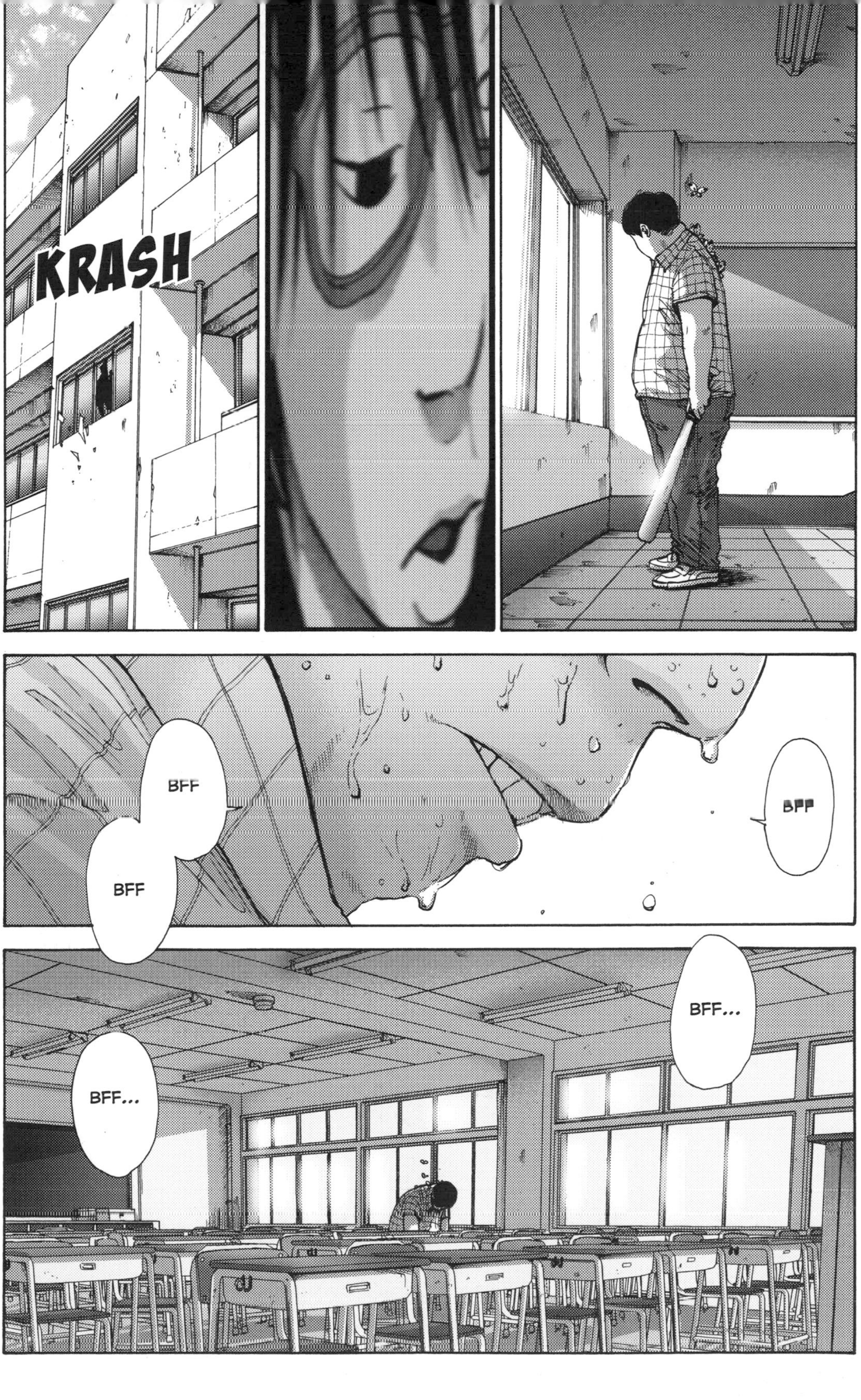
KRASH
BFF
BFF
BFF
BFF...
BFF...

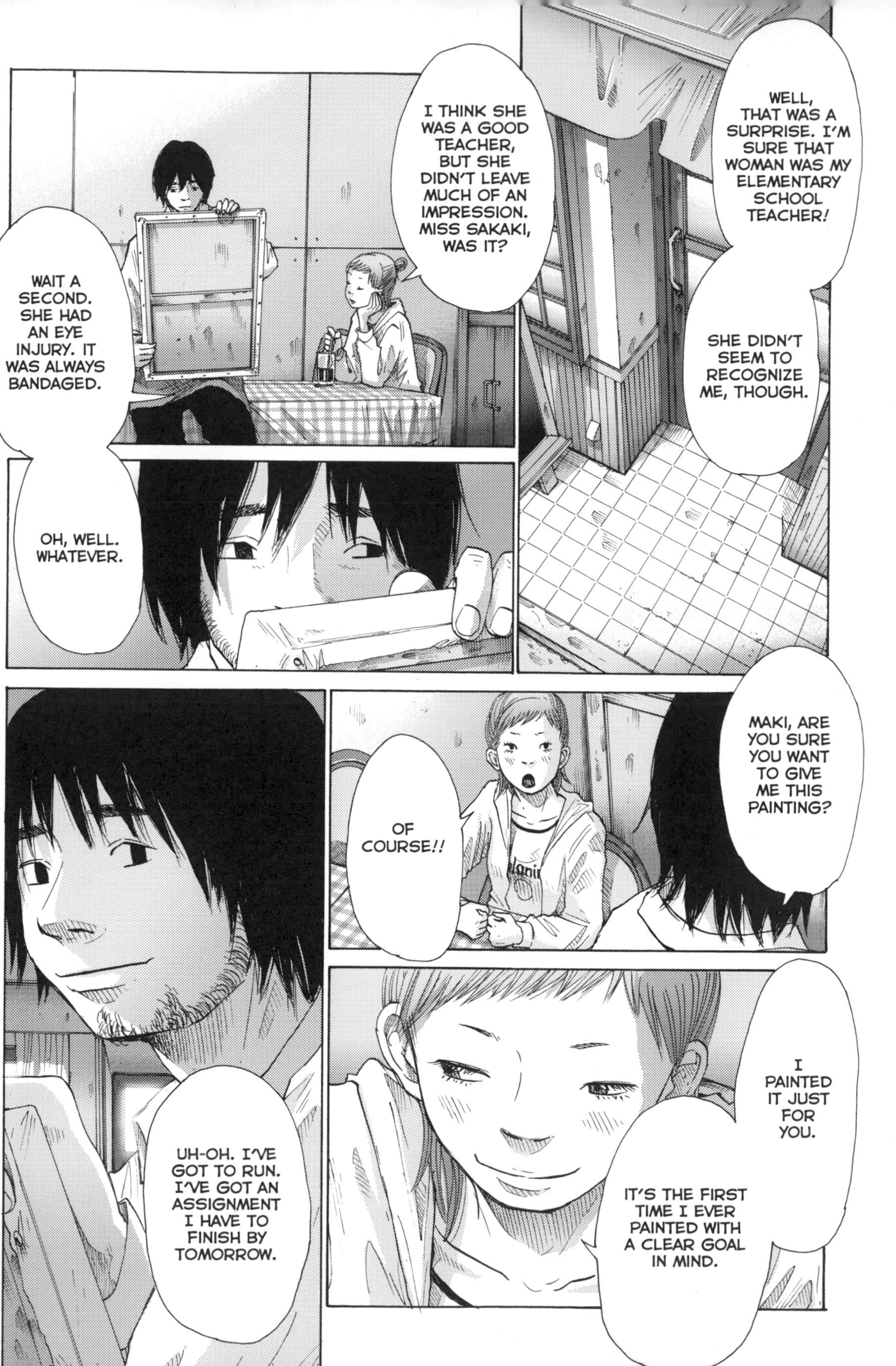
WELL, THAT WAS A SURPRISE. I'M SURE THAT WOMAN WAS MY ELEMENTARY SCHOOL TEACHER!
SHE DIDN'T SEEM TO RECOGNIZE ME, THOUGH.
I THINK SHE WAS A GOOD TEACHER, BUT SHE DIDN'T LEAVE MUCH OF AN IMPRESSION. MISS SAKAKI, WAS IT?
WAIT A SECOND. SHE HAD AN EYE INJURY. IT WAS ALWAYS BANDAGED.
OH, WELL. WHATEVER.
MAKI, ARE YOU SURE YOU WANT TO GIVE ME THIS PAINTING?
OF COURSE!!
I PAINTED IT JUST FOR YOU.
IT'S THE FIRST TIME I EVER PAINTED WITH A CLEAR GOAL IN MIND.
UH-OH. I'VE GOT TO RUN. I'VE GOT AN ASSIGNMENT I HAVE TO FINISH BY TOMORROW.

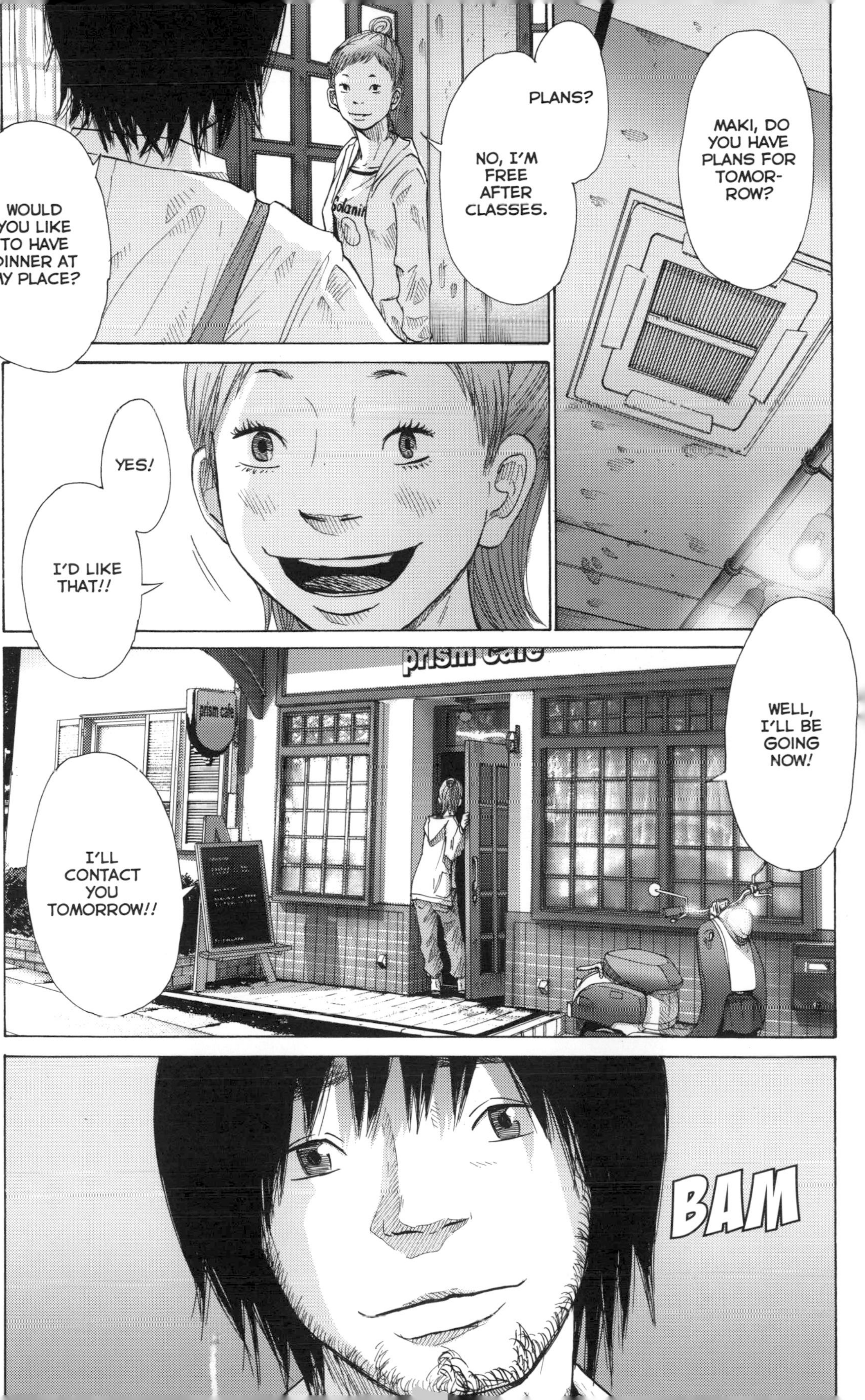
MAKI, DO YOU HAVE PLANS FOR TOMOR-ROW?
PLANS?
NO, I'M FREE AFTER CLASSES.
WOULD YOU LIKE TO HAVE DINNER AT MY PLACE?
YES!
I'D LIKE THAT!!
prism cafe
prism cafe
WELL, I'LL BE GOING NOW!
I'LL CONTACT YOU TOMORROW!!
BAM

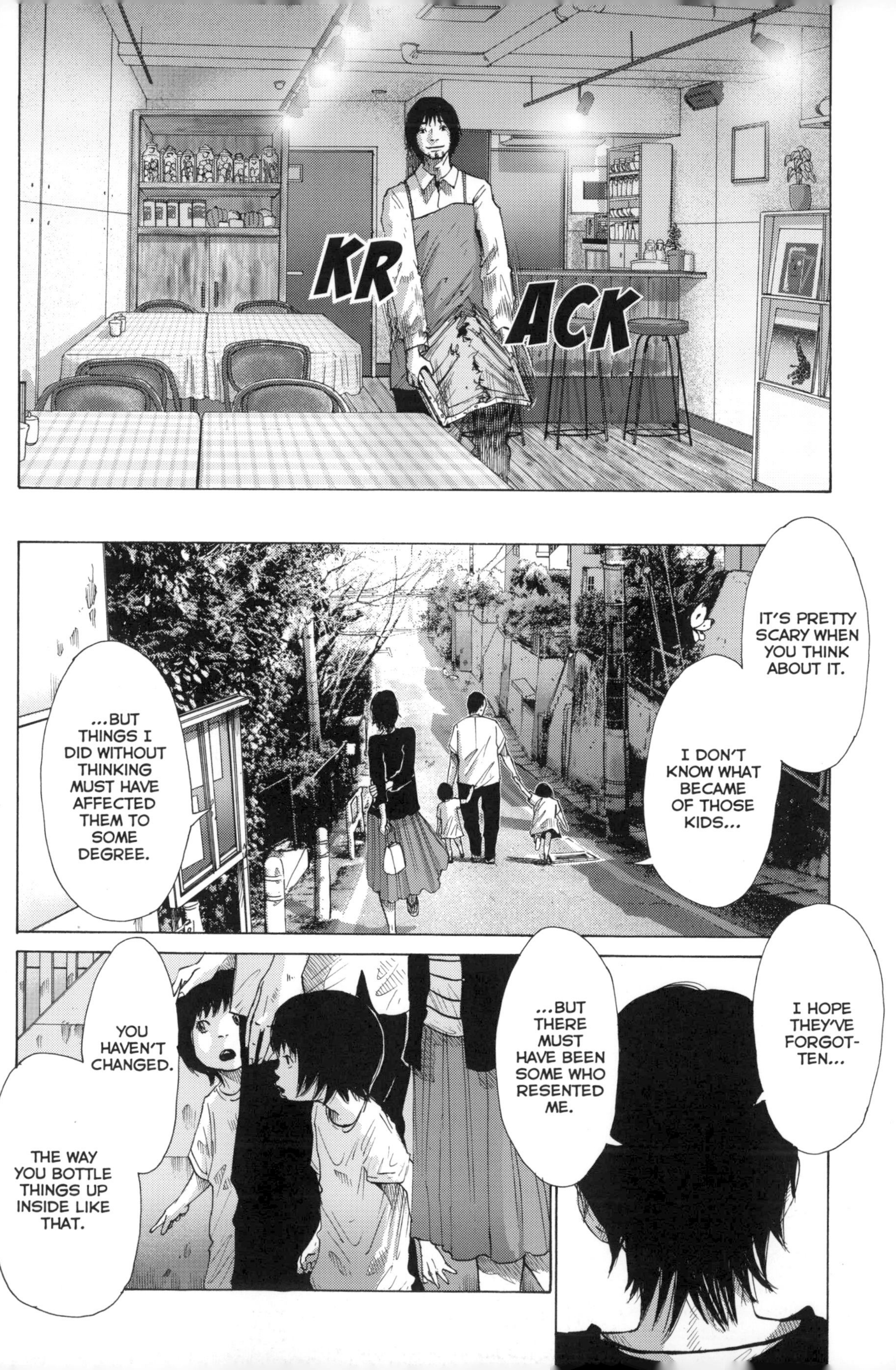
KRACK
IT'S PRETTY SCARY WHEN YOU THINK ABOUT IT.
I DON'T KNOW WHAT BECAME OF THOSE KIDS...
...BUT THINGS I DID WITHOUT THINKING MUST HAVE AFFECTED THEM TO SOME DEGREE.
I HOPE THEY'VE FORGOT-TEN...
...BUT THERE MUST HAVE BEEN SOME WHO RESENTED ME.
YOU HAVEN'T CHANGED.
THE WAY YOU BOTTLE THINGS UP INSIDE LIKE THAT.

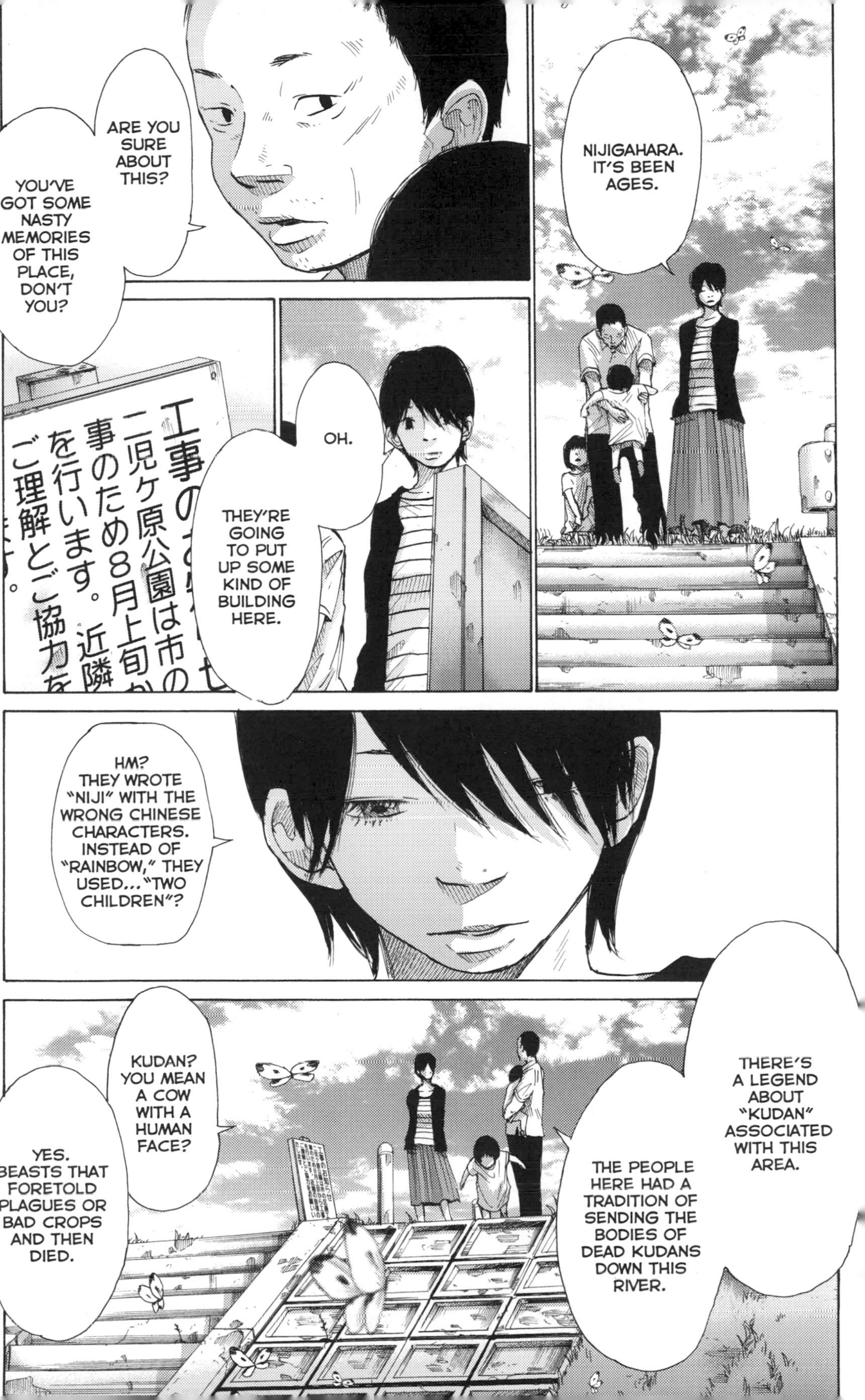
NIJIGAHARA. IT'S BEEN AGES.
ARE YOU SURE ABOUT THIS?
YOU'VE GOT SOME NASTY MEMORIES OF THIS PLACE, DON'T YOU?
OH.
THEY'RE GOING TO PUT UP SOME KIND OF BUILDING HERE.
工事の
二児ケ原公園は市の
事のため8月上旬か
を行います。近隣
ご理解とご協力を
HM? THEY WROTE "NIJI" WITH THE WRONG CHINESE CHARACTERS. INSTEAD OF "RAINBOW," THEY USED... "TWO CHILDREN"?
THERE'S A LEGEND ABOUT "KUDAN" ASSOCIATED WITH THIS AREA.
THE PEOPLE HERE HAD A TRADITION OF SENDING THE BODIES OF DEAD KUDANS DOWN THIS RIVER.
KUDAN? YOU MEAN A COW WITH A HUMAN FACE?
YES. BEASTS THAT FORETOLD PLAGUES OR BAD CROPS AND THEN DIED.

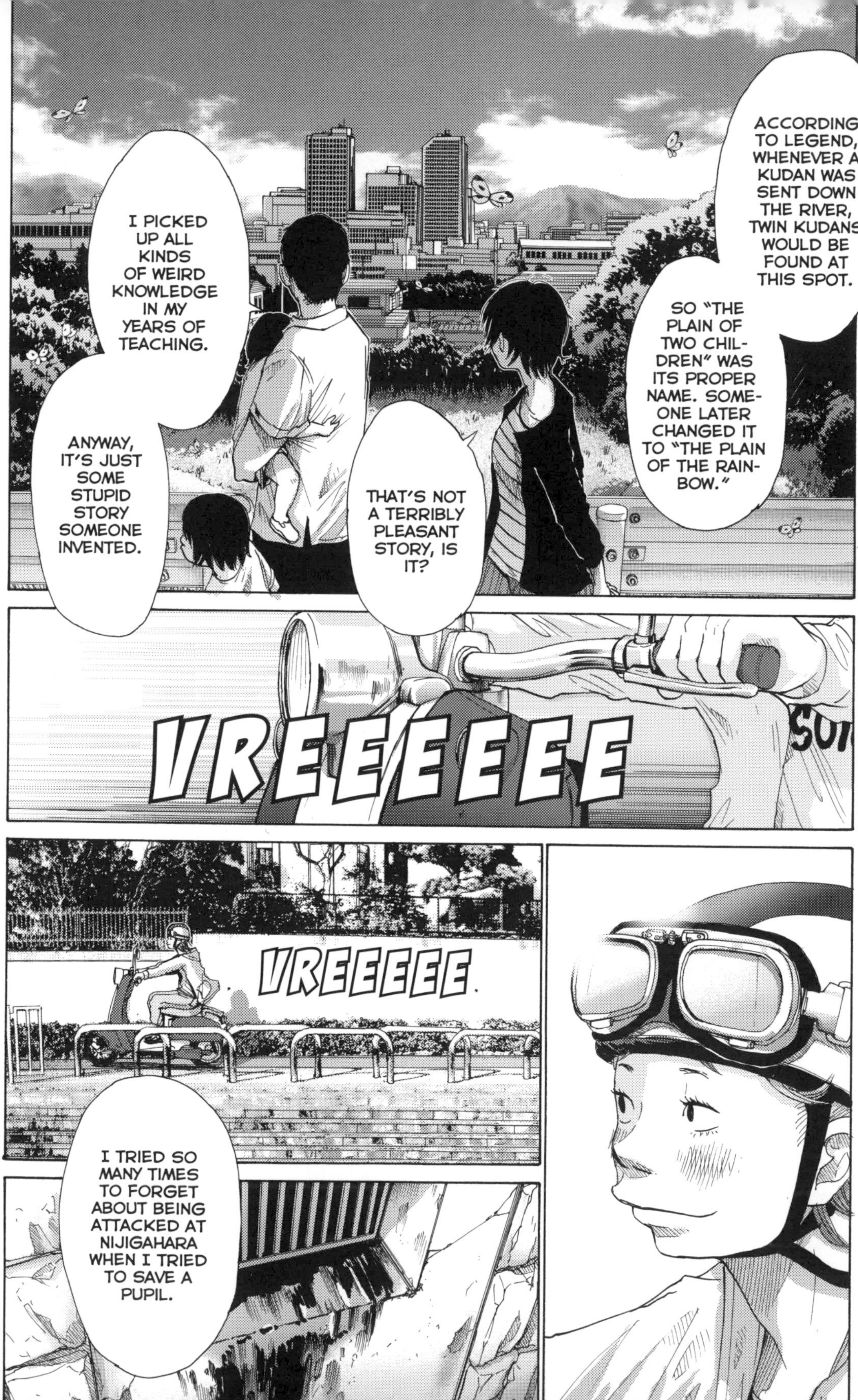
ACCORDING TO LEGEND, WHENEVER A KUDAN WAS SENT DOWN THE RIVER, TWIN KUDANS WOULD BE FOUND AT THIS SPOT.
SO "THE PLAIN OF TWO CHIL-DREN" WAS ITS PROPER NAME. SOME-ONE LATER CHANGED IT TO "THE PLAIN OF THE RAIN-BOW."
THAT'S NOT A TERRIBLY PLEASANT STORY, IS IT?
I PICKED UP ALL KINDS OF WEIRD KNOWLEDGE IN MY YEARS OF TEACHING.
ANYWAY, IT'S JUST SOME STUPID STORY SOMEONE INVENTED.
VREEEEEEE
VREEEEEE
I TRIED SO MANY TIMES TO FORGET ABOUT BEING ATTACKED AT NIJIGAHARA WHEN I TRIED TO SAVE A PUPIL.

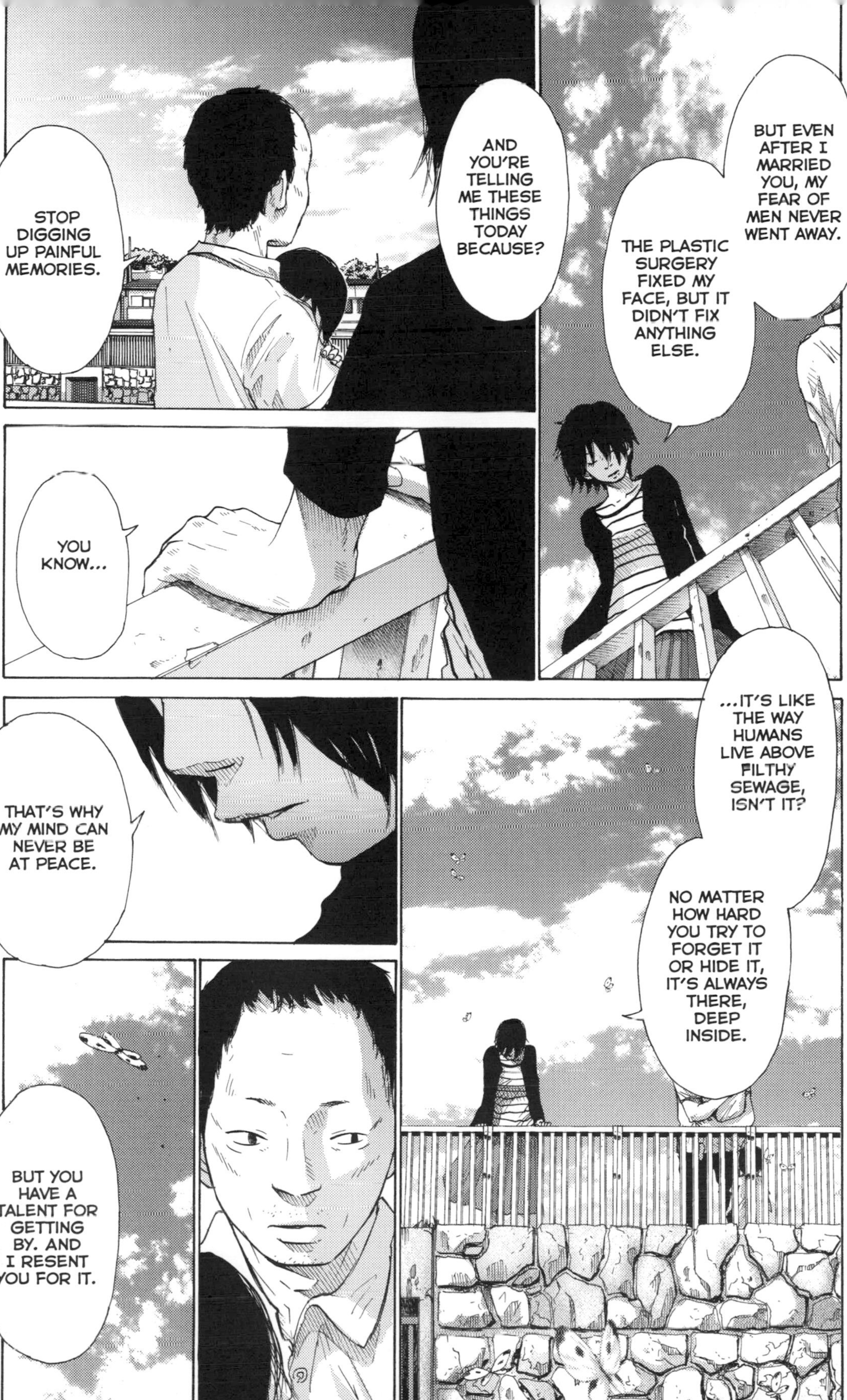
BUT EVEN AFTER I MARRIED YOU, MY FEAR OF MEN NEVER WENT AWAY.
THE PLASTIC SURGERY FIXED MY FACE, BUT IT DIDN'T FIX ANYTHING ELSE.
AND YOU'RE TELLING ME THESE THINGS TODAY BECAUSE?
STOP DIGGING UP PAINFUL MEMORIES.
YOU KNOW...
...IT'S LIKE THE WAY HUMANS LIVE ABOVE FILTHY SEWAGE, ISN'T IT?
NO MATTER HOW HARD YOU TRY TO FORGET IT OR HIDE IT, IT'S ALWAYS THERE, DEEP INSIDE.
THAT'S WHY MY MIND CAN NEVER BE AT PEACE.
BUT YOU HAVE A TALENT FOR GETTING BY. AND I RESENT YOU FOR IT.

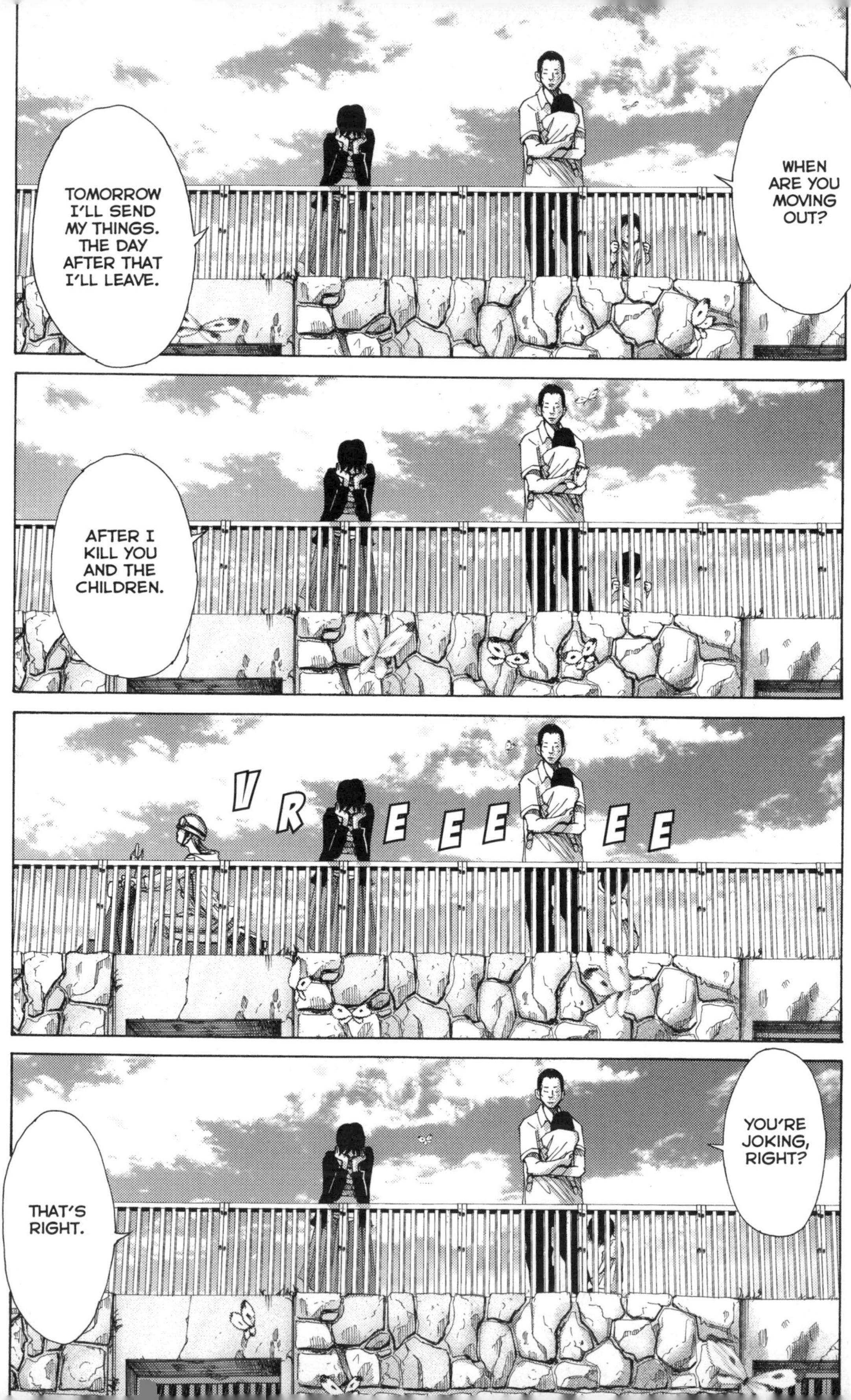
WHEN ARE YOU MOVING OUT?
TOMORROW I'LL SEND MY THINGS. THE DAY AFTER THAT I'LL LEAVE.
AFTER I KILL YOU AND THE CHILDREN.
VREEEEE
YOU'RE JOKING, RIGHT?
THAT'S RIGHT.

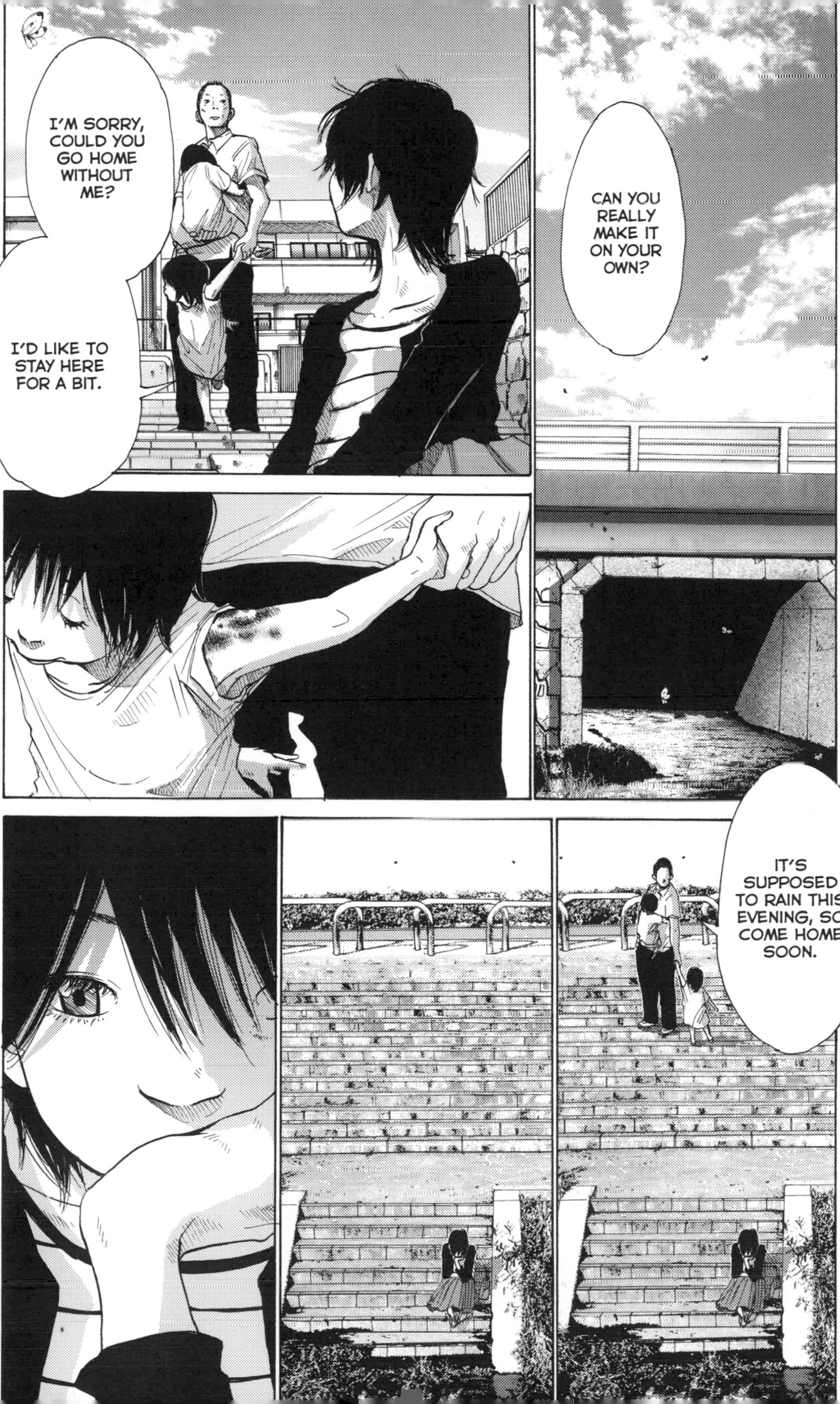
CAN YOU REALLY MAKE IT ON YOUR OWN?
I'M SORRY, COULD YOU GO HOME WITHOUT ME?
I'D LIKE TO STAY HERE FOR A BIT.
IT'S SUPPOSED TO RAIN THIS EVENING, SO COME HOME SOON.

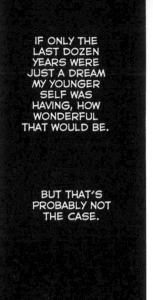

IF ONLY THE LAST DOZEN YEARS WERE JUST A DREAM MY YOUNGER SELF WAS HAVING, HOW WONDERFUL THAT WOULD BE.

BUT THAT'S PROBABLY NOT THE CASE.

I'M SORRY.

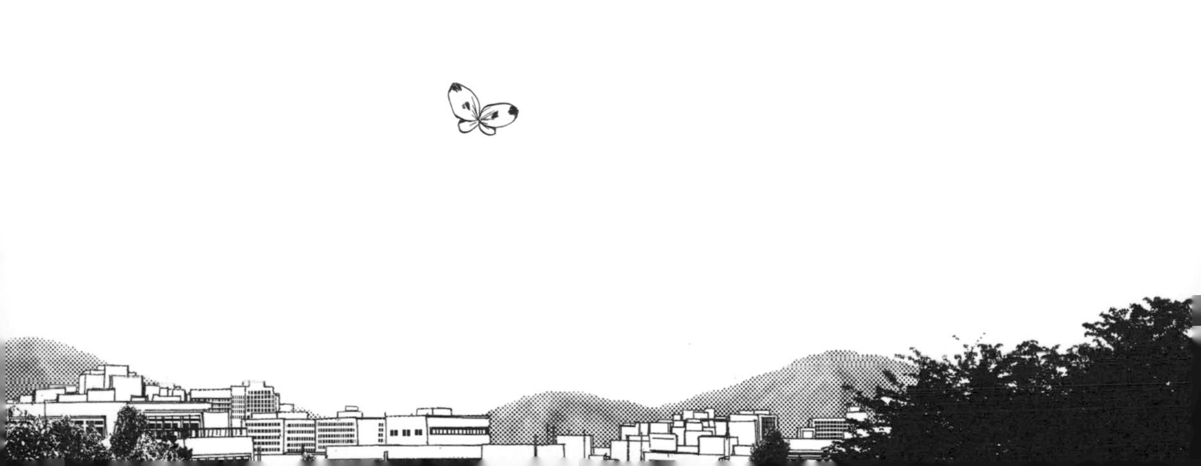

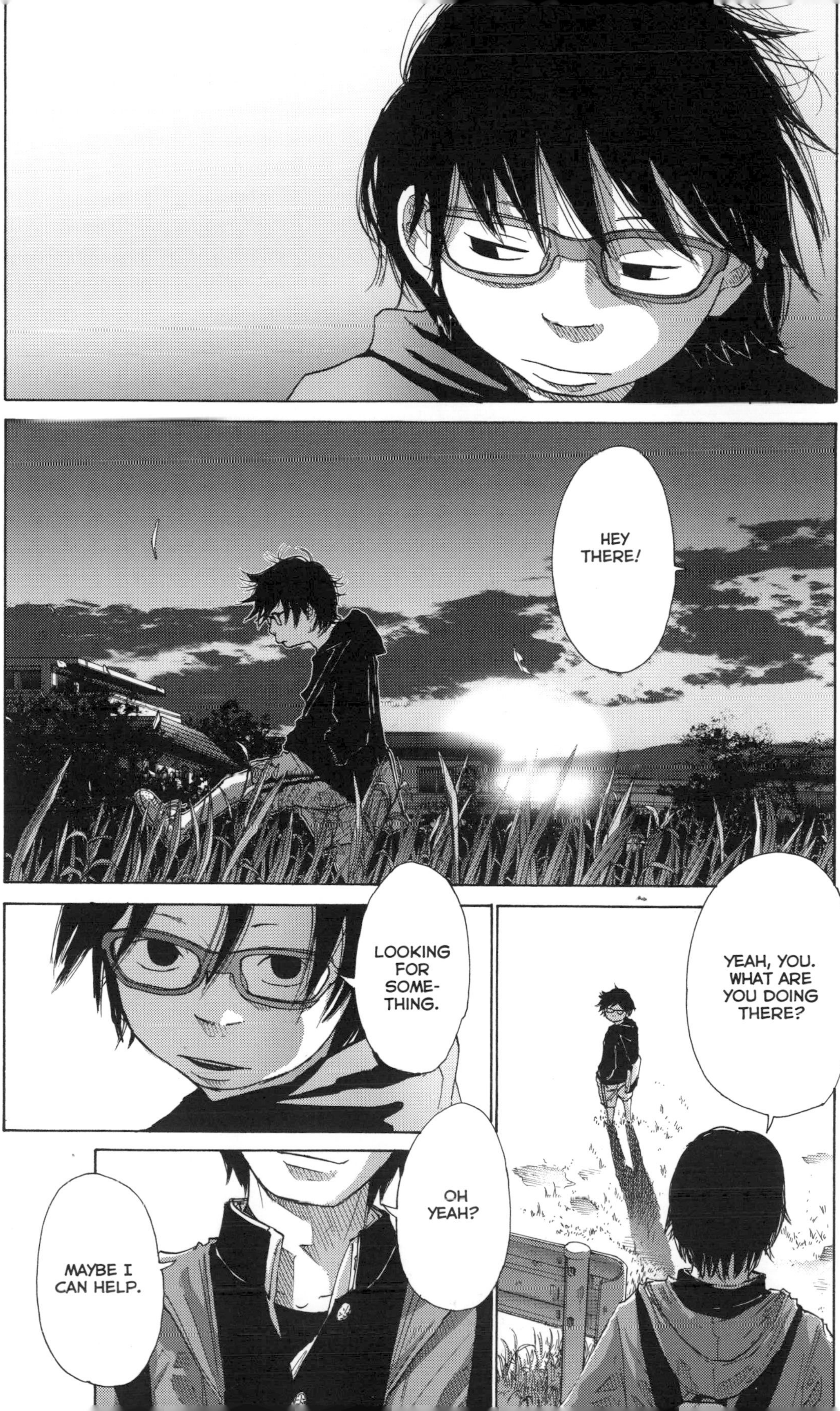
HEY THERE!
YEAH, YOU. WHAT ARE YOU DOING THERE?
LOOKING FOR SOME-THING.
OH YEAH?
MAYBE I CAN HELP.

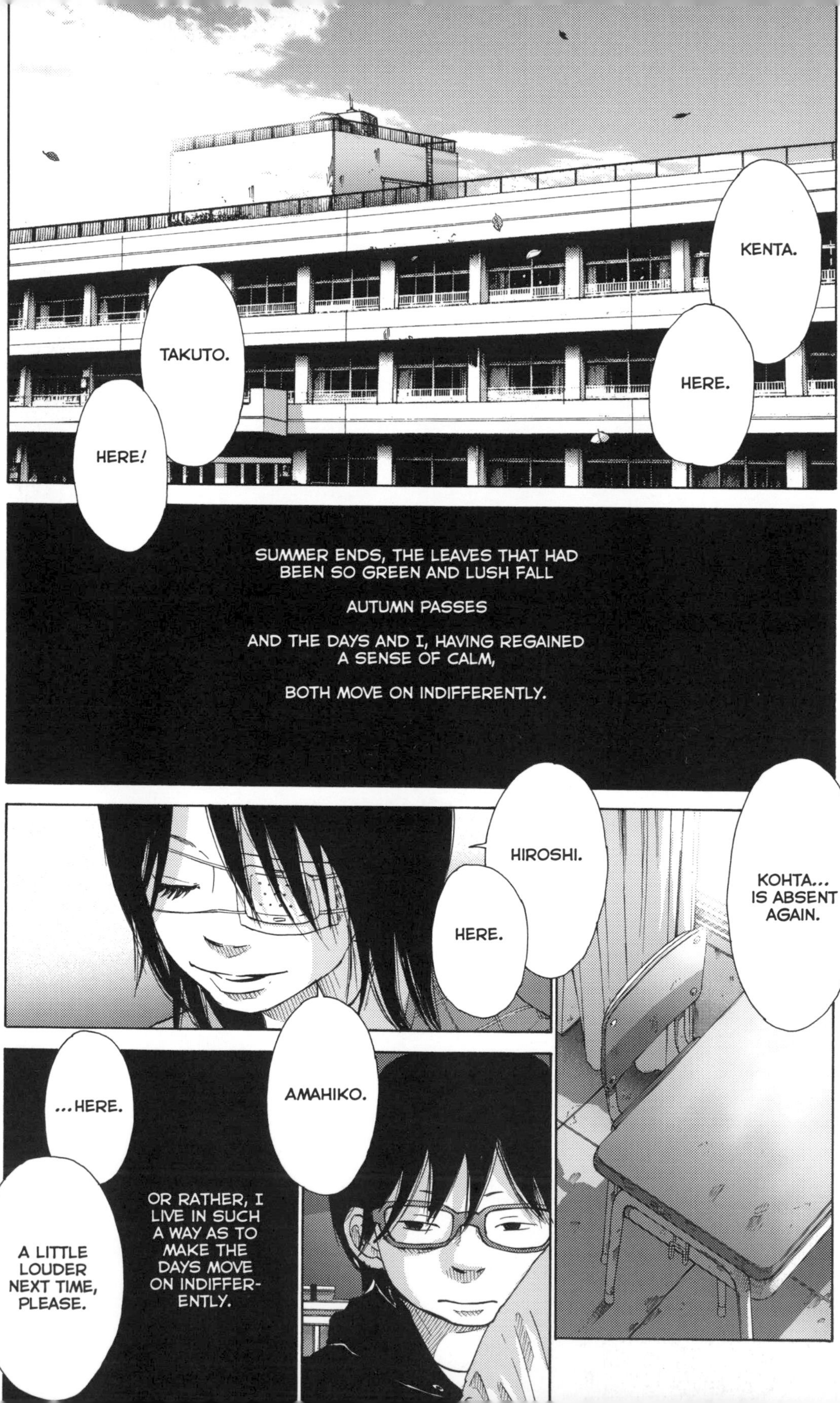
KENTA.
HERE.
TAKUTO.
HERE!
SUMMER ENDS, THE LEAVES THAT HAD BEEN SO GREEN AND LUSH FALL
AUTUMN PASSES
AND THE DAYS AND I, HAVING REGAINED A SENSE OF CALM,
BOTH MOVE ON INDIFFERENTLY.
KOHTA... IS ABSENT AGAIN.
HIROSHI.
HERE.
AMAHIKO.
...HERE.
A LITTLE LOUDER NEXT TIME, PLEASE.
OR RATHER, I LIVE IN SUCH A WAY AS TO MAKE THE DAYS MOVE ON INDIFFER-ENTLY.

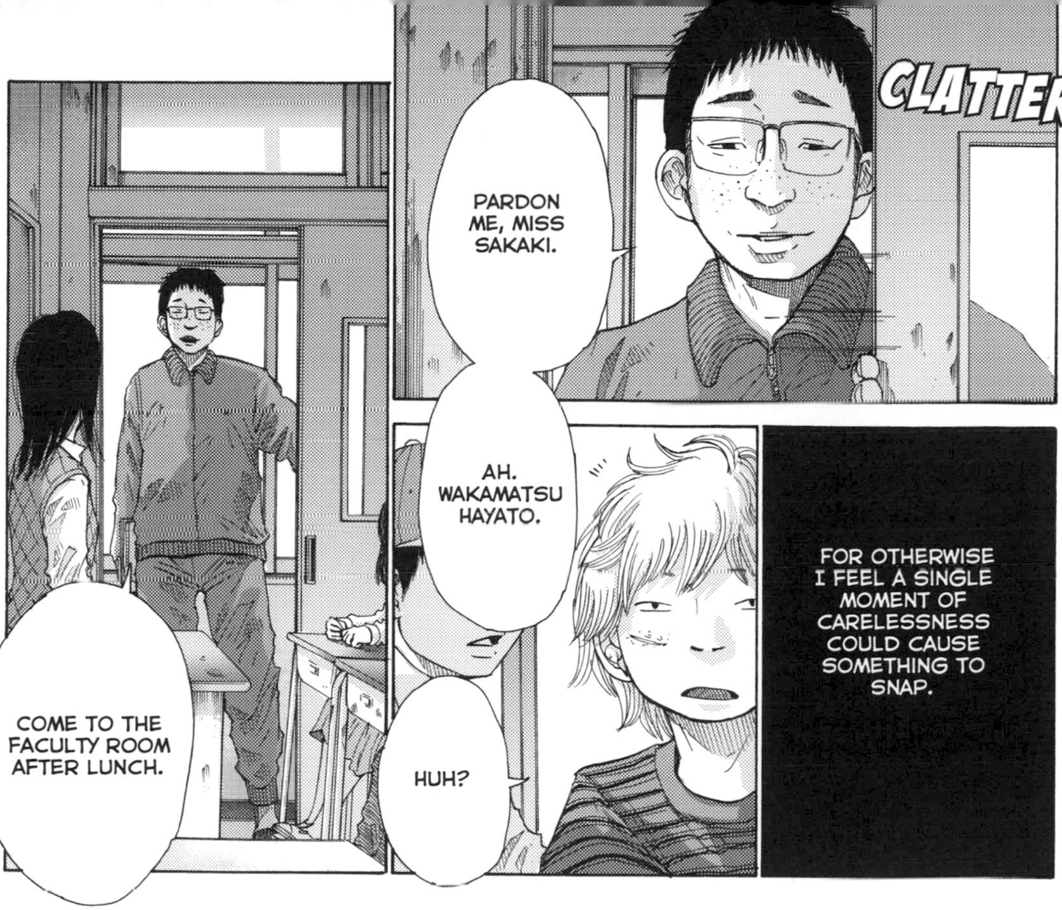
CLATTER
PARDON ME, MISS SAKAKI.
FOR OTHERWISE I FEEL A SINGLE MOMENT OF CARELESSNESS COULD CAUSE SOMETHING TO SNAP.
AH. WAKAMATSU HAYATO.
HUH?
COME TO THE FACULTY ROOM AFTER LUNCH.

CHAPTER 7

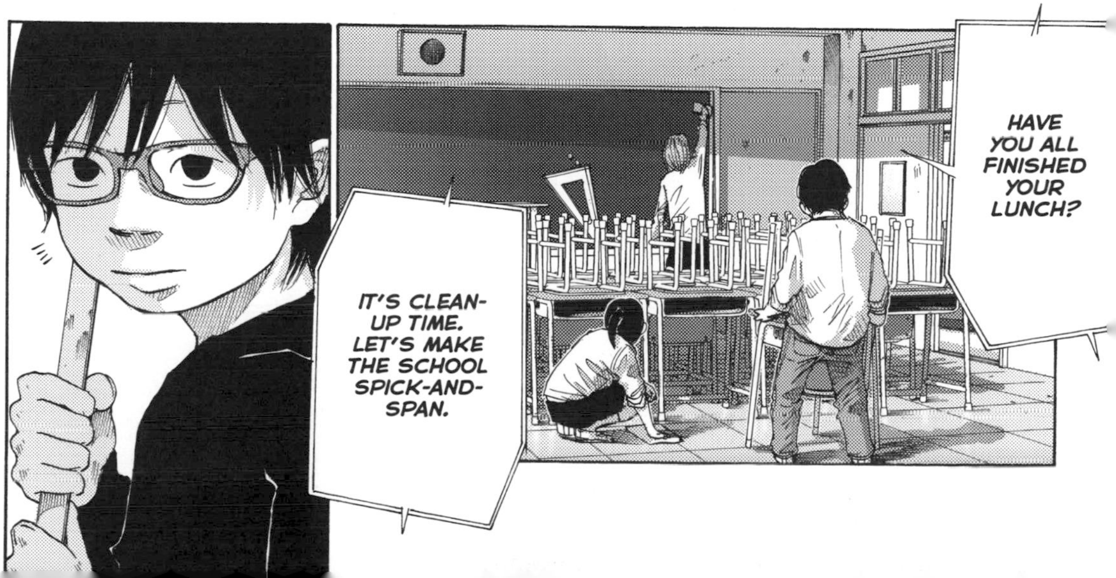
HAVE YOU ALL FINISHED YOUR LUNCH?
IT'S CLEAN-UP TIME. LET'S MAKE THE SCHOOL SPICK-AND-SPAN.

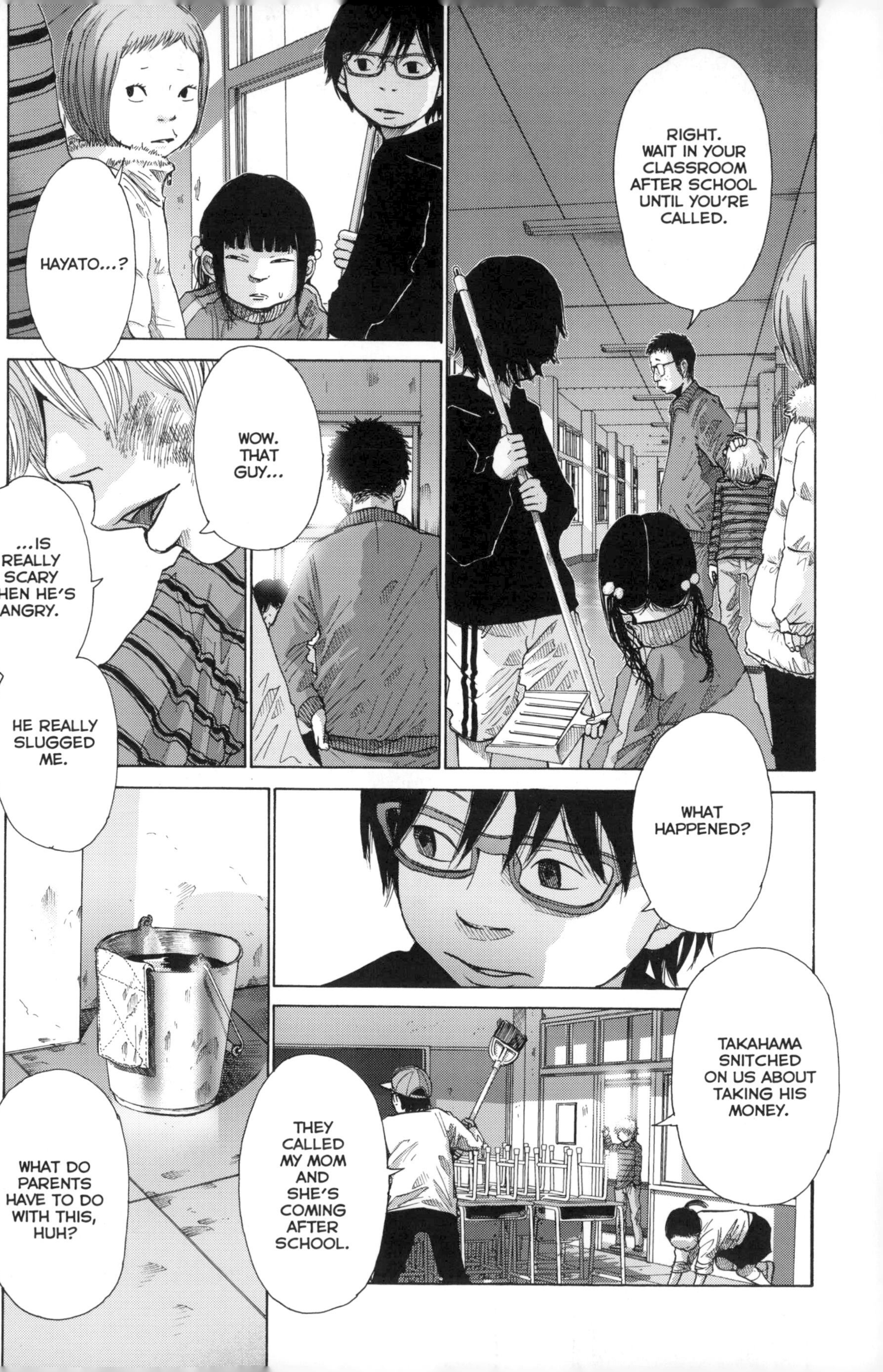
RIGHT. WAIT IN YOUR CLASSROOM AFTER SCHOOL UNTIL YOU'RE CALLED.
HAYATO...?
WOW. THAT GUY...
...IS REALLY SCARY WHEN HE'S ANGRY.
HE REALLY SLUGGED ME.
WHAT HAPPENED?
TAKAHAMA SNITCHED ON US ABOUT TAKING HIS MONEY.
THEY CALLED MY MOM AND SHE'S COMING AFTER SCHOOL.
WHAT DO PARENTS HAVE TO DO WITH THIS, HUH?

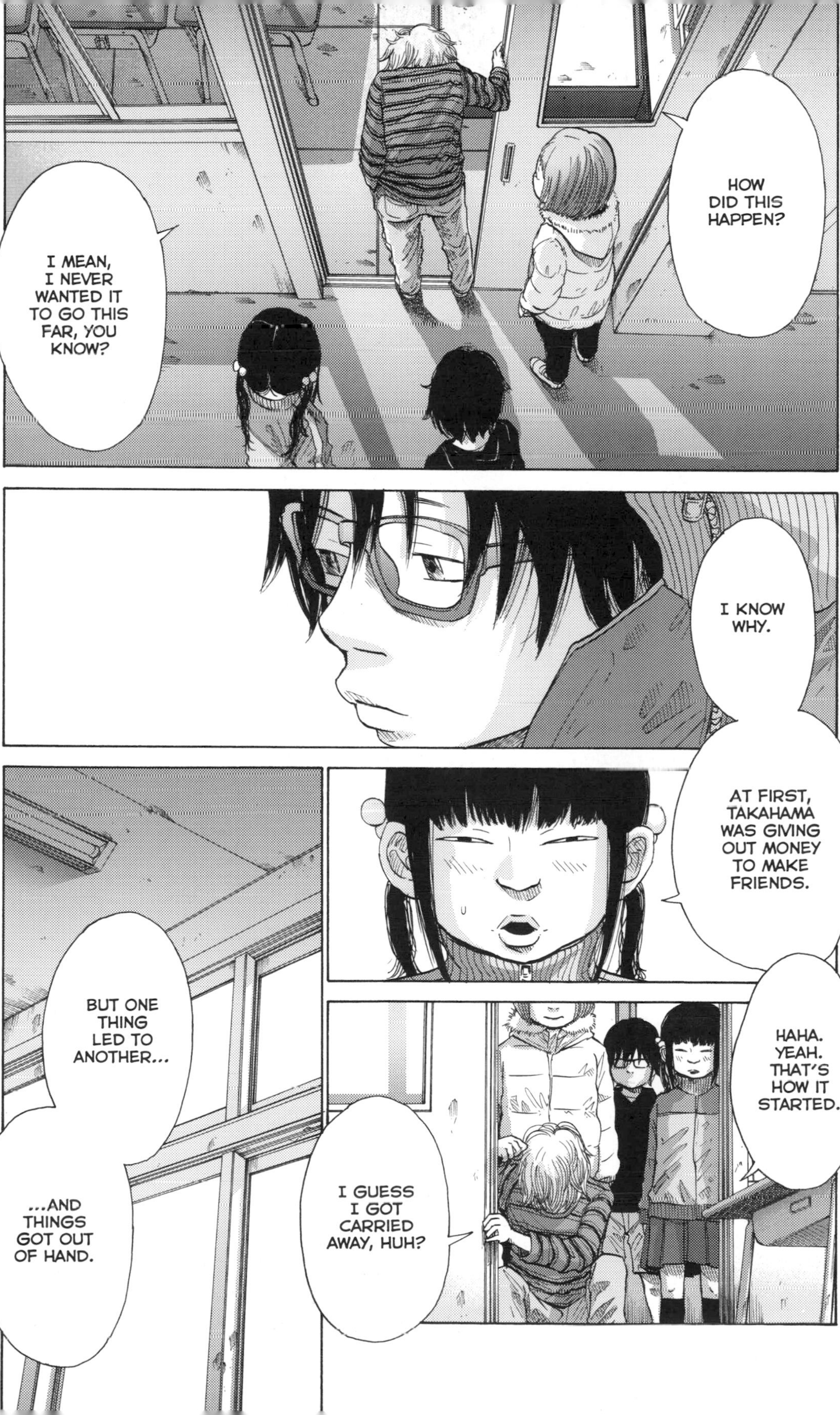
HOW DID THIS HAPPEN?
I MEAN, I NEVER WANTED IT TO GO THIS FAR, YOU KNOW?
I KNOW WHY.
AT FIRST, TAKAHAMA WAS GIVING OUT MONEY TO MAKE FRIENDS.
HAHA. YEAH. THAT'S HOW IT STARTED.
I GUESS I GOT CARRIED AWAY, HUH?
BUT ONE THING LED TO ANOTHER...
...AND THINGS GOT OUT OF HAND.

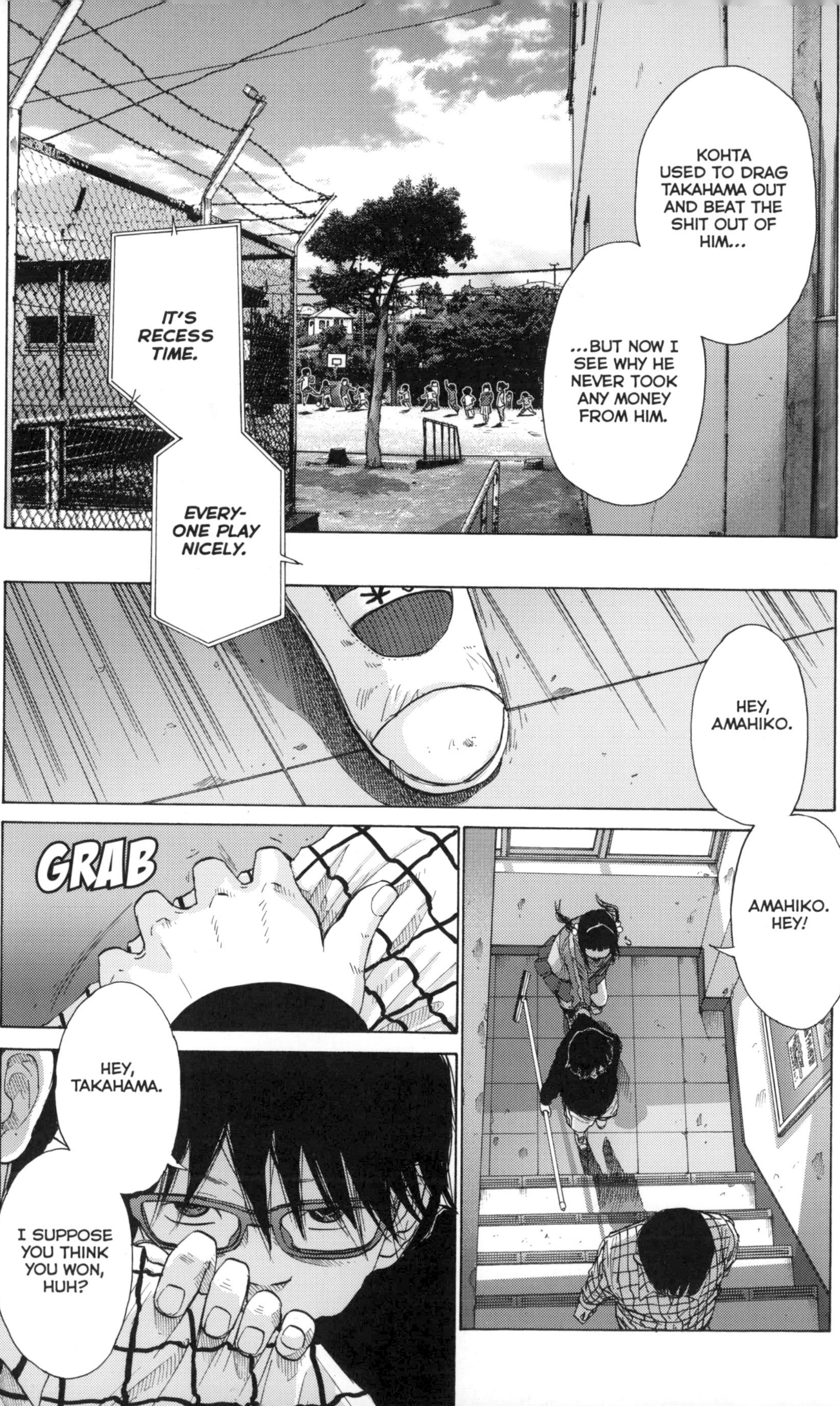
KOHTA USED TO DRAG TAKAHAMA OUT AND BEAT THE SHIT OUT OF HIM...
...BUT NOW I SEE WHY HE NEVER TOOK ANY MONEY FROM HIM.
IT'S RECESS TIME.
EVERY-ONE PLAY NICELY.
HEY, AMAHIKO.
AMAHIKO. HEY!
GRAB
HEY, TAKAHAMA.
I SUPPOSE YOU THINK YOU WON, HUH?

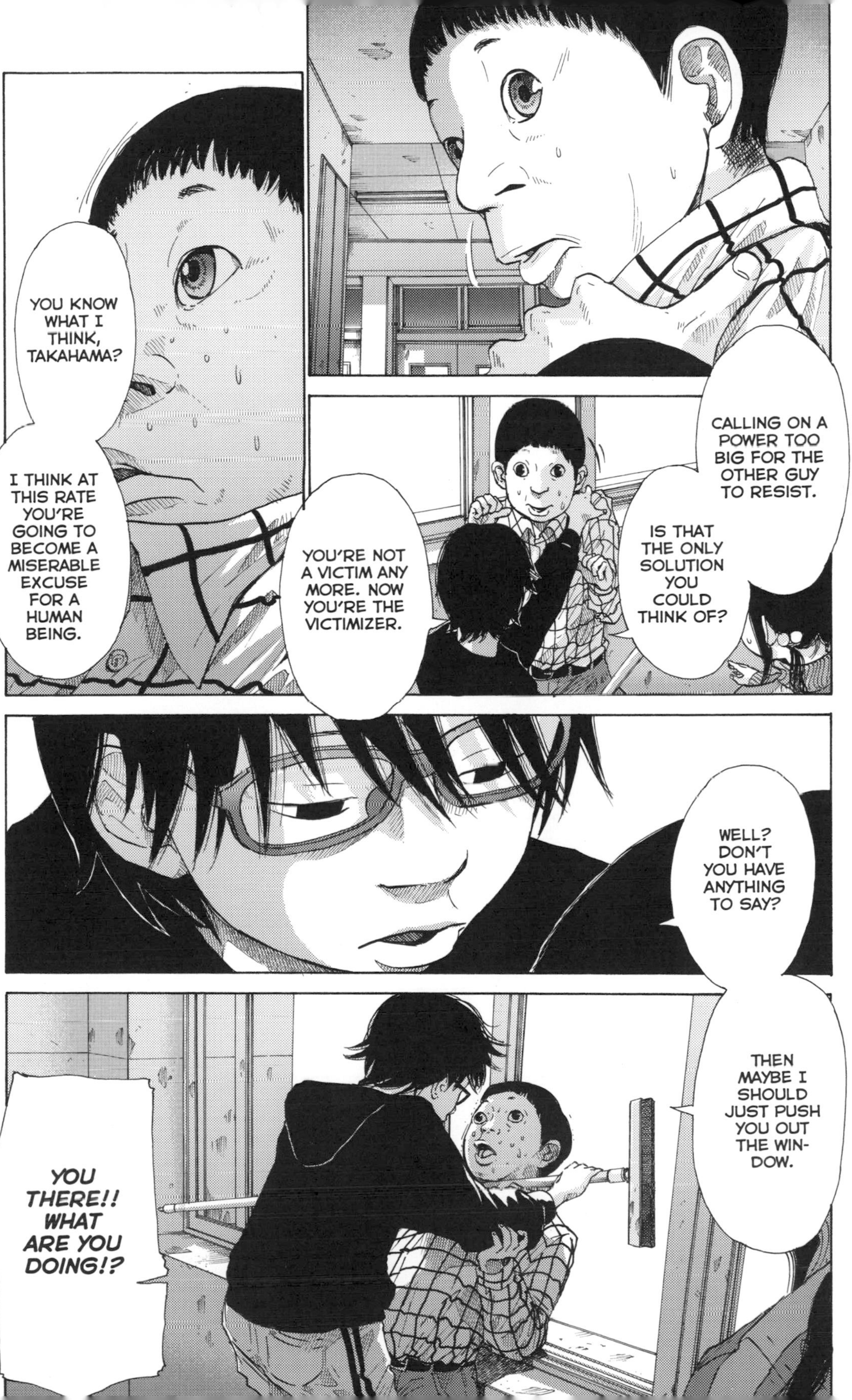
CALLING ON A POWER TOO BIG FOR THE OTHER GUY TO RESIST.
IS THAT THE ONLY SOLUTION YOU COULD THINK OF?
YOU'RE NOT A VICTIM ANY MORE. NOW YOU'RE THE VICTIMIZER.
YOU KNOW WHAT I THINK, TAKAHAMA?
I THINK AT THIS RATE YOU'RE GOING TO BECOME A MISERABLE EXCUSE FOR A HUMAN BEING.
WELL? DON'T YOU HAVE ANYTHING TO SAY?
THEN MAYBE I SHOULD JUST PUSH YOU OUT THE WIN-DOW.
YOU THERE!! WHAT ARE YOU DOING!?

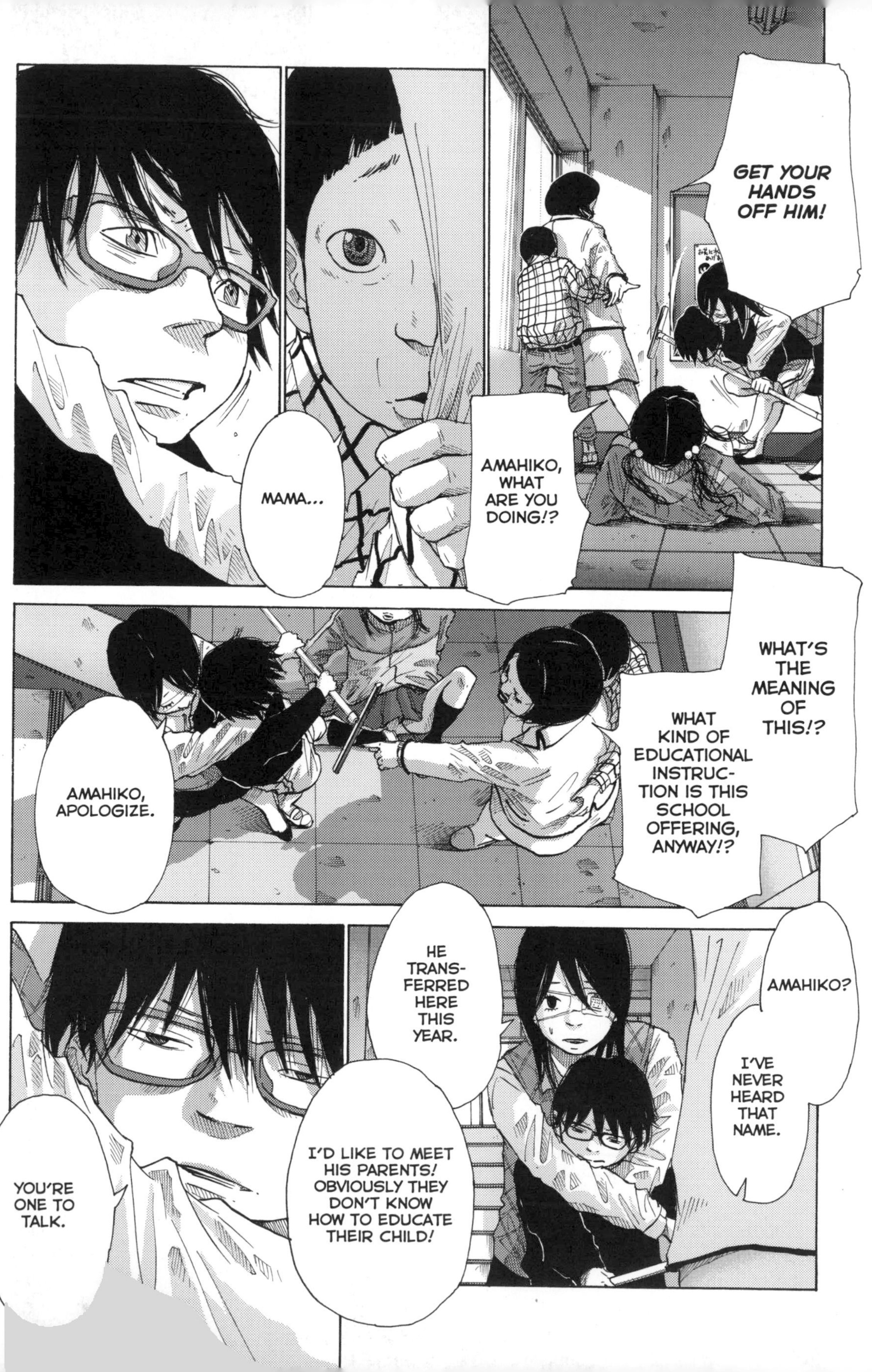
GET YOUR HANDS OFF HIM!
AMAHIKO, WHAT ARE YOU DOING!?
MAMA...
WHAT'S THE MEANING OF THIS!?
WHAT KIND OF EDUCATIONAL INSTRUC-TION IS THIS SCHOOL OFFERING, ANYWAY!?
AMAHIKO, APOLOGIZE.
AMAHIKO?
I'VE NEVER HEARD THAT NAME.
HE TRANS-FERRED HERE THIS YEAR.
I'D LIKE TO MEET HIS PARENTS! OBVIOUSLY THEY DON'T KNOW HOW TO EDUCATE THEIR CHILD!
YOU'RE ONE TO TALK.

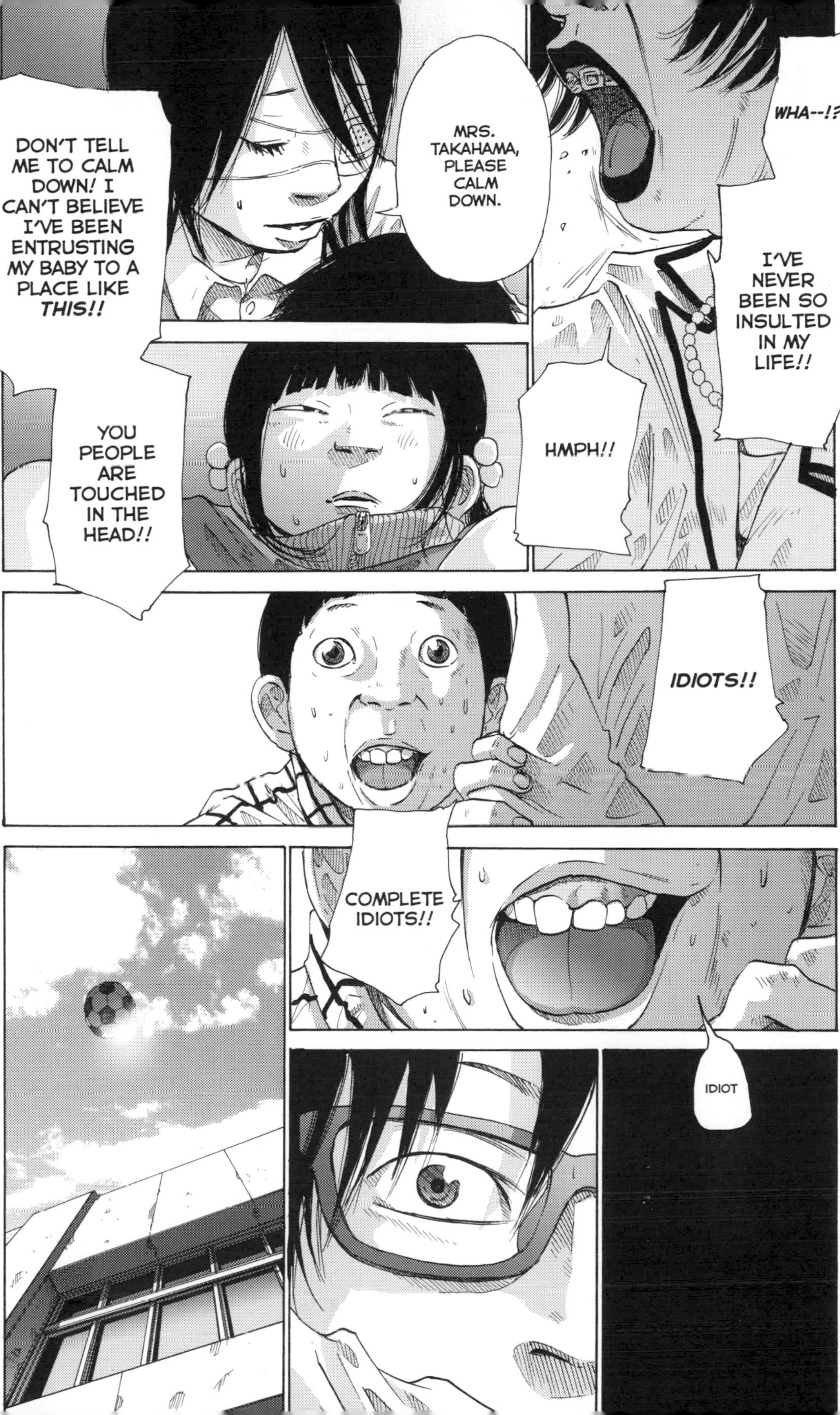
WHA--!?
I'VE NEVER BEEN SO INSULTED IN MY LIFE!!
HMPH!!
MRS. TAKAHAMA, PLEASE CALM DOWN.
DON'T TELL ME TO CALM DOWN! I CAN'T BELIEVE I'VE BEEN ENTRUSTING MY BABY TO A PLACE LIKE THIS!!
YOU PEOPLE ARE TOUCHED IN THE HEAD!!
IDIOTS!!
COMPLETE IDIOTS!!
IDIOT

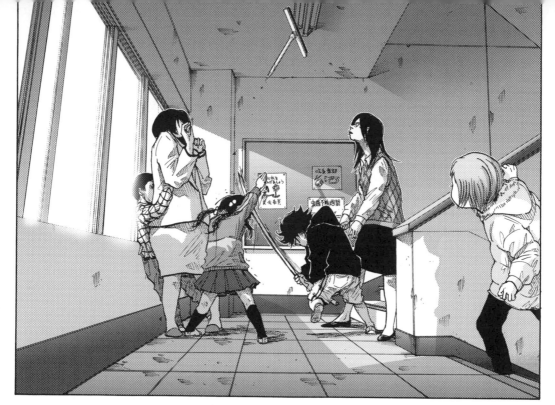

WHY...?

WHY DID
YOU
PROTECT
HIM?

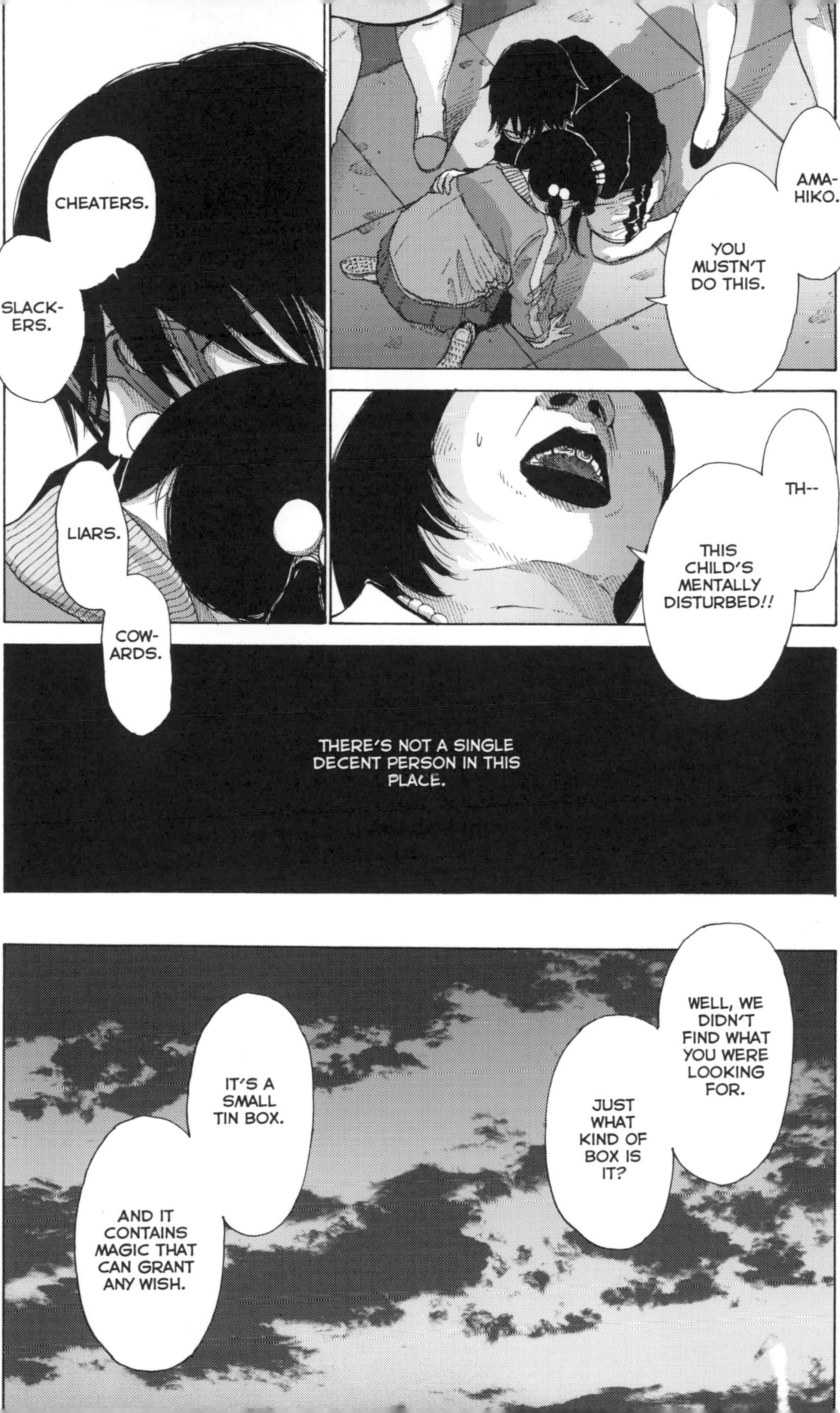
AMA-HIKO.
YOU MUSTN'T DO THIS.
TH--
THIS CHILD'S MENTALLY DISTURBED!!
CHEATERS.
SLACK-ERS.
LIARS.
COW-ARDS.
THERE'S NOT A SINGLE DECENT PERSON IN THIS PLACE.
WELL, WE DIDN'T FIND WHAT YOU WERE LOOKING FOR.
JUST WHAT KIND OF BOX IS IT?
IT'S A SMALL TIN BOX.
AND IT CONTAINS MAGIC THAT CAN GRANT ANY WISH.

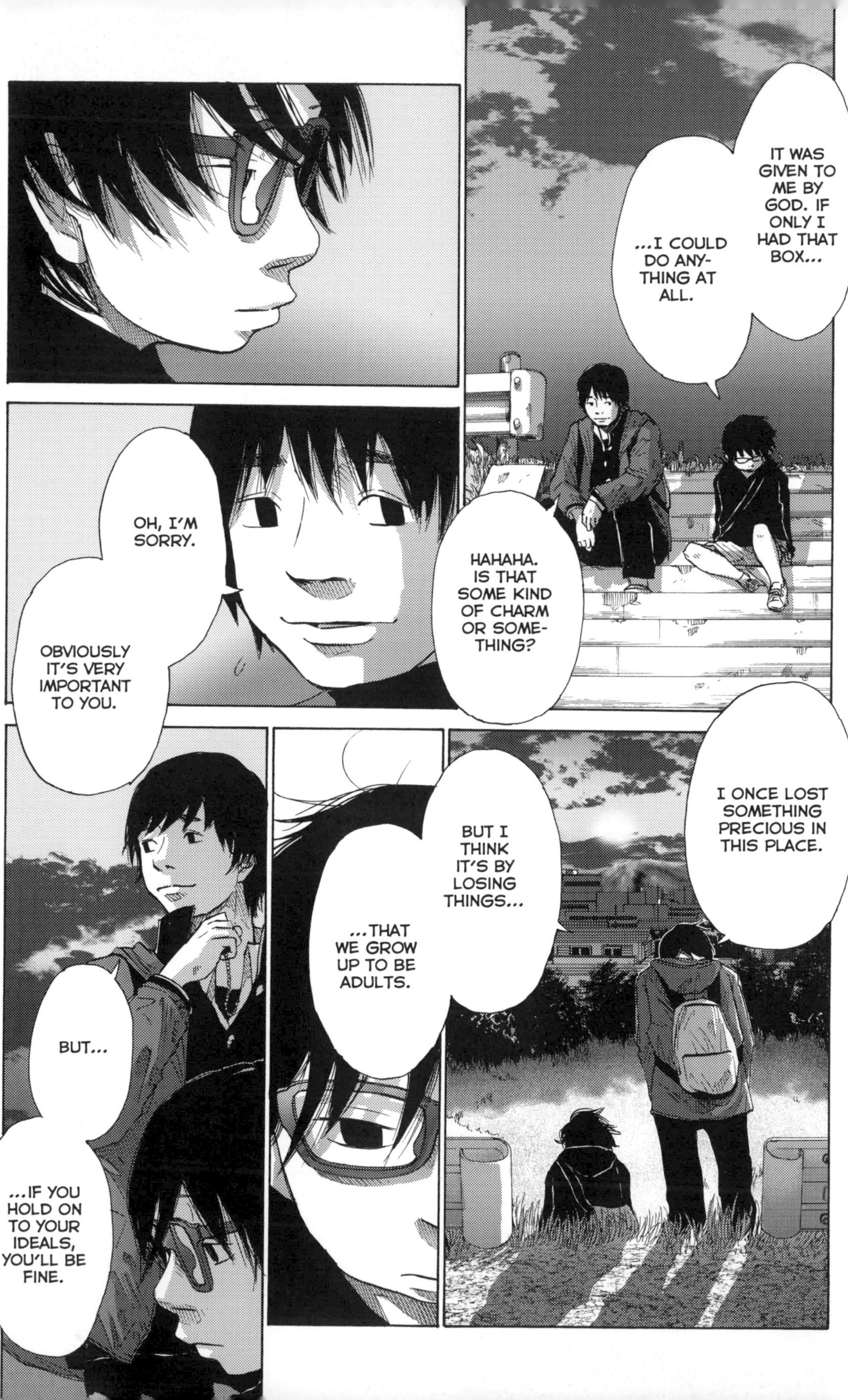
IT WAS GIVEN TO ME BY GOD. IF ONLY I HAD THAT BOX...
...I COULD DO ANYTHING AT ALL.
HAHAHA. IS THAT SOME KIND OF CHARM OR SOMETHING?
OH, I'M SORRY.
OBVIOUSLY IT'S VERY IMPORTANT TO YOU.
I ONCE LOST SOMETHING PRECIOUS IN THIS PLACE.
BUT I THINK IT'S BY LOSING THINGS...
...THAT WE GROW UP TO BE ADULTS.
BUT...
...IF YOU HOLD ON TO YOUR IDEALS, YOU'LL BE FINE.

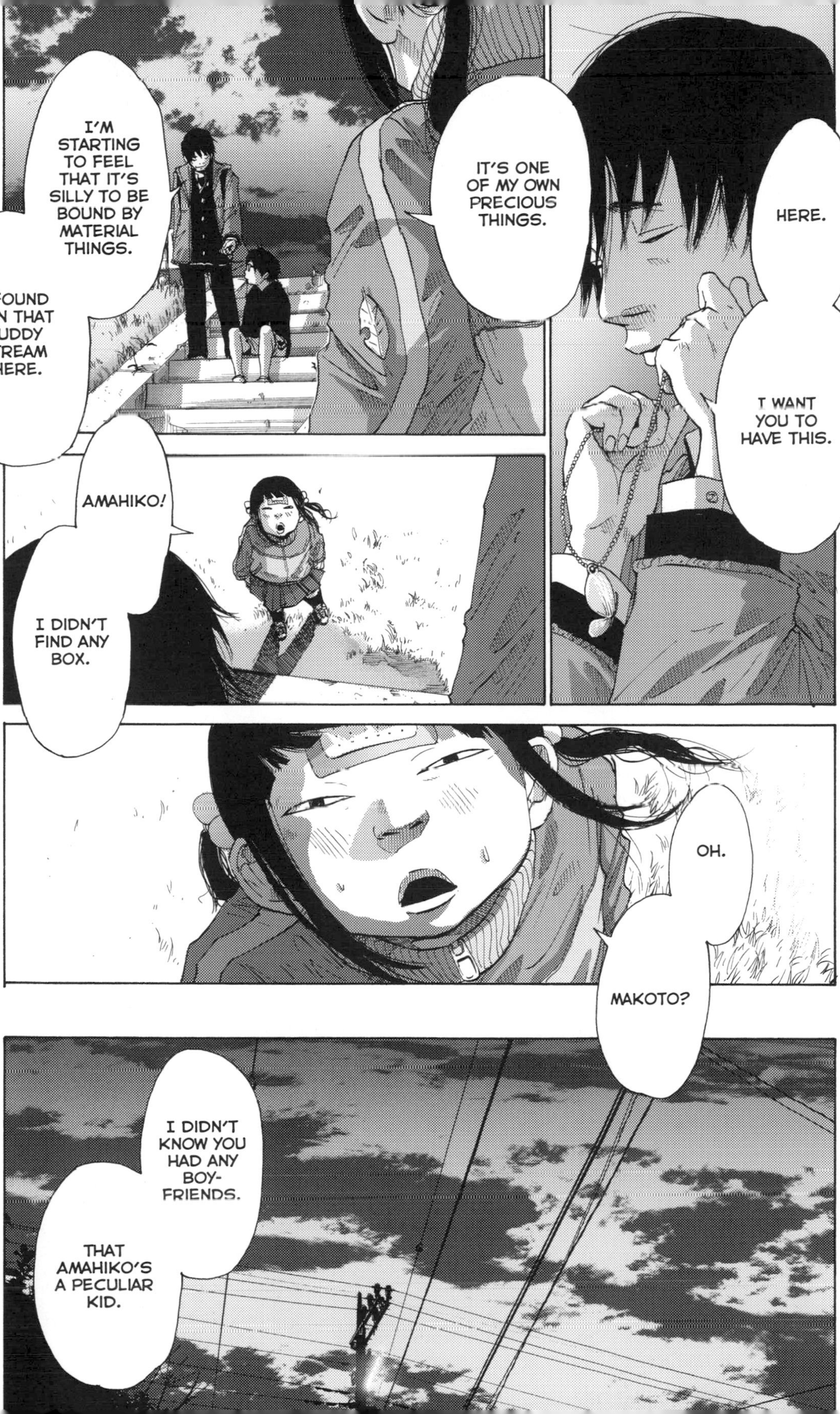
HERE.
I WANT YOU TO HAVE THIS.
IT'S ONE OF MY OWN PRECIOUS THINGS.
I'M STARTING TO FEEL THAT IT'S SILLY TO BE BOUND BY MATERIAL THINGS.
I FOUND IT IN THAT MUDDY STREAM THERE.
AMAHIKO!
I DIDN'T FIND ANY BOX.
OH.
MAKOTO?
I DIDN'T KNOW YOU HAD ANY BOY-FRIENDS.
THAT AMAHIKO'S A PECULIAR KID.

REALLY.

REALLY?

BY THE WAY. YOU'VE BEEN READING MY DIARY, HAVEN'T YOU?

NO I HAVEN'T.

GRAB

YES. I'M LYING.

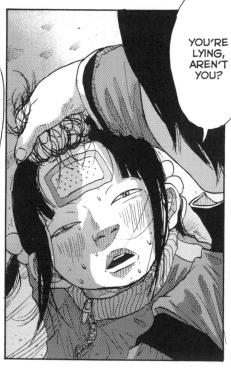

YOU'RE LYING, AREN'T YOU?

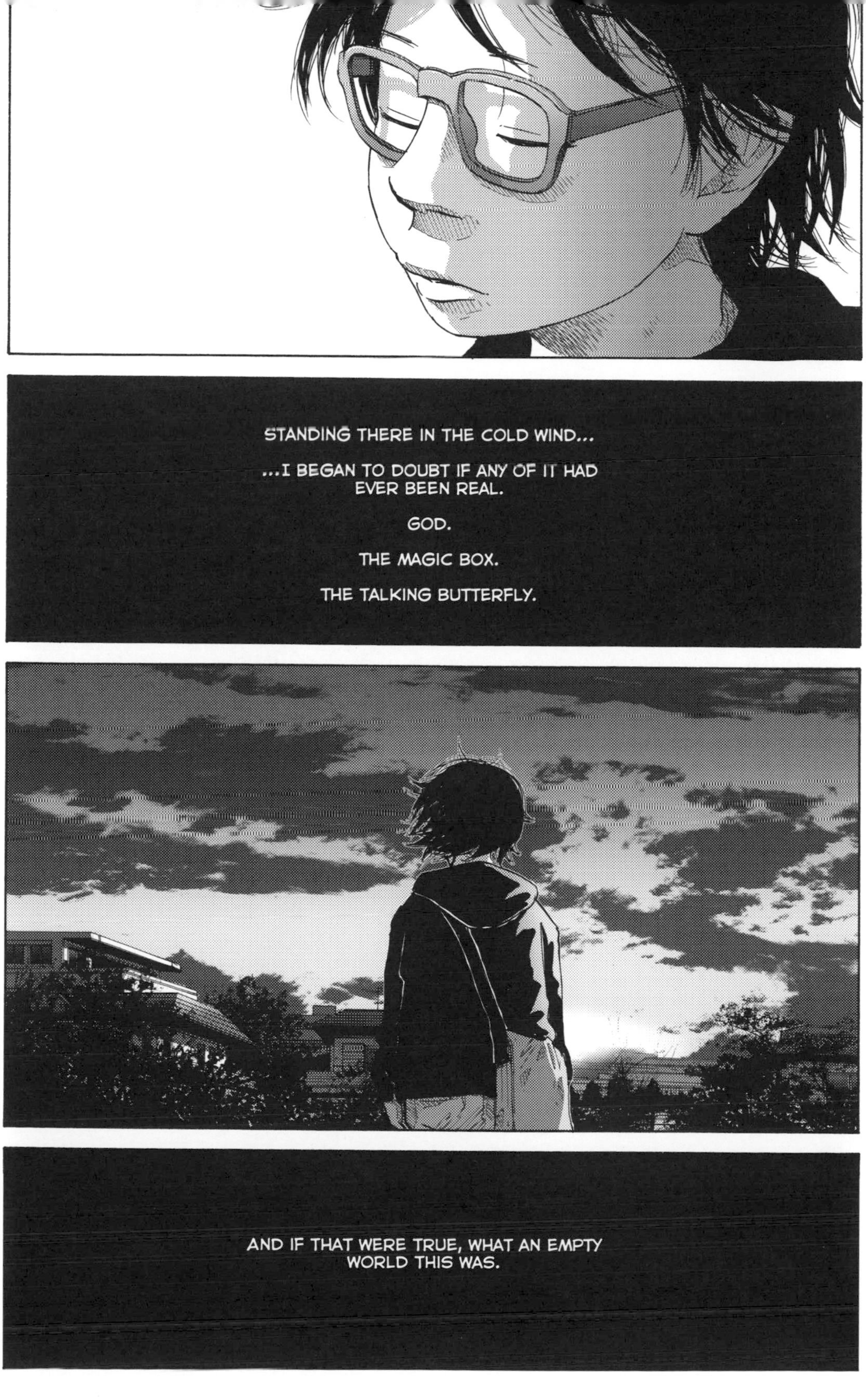
STANDING THERE IN THE COLD WIND...
...I BEGAN TO DOUBT IF ANY OF IT HAD EVER BEEN REAL.
GOD.
THE MAGIC BOX.
THE TALKING BUTTERFLY.
AND IF THAT WERE TRUE, WHAT AN EMPTY WORLD THIS WAS.

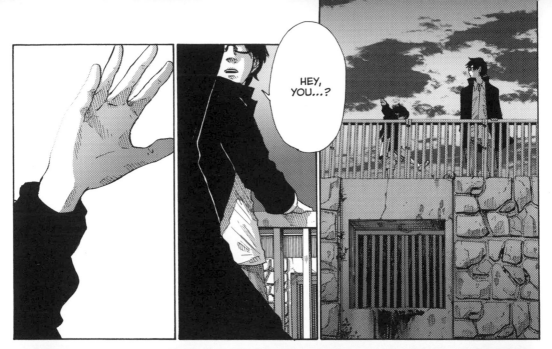

HEY,
YOU...?

FEELING SOME BLACK THING BEGIN TO SPILL OVER...

...I STEPPED OUT INTO THAT EMPTY WORLD.

THE RAIN THAT HAD BEEN FALLING SINCE NIGHT
HAS AT LAST LET UP.

YET THE LOW-HANGING, LEADEN SKY THREATENS TO
UNLEASH ANOTHER ROUND.

ON DAMP DAYS SUCH AS THIS, I RECALL THE EVENTS
OF THOSE DAYS.

OR PERHAPS
I SHOULD
SAY I
RECALL
THEM MORE.

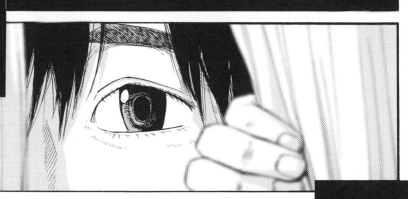

I HAVE LITTLE
DIFFICULTY
RECALLING
MEMORIES
I RUMINATE
OVER ON A
DAILY BASIS.

BUT TODAY
THEY COME
BACK TO ME
EVEN MORE
VIVIDLY.

DING
DONG

UM!
HELLO!

IT'S
MAKI.

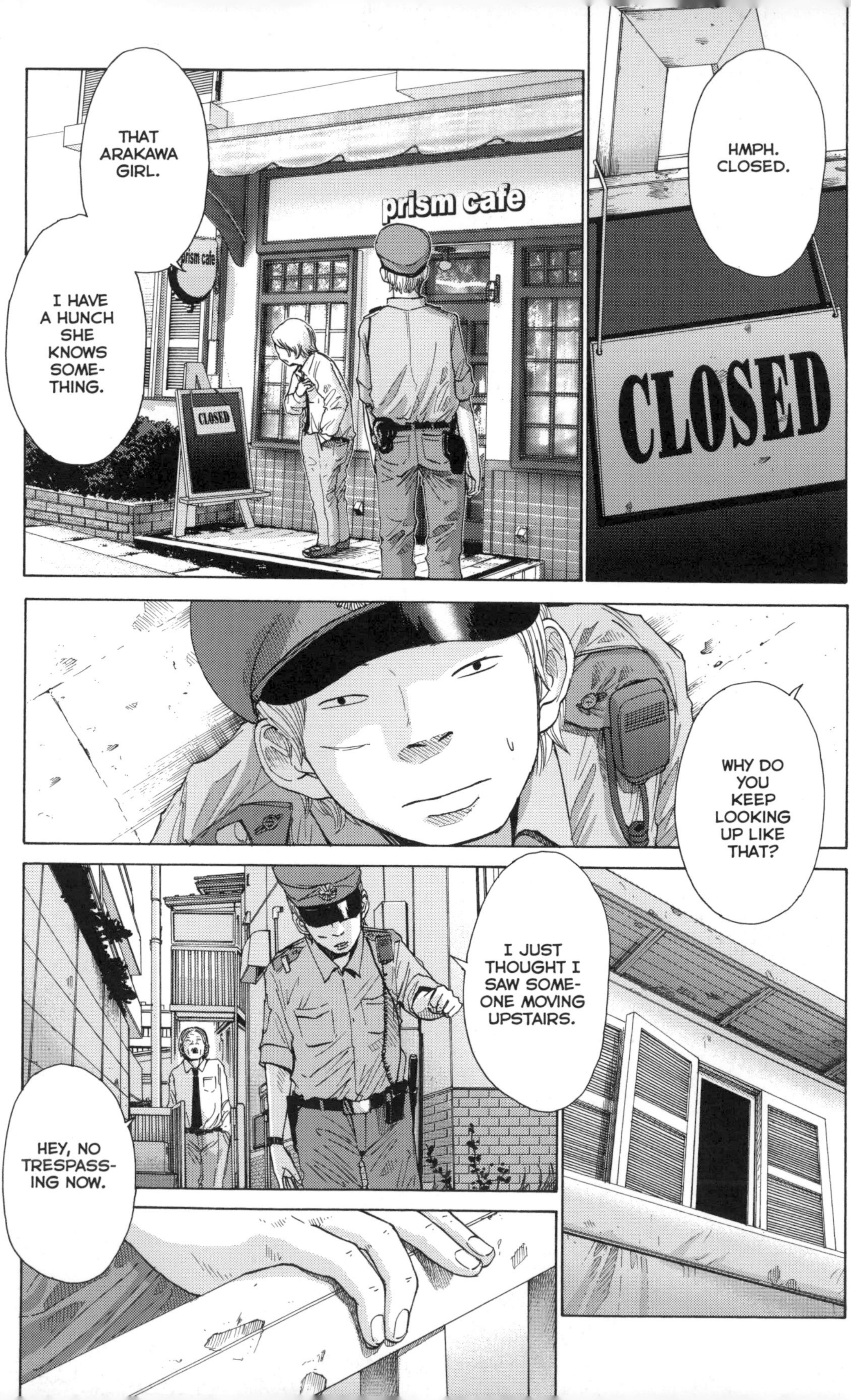
HMPH. CLOSED.
CLOSED
THAT ARAKAWA GIRL.
prism cafe
I HAVE A HUNCH SHE KNOWS SOME-THING.
WHY DO YOU KEEP LOOKING UP LIKE THAT?
I JUST THOUGHT I SAW SOME-ONE MOVING UPSTAIRS.
HEY, NO TRESPASS-ING NOW.

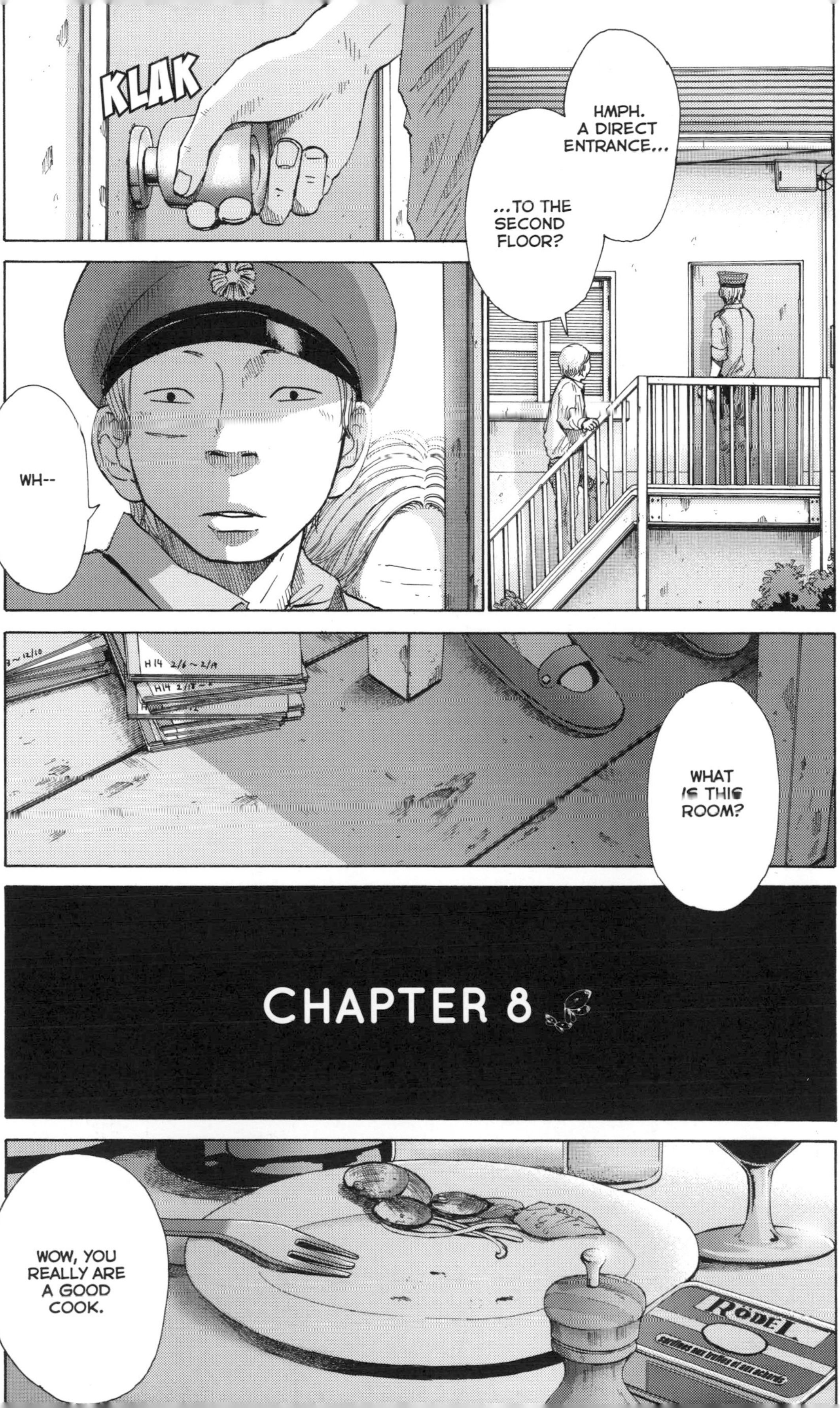
HMPH. A DIRECT ENTRANCE...
...TO THE SECOND FLOOR?
KLAK
WH--
WHAT IS THIS ROOM?
CHAPTER 8
WOW, YOU REALLY ARE A GOOD COOK.
RÖDEL

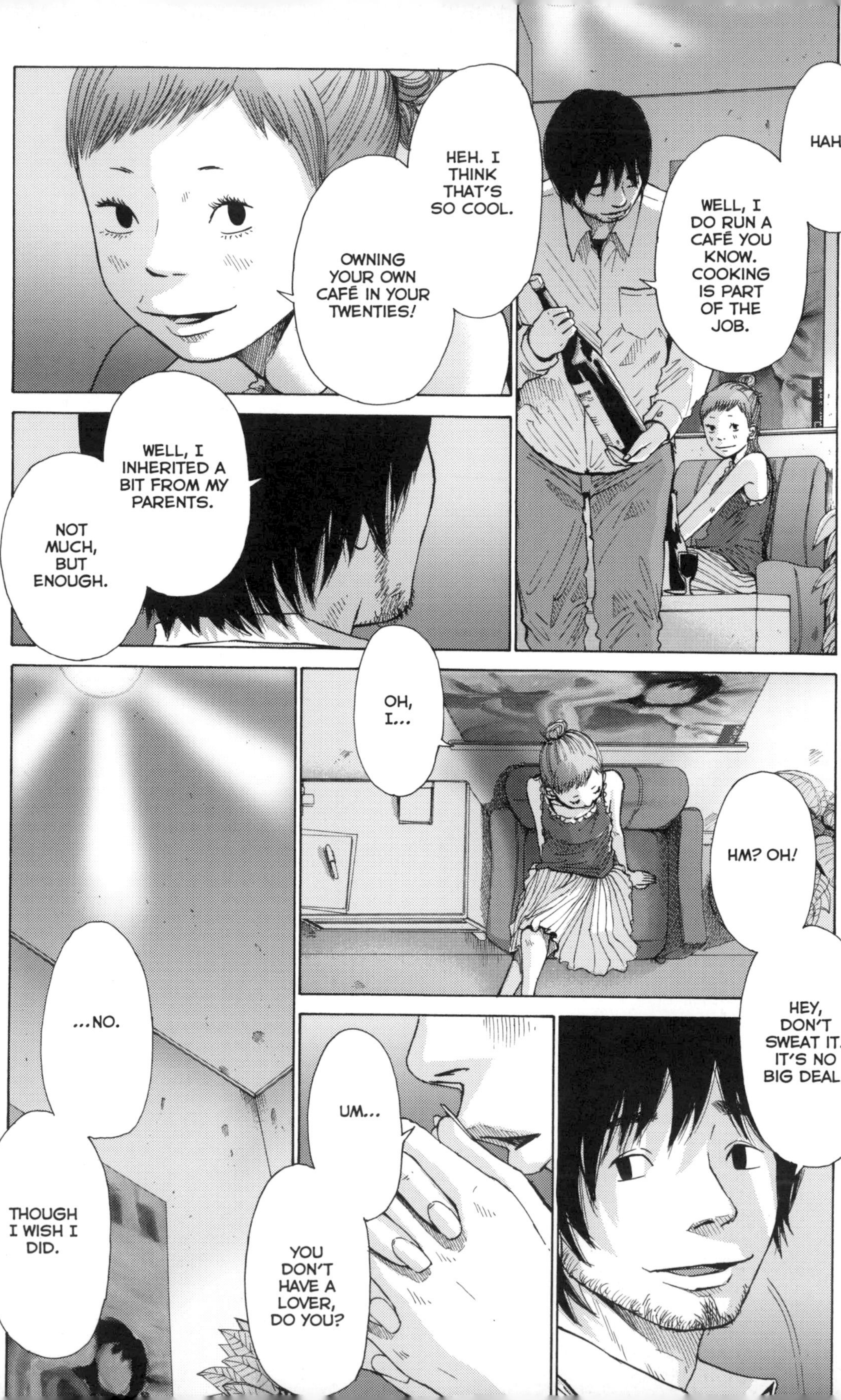
HAHA.
WELL, I DO RUN A CAFÉ YOU KNOW. COOKING IS PART OF THE JOB.
HEH. I THINK THAT'S SO COOL.
OWNING YOUR OWN CAFÉ IN YOUR TWENTIES!
WELL, I INHERITED A BIT FROM MY PARENTS.
NOT MUCH, BUT ENOUGH.
OH, I...
HM? OH!
HEY, DON'T SWEAT IT. IT'S NO BIG DEAL.
UM...
YOU DON'T HAVE A LOVER, DO YOU?
...NO.
THOUGH I WISH I DID.

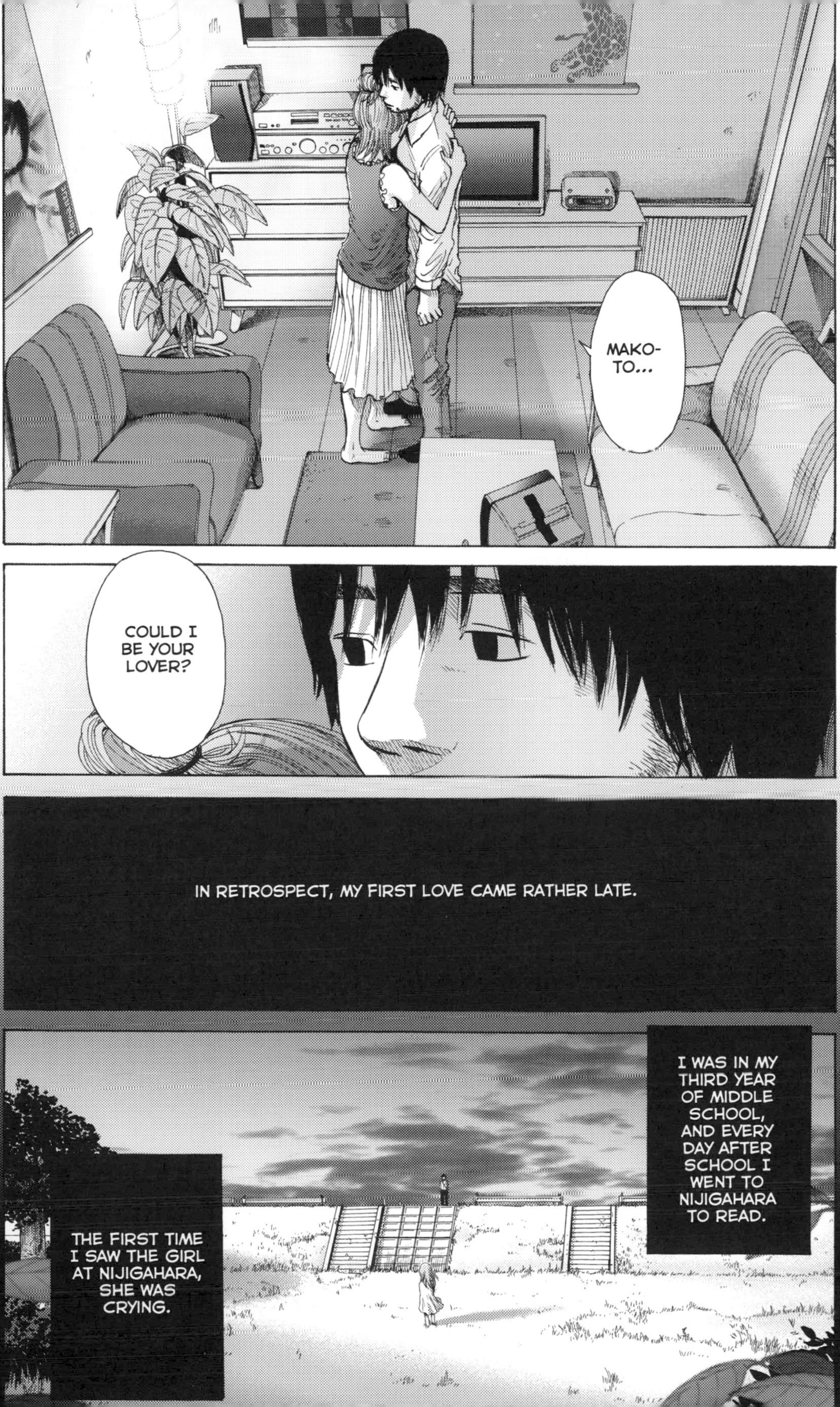
MAKO-TO...
COULD I BE YOUR LOVER?
IN RETROSPECT, MY FIRST LOVE CAME RATHER LATE.
I WAS IN MY THIRD YEAR OF MIDDLE SCHOOL, AND EVERY DAY AFTER SCHOOL I WENT TO NIJIGAHARA TO READ.
THE FIRST TIME I SAW THE GIRL AT NIJIGAHARA, SHE WAS CRYING.

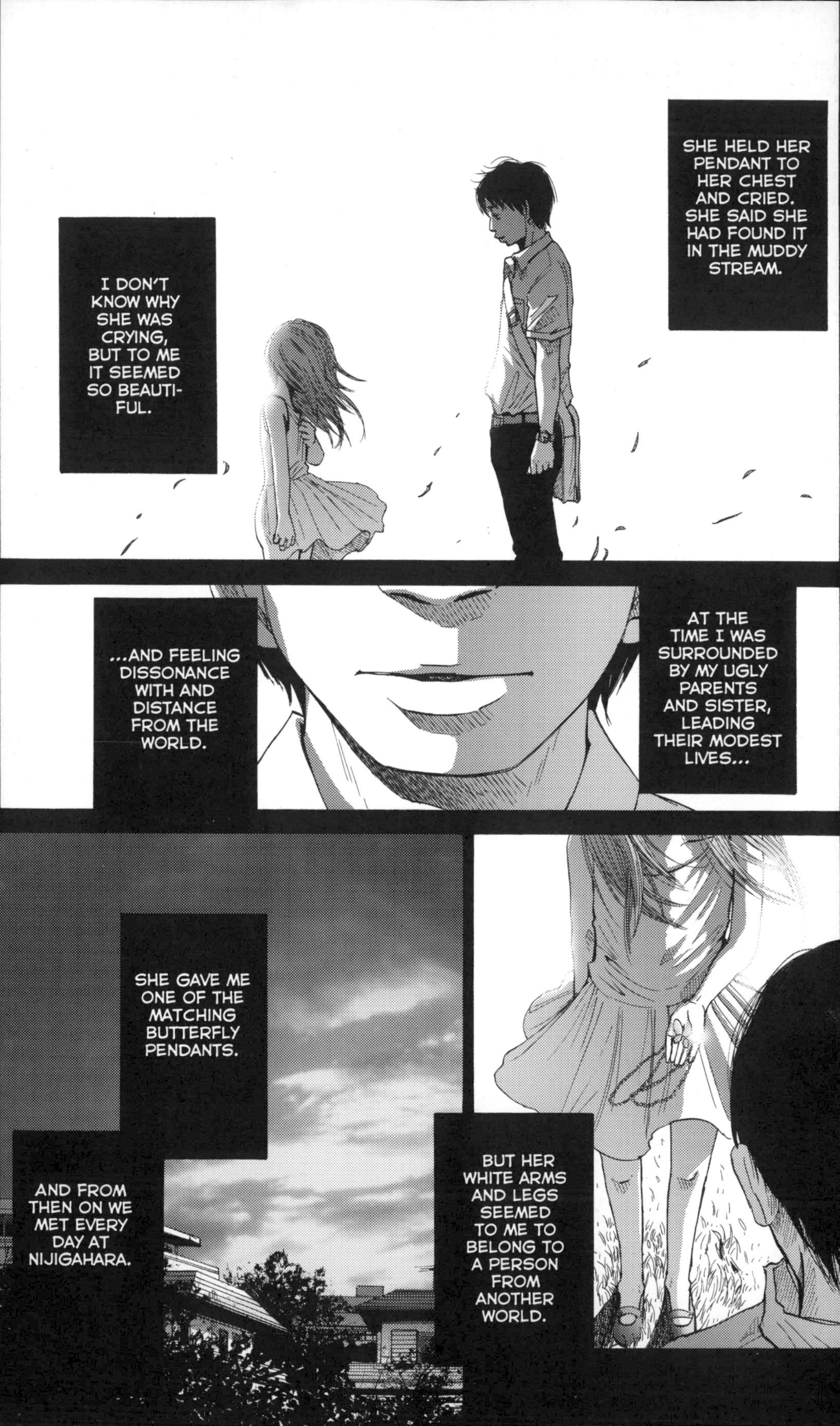
SHE HELD HER PENDANT TO HER CHEST AND CRIED. SHE SAID SHE HAD FOUND IT IN THE MUDDY STREAM.
I DON'T KNOW WHY SHE WAS CRYING, BUT TO ME IT SEEMED SO BEAUTI-FUL.
AT THE TIME I WAS SURROUNDED BY MY UGLY PARENTS AND SISTER, LEADING THEIR MODEST LIVES...
...AND FEELING DISSONANCE WITH AND DISTANCE FROM THE WORLD.
BUT HER WHITE ARMS AND LEGS SEEMED TO ME TO BELONG TO A PERSON FROM ANOTHER WORLD.
SHE GAVE ME ONE OF THE MATCHING BUTTERFLY PENDANTS.
AND FROM THEN ON WE MET EVERY DAY AT NIJIGAHARA.

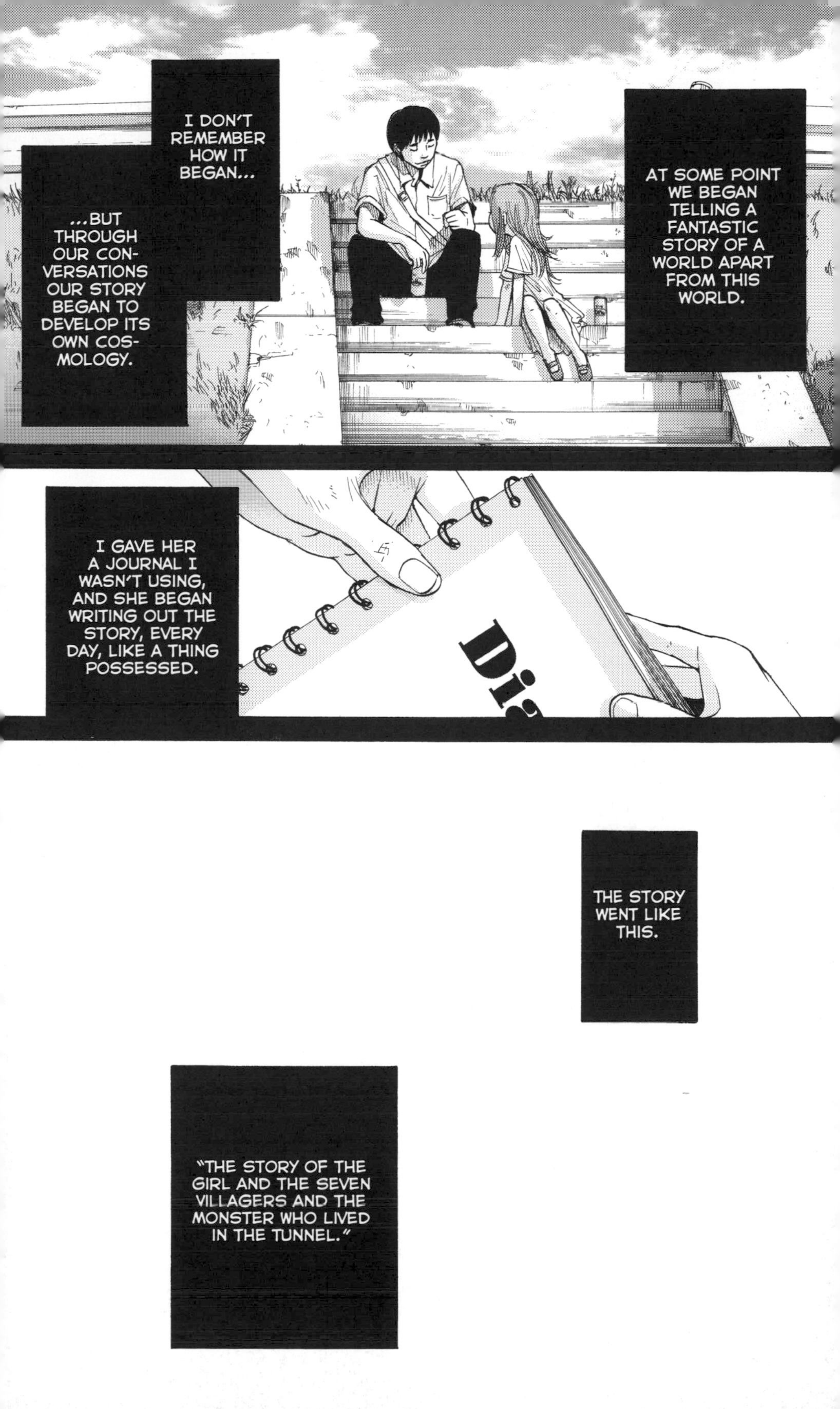
AT SOME POINT WE BEGAN TELLING A FANTASTIC STORY OF A WORLD APART FROM THIS WORLD.
I DON'T REMEMBER HOW IT BEGAN...
...BUT THROUGH OUR CONVERSATIONS OUR STORY BEGAN TO DEVELOP ITS OWN COSMOLOGY.
I GAVE HER A JOURNAL I WASN'T USING, AND SHE BEGAN WRITING OUT THE STORY, EVERY DAY, LIKE A THING POSSESSED.
THE STORY WENT LIKE THIS.
"THE STORY OF THE GIRL AND THE SEVEN VILLAGERS AND THE MONSTER WHO LIVED IN THE TUNNEL."

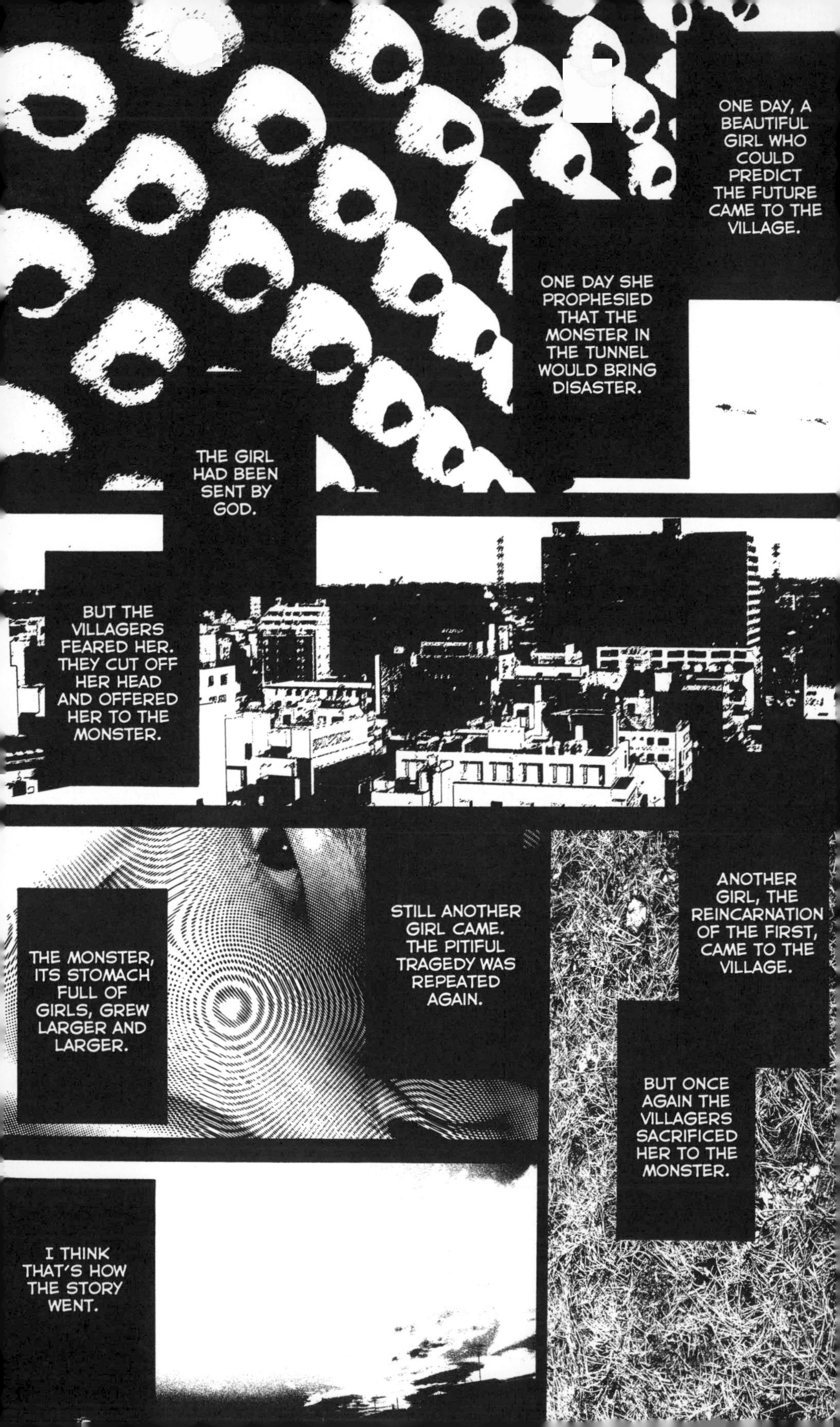
ONE DAY, A BEAUTIFUL GIRL WHO COULD PREDICT THE FUTURE CAME TO THE VILLAGE.
ONE DAY SHE PROPHESIED THAT THE MONSTER IN THE TUNNEL WOULD BRING DISASTER.
THE GIRL HAD BEEN SENT BY GOD.
BUT THE VILLAGERS FEARED HER. THEY CUT OFF HER HEAD AND OFFERED HER TO THE MONSTER.
ANOTHER GIRL, THE REINCARNATION OF THE FIRST, CAME TO THE VILLAGE.
BUT ONCE AGAIN THE VILLAGERS SACRIFICED HER TO THE MONSTER.
STILL ANOTHER GIRL CAME. THE PITIFUL TRAGEDY WAS REPEATED AGAIN.
THE MONSTER, ITS STOMACH FULL OF GIRLS, GREW LARGER AND LARGER.
I THINK THAT'S HOW THE STORY WENT.

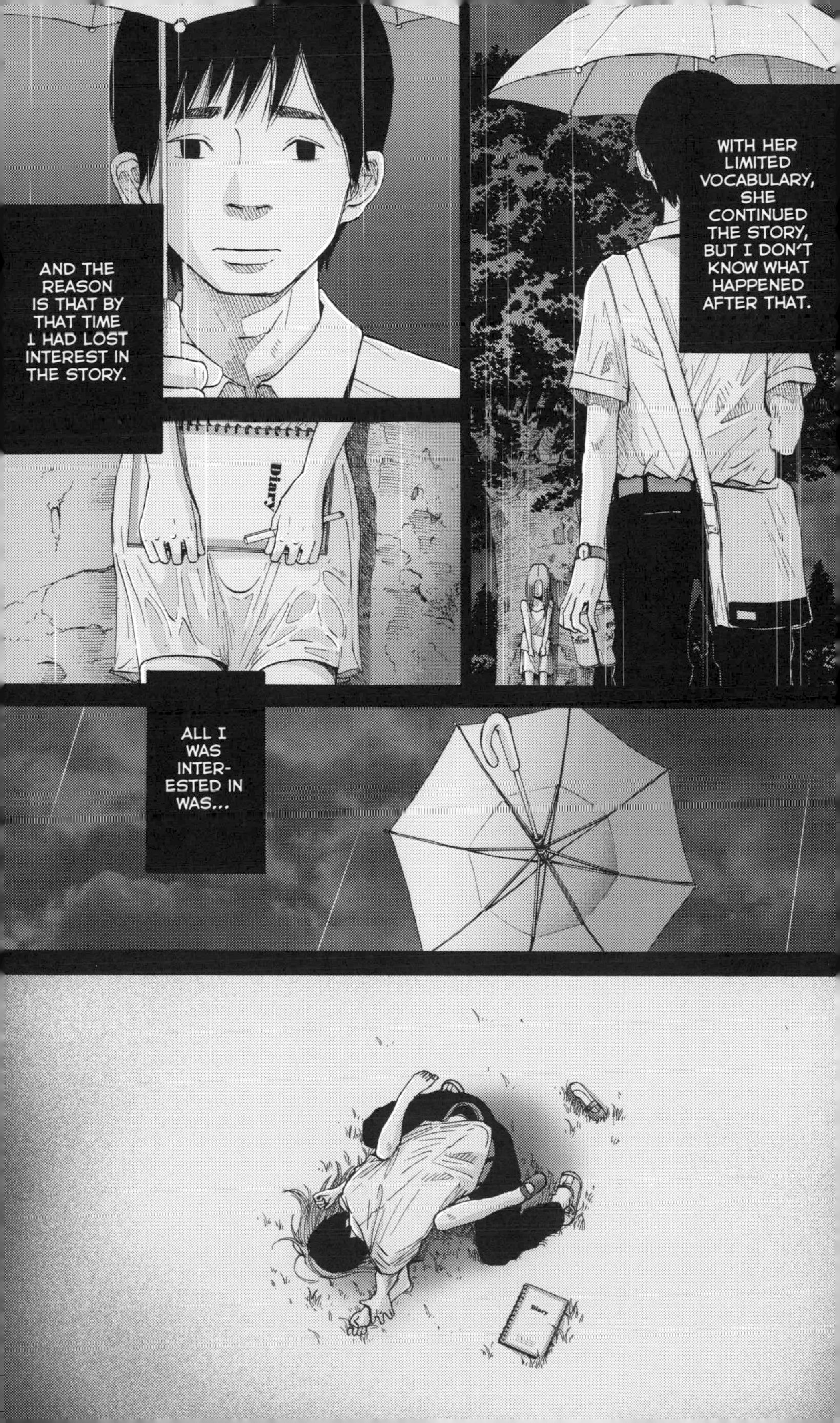

WITH HER LIMITED VOCABULARY, SHE CONTINUED THE STORY, BUT I DON'T KNOW WHAT HAPPENED AFTER THAT.
AND THE REASON IS THAT BY THAT TIME I HAD LOST INTEREST IN THE STORY.
Diary
ALL I WAS INTER- ESTED IN WAS...

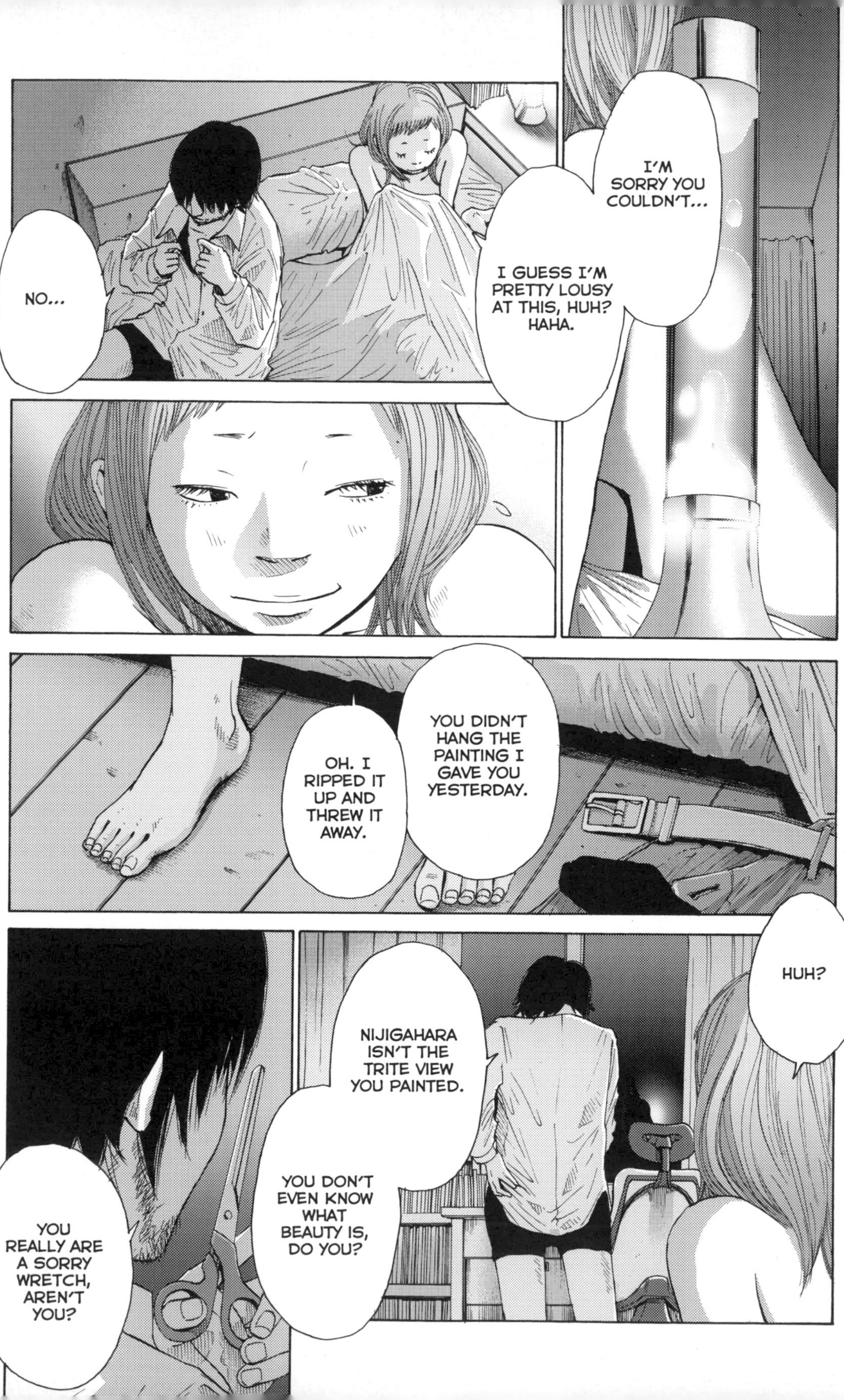
I'M SORRY YOU COULDN'T...
I GUESS I'M PRETTY LOUSY AT THIS, HUH? HAHA.
NO...
YOU DIDN'T HANG THE PAINTING I GAVE YOU YESTERDAY.
OH. I RIPPED IT UP AND THREW IT AWAY.
HUH?
NIJIGAHARA ISN'T THE TRITE VIEW YOU PAINTED.
YOU DON'T EVEN KNOW WHAT BEAUTY IS, DO YOU?
YOU REALLY ARE A SORRY WRETCH, AREN'T YOU?

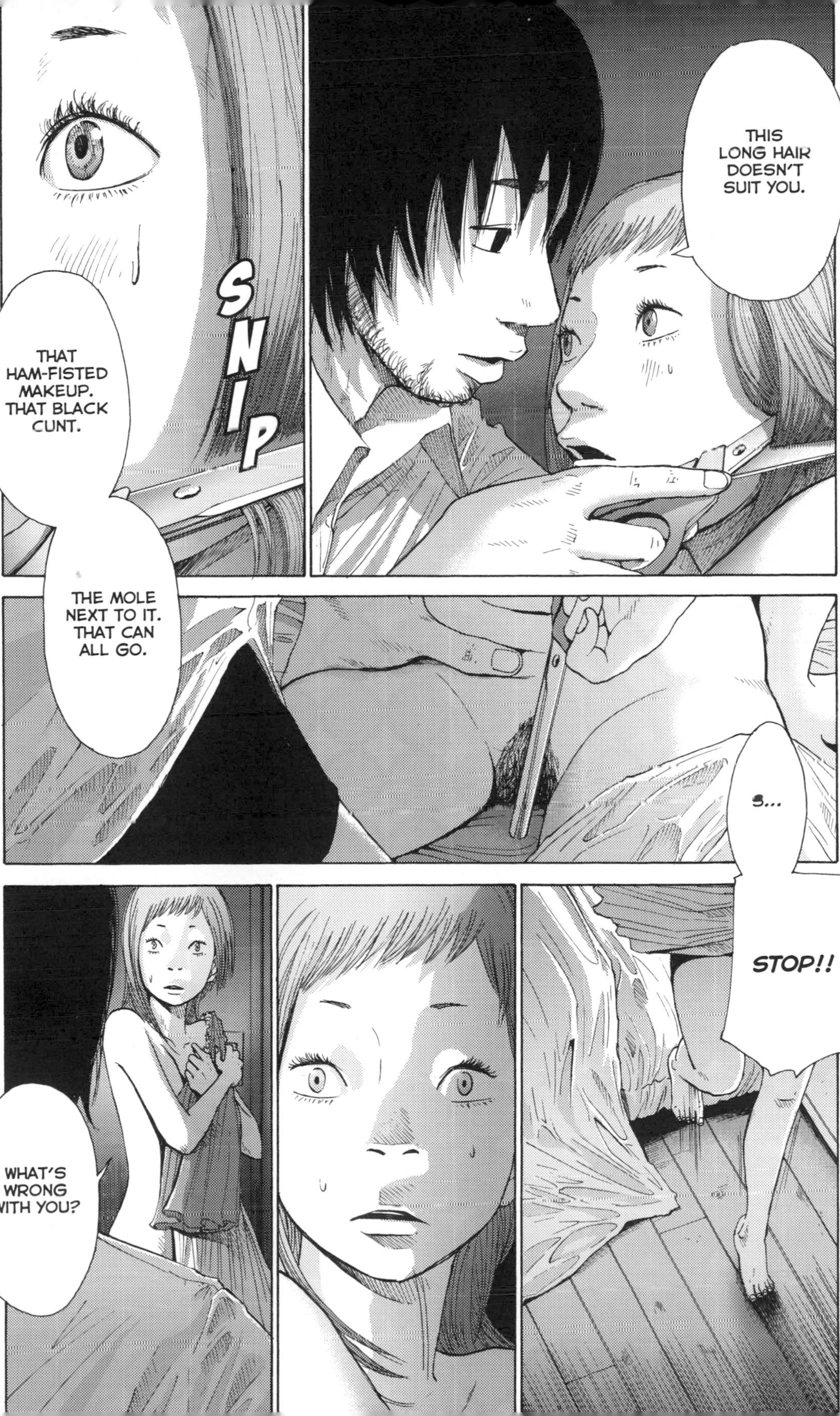
THIS LONG HAIR DOESN'T SUIT YOU.
SNIP
THAT HAM-FISTED MAKEUP. THAT BLACK CUNT.
THE MOLE NEXT TO IT. THAT CAN ALL GO.
S...
STOP!!
WHAT'S WRONG WITH YOU?

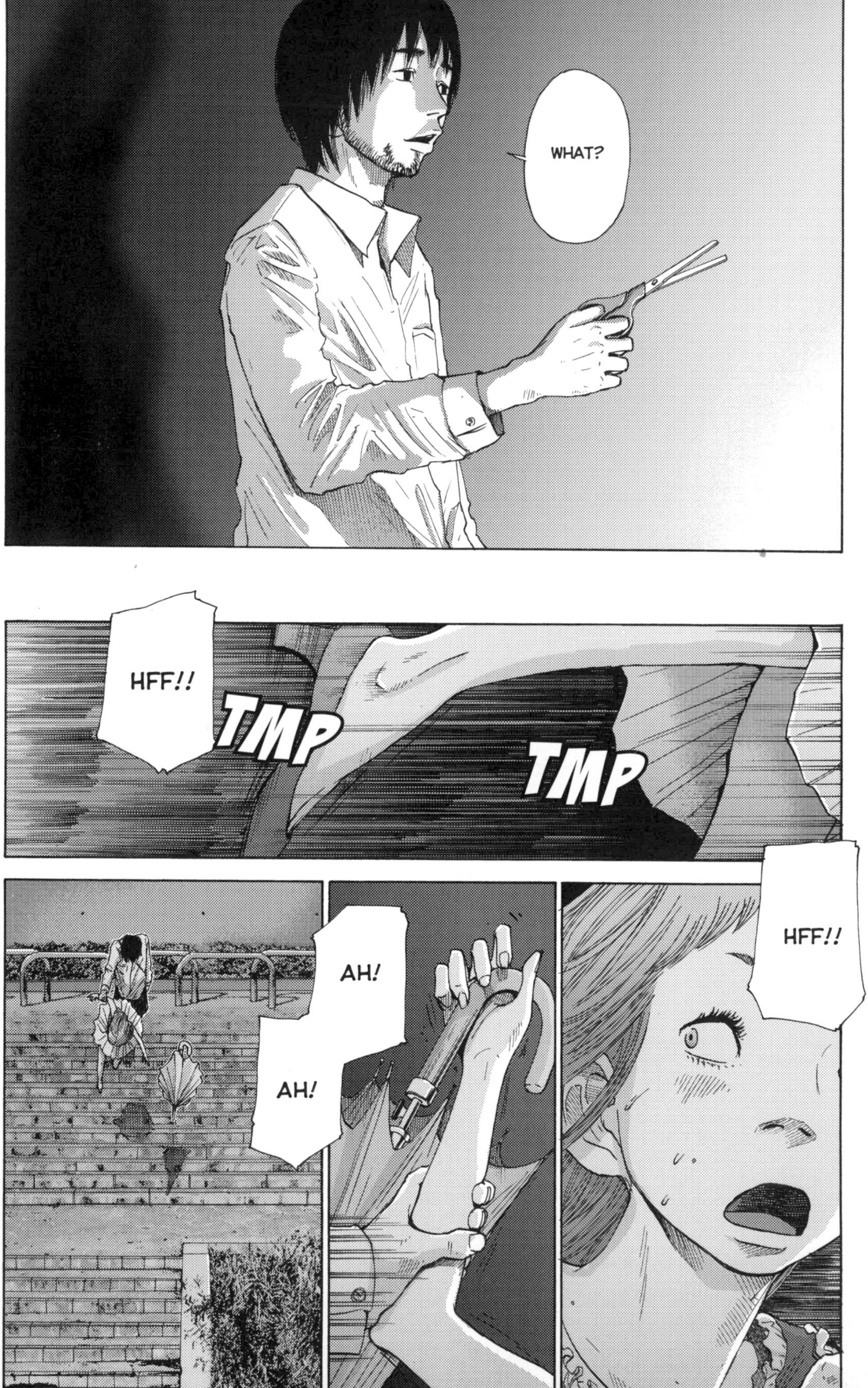
WHAT?
HFF!!
TMP
TMP
HFF!!
AH!
AH!

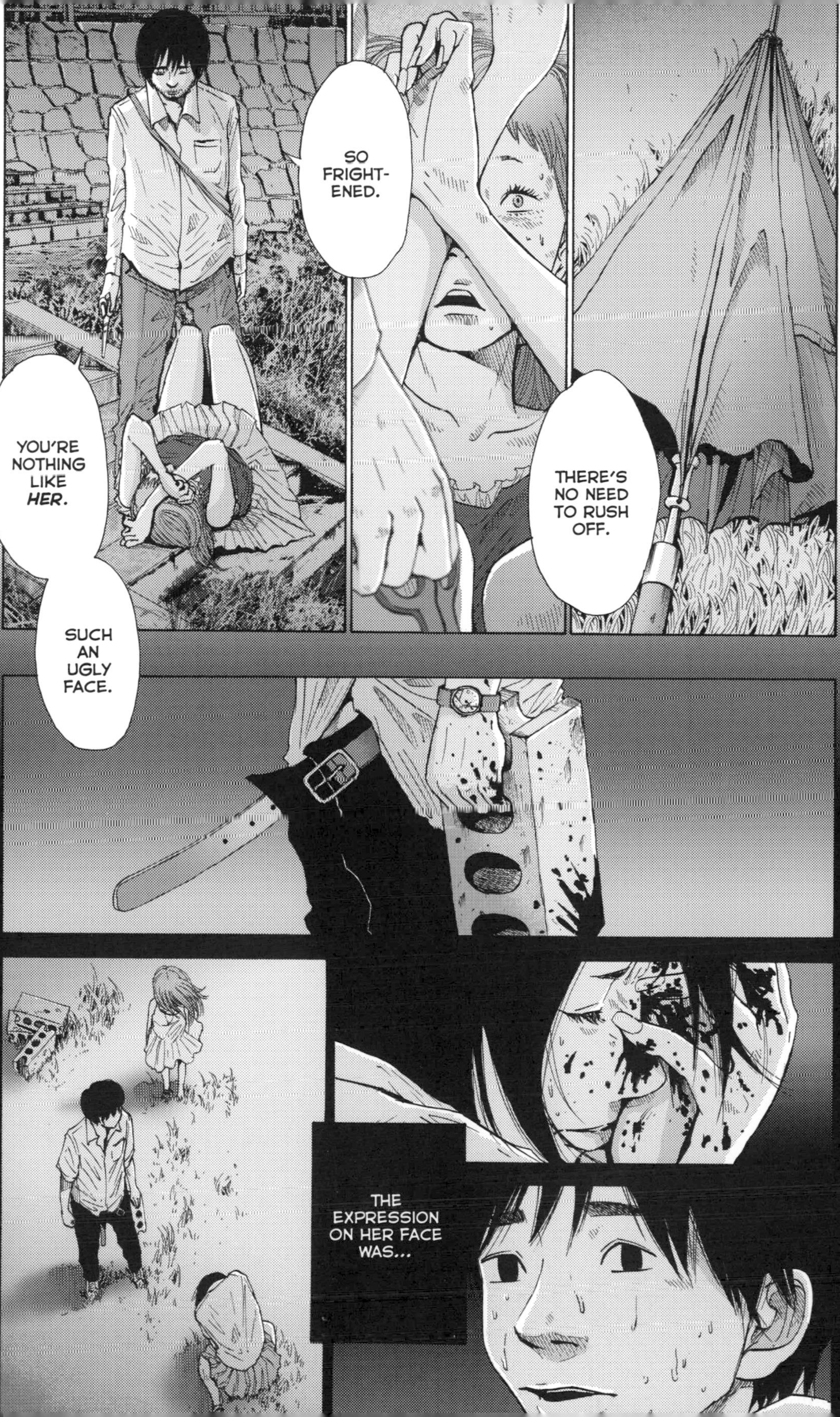
THERE'S NO NEED TO RUSH OFF.
SO FRIGHT-ENED.
YOU'RE NOTHING LIKE *HER*.
SUCH AN UGLY FACE.
THE EXPRESSION ON HER FACE WAS...

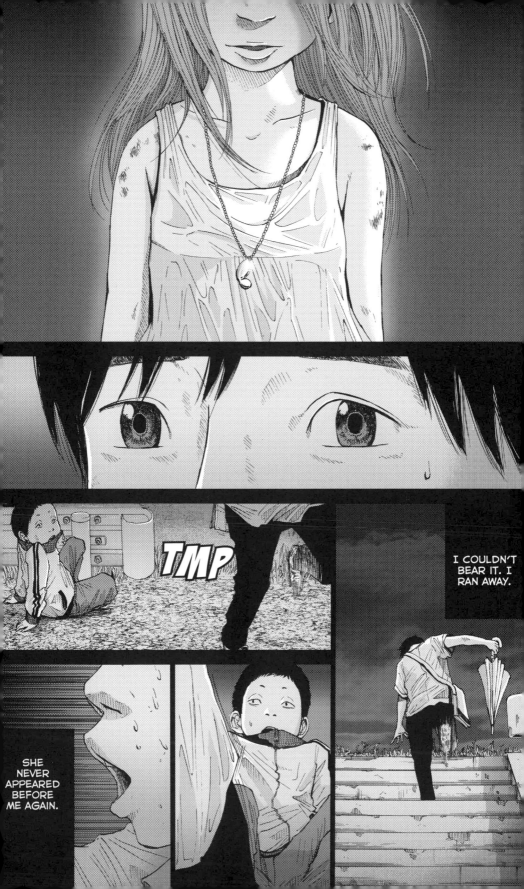

TMP

I COULDN'T BEAR IT. I RAN AWAY.

SHE NEVER APPEARED BEFORE ME AGAIN.

I'M SO FULL OF REGRET.

LATER, I HAPPENED TO LEARN THAT THE STORY IN THAT BOOK HAD SPREAD AMONG THE LOCAL CHILDREN.

TO THINK THAT NO MATTER HOW I SEARCHED FOR HER I COULD NOT FIND HER, AND YET THE STORY SHE MADE CONTINUED TO LIVE ON...

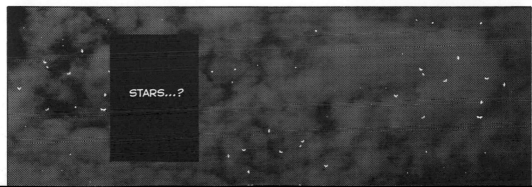

STARS...?

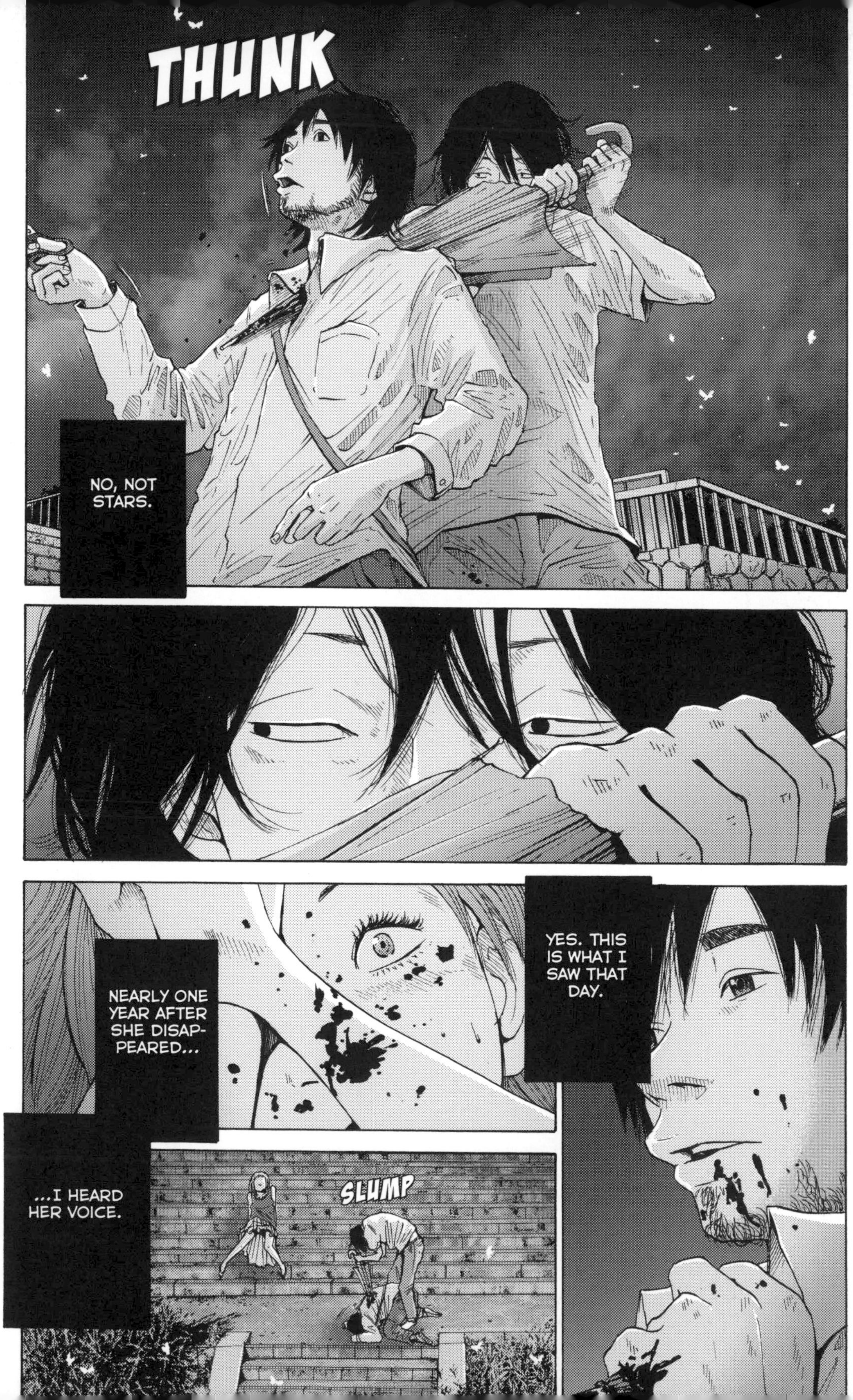
THUNK
NO, NOT STARS.
YES. THIS IS WHAT I SAW THAT DAY.
NEARLY ONE YEAR AFTER SHE DISAPPEARED...
SLUMP
...I HEARD HER VOICE.

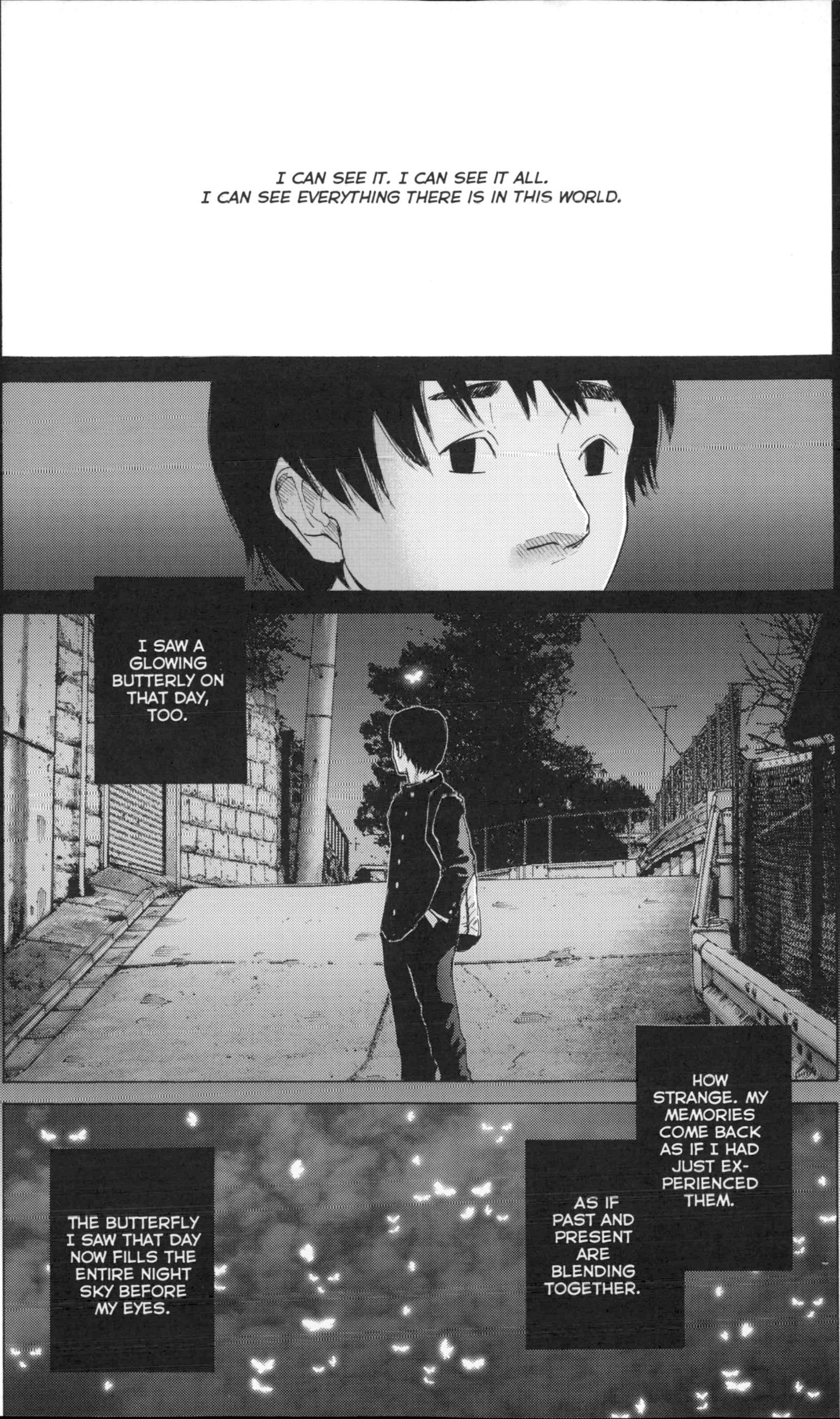
I CAN SEE IT. I CAN SEE IT ALL.
I CAN SEE EVERYTHING THERE IS IN THIS WORLD.
I SAW A GLOWING BUTTERLY ON THAT DAY, TOO.
HOW STRANGE. MY MEMORIES COME BACK AS IF I HAD JUST EXPERIENCED THEM.
AS IF PAST AND PRESENT ARE BLENDING TOGETHER.
THE BUTTERFLY I SAW THAT DAY NOW FILLS THE ENTIRE NIGHT SKY BEFORE MY EYES.

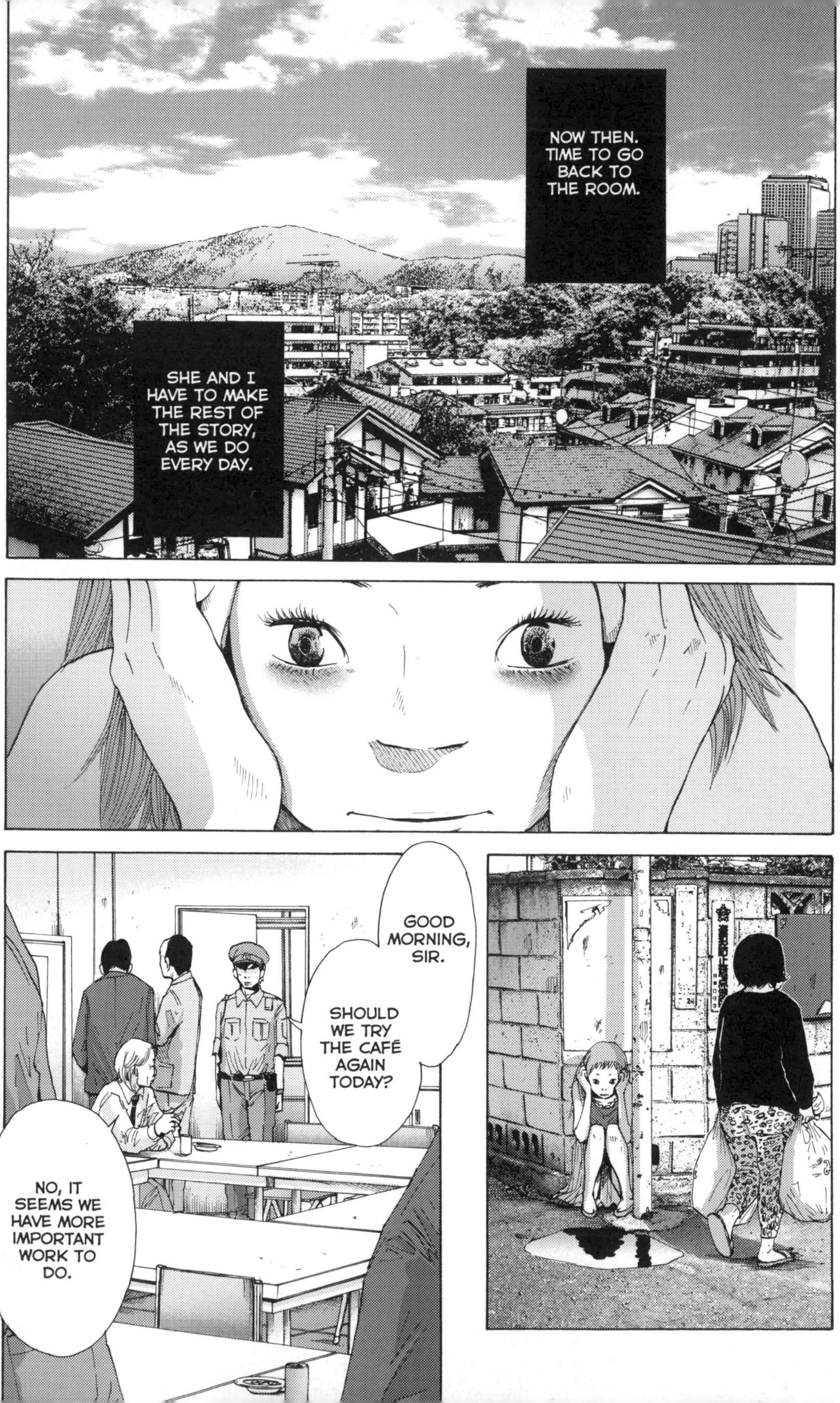
NOW THEN. TIME TO GO BACK TO THE ROOM.
SHE AND I HAVE TO MAKE THE REST OF THE STORY, AS WE DO EVERY DAY.
GOOD MORNING, SIR.
SHOULD WE TRY THE CAFÉ AGAIN TODAY?
NO, IT SEEMS WE HAVE MORE IMPORTANT WORK TO DO.

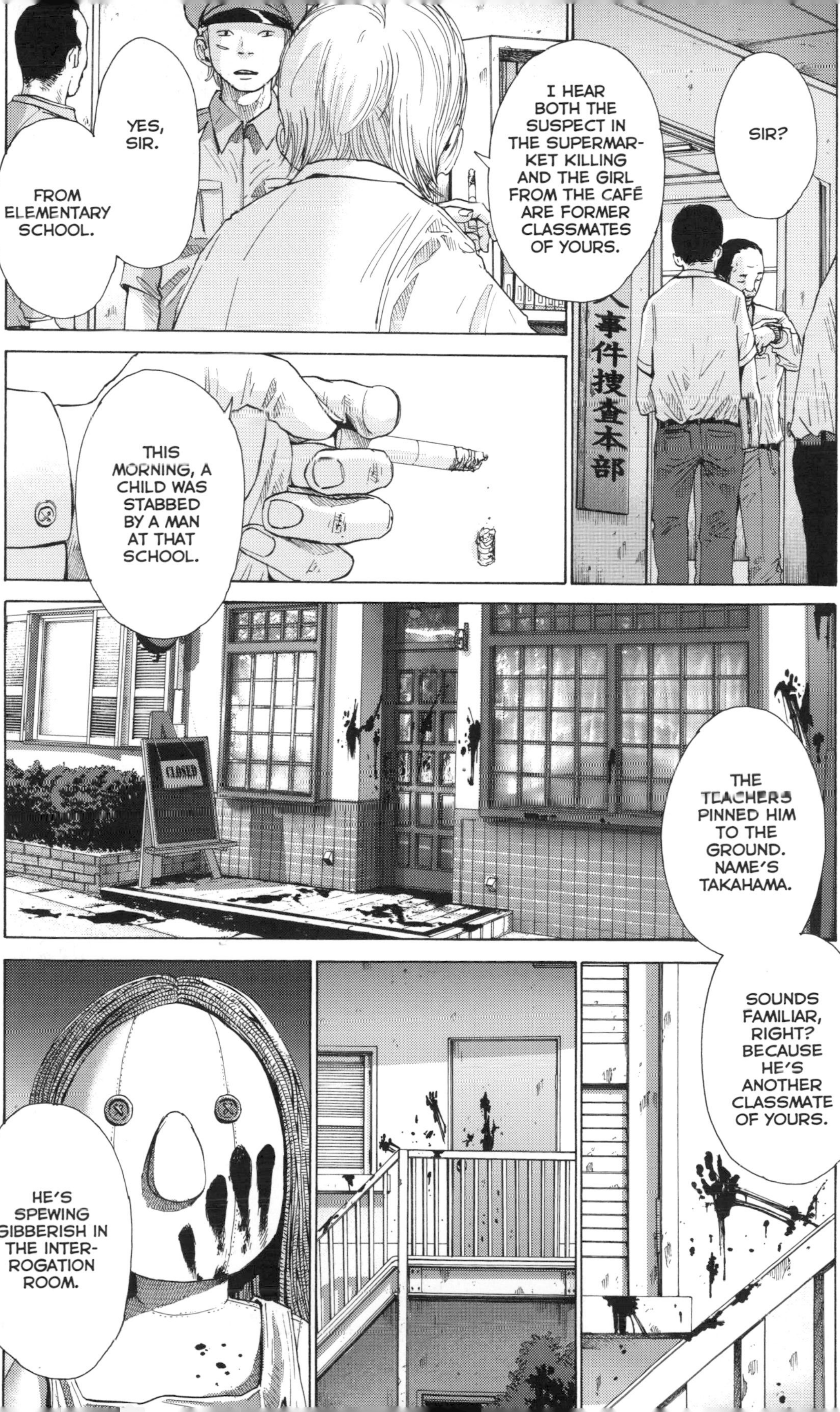
SIR?
事件捜査本部
I HEAR BOTH THE SUSPECT IN THE SUPERMAR-KET KILLING AND THE GIRL FROM THE CAFÉ ARE FORMER CLASSMATES OF YOURS.
YES, SIR.
FROM ELEMENTARY SCHOOL.
THIS MORNING, A CHILD WAS STABBED BY A MAN AT THAT SCHOOL.
THE TEACHERS PINNED HIM TO THE GROUND. NAME'S TAKAHAMA.
CLOSED
SOUNDS FAMILIAR, RIGHT? BECAUSE HE'S ANOTHER CLASSMATE OF YOURS.
HE'S SPEWING GIBBERISH IN THE INTER-ROGATION ROOM.

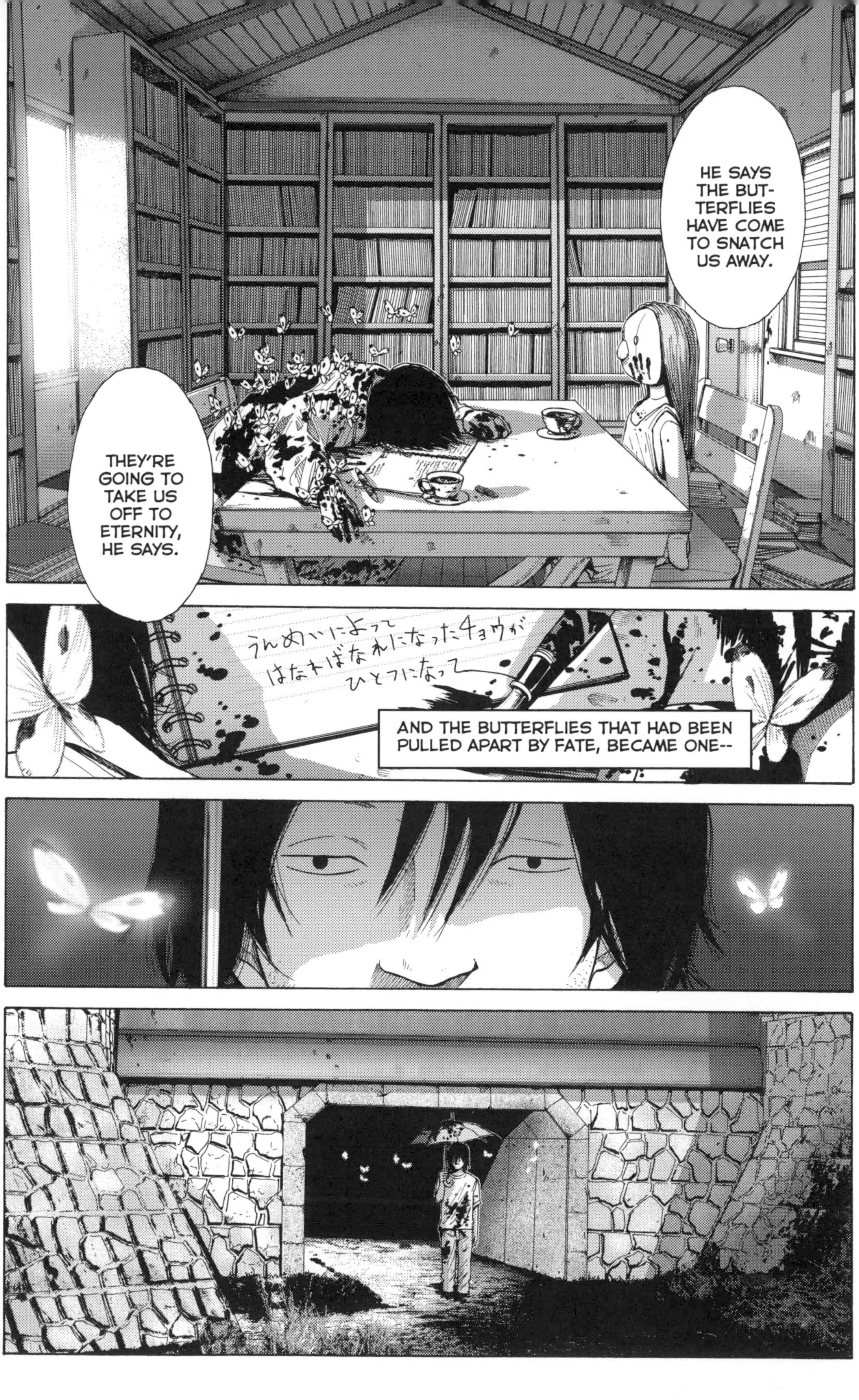
HE SAYS THE BUTTERFLIES HAVE COME TO SNATCH US AWAY.
THEY'RE GOING TO TAKE US OFF TO ETERNITY, HE SAYS.
うんめいによって
はなればなれになったチョウが
ひとつになって
AND THE BUTTERFLIES THAT HAD BEEN PULLED APART BY FATE, BECAME ONE--

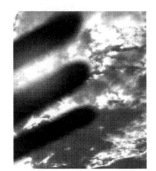

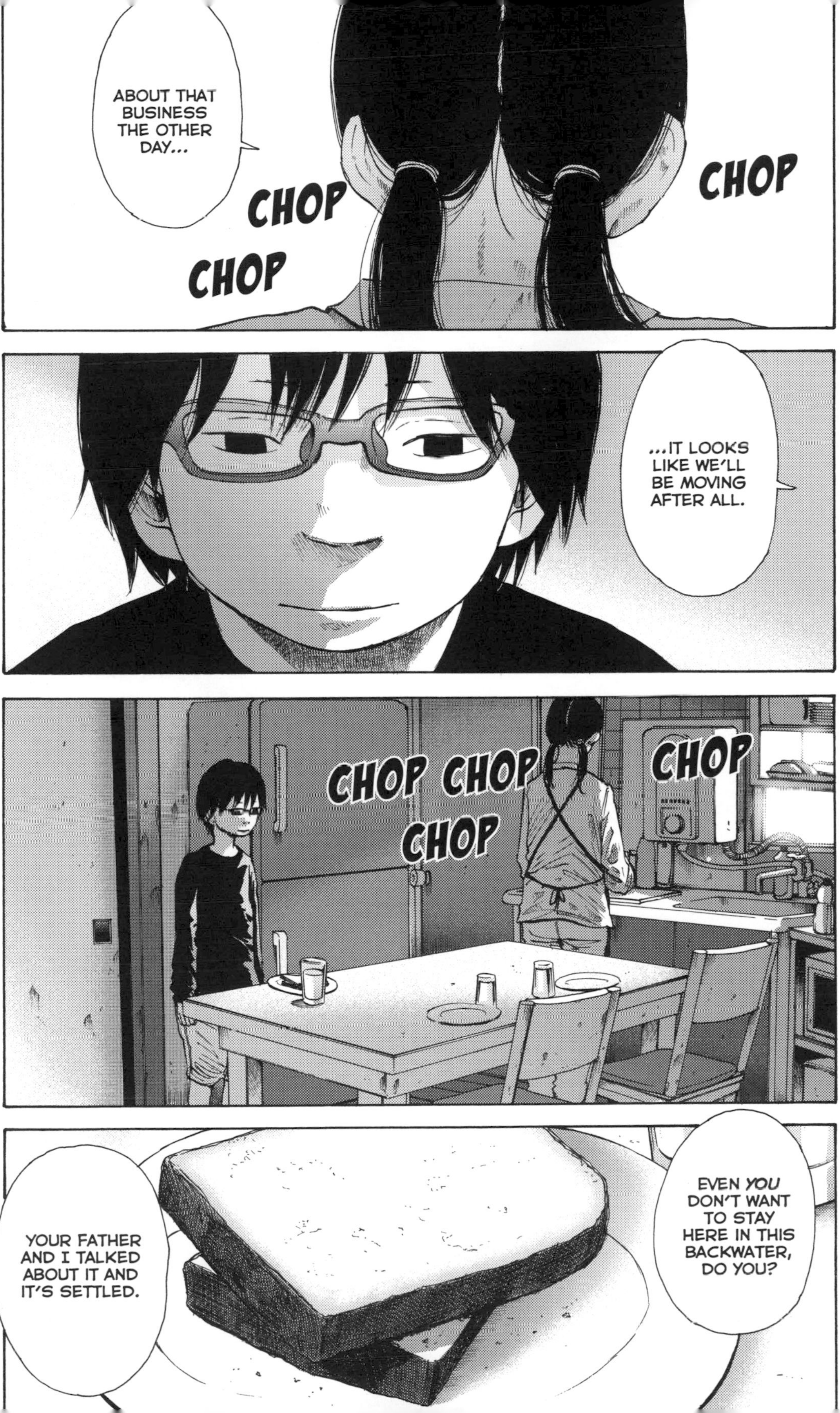
ABOUT THAT BUSINESS THE OTHER DAY...
CHOP
CHOP
CHOP
...IT LOOKS LIKE WE'LL BE MOVING AFTER ALL.
CHOP
CHOP CHOP
CHOP
EVEN *YOU* DON'T WANT TO STAY HERE IN THIS BACKWATER, DO YOU?
YOUR FATHER AND I TALKED ABOUT IT AND IT'S SETTLED.

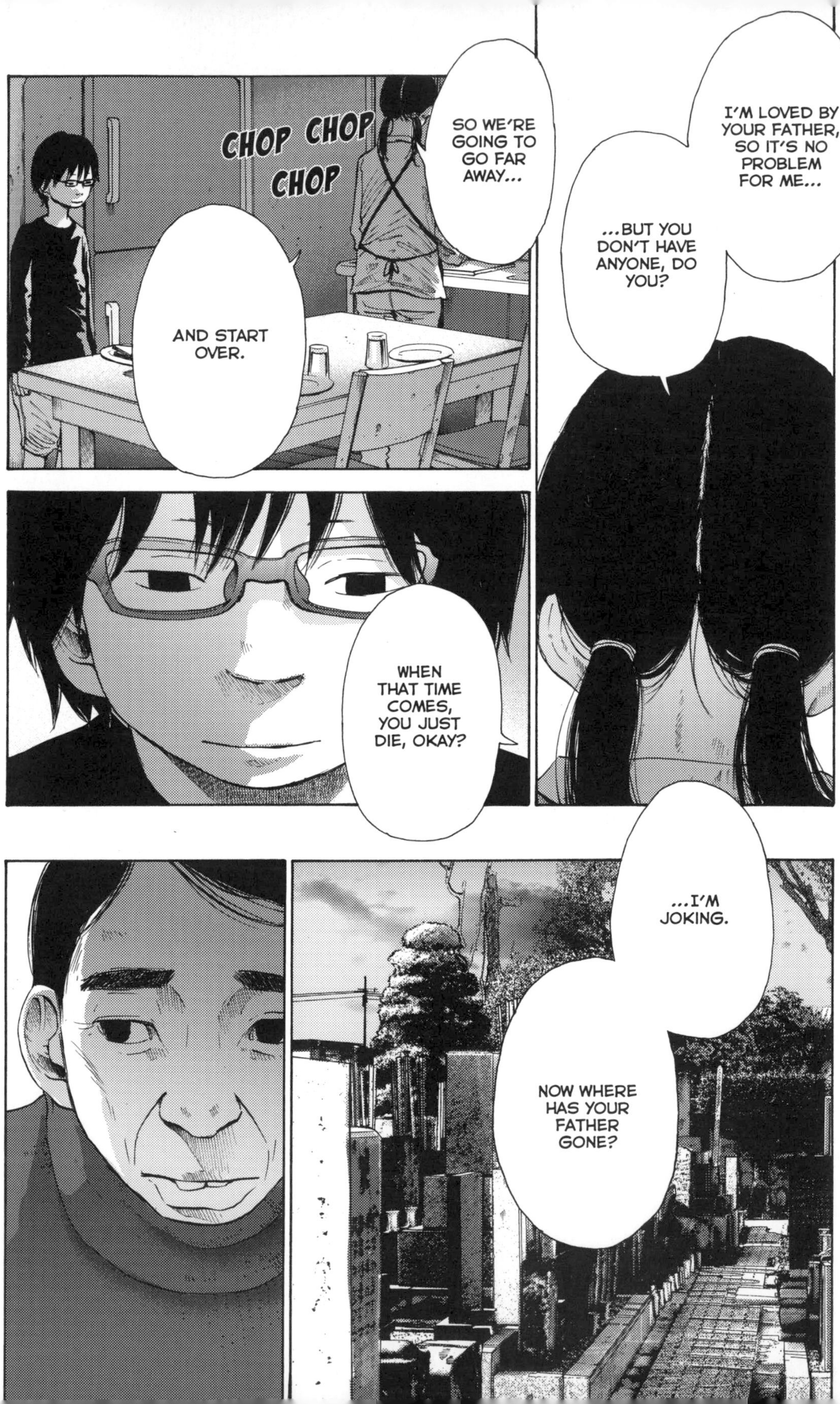
I'M LOVED BY YOUR FATHER, SO IT'S NO PROBLEM FOR ME...
...BUT YOU DON'T HAVE ANYONE, DO YOU?
CHOP CHOP CHOP
SO WE'RE GOING TO GO FAR AWAY...
AND START OVER.
WHEN THAT TIME COMES, YOU JUST DIE, OKAY?
...I'M JOKING.
NOW WHERE HAS YOUR FATHER GONE?

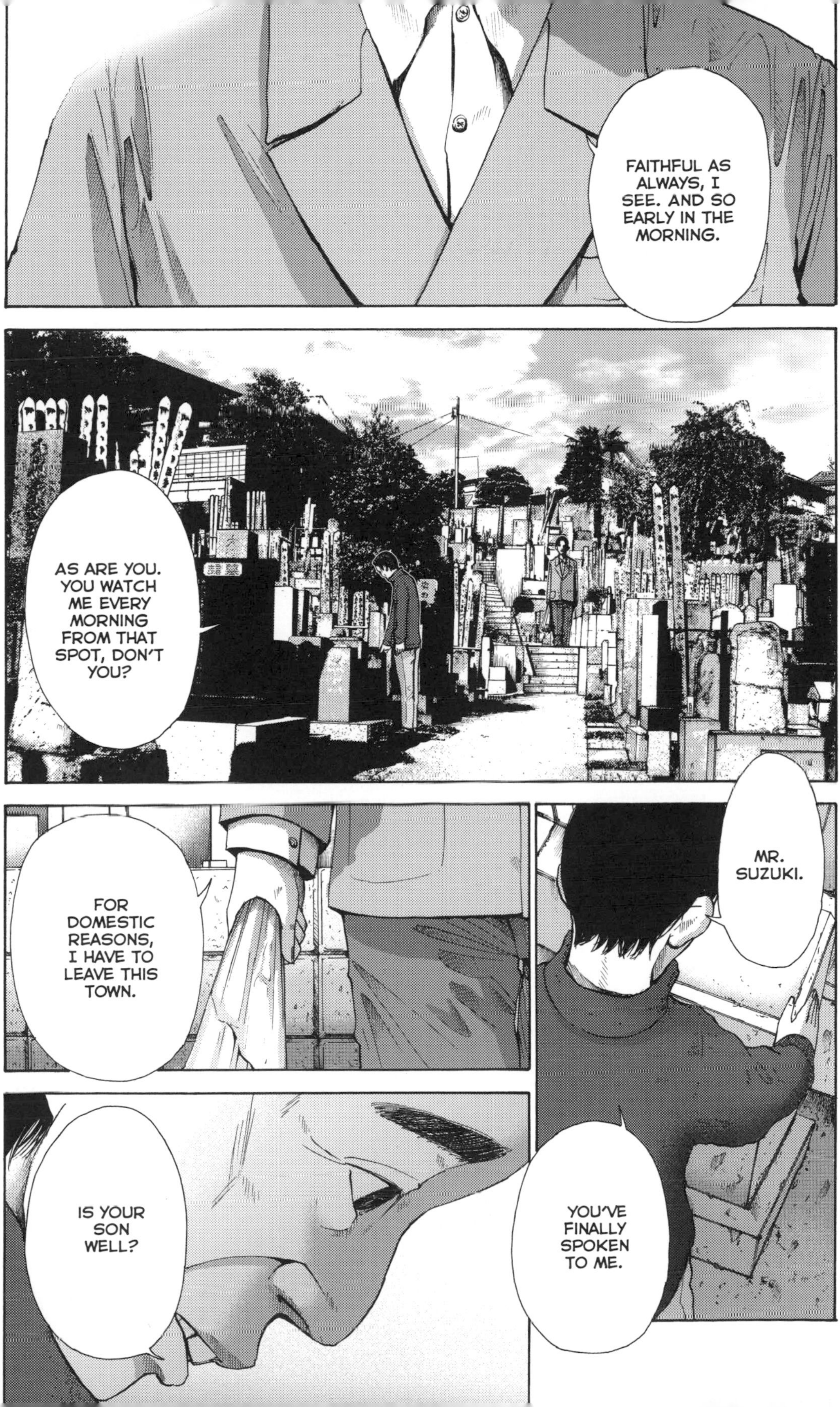
FAITHFUL AS ALWAYS, I SEE. AND SO EARLY IN THE MORNING.
AS ARE YOU. YOU WATCH ME EVERY MORNING FROM THAT SPOT, DON'T YOU?
MR. SUZUKI.
YOU'VE FINALLY SPOKEN TO ME.
FOR DOMESTIC REASONS, I HAVE TO LEAVE THIS TOWN.
IS YOUR SON WELL?

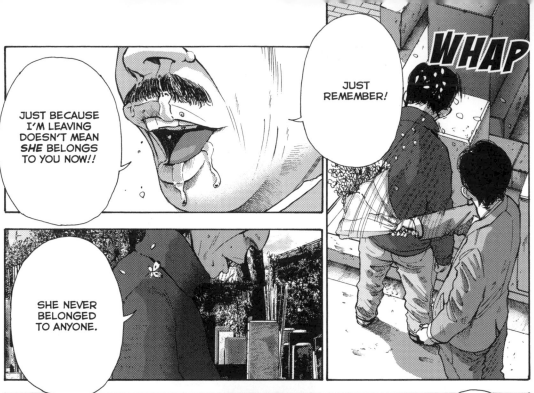

WHAP

JUST REMEMBER!

JUST BECAUSE I'M LEAVING DOESN'T MEAN *SHE* BELONGS TO YOU NOW!!

SHE NEVER BELONGED TO ANYONE.

SHE ALWAYS HAD HER EYES ON SOMETHING MUCH FARTHER AWAY.

YOU CAN'T IMAGINE MY LONELINESS.

I'M JUST WAITING FOR MY DAY OF JUDGMENT.

SEE?

I'M SURE SHE'S SOMEWHERE WATCHING ME THIS VERY MOMENT.

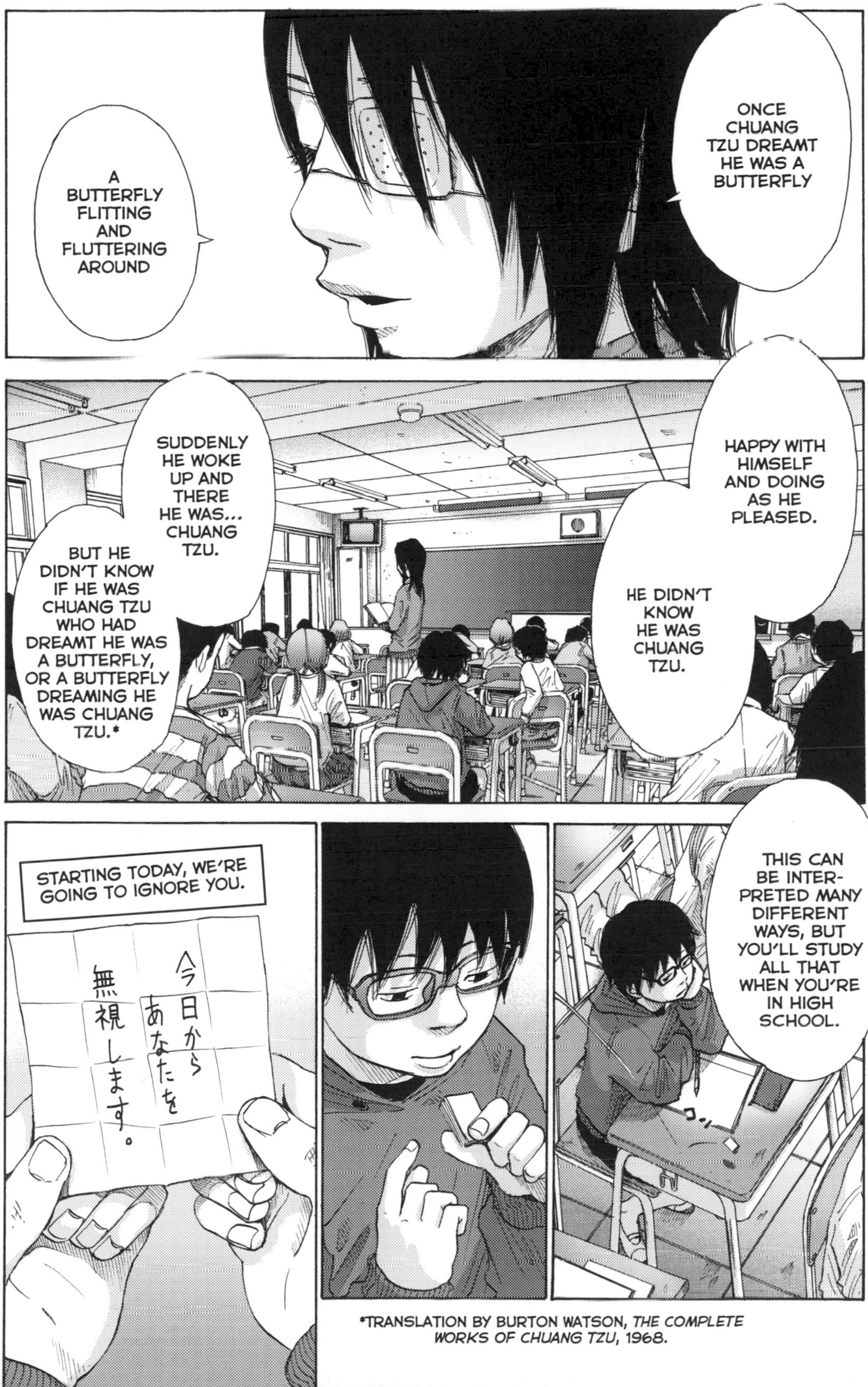
ONCE CHUANG TZU DREAMT HE WAS A BUTTERFLY
A BUTTERFLY FLITTING AND FLUTTERING AROUND
HAPPY WITH HIMSELF AND DOING AS HE PLEASED.
HE DIDN'T KNOW HE WAS CHUANG TZU.
SUDDENLY HE WOKE UP AND THERE HE WAS... CHUANG TZU.
BUT HE DIDN'T KNOW IF HE WAS CHUANG TZU WHO HAD DREAMT HE WAS A BUTTERFLY, OR A BUTTERFLY DREAMING HE WAS CHUANG TZU.*
THIS CAN BE INTER-PRETED MANY DIFFERENT WAYS, BUT YOU'LL STUDY ALL THAT WHEN YOU'RE IN HIGH SCHOOL.
STARTING TODAY, WE'RE GOING TO IGNORE YOU.
今日からあなたを無視します。

*TRANSLATION BY BURTON WATSON, *THE COMPLETE WORKS OF CHUANG TZU*, 1968.

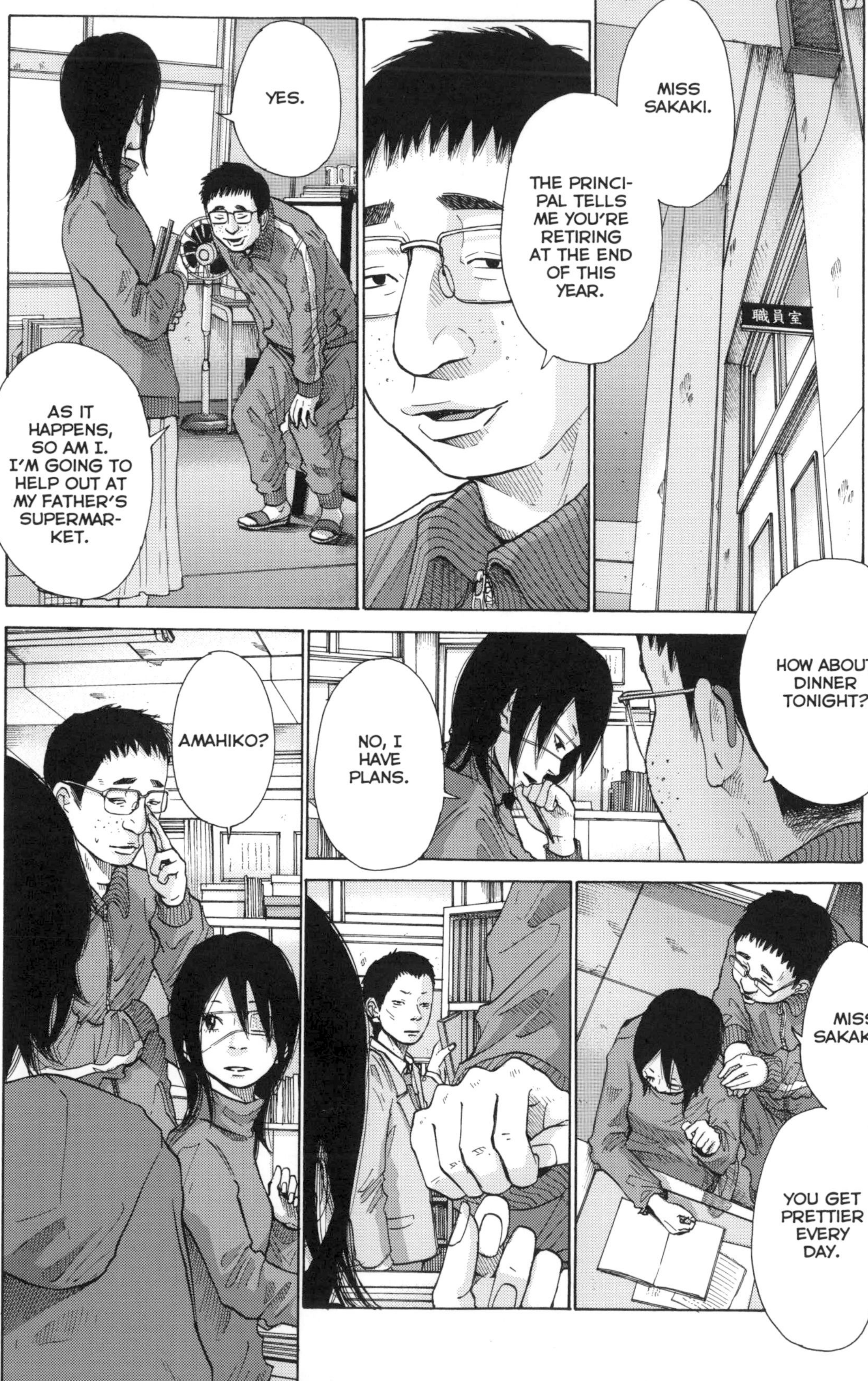
MISS SAKAKI.
THE PRINCIPAL TELLS ME YOU'RE RETIRING AT THE END OF THIS YEAR.
職員室
YES.
AS IT HAPPENS, SO AM I. I'M GOING TO HELP OUT AT MY FATHER'S SUPERMARKET.
HOW ABOUT DINNER TONIGHT?
NO, I HAVE PLANS.
MISS SAKAKI...
YOU GET PRETTIER EVERY DAY.
AMAHIKO?

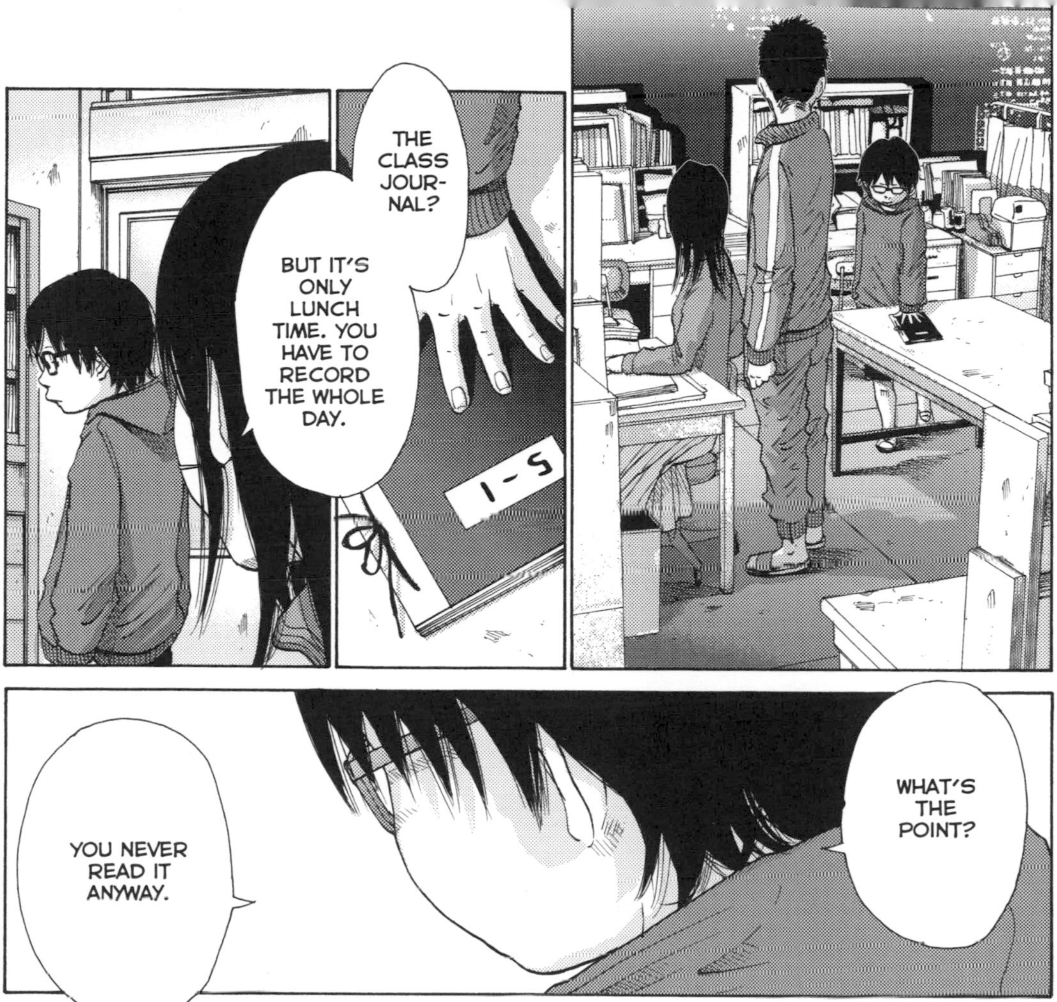
THE CLASS JOURNAL?
BUT IT'S ONLY LUNCH TIME. YOU HAVE TO RECORD THE WHOLE DAY.
WHAT'S THE POINT?
YOU NEVER READ IT ANYWAY.

CHAPTER 9

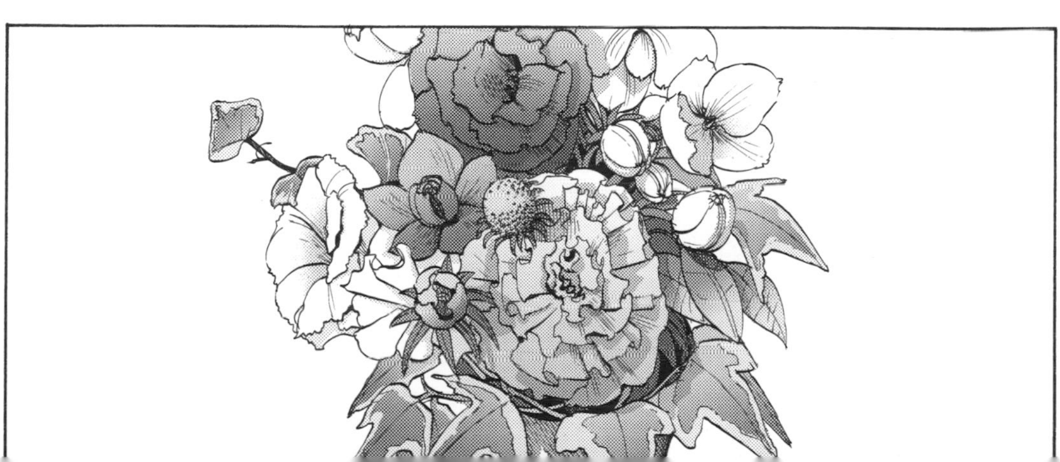

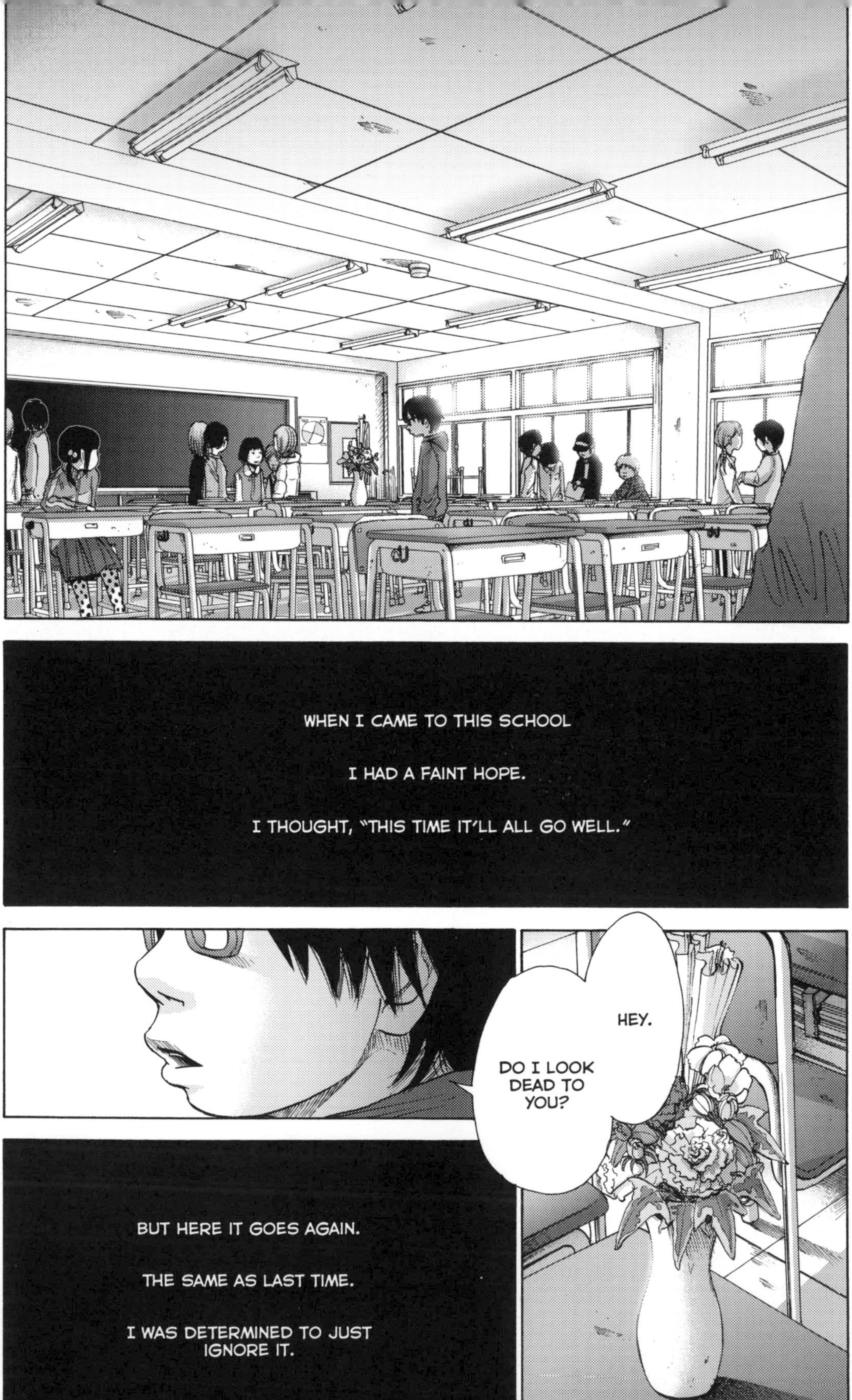
WHEN I CAME TO THIS SCHOOL
I HAD A FAINT HOPE.
I THOUGHT, "THIS TIME IT'LL ALL GO WELL."
HEY.
DO I LOOK DEAD TO YOU?
BUT HERE IT GOES AGAIN.
THE SAME AS LAST TIME.
I WAS DETERMINED TO JUST IGNORE IT.

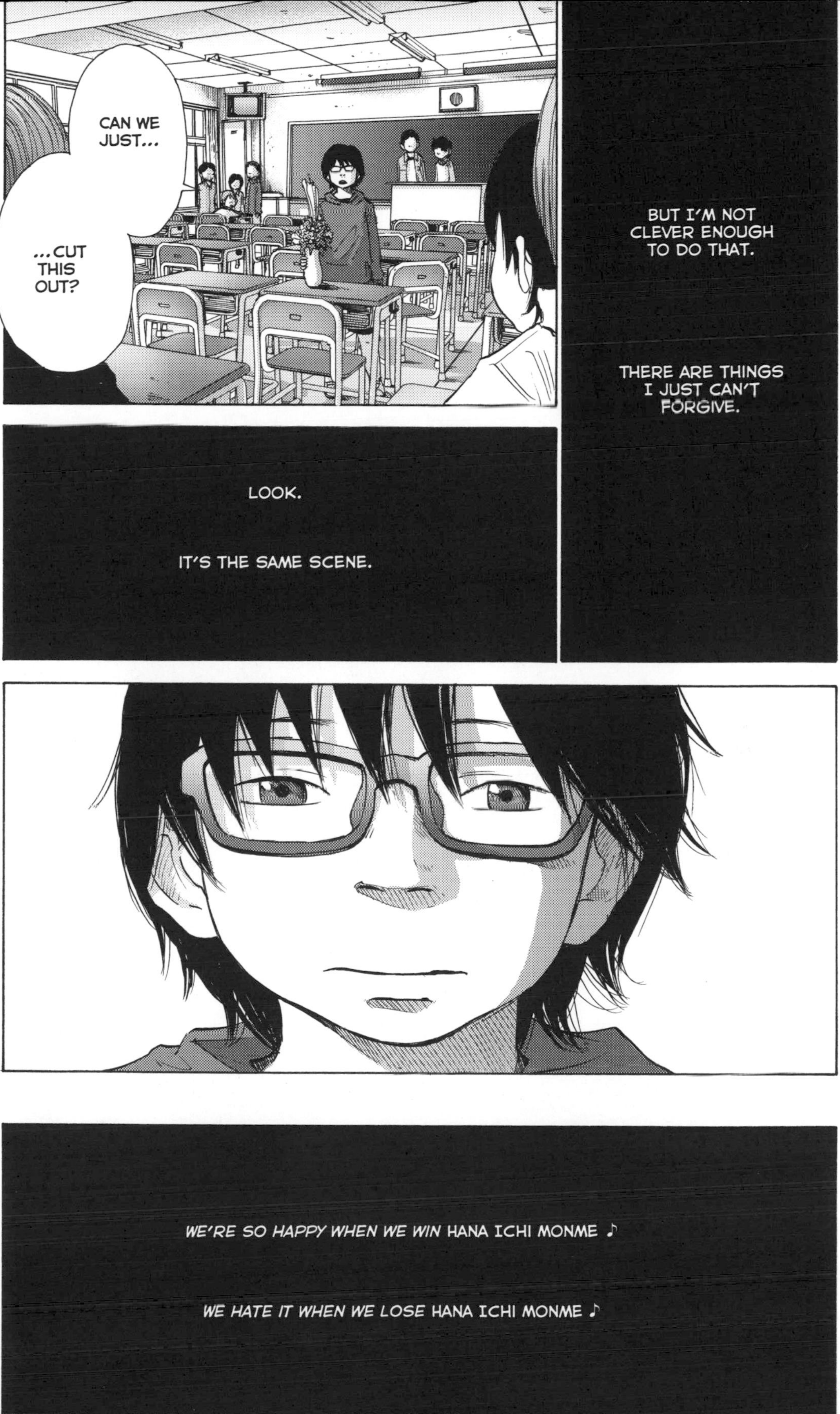

BUT I'M NOT CLEVER ENOUGH TO DO THAT.
THERE ARE THINGS I JUST CAN'T FORGIVE.
CAN WE JUST...
...CUT THIS OUT?
LOOK.
IT'S THE SAME SCENE.
WE'RE SO HAPPY WHEN WE WIN HANA ICHI MONME ♪
WE HATE IT WHEN WE LOSE HANA ICHI MONME ♪

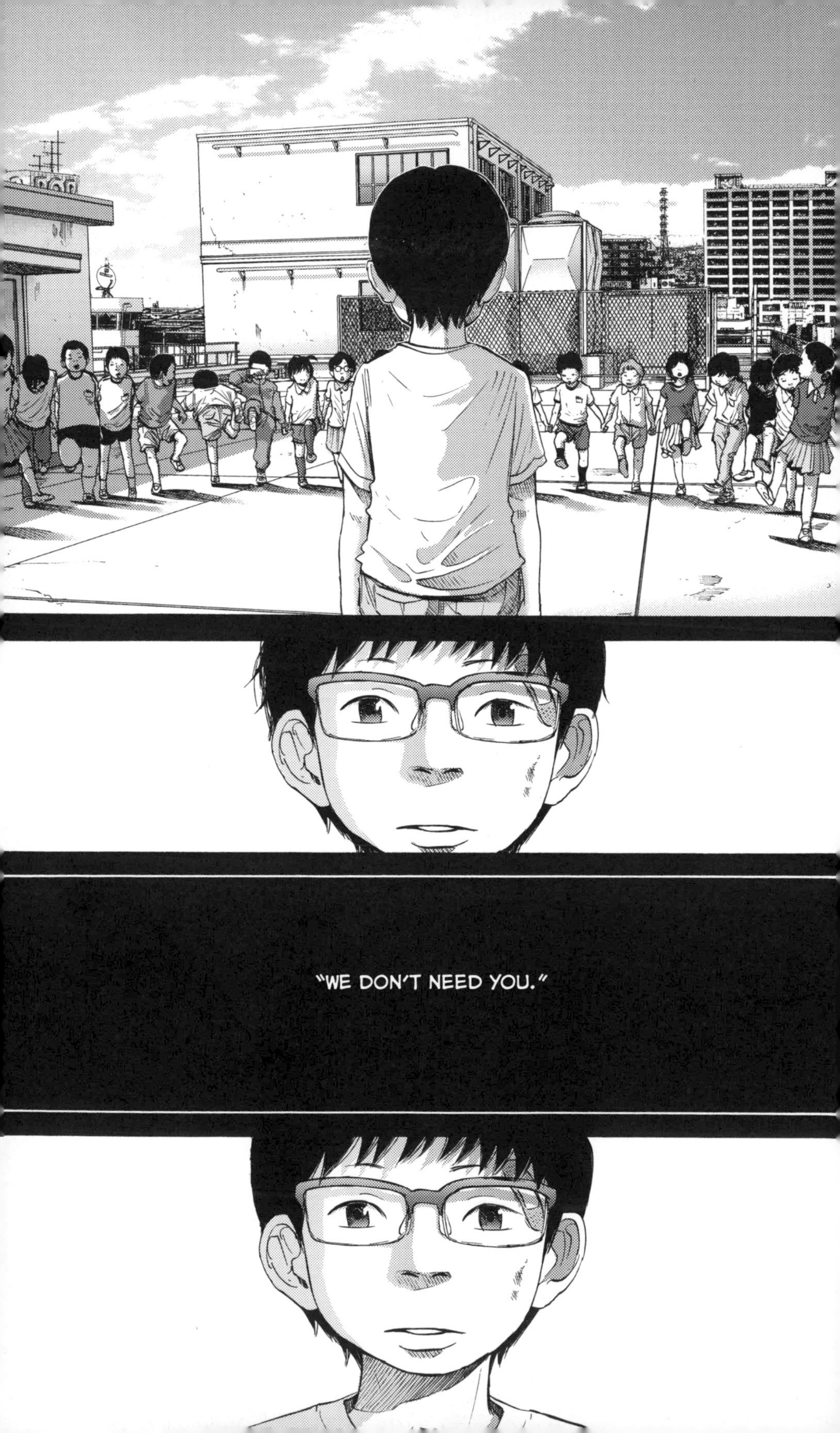
"WE DON'T NEED YOU."

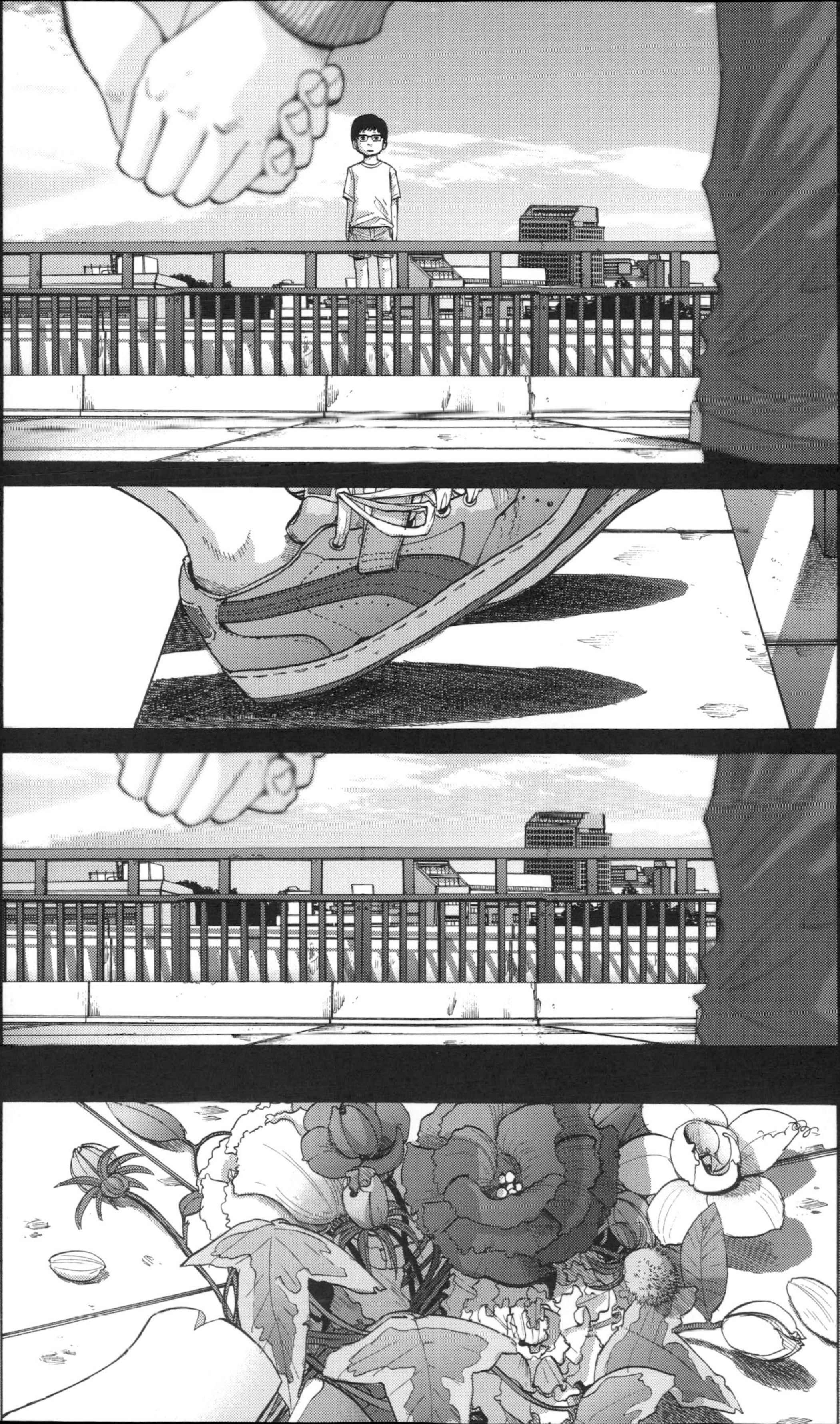

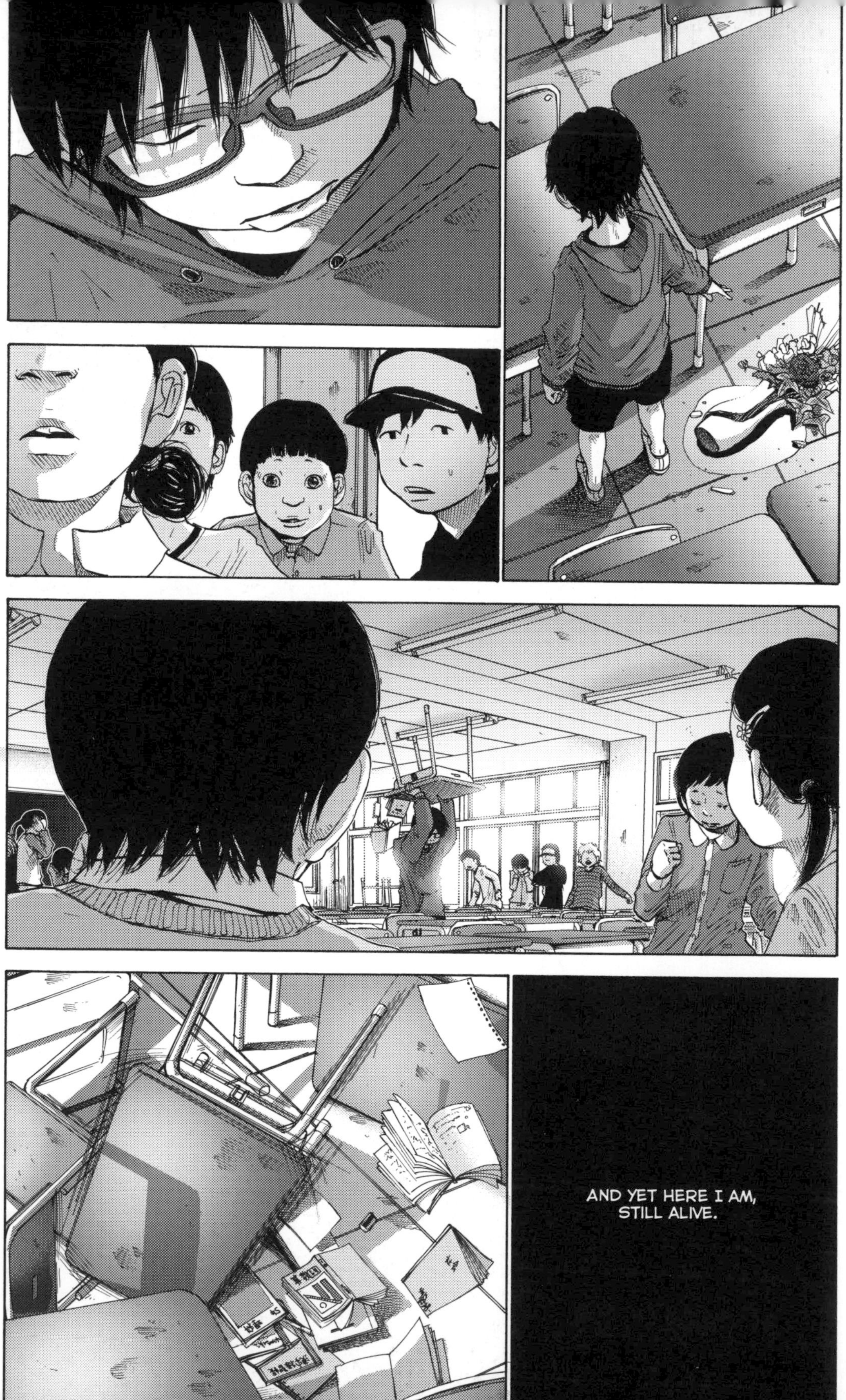
AND YET HERE I AM,
STILL ALIVE.

WHETHER IT WAS LUCK OR SOME WHIM OF GOD

I AM MADE TO LIVE.

WHAT MORE DO YOU WANT ME TO DO?

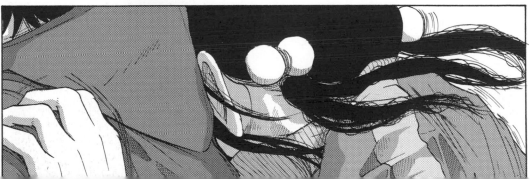

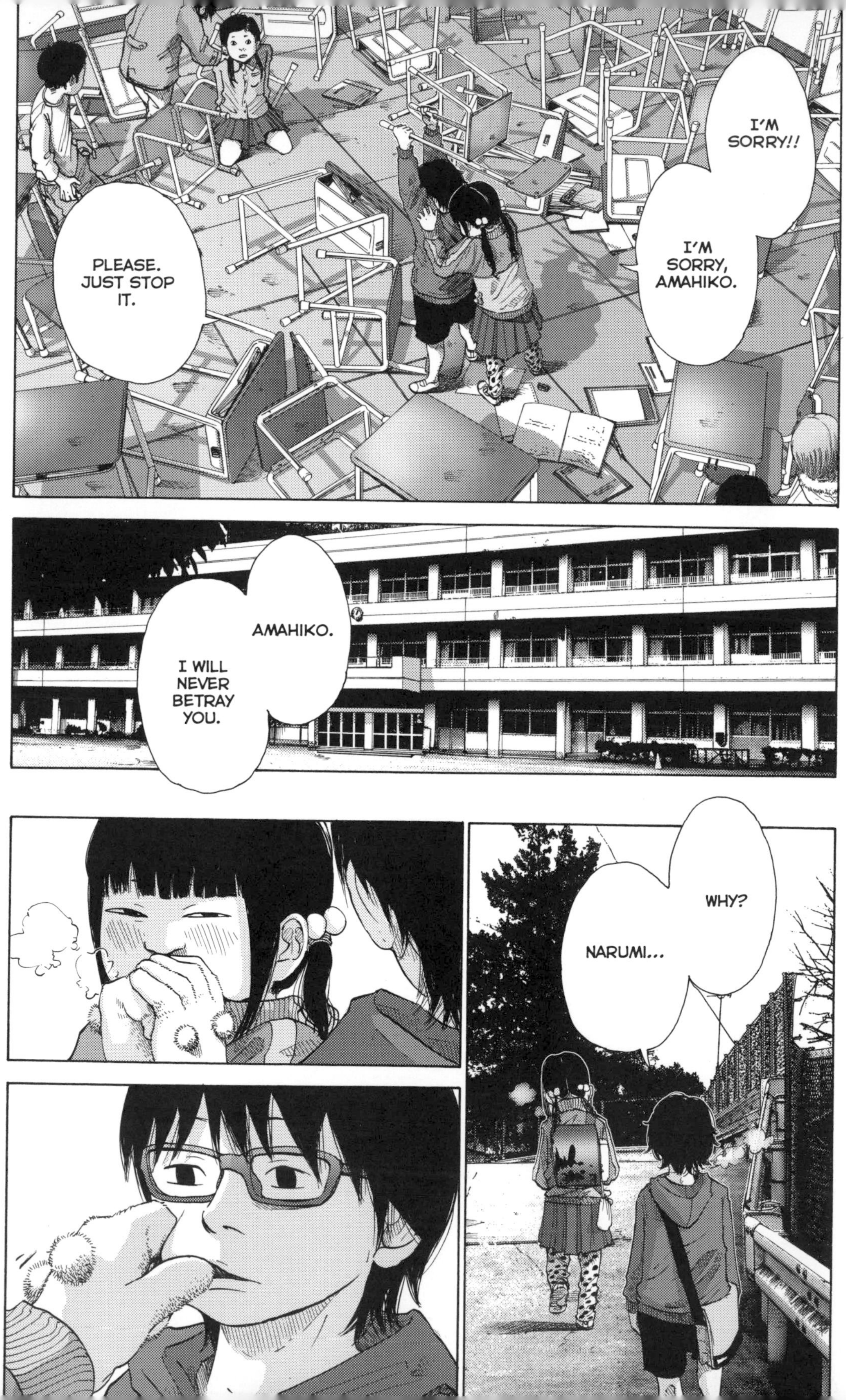
I'M SORRY!!
I'M SORRY, AMAHIKO.
PLEASE. JUST STOP IT.
AMAHIKO.
I WILL NEVER BETRAY YOU.
WHY?
NARUMI...

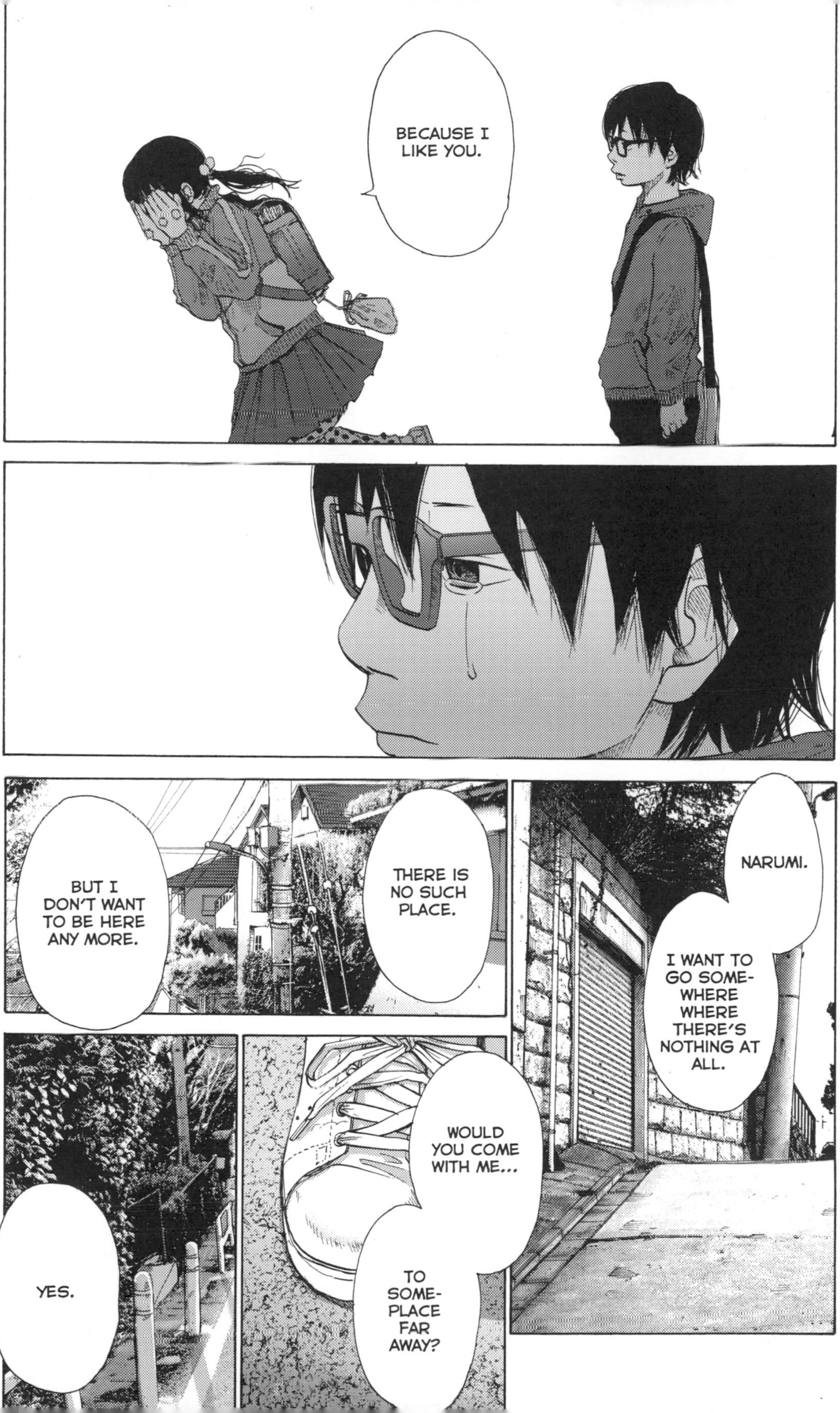
BECAUSE I LIKE YOU.
NARUMI.
I WANT TO GO SOME-WHERE WHERE THERE'S NOTHING AT ALL.
THERE IS NO SUCH PLACE.
BUT I DON'T WANT TO BE HERE ANY MORE.
WOULD YOU COME WITH ME...
TO SOME-PLACE FAR AWAY?
YES.

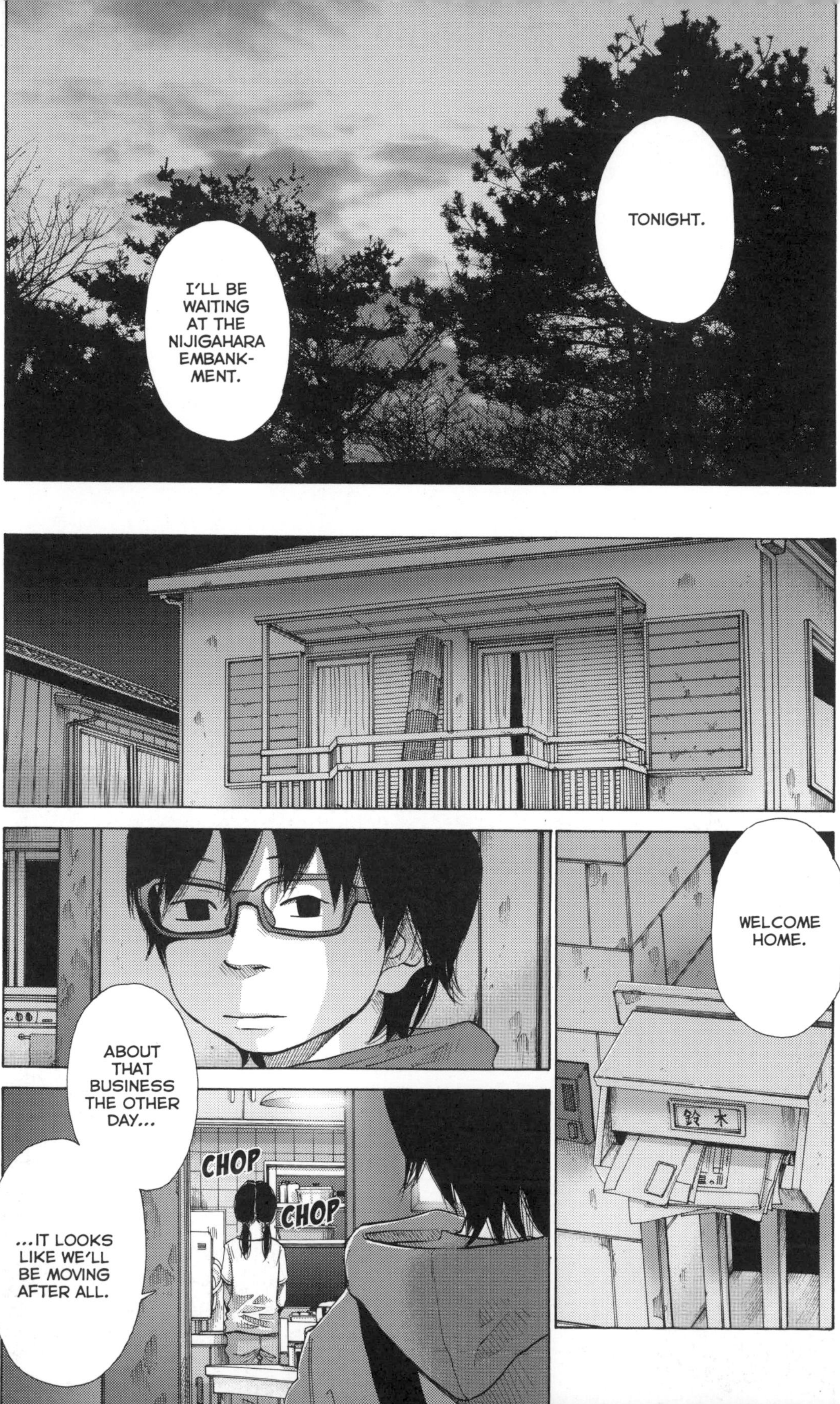
TONIGHT.
I'LL BE WAITING AT THE NIJIGAHARA EMBANK-MENT.
WELCOME HOME.
鈴木
ABOUT THAT BUSINESS THE OTHER DAY...
CHOP
CHOP
...IT LOOKS LIKE WE'LL BE MOVING AFTER ALL.

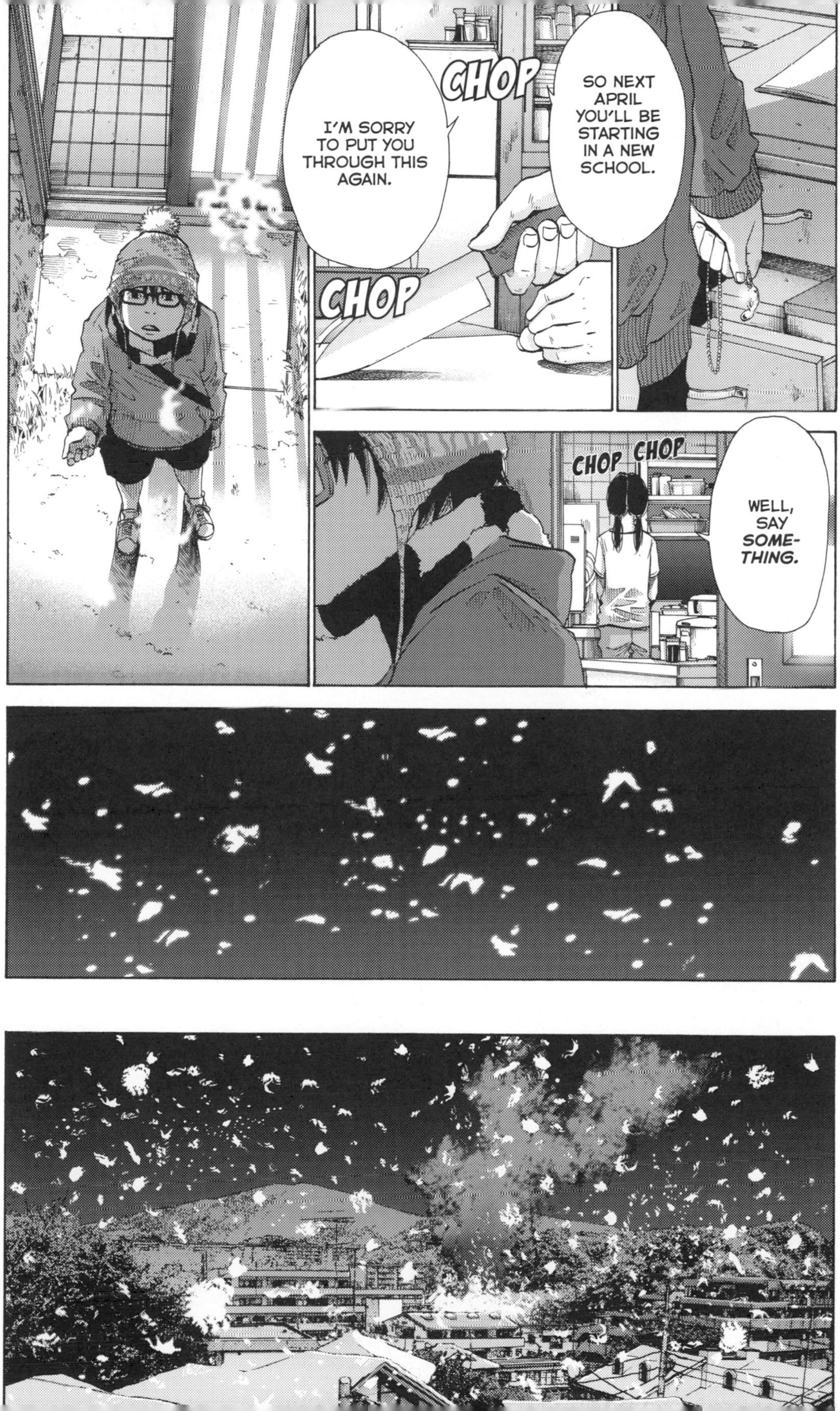
SO NEXT APRIL YOU'LL BE STARTING IN A NEW SCHOOL.
CHOP
I'M SORRY TO PUT YOU THROUGH THIS AGAIN.
CHOP
CHOP CHOP
WELL, SAY *SOME-THING.*

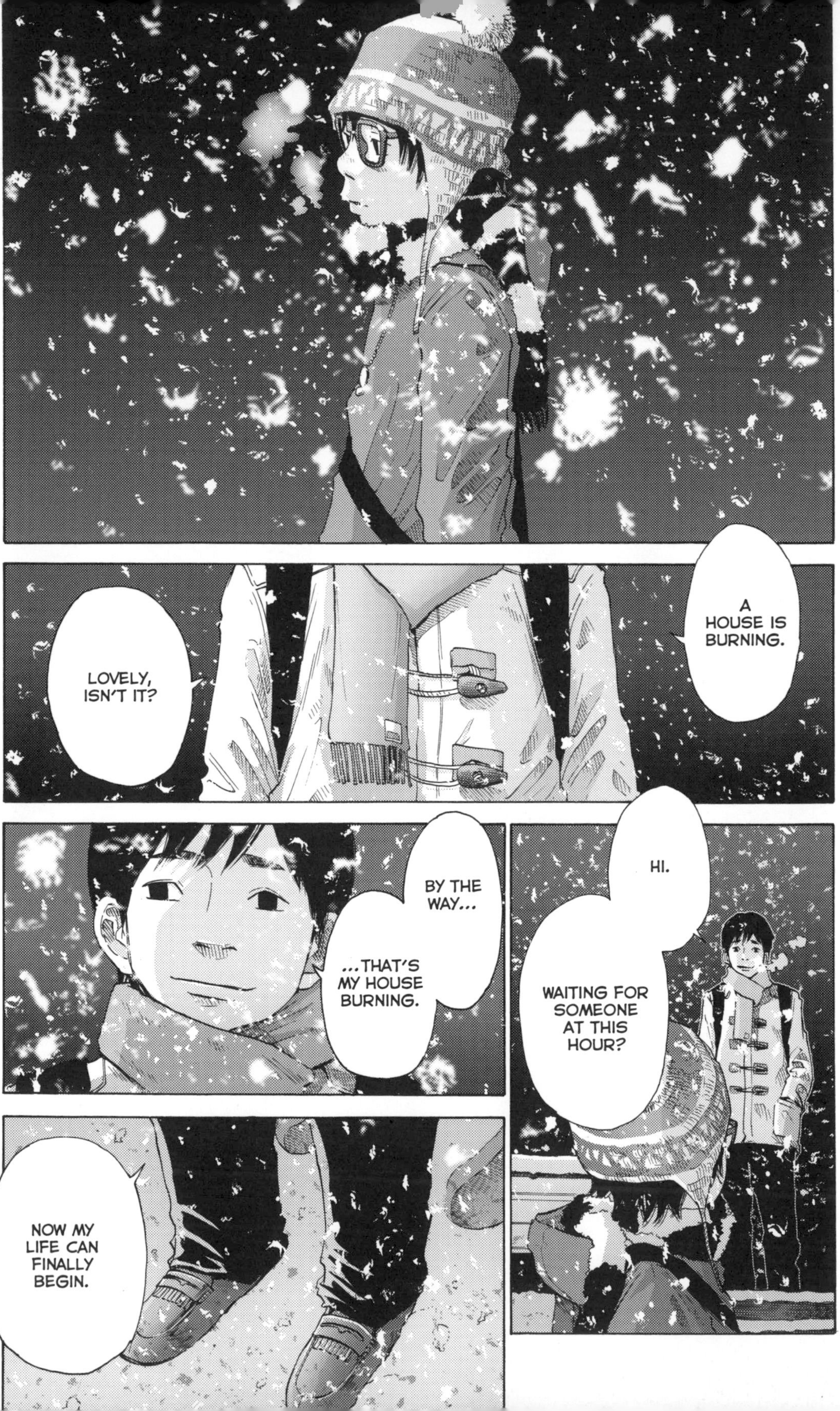
A HOUSE IS BURNING.
LOVELY, ISN'T IT?
HI.
WAITING FOR SOMEONE AT THIS HOUR?
BY THE WAY...
...THAT'S MY HOUSE BURNING.
NOW MY LIFE CAN FINALLY BEGIN.

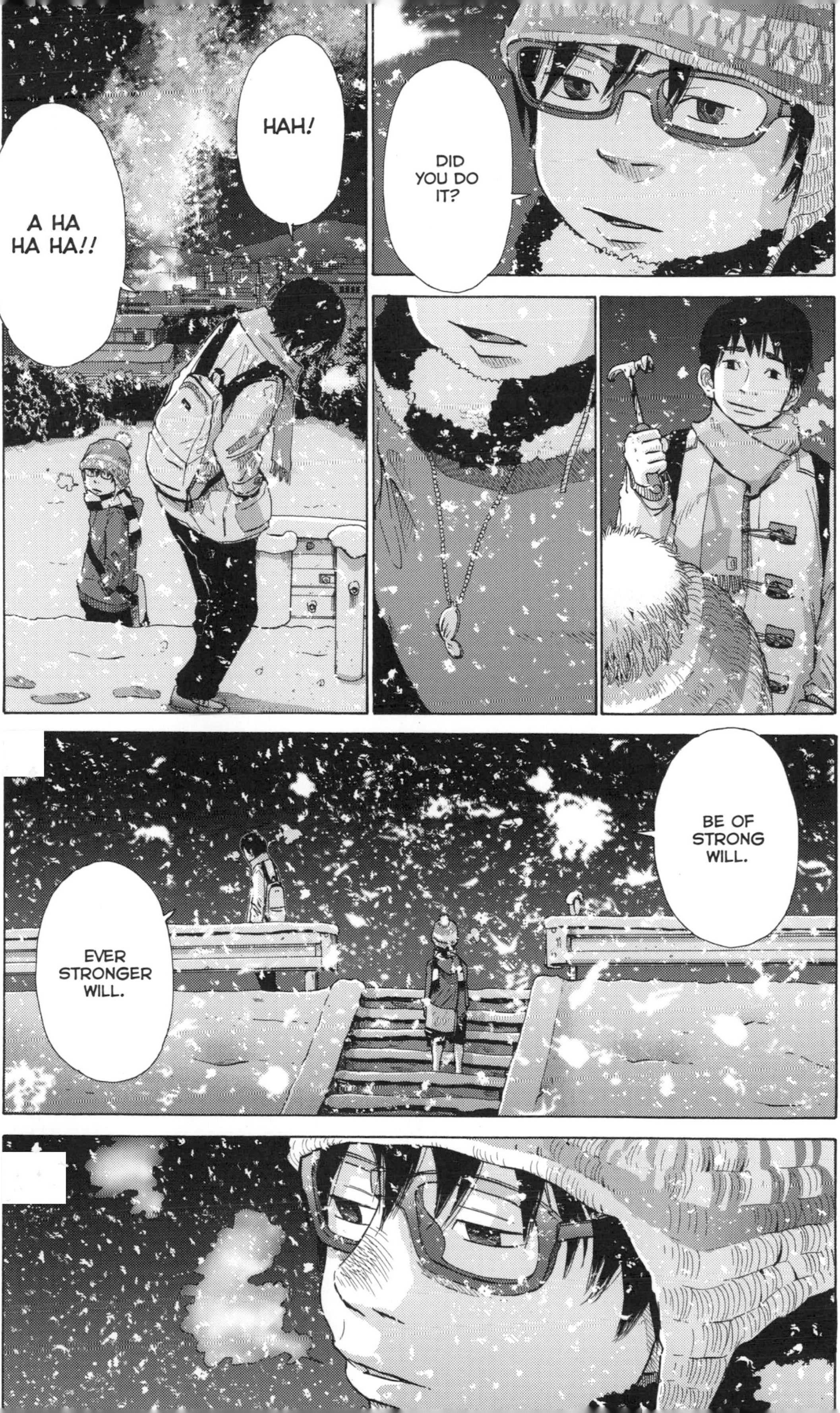
DID YOU DO IT?
HAH!
A HA HA HA!!
BE OF STRONG WILL.
EVER STRONGER WILL.

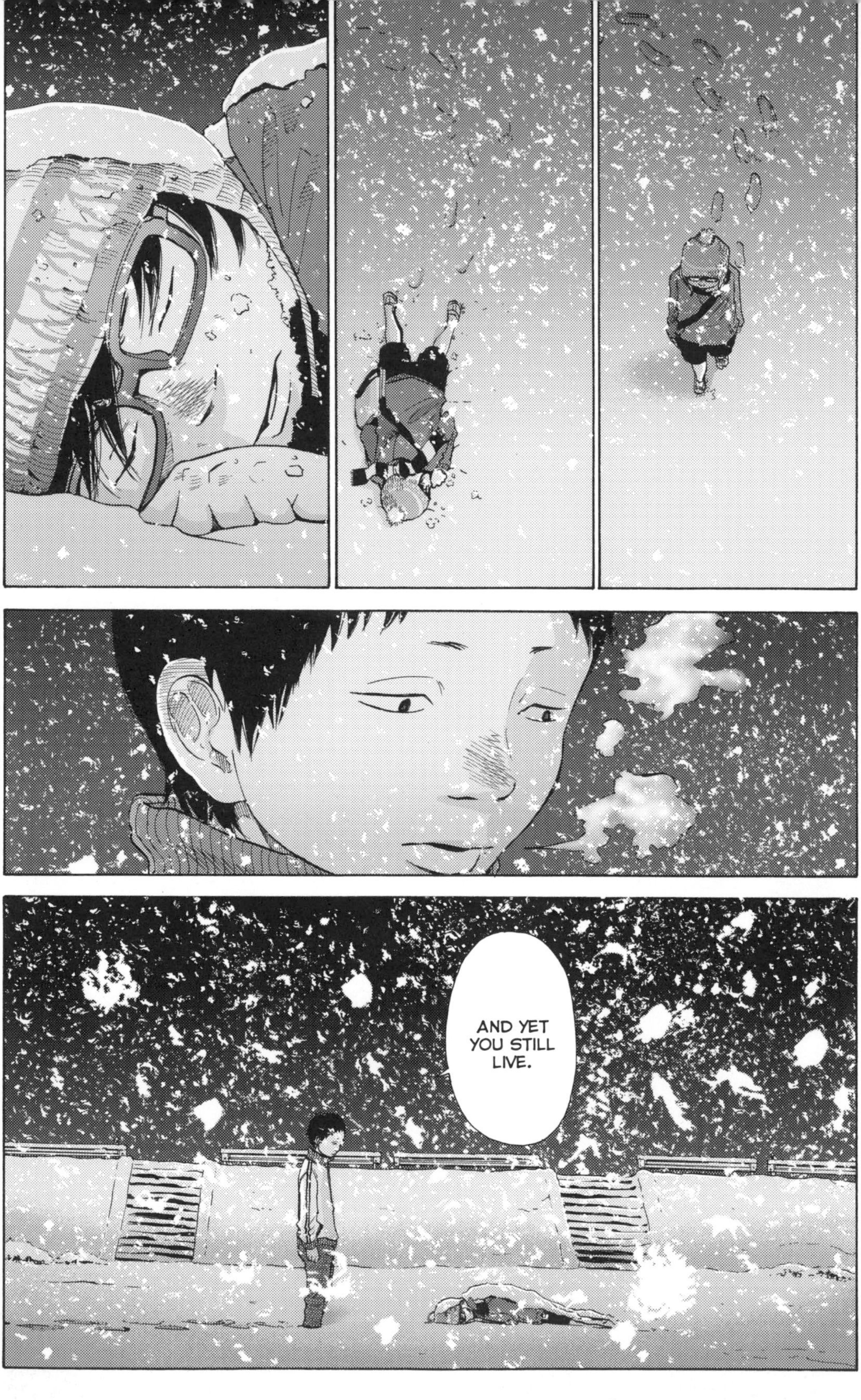
AND YET YOU STILL LIVE.

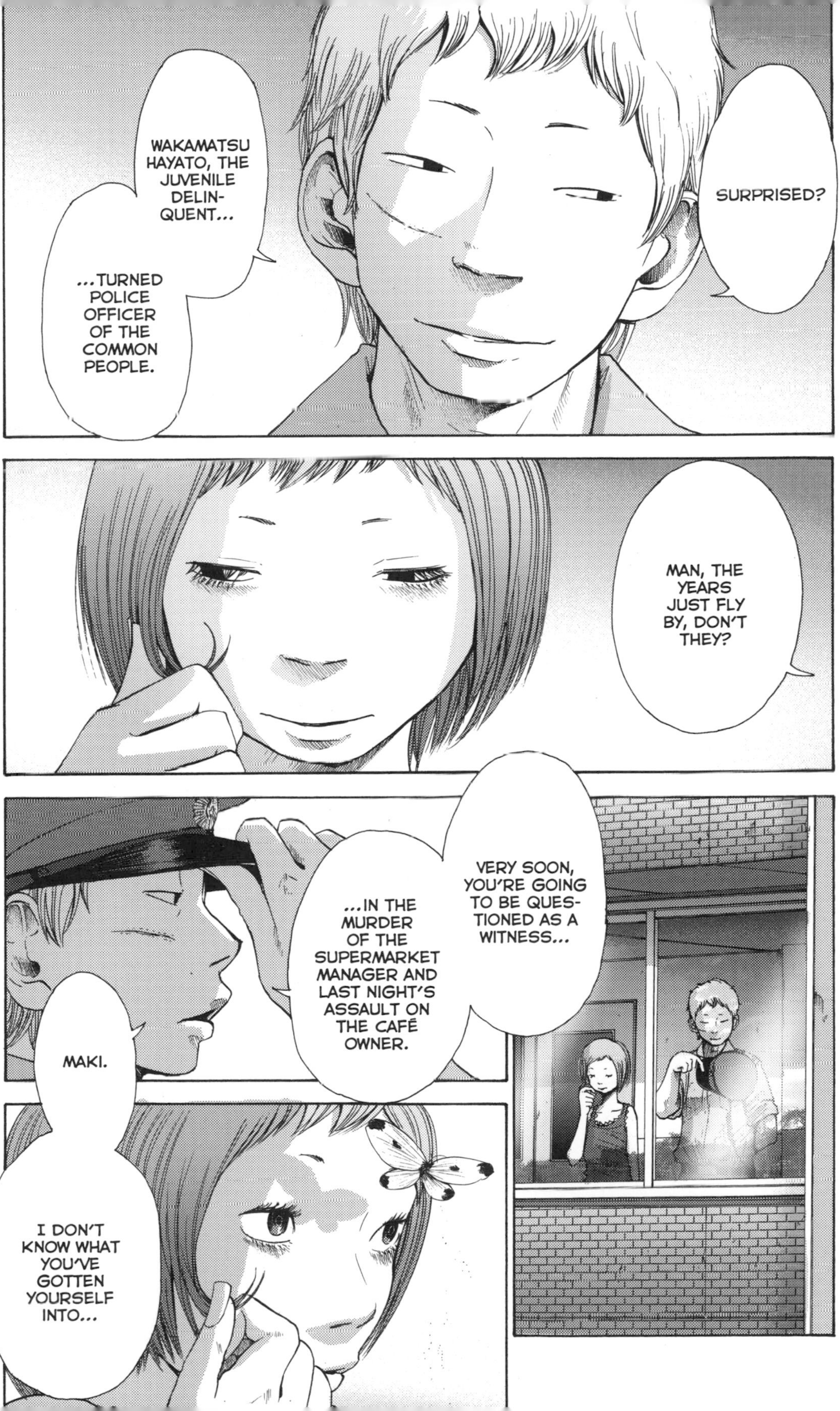
SURPRISED?
WAKAMATSU HAYATO, THE JUVENILE DELINQUENT...
...TURNED POLICE OFFICER OF THE COMMON PEOPLE.
MAN, THE YEARS JUST FLY BY, DON'T THEY?
VERY SOON, YOU'RE GOING TO BE QUESTIONED AS A WITNESS...
...IN THE MURDER OF THE SUPERMARKET MANAGER AND LAST NIGHT'S ASSAULT ON THE CAFÉ OWNER.
MAKI.
I DON'T KNOW WHAT YOU'VE GOTTEN YOURSELF INTO...

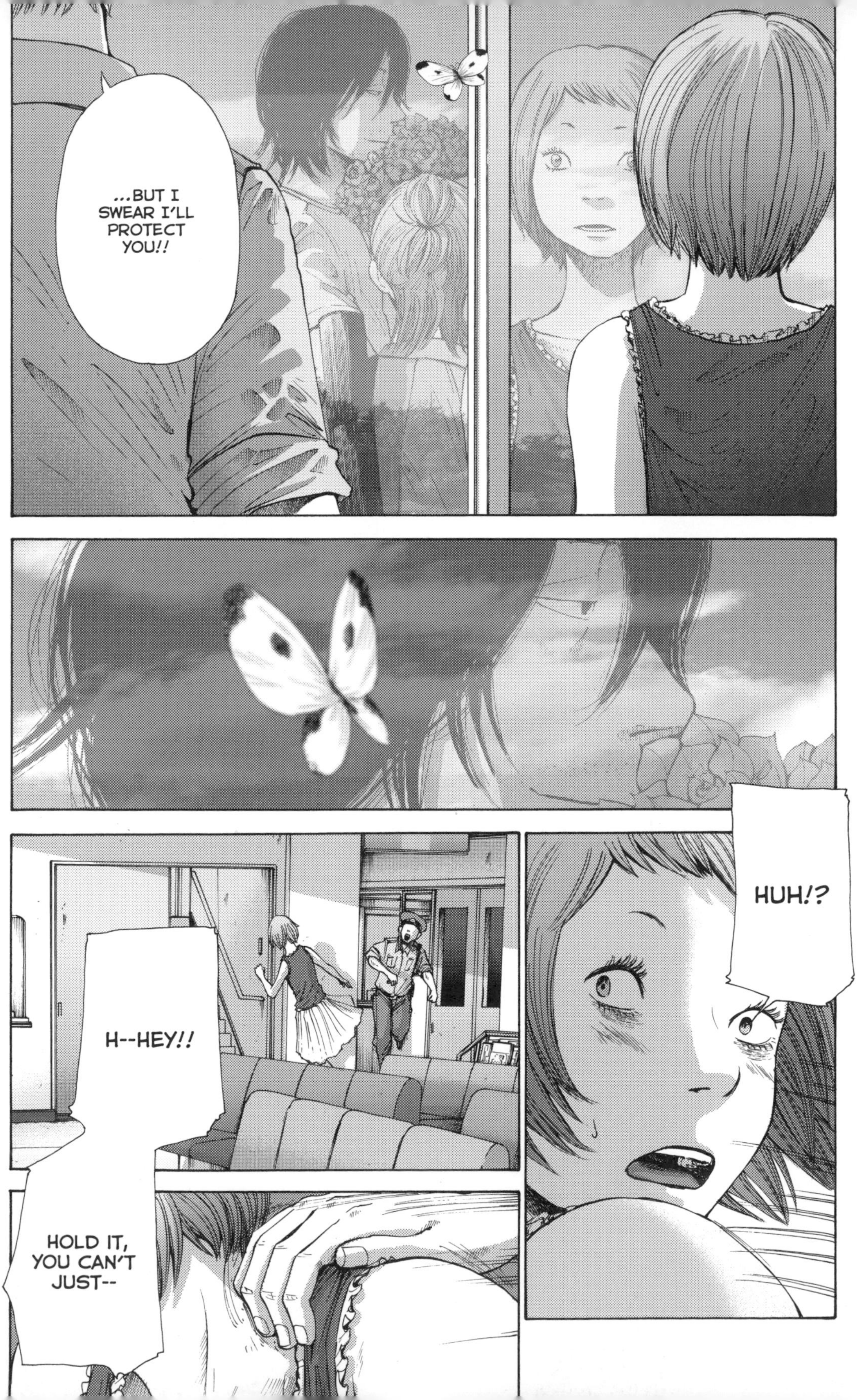
...BUT I SWEAR I'LL PROTECT YOU!!
HUH!?
H--HEY!!
HOLD IT, YOU CAN'T JUST--

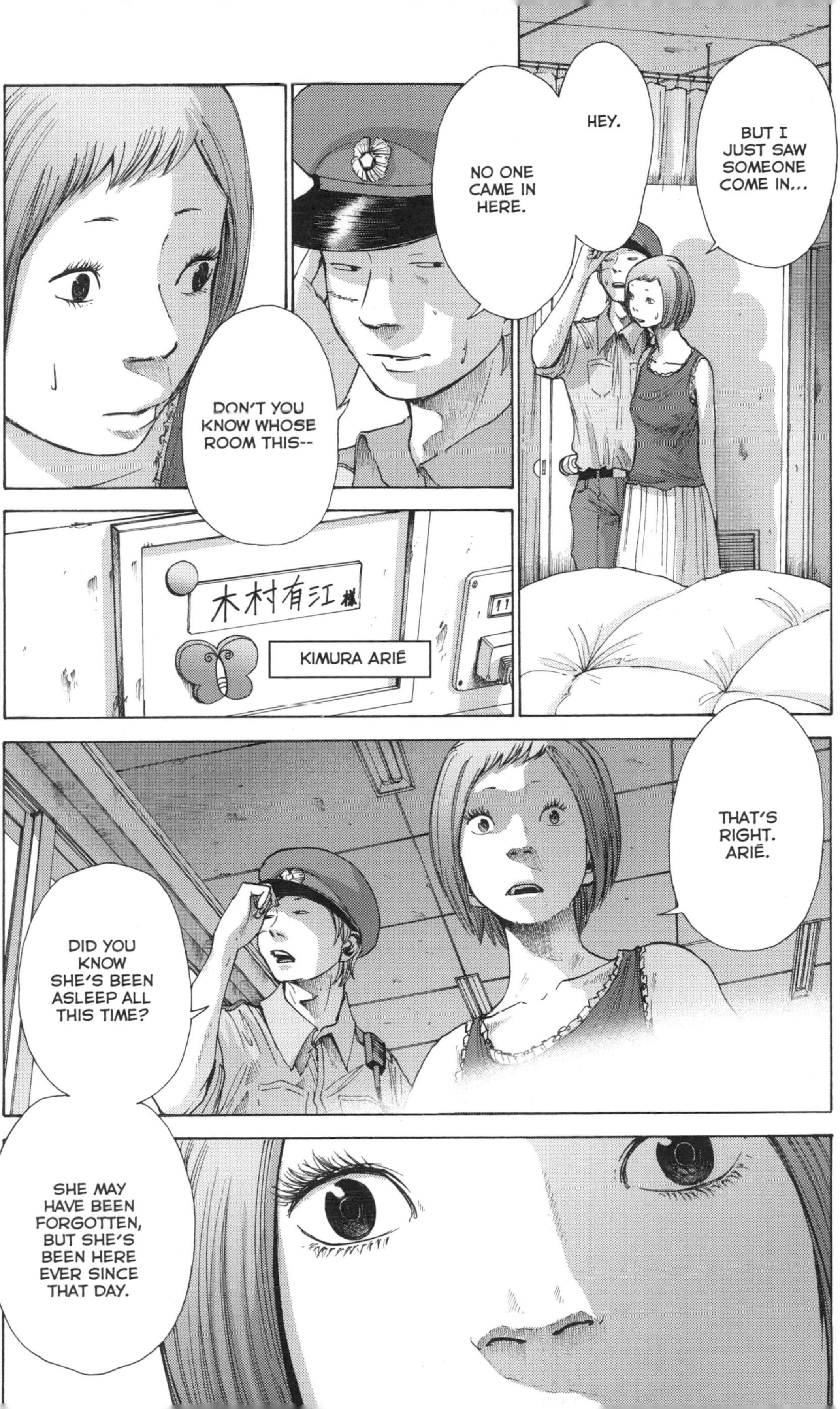
BUT I JUST SAW SOMEONE COME IN...
HEY.
NO ONE CAME IN HERE.
DON'T YOU KNOW WHOSE ROOM THIS--
木村有江 様
KIMURA ARIÉ
THAT'S RIGHT. ARIÉ.
DID YOU KNOW SHE'S BEEN ASLEEP ALL THIS TIME?
SHE MAY HAVE BEEN FORGOTTEN, BUT SHE'S BEEN HERE EVER SINCE THAT DAY.

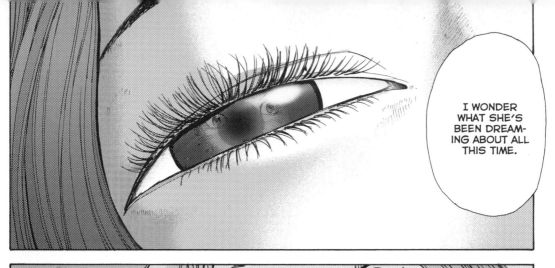

I WONDER WHAT SHE'S BEEN DREAMING ABOUT ALL THIS TIME.

IT'S BEEN NAGGING MY CONSCIENCE FOR TEN YEARS.

WHY?

WHY THE HELL DID WE DO THAT?

HUH?

FLOWERS?

BECAUSE OF THE RAIN THE OTHER DAY, THE WATER LEVEL
HAS RISEN AND IT'S HARD TO WALK.

TODAY, AGAIN,

I LET THE GLOWING BUTTERFLY LEAD ME

AND WANDER THE TUNNELS.

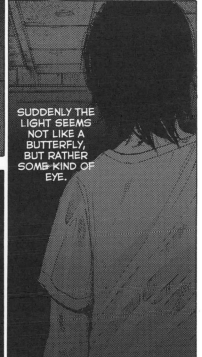

SUDDENLY THE
LIGHT SEEMS
NOT LIKE A
BUTTERFLY,
BUT RATHER
SOME KIND OF
EYE.

I REMEMBER THE STORY OF THE MONSTER IN
THE TUNNEL

THAT SHE USED TO TALK ABOUT IN
ELEMENTARY SCHOOL.

IS THIS ONE-EYED MONSTER

TRYING TO TELL ME SOMETHING?

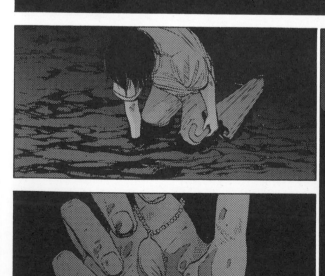

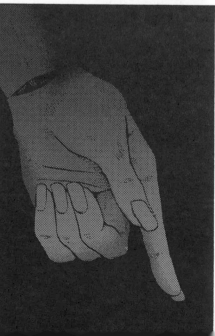

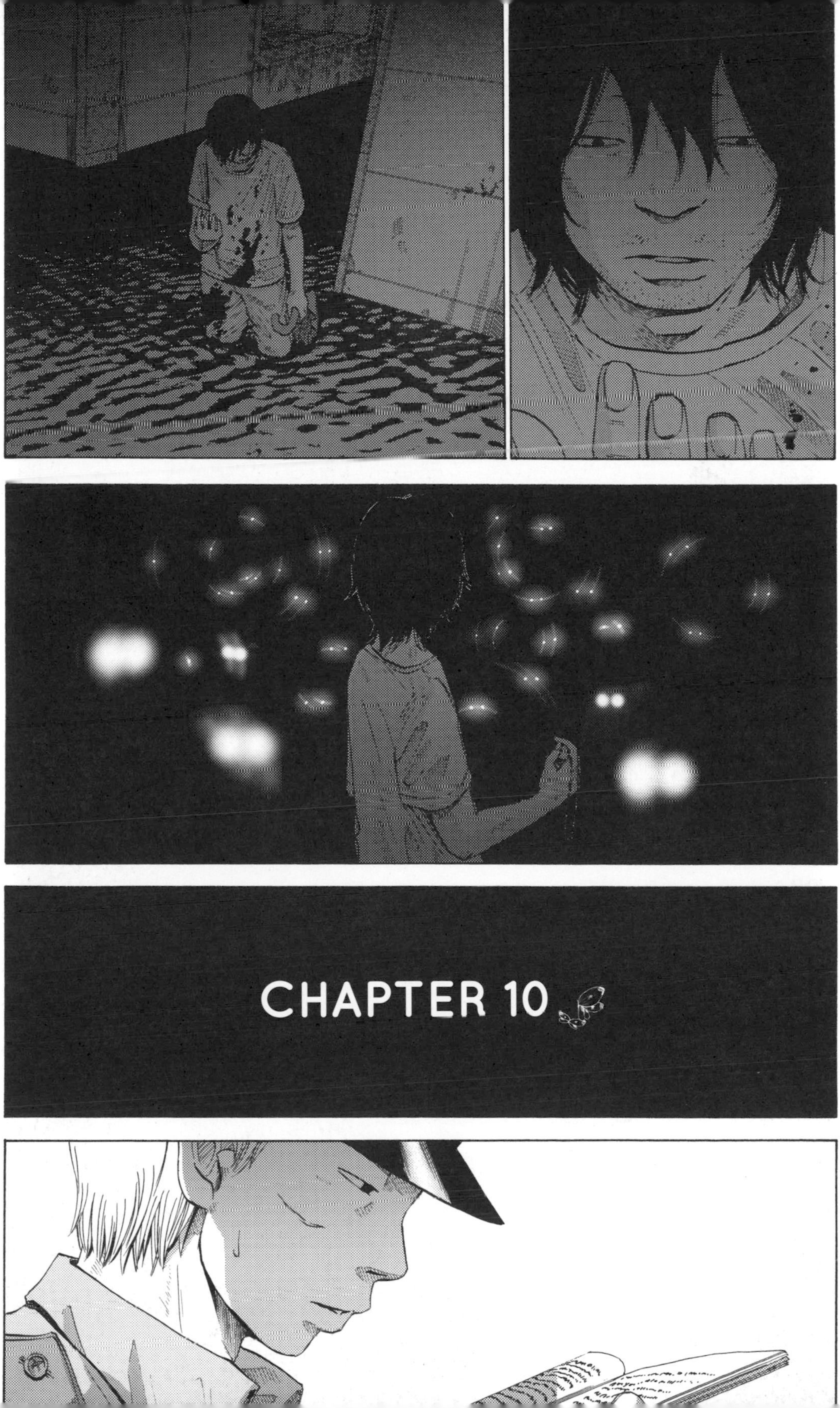
CHAPTER 10

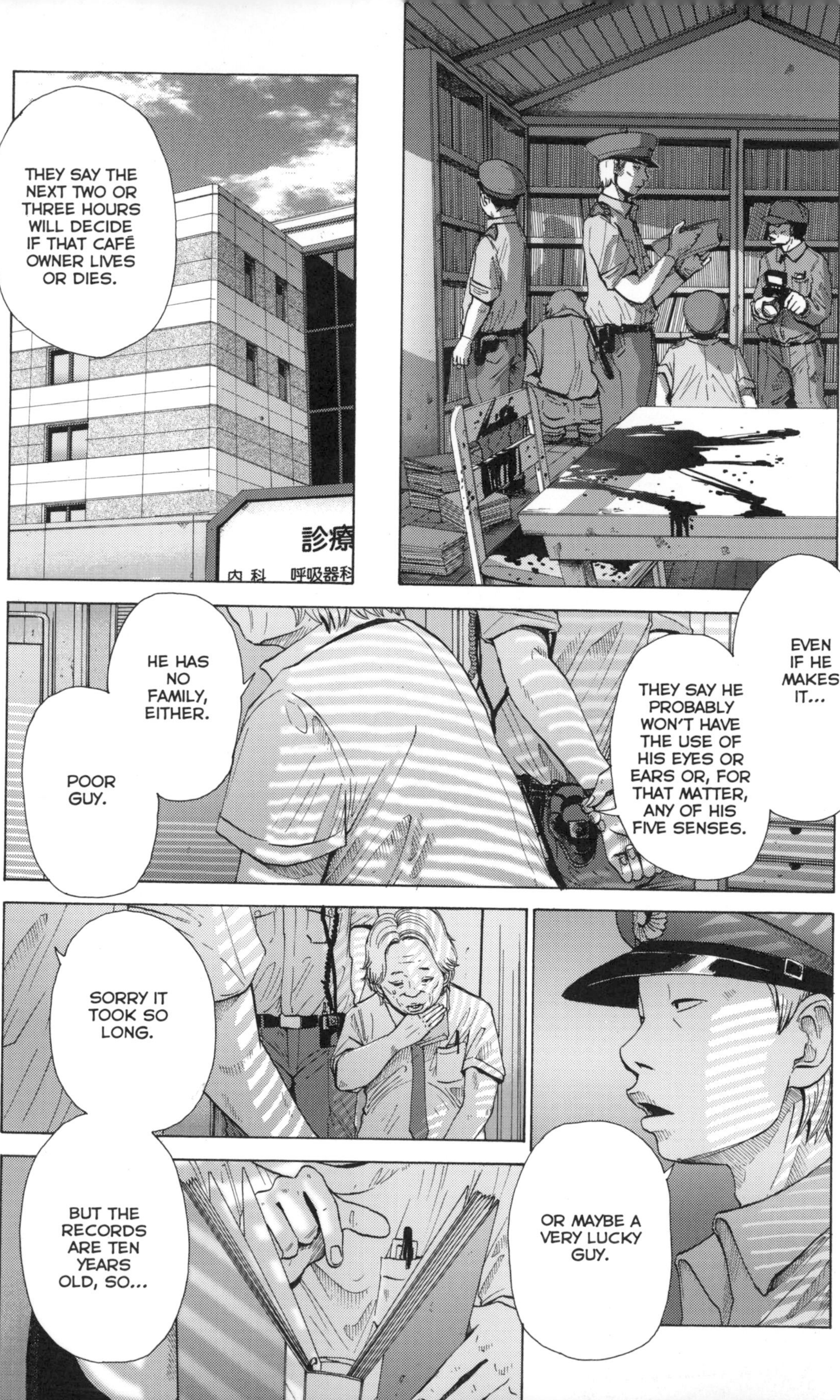
THEY SAY THE NEXT TWO OR THREE HOURS WILL DECIDE IF THAT CAFÉ OWNER LIVES OR DIES.
診療
内科 呼吸器科
EVEN IF HE MAKES IT...
THEY SAY HE PROBABLY WON'T HAVE THE USE OF HIS EYES OR EARS OR, FOR THAT MATTER, ANY OF HIS FIVE SENSES.
HE HAS NO FAMILY, EITHER.
POOR GUY.
OR MAYBE A VERY LUCKY GUY.
SORRY IT TOOK SO LONG.
BUT THE RECORDS ARE TEN YEARS OLD, SO...

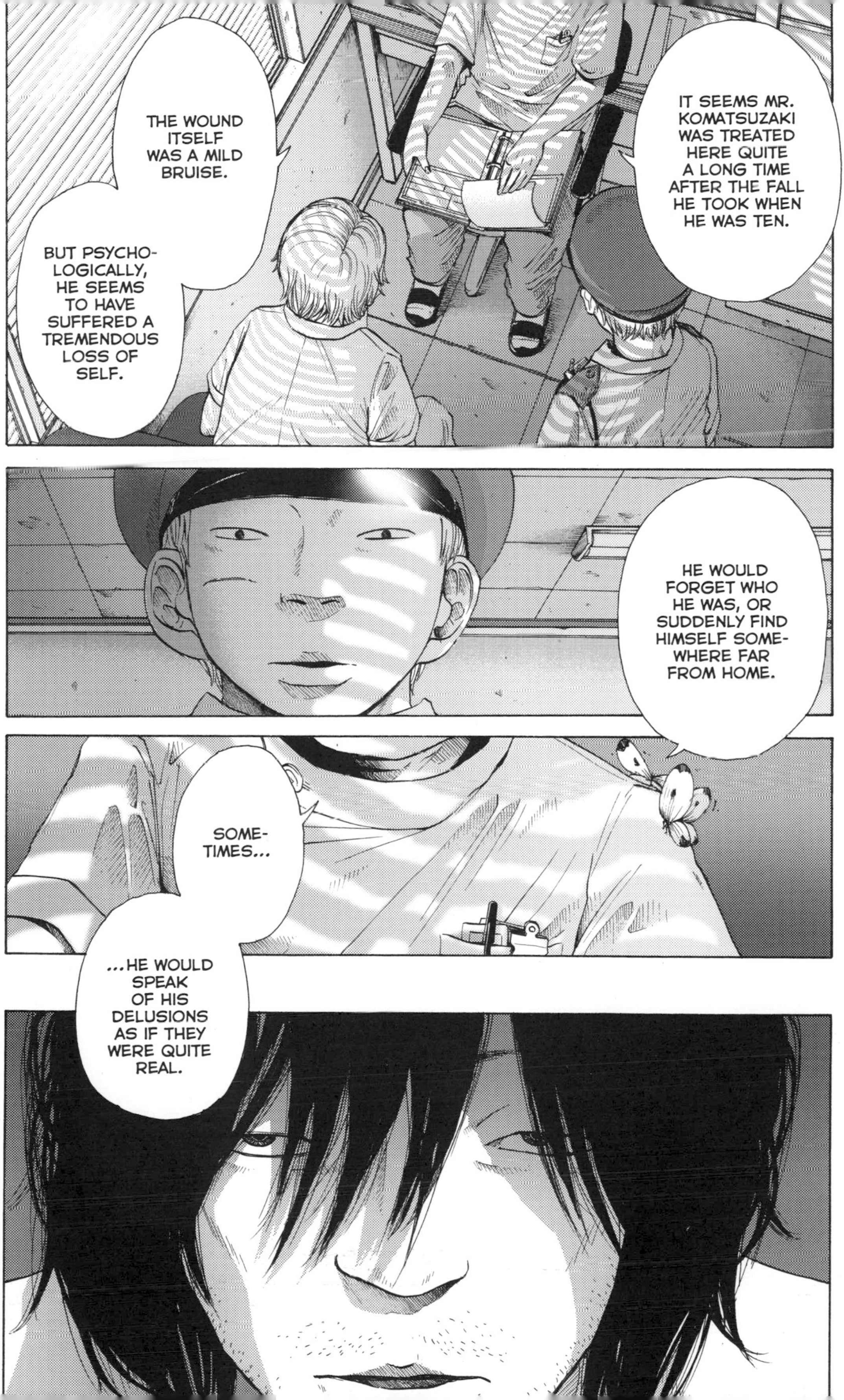
IT SEEMS MR. KOMATSUZAKI WAS TREATED HERE QUITE A LONG TIME AFTER THE FALL HE TOOK WHEN HE WAS TEN.
THE WOUND ITSELF WAS A MILD BRUISE.
BUT PSYCHO-LOGICALLY, HE SEEMS TO HAVE SUFFERED A TREMENDOUS LOSS OF SELF.
HE WOULD FORGET WHO HE WAS, OR SUDDENLY FIND HIMSELF SOME-WHERE FAR FROM HOME.
SOME-TIMES...
...HE WOULD SPEAK OF HIS DELUSIONS AS IF THEY WERE QUITE REAL.

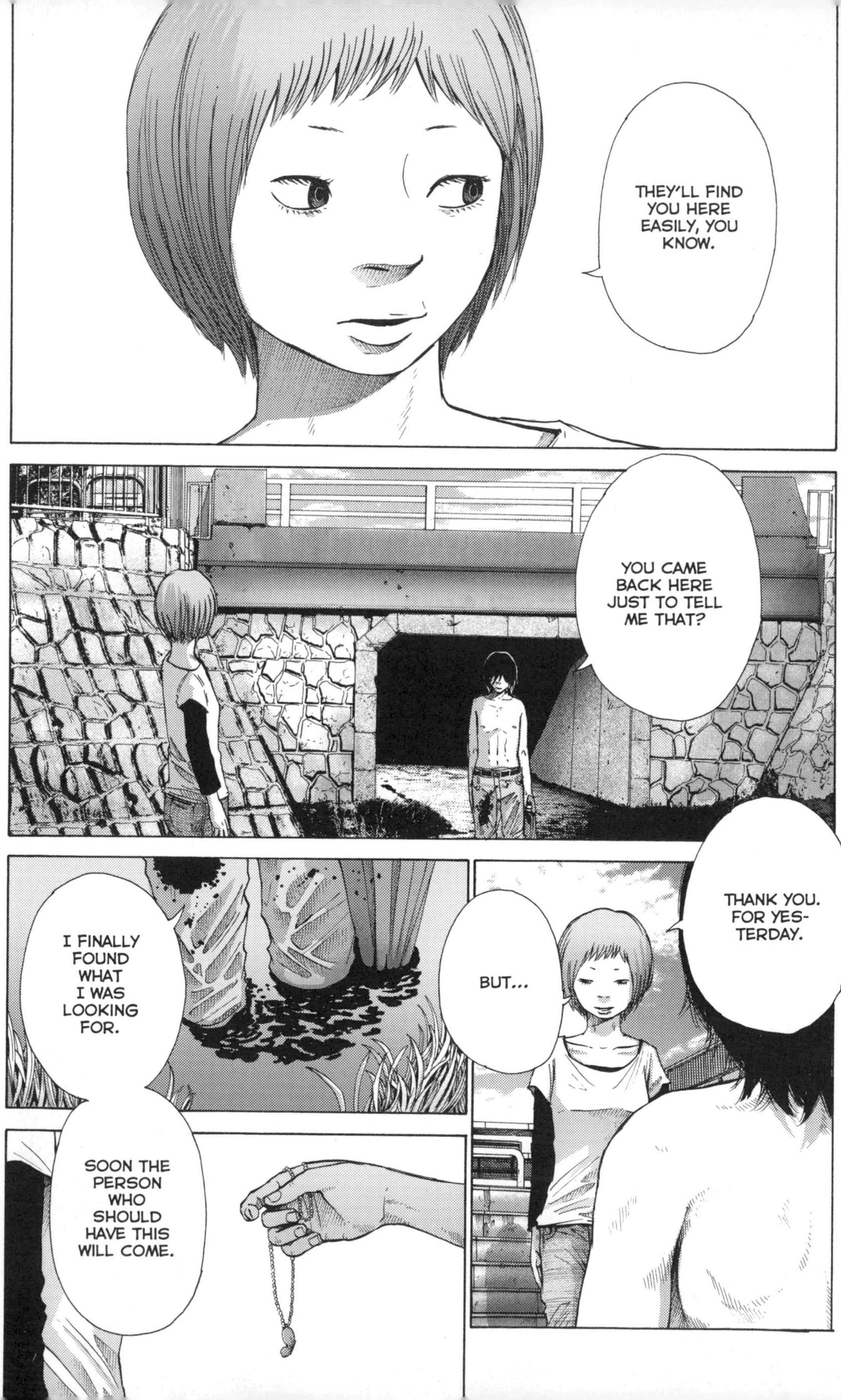
THEY'LL FIND YOU HERE EASILY, YOU KNOW.
YOU CAME BACK HERE JUST TO TELL ME THAT?
THANK YOU. FOR YES-TERDAY.
BUT...
I FINALLY FOUND WHAT I WAS LOOKING FOR.
SOON THE PERSON WHO SHOULD HAVE THIS WILL COME.

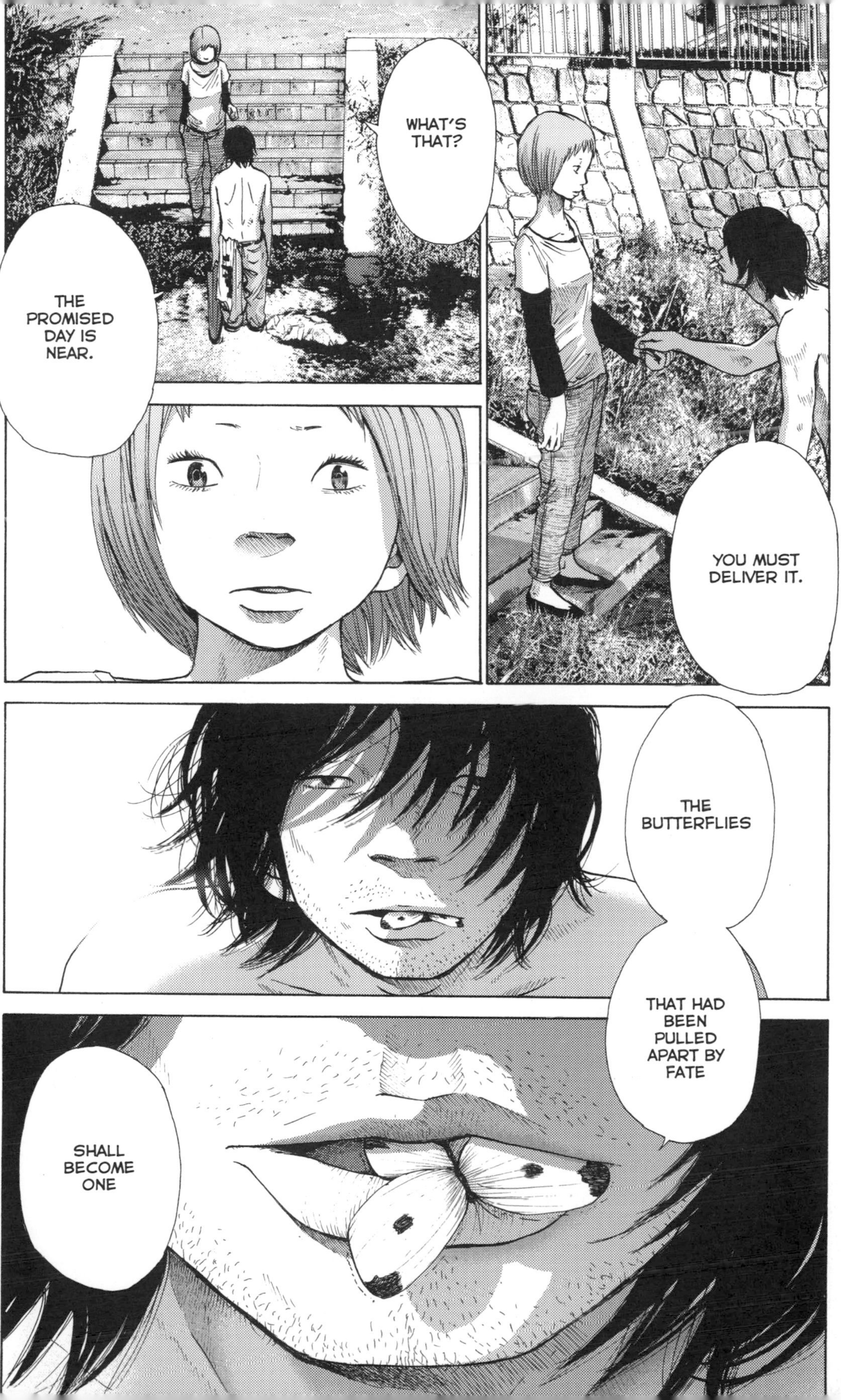
WHAT'S THAT?
YOU MUST DELIVER IT.
THE PROMISED DAY IS NEAR.
THE BUTTERFLIES
THAT HAD BEEN PULLED APART BY FATE
SHALL BECOME ONE

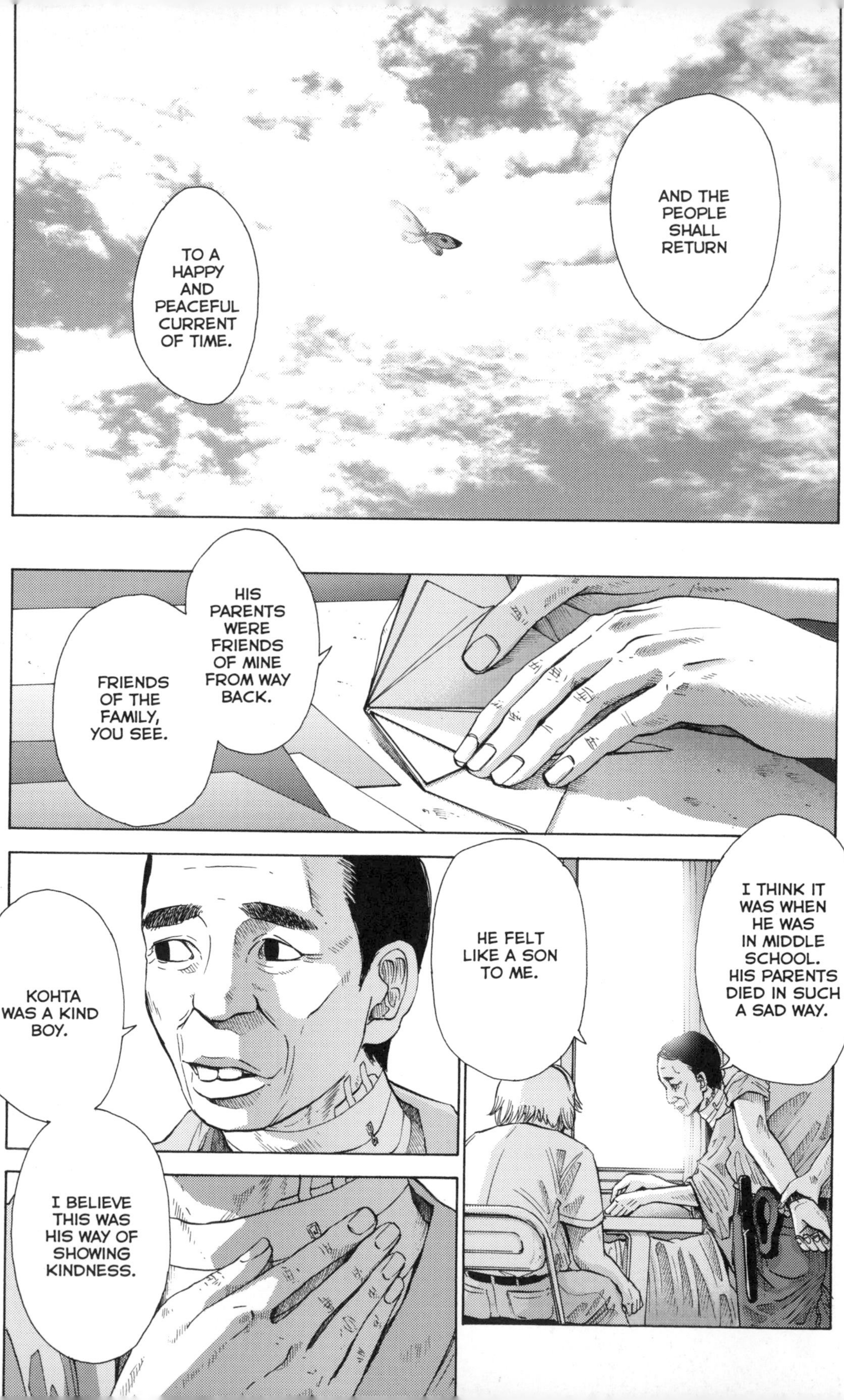
AND THE PEOPLE SHALL RETURN
TO A HAPPY AND PEACEFUL CURRENT OF TIME.
HIS PARENTS WERE FRIENDS OF MINE FROM WAY BACK.
FRIENDS OF THE FAMILY, YOU SEE.
I THINK IT WAS WHEN HE WAS IN MIDDLE SCHOOL. HIS PARENTS DIED IN SUCH A SAD WAY.
HE FELT LIKE A SON TO ME.
KOHTA WAS A KIND BOY.
I BELIEVE THIS WAS HIS WAY OF SHOWING KINDNESS.

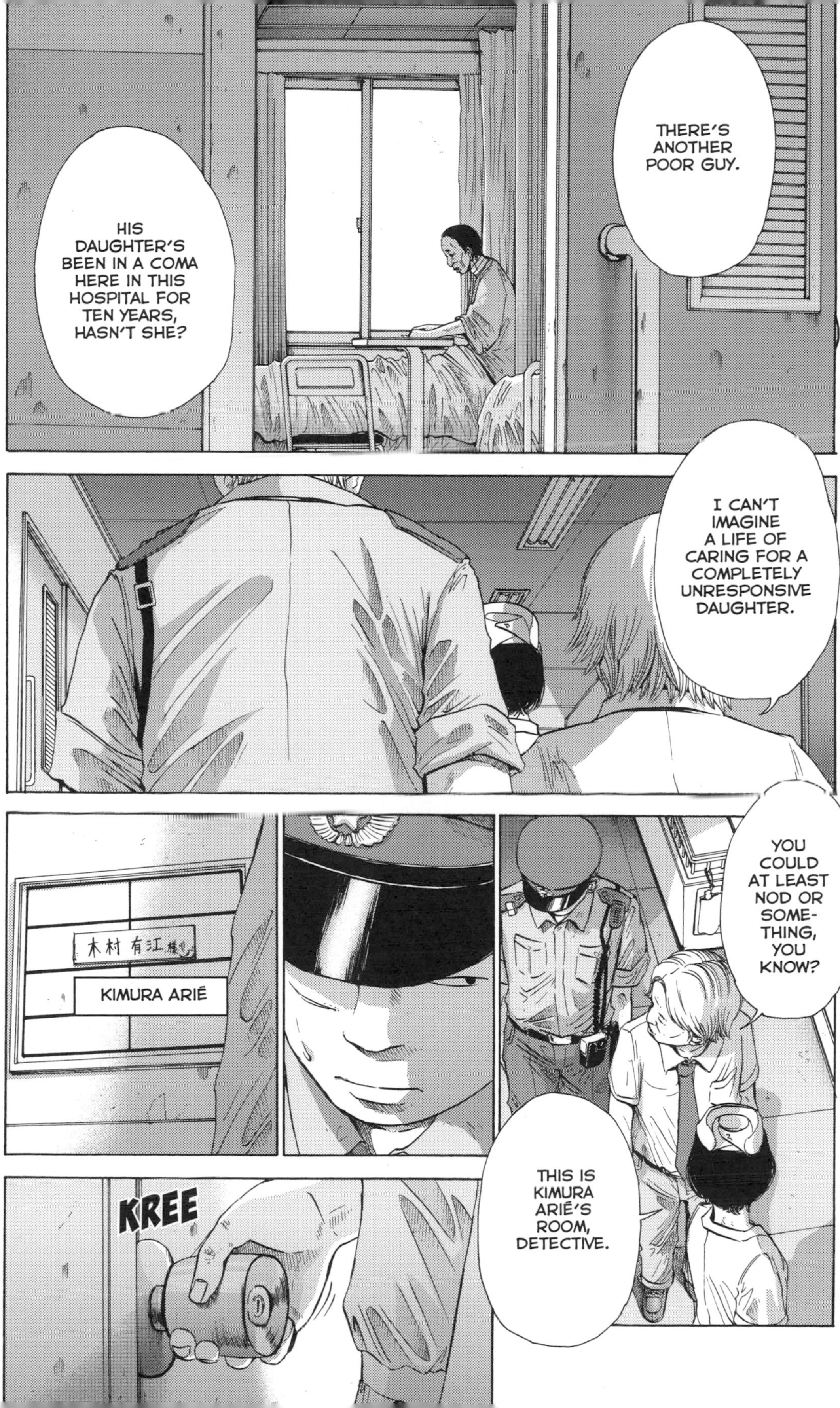
THERE'S ANOTHER POOR GUY.
HIS DAUGHTER'S BEEN IN A COMA HERE IN THIS HOSPITAL FOR TEN YEARS, HASN'T SHE?
I CAN'T IMAGINE A LIFE OF CARING FOR A COMPLETELY UNRESPONSIVE DAUGHTER.
YOU COULD AT LEAST NOD OR SOME-THING, YOU KNOW?
木村有江
KIMURA ARIÉ
THIS IS KIMURA ARIÉ'S ROOM, DETECTIVE.
KREE

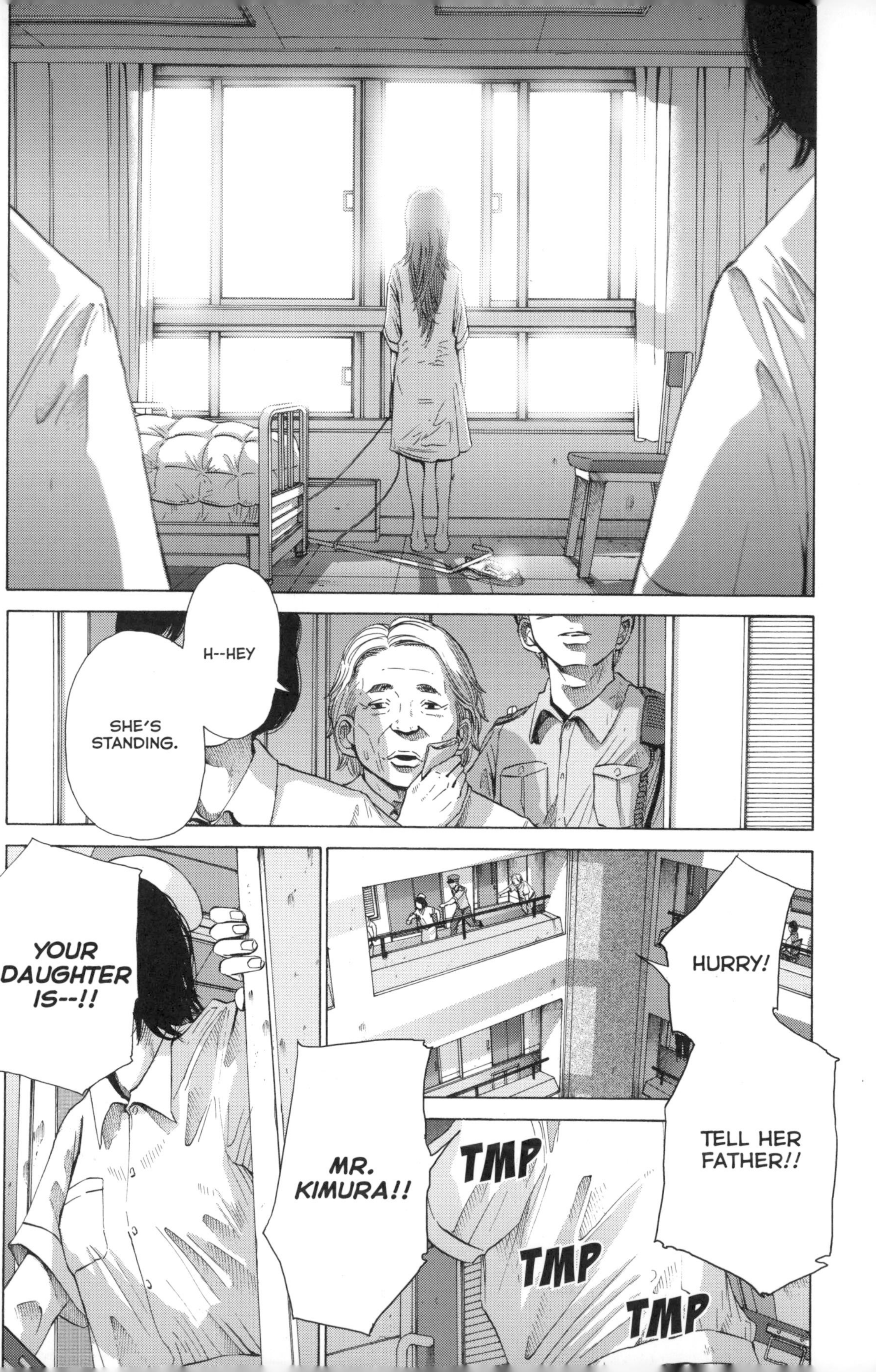
H--HEY
SHE'S STANDING.
HURRY!
TELL HER FATHER!!
MR. KIMURA!!
TMP
TMP
TMP
YOUR DAUGHTER IS--!!

AH...

WH...

WHY!?

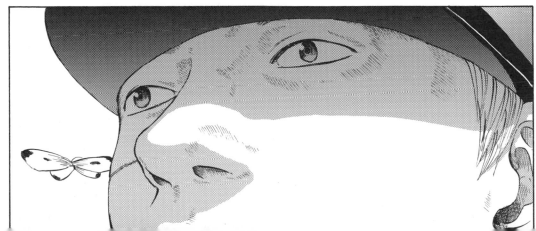

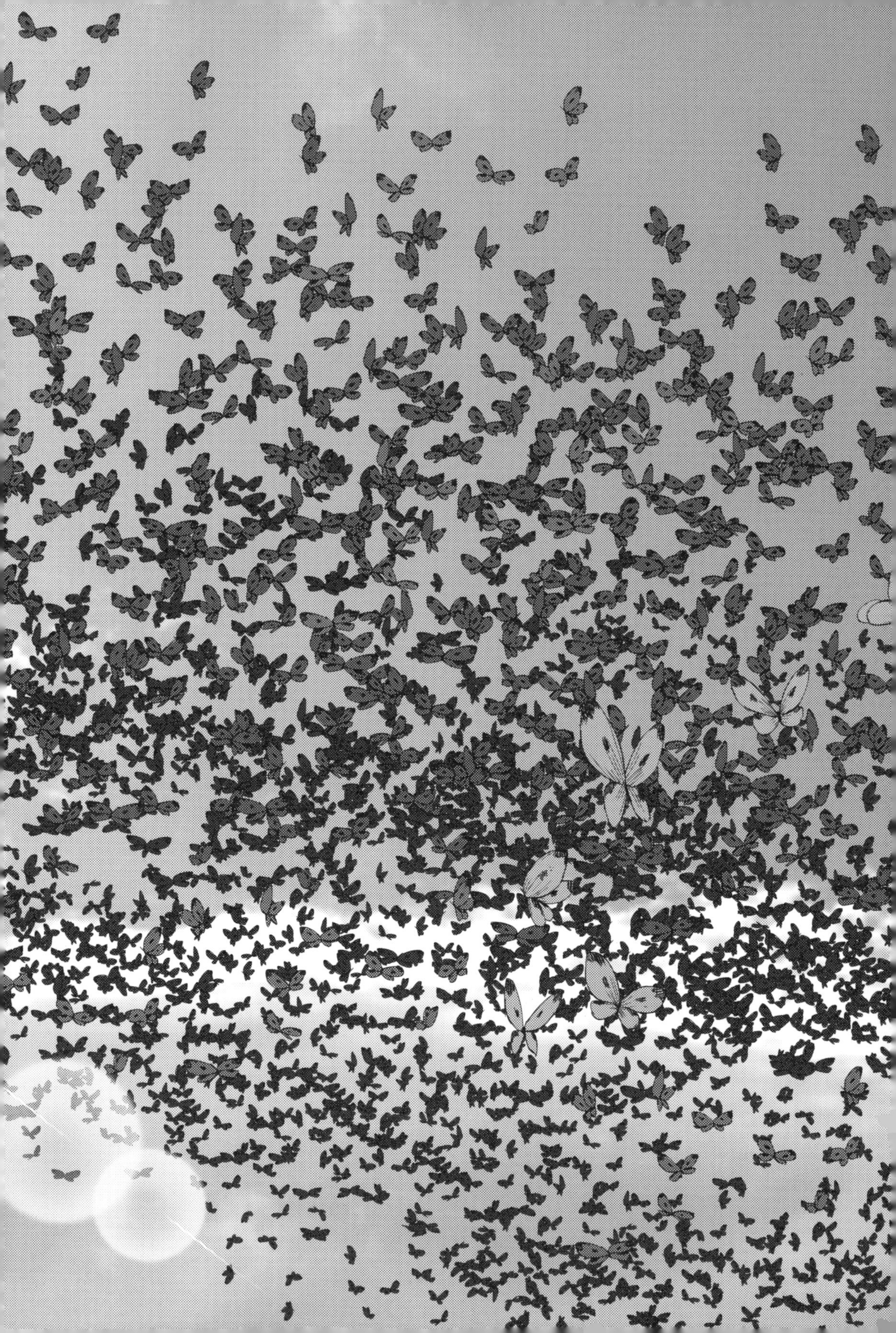

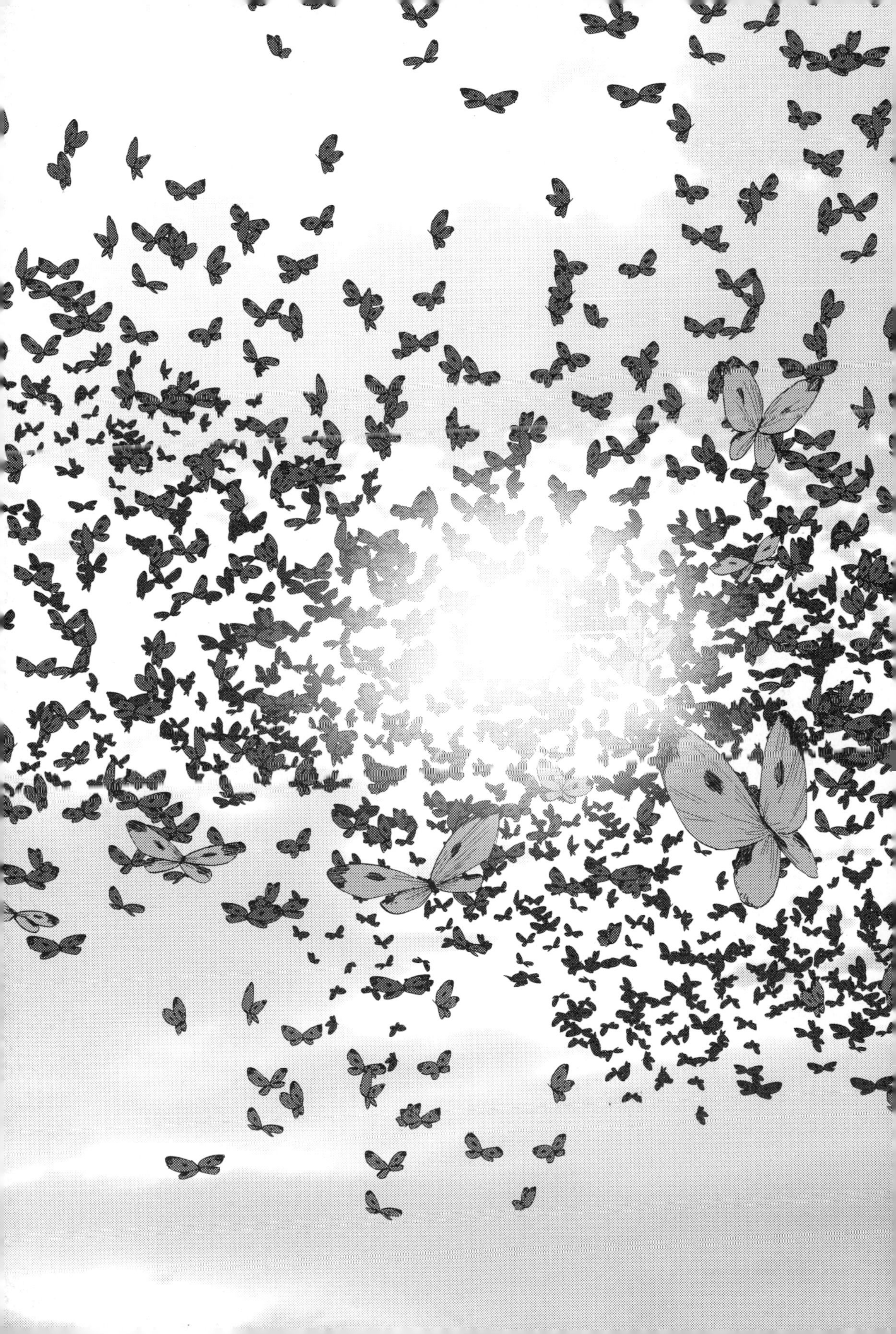

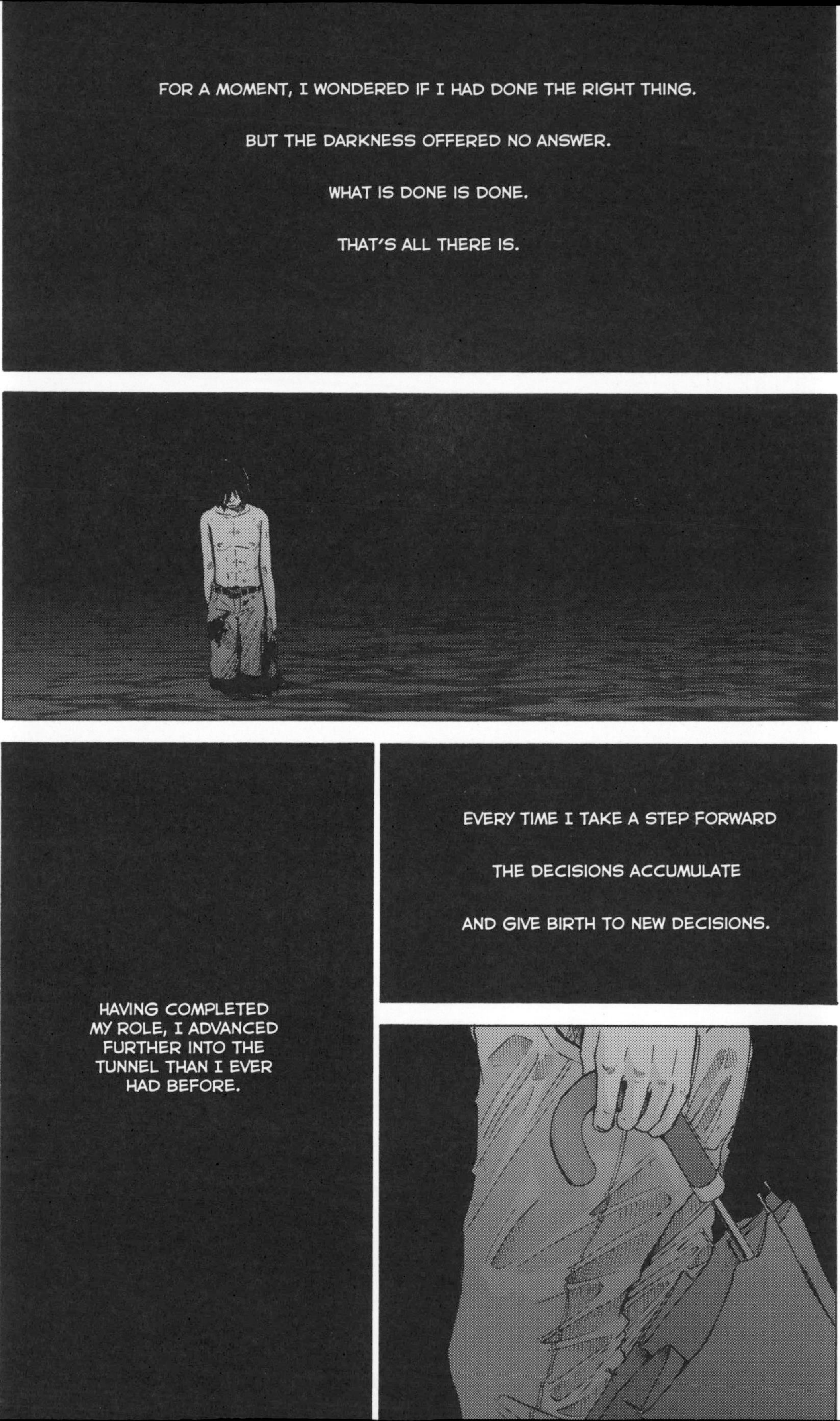

FOR A MOMENT, I WONDERED IF I HAD DONE THE RIGHT THING.

BUT THE DARKNESS OFFERED NO ANSWER.

WHAT IS DONE IS DONE.

THAT'S ALL THERE IS.

EVERY TIME I TAKE A STEP FORWARD

THE DECISIONS ACCUMULATE

AND GIVE BIRTH TO NEW DECISIONS.

HAVING COMPLETED
MY ROLE, I ADVANCED
FURTHER INTO THE
TUNNEL THAN I EVER
HAD BEFORE.

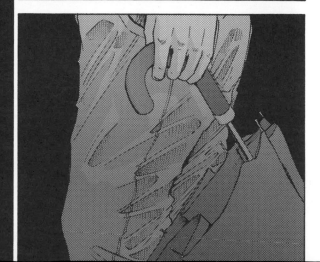

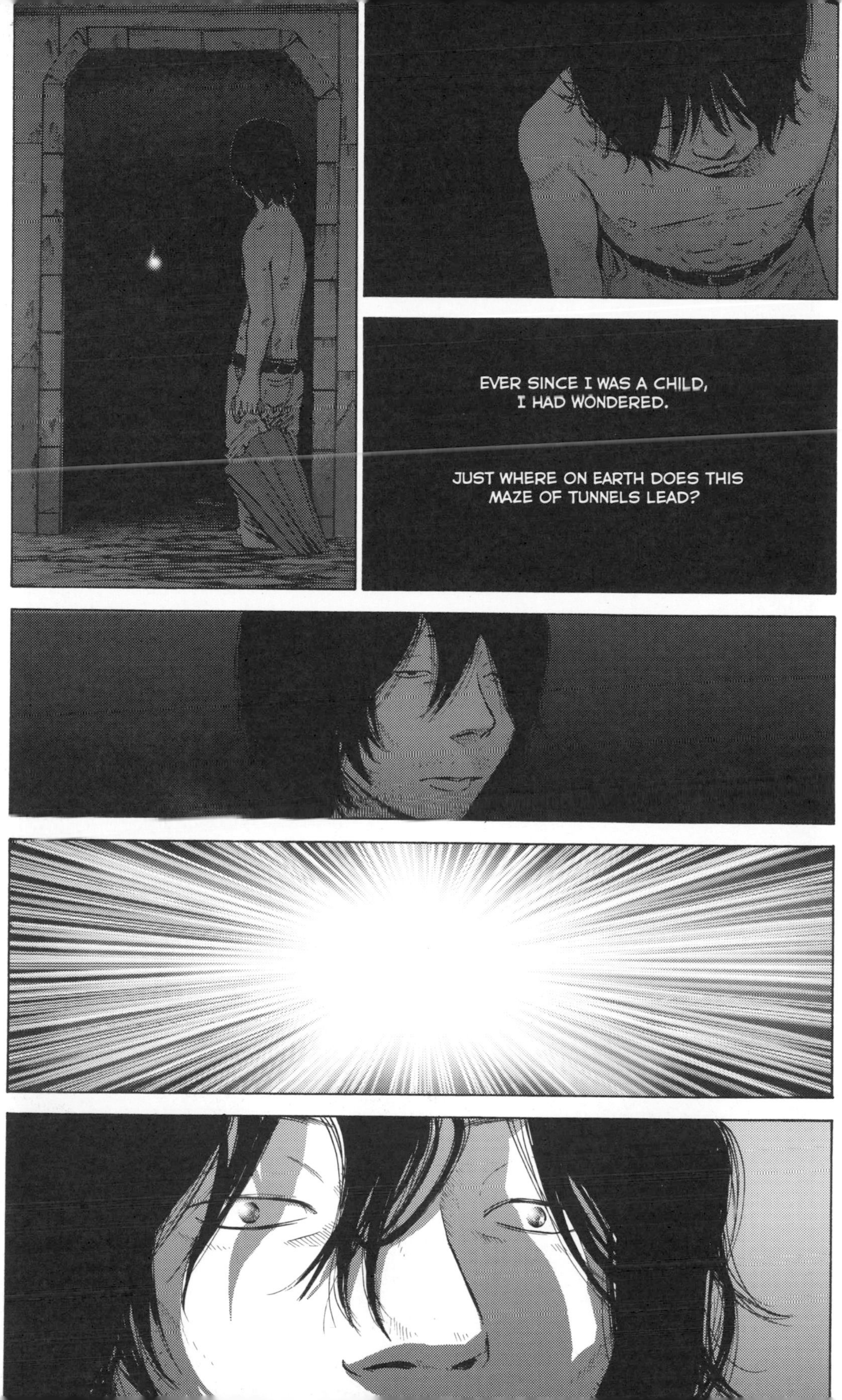
EVER SINCE I WAS A CHILD, I HAD WONDERED.
JUST WHERE ON EARTH DOES THIS MAZE OF TUNNELS LEAD?

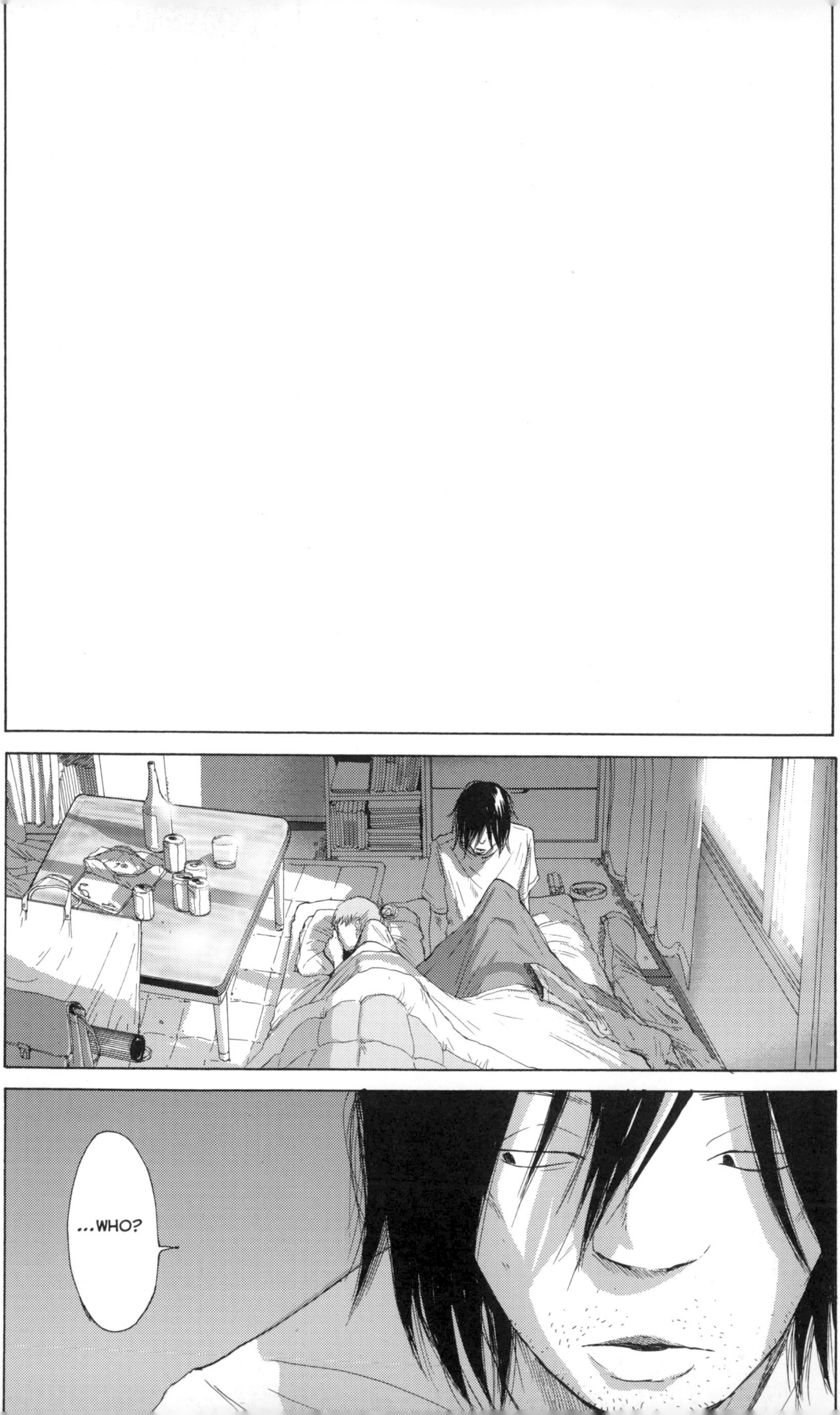
...WHO?

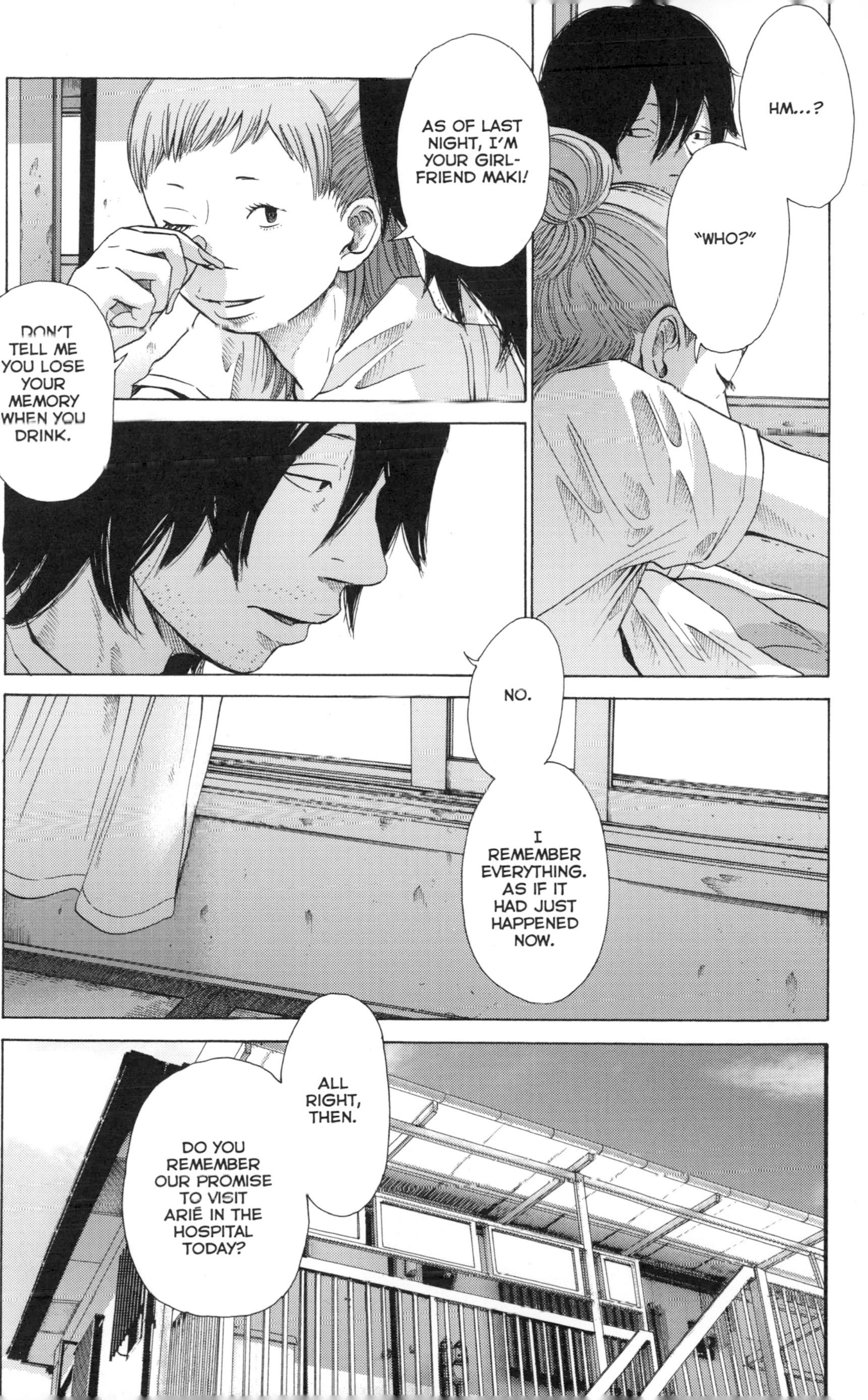
HM...?
"WHO?"
AS OF LAST NIGHT, I'M YOUR GIRL-FRIEND MAKI!
DON'T TELL ME YOU LOSE YOUR MEMORY WHEN YOU DRINK.
NO.
I REMEMBER EVERYTHING. AS IF IT HAD JUST HAPPENED NOW.
ALL RIGHT, THEN.
DO YOU REMEMBER OUR PROMISE TO VISIT ARIÉ IN THE HOSPITAL TODAY?

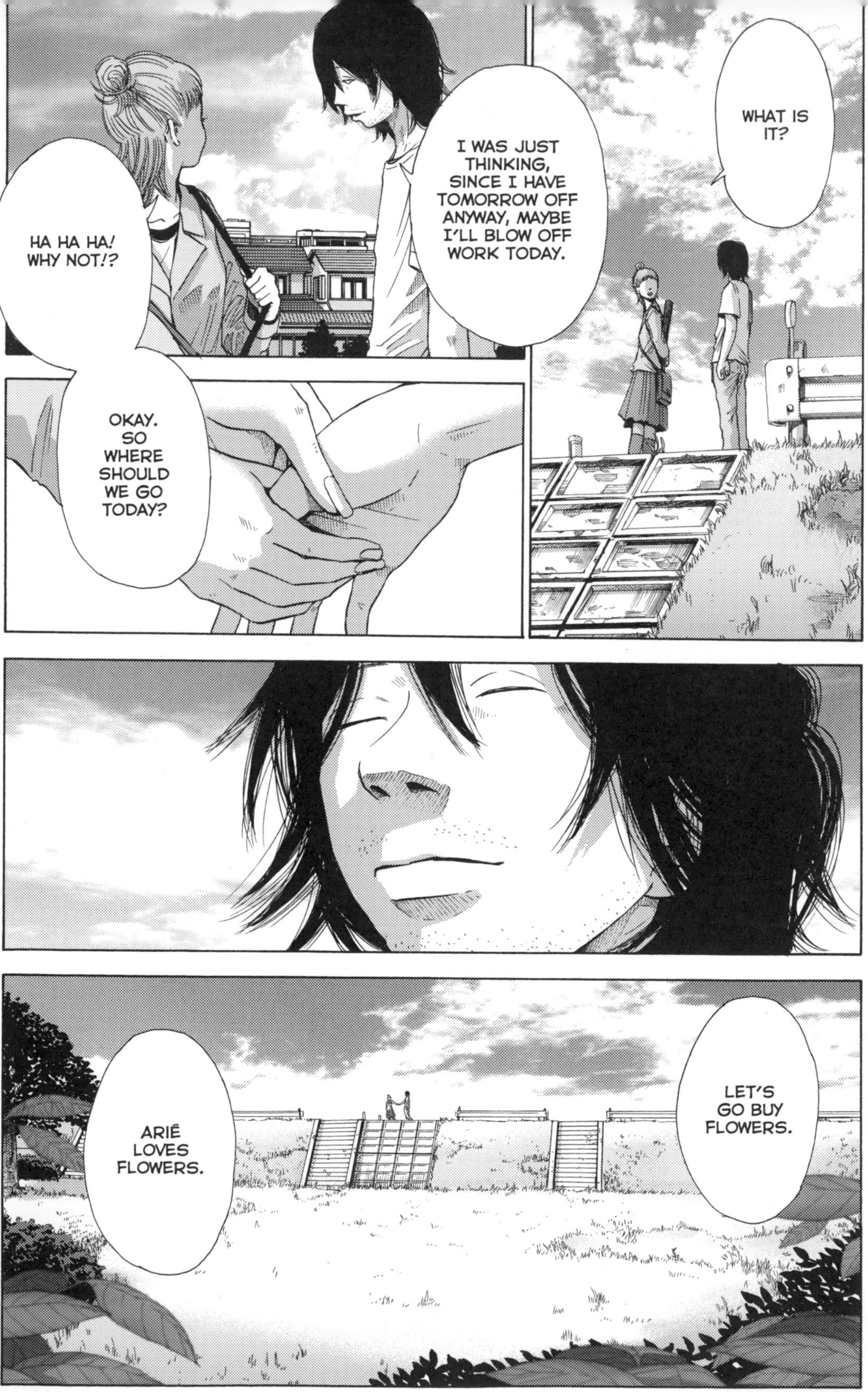
WHAT IS IT?
I WAS JUST THINKING, SINCE I HAVE TOMORROW OFF ANYWAY, MAYBE I'LL BLOW OFF WORK TODAY.
HA HA HA! WHY NOT!?
OKAY. SO WHERE SHOULD WE GO TODAY?
LET'S GO BUY FLOWERS.
ARIÉ LOVES FLOWERS.

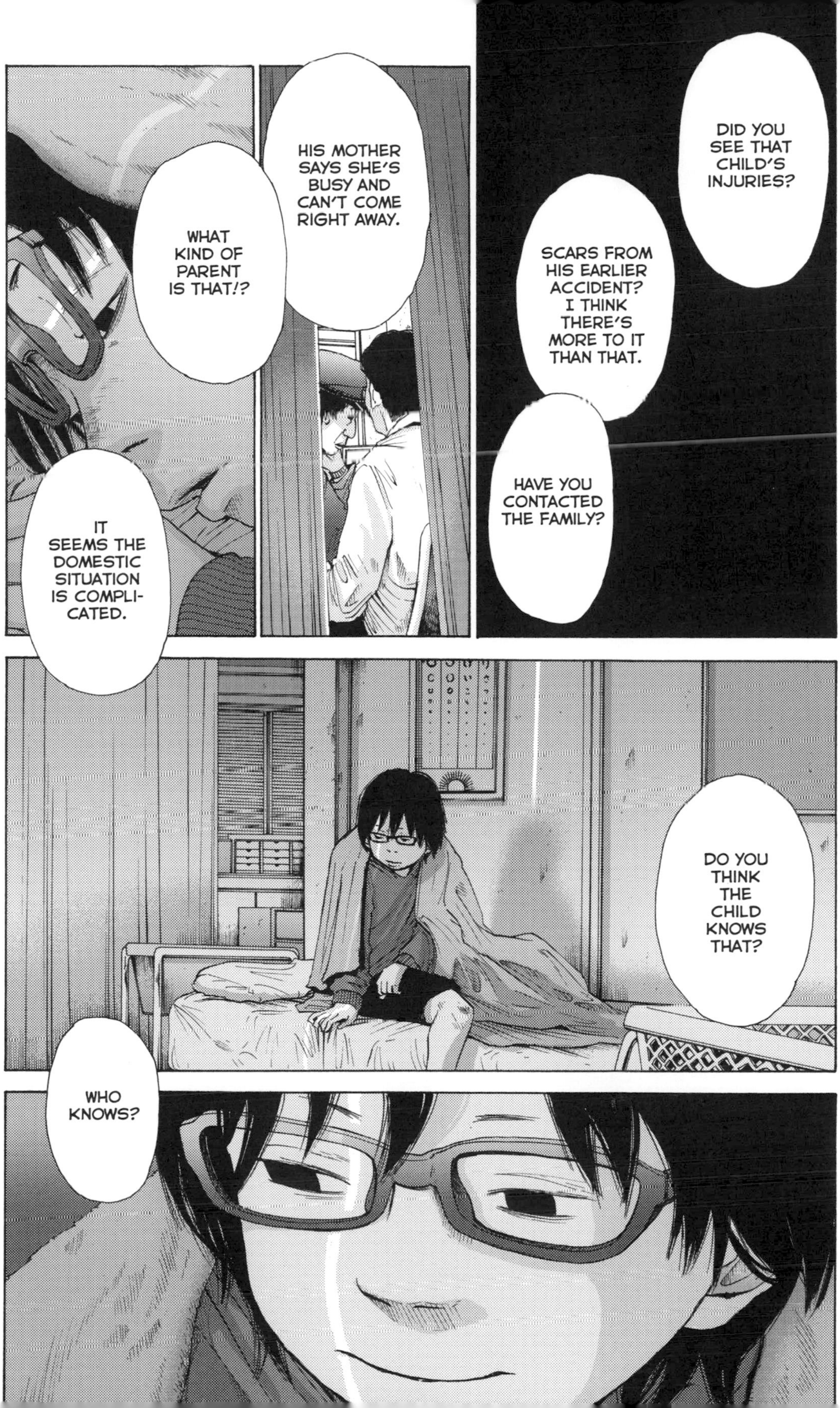
DID YOU SEE THAT CHILD'S INJURIES?
SCARS FROM HIS EARLIER ACCIDENT? I THINK THERE'S MORE TO IT THAN THAT.
HAVE YOU CONTACTED THE FAMILY?
HIS MOTHER SAYS SHE'S BUSY AND CAN'T COME RIGHT AWAY.
WHAT KIND OF PARENT IS THAT!?
IT SEEMS THE DOMESTIC SITUATION IS COMPLICATED.
DO YOU THINK THE CHILD KNOWS THAT?
WHO KNOWS?

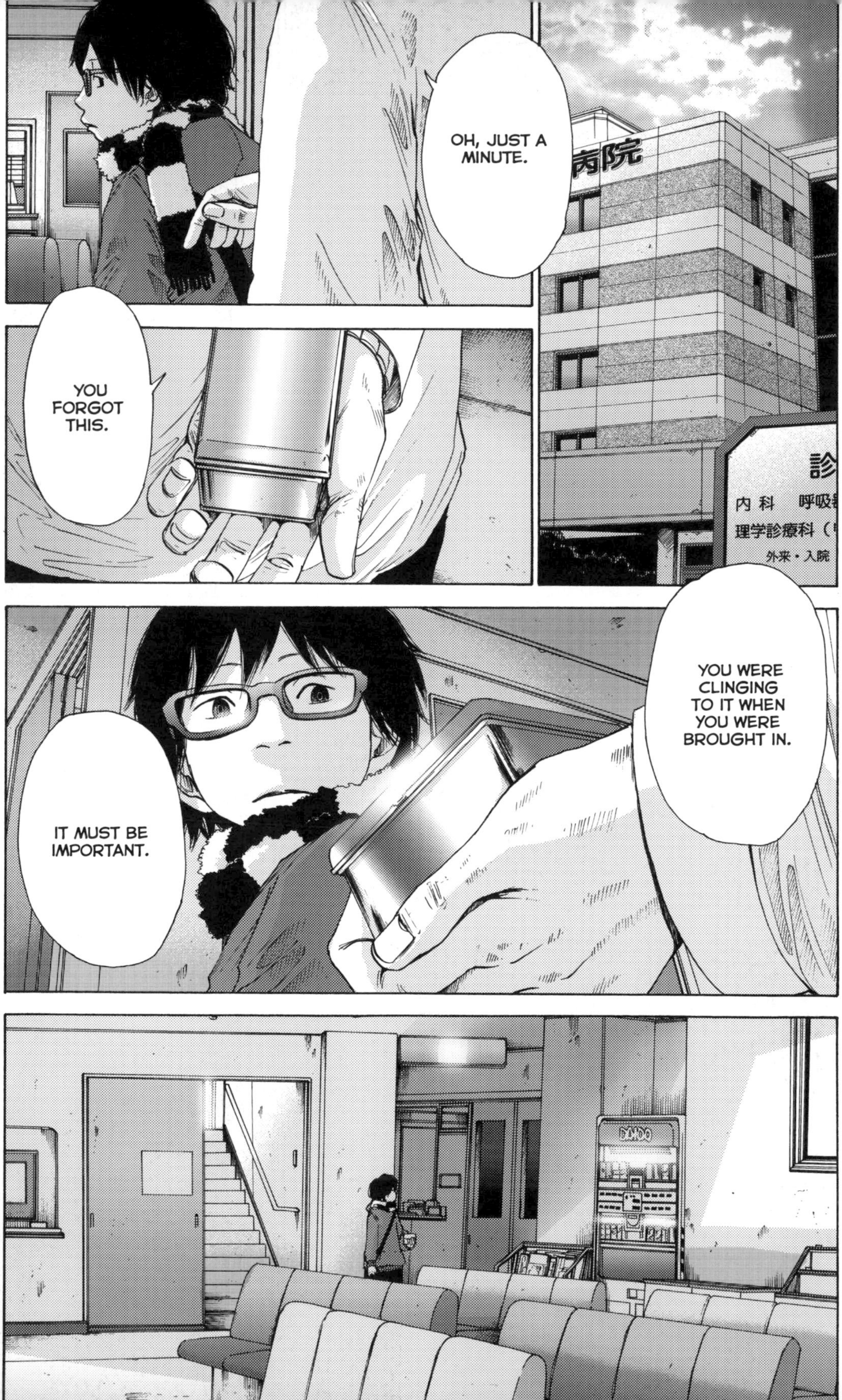
内科
理学診療科
外来・入院
OH, JUST A MINUTE.
YOU FORGOT THIS.
YOU WERE CLINGING TO IT WHEN YOU WERE BROUGHT IN.
IT MUST BE IMPORTANT.

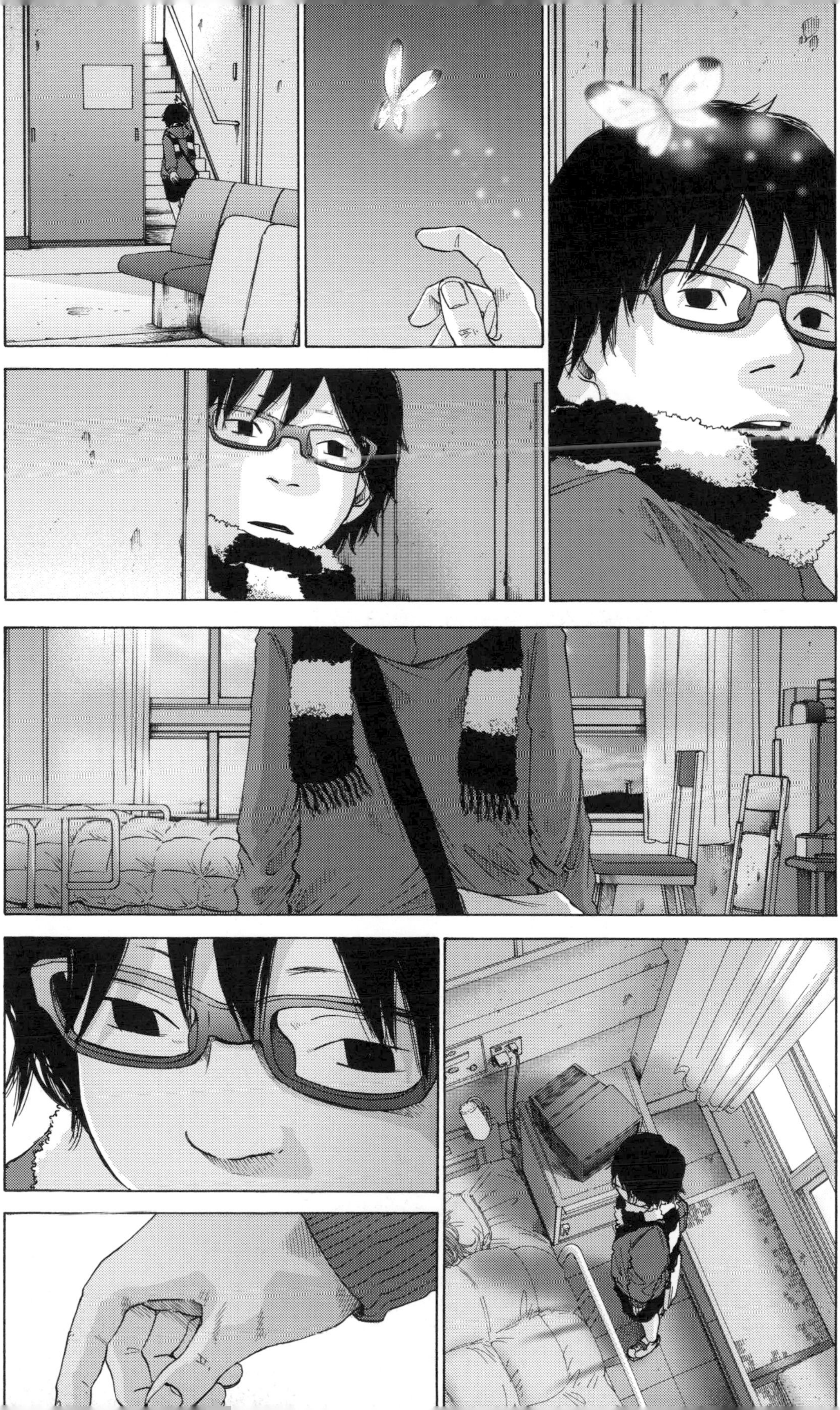

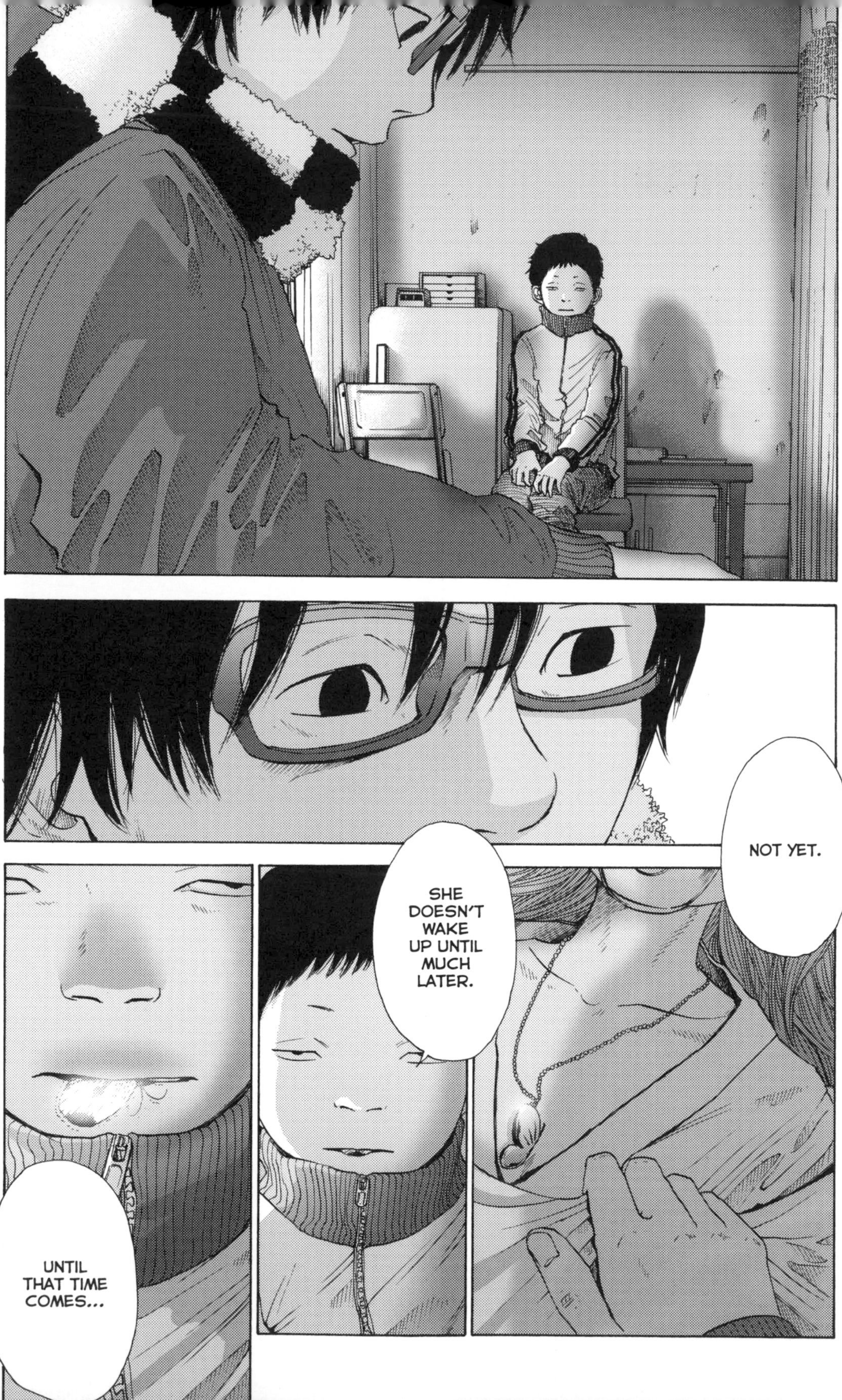
NOT YET.
SHE DOESN'T WAKE UP UNTIL MUCH LATER.
UNTIL THAT TIME COMES...

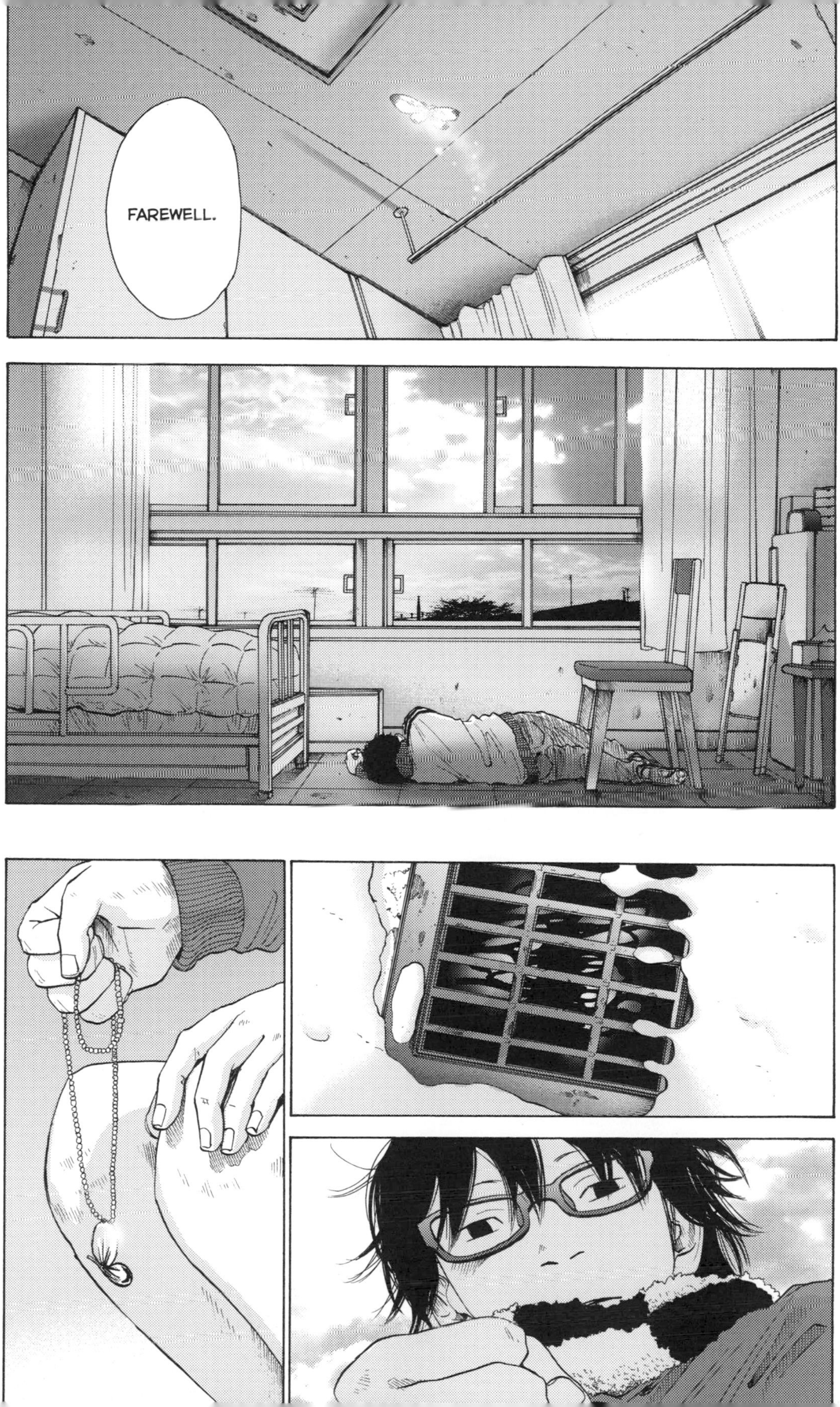
FAREWELL.

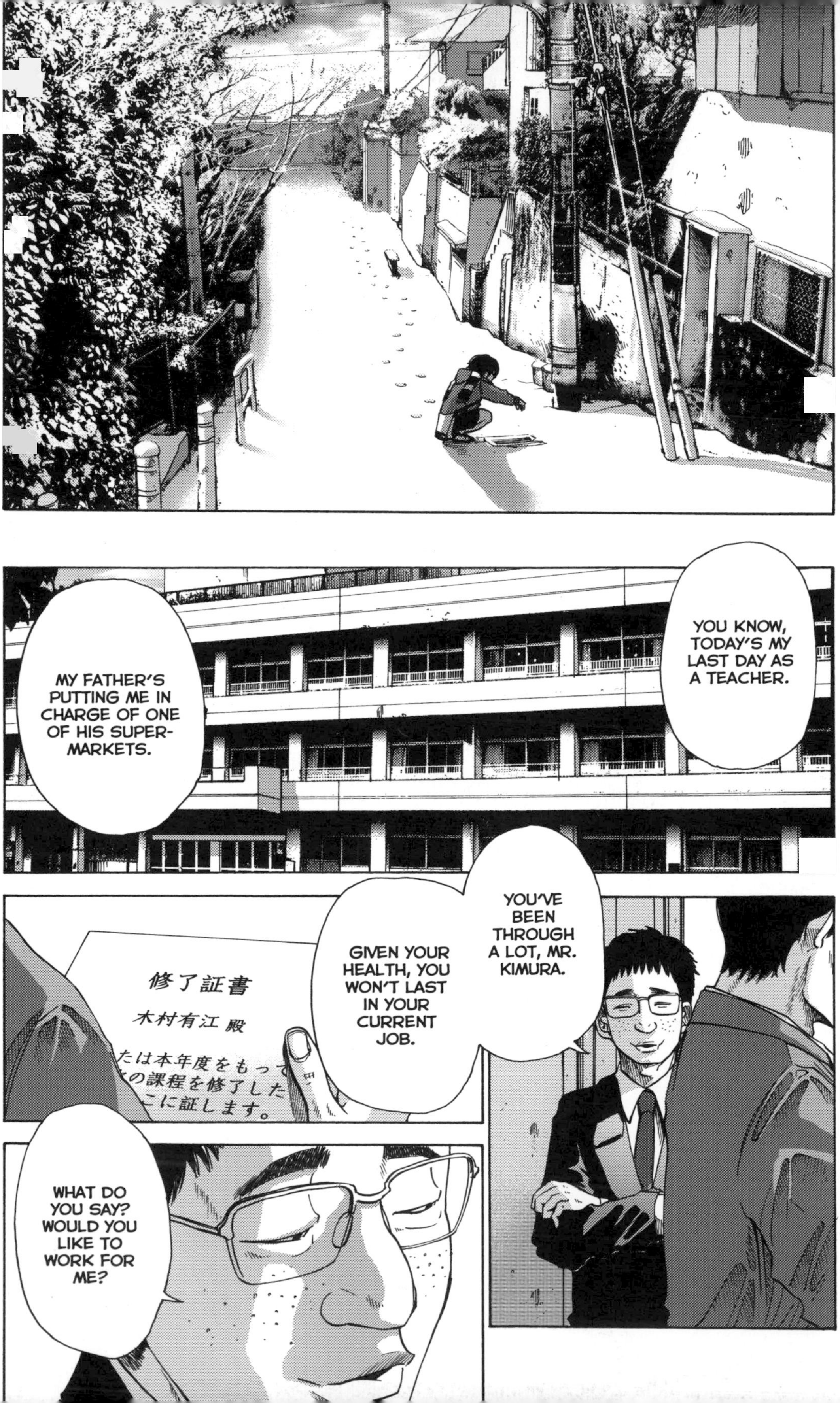
YOU KNOW, TODAY'S MY LAST DAY AS A TEACHER.
MY FATHER'S PUTTING ME IN CHARGE OF ONE OF HIS SUPER-MARKETS.
YOU'VE BEEN THROUGH A LOT, MR. KIMURA.
修了証書
木村有江 殿
GIVEN YOUR HEALTH, YOU WON'T LAST IN YOUR CURRENT JOB.
WHAT DO YOU SAY? WOULD YOU LIKE TO WORK FOR ME?

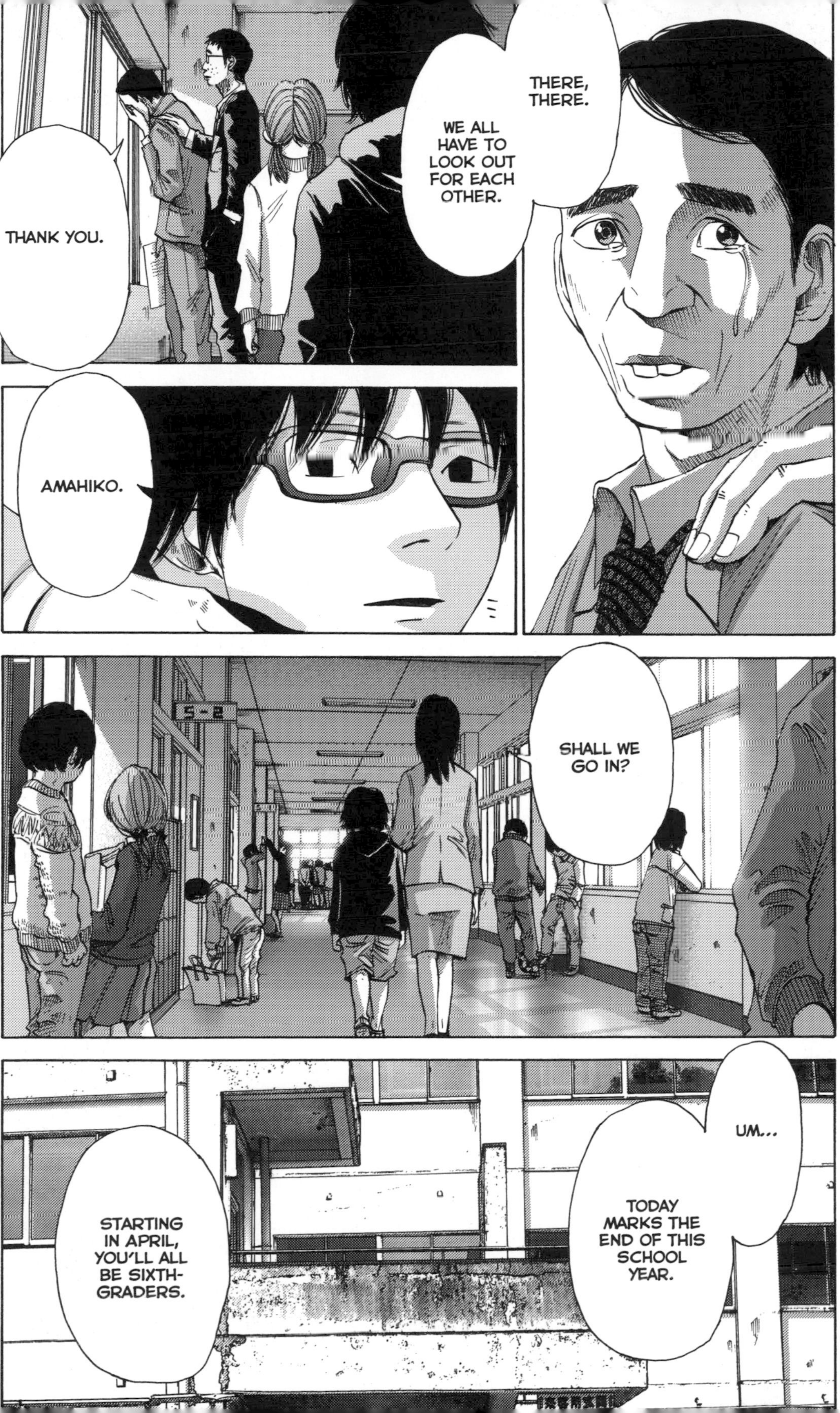
THERE, THERE.
WE ALL HAVE TO LOOK OUT FOR EACH OTHER.
THANK YOU.
AMAHIKO.
5-2
SHALL WE GO IN?
UM...
TODAY MARKS THE END OF THIS SCHOOL YEAR.
STARTING IN APRIL, YOU'LL ALL BE SIXTH-GRADERS.

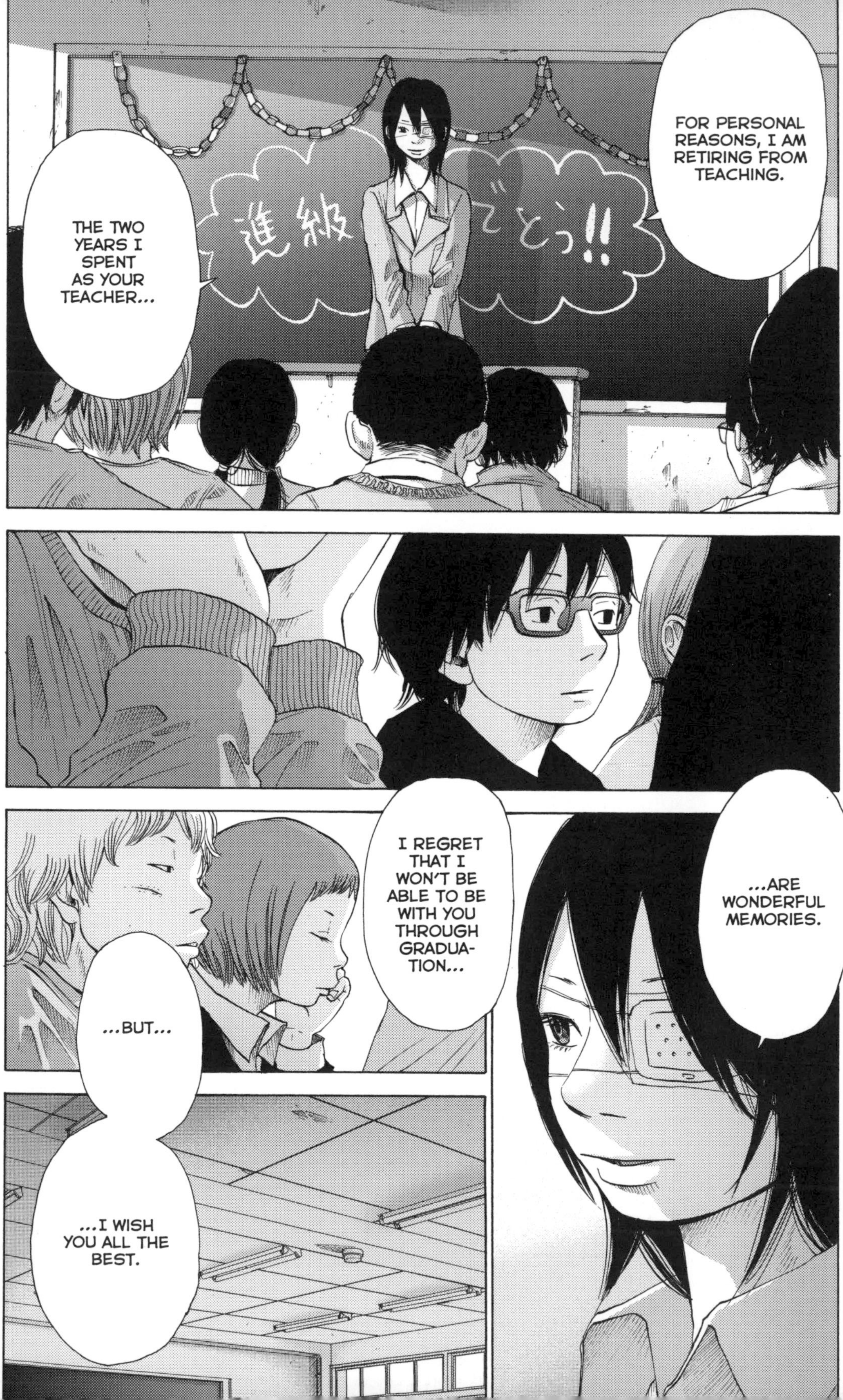
FOR PERSONAL REASONS, I AM RETIRING FROM TEACHING.
進級 でとっ!!
THE TWO YEARS I SPENT AS YOUR TEACHER...
...ARE WONDERFUL MEMORIES.
I REGRET THAT I WON'T BE ABLE TO BE WITH YOU THROUGH GRADUA-TION...
...BUT...
...I WISH YOU ALL THE BEST.

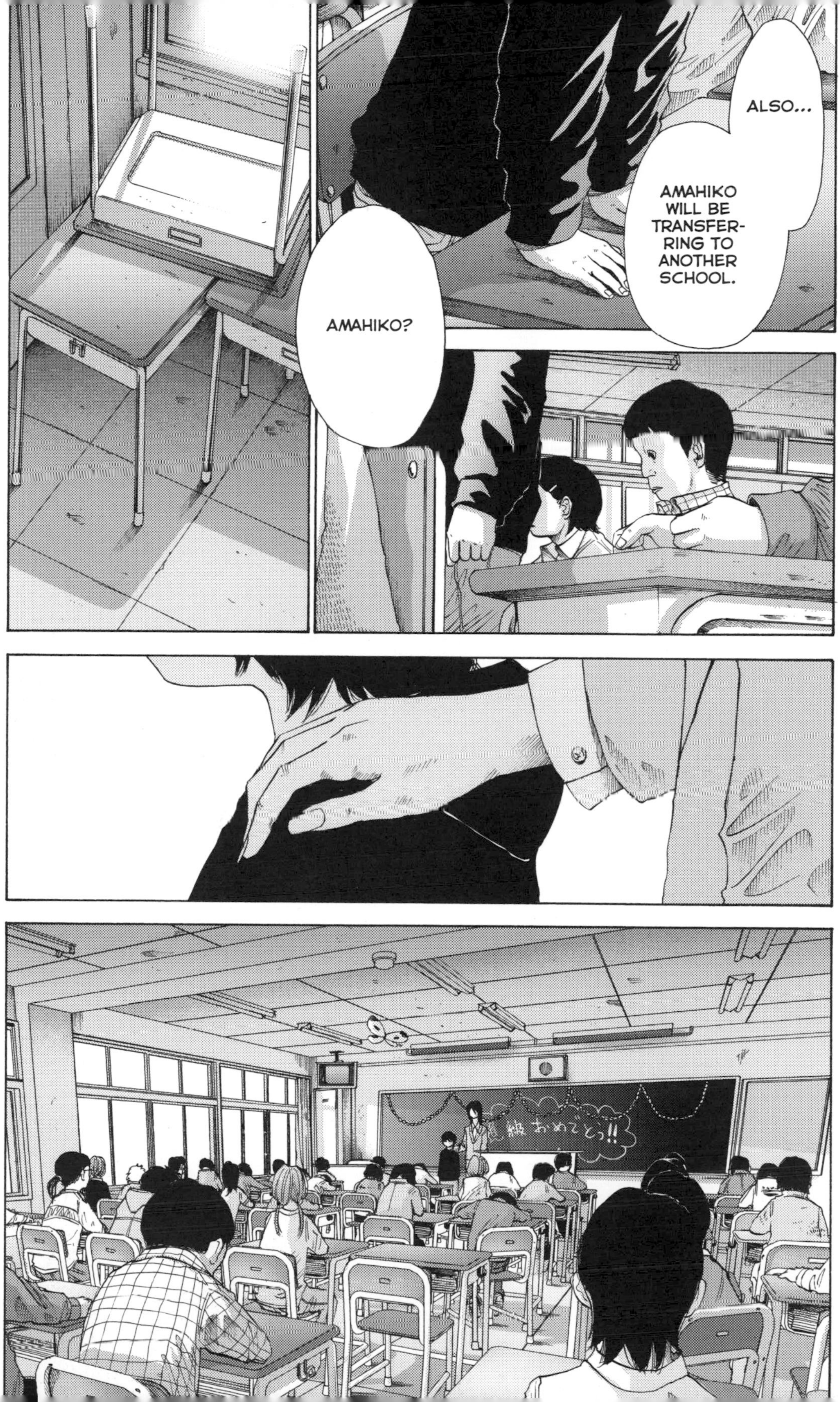
ALSO...
AMAHIKO WILL BE TRANSFER-RING TO ANOTHER SCHOOL.
AMAHIKO?

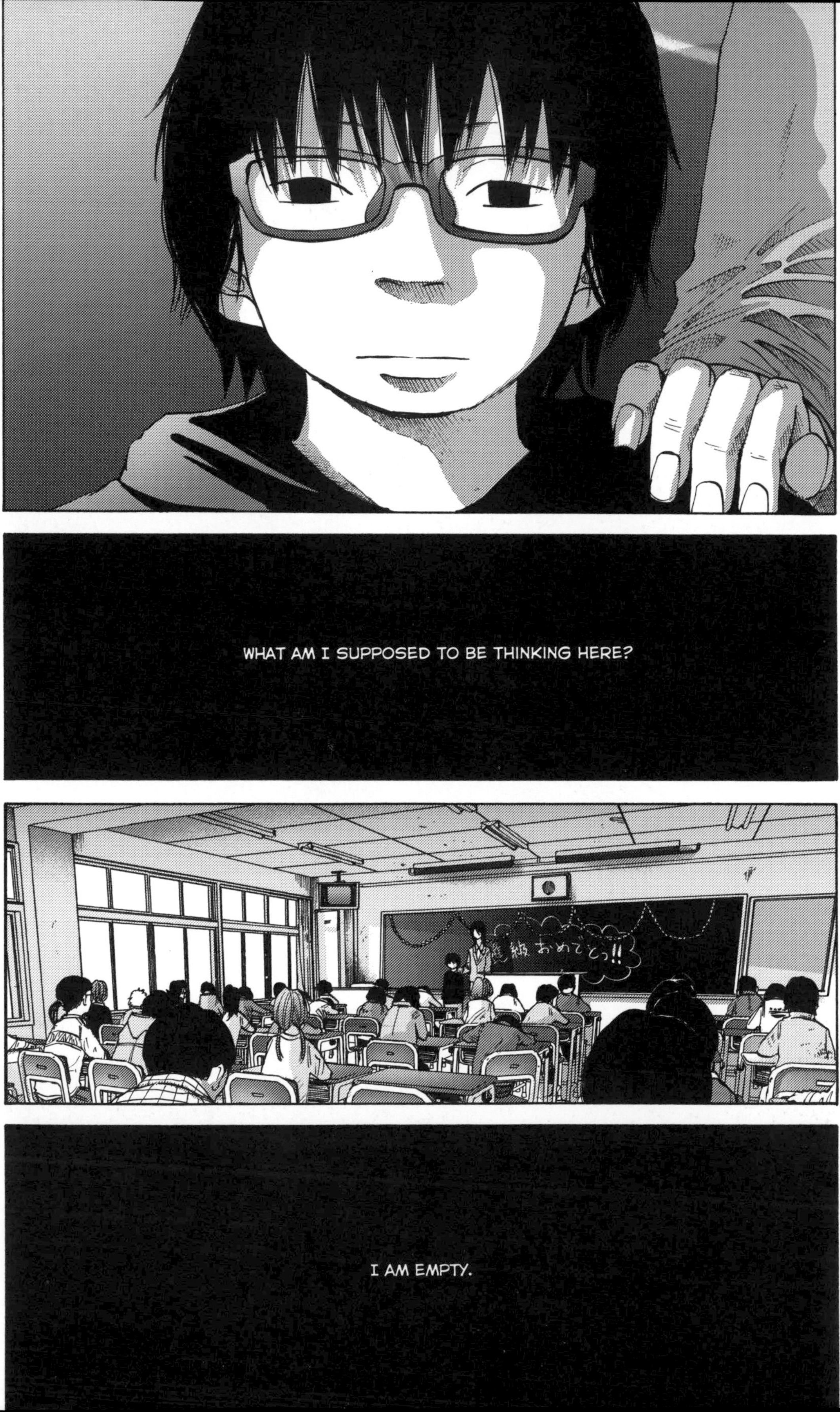
WHAT AM I SUPPOSED TO BE THINKING HERE?
I AM EMPTY.

THE SUNSET THAT DAY

WAS REDDER THAN USUAL.

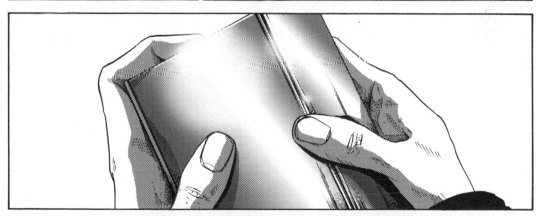

IN THIS BOX IS MAGIC THAT WILL GRANT JUST ONE WISH.
ANY WISH.

IF I WANTED TO

I COULD END THE WORLD RIGHT NOW.

THESE ARE MY
MEMORIES OF
WHEN I WAS TEN
YEARS OLD.

I HAVEN'T GOT A
CLUE WHAT I DID
WITH THAT TIN BOX
ON THAT DAY, OR
EVEN WHERE IT IS
NOW.

BUT OBVIOUSLY THE
WORLD HASN'T ENDED.

AND THIS BARREN
WORLD IS NOT MUCH
DIFFERENT NOW FROM
WHAT IT WAS THEN.

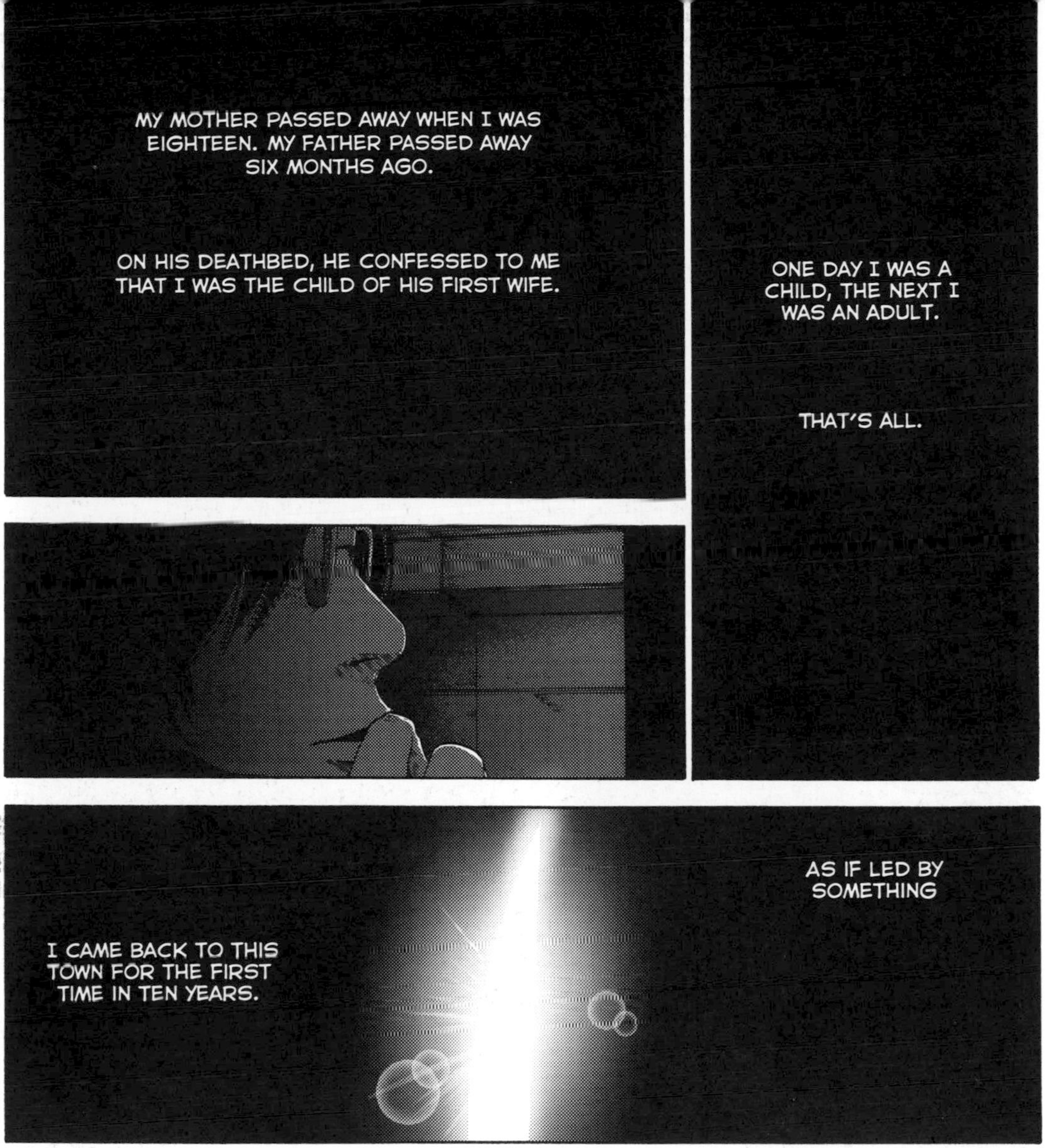
ONE DAY I WAS A CHILD, THE NEXT I WAS AN ADULT.
THAT'S ALL.
MY MOTHER PASSED AWAY WHEN I WAS EIGHTEEN. MY FATHER PASSED AWAY SIX MONTHS AGO.
ON HIS DEATHBED, HE CONFESSED TO ME THAT I WAS THE CHILD OF HIS FIRST WIFE.
AS IF LED BY SOMETHING
I CAME BACK TO THIS TOWN FOR THE FIRST TIME IN TEN YEARS.

CHAPTER 11

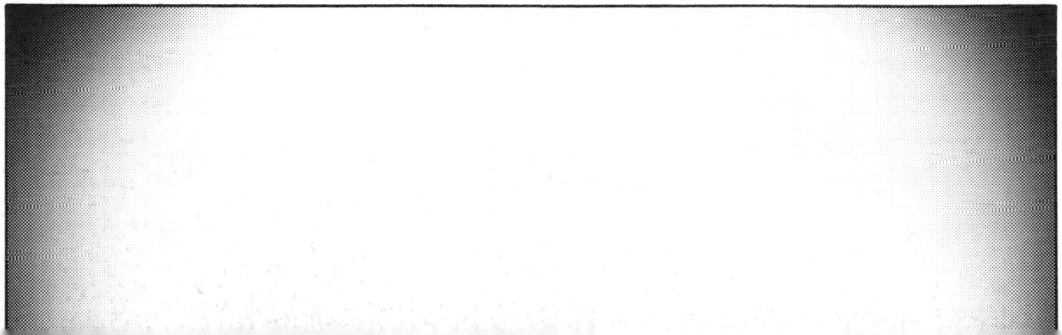

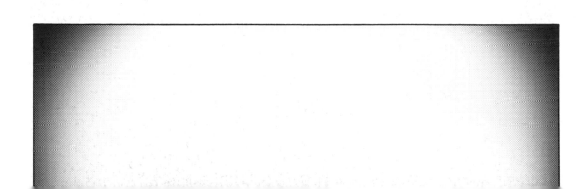

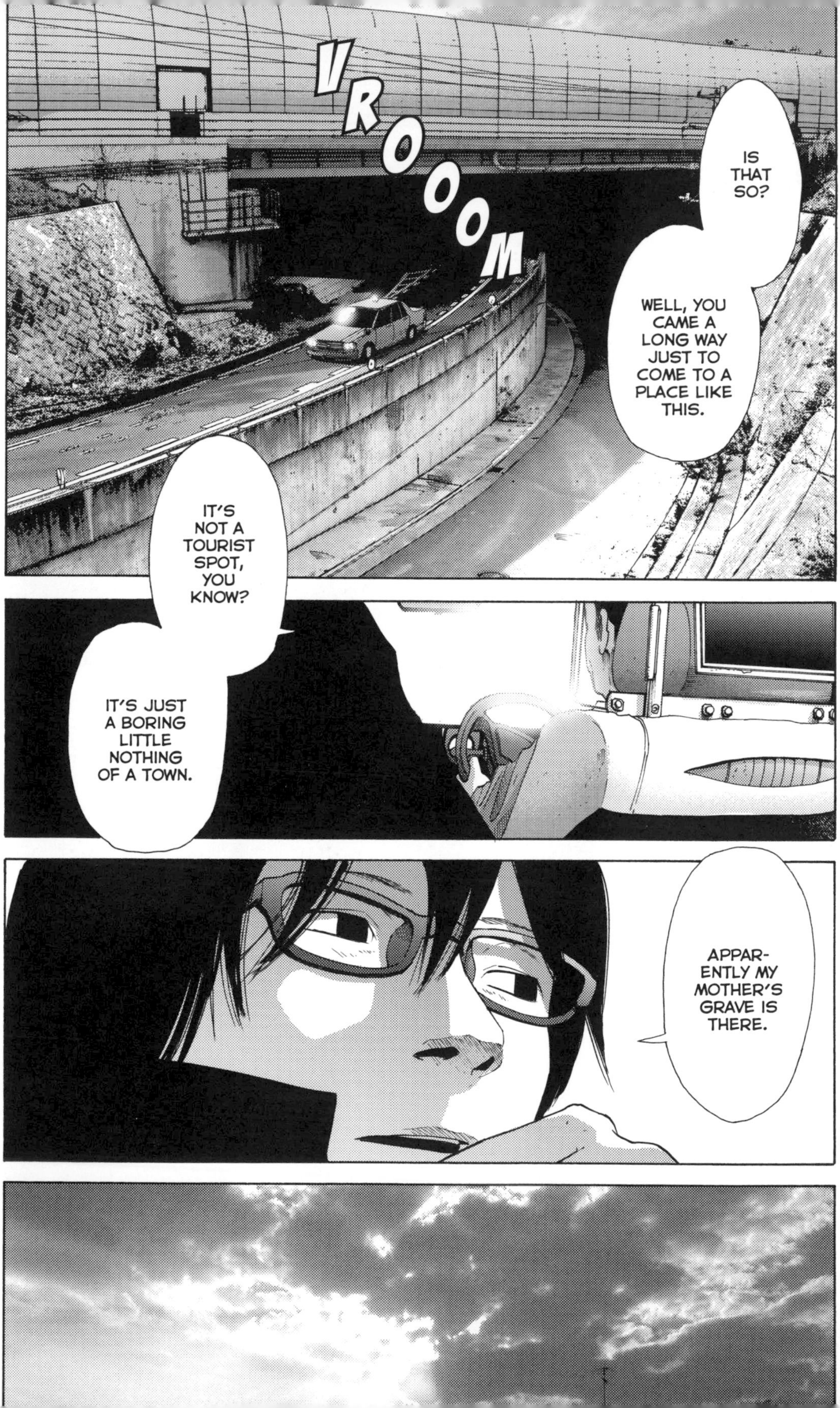
IS THAT SO?
WELL, YOU CAME A LONG WAY JUST TO COME TO A PLACE LIKE THIS.
VROOOM
IT'S NOT A TOURIST SPOT, YOU KNOW?
IT'S JUST A BORING LITTLE NOTHING OF A TOWN.
APPAR-ENTLY MY MOTHER'S GRAVE IS THERE.

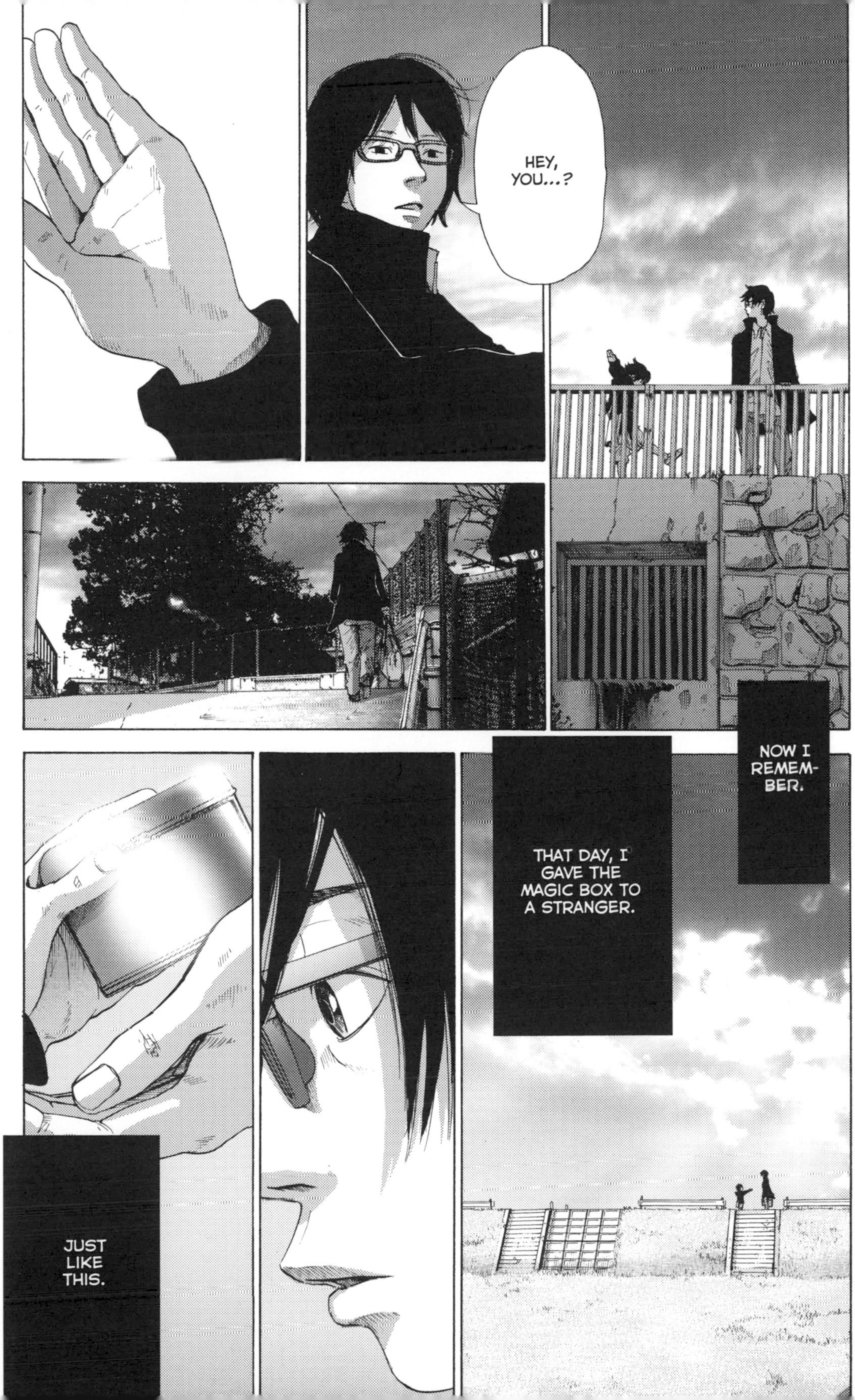
NOW I REMEMBER.
HEY, YOU...?
THAT DAY, I GAVE THE MAGIC BOX TO A STRANGER.
JUST LIKE THIS.

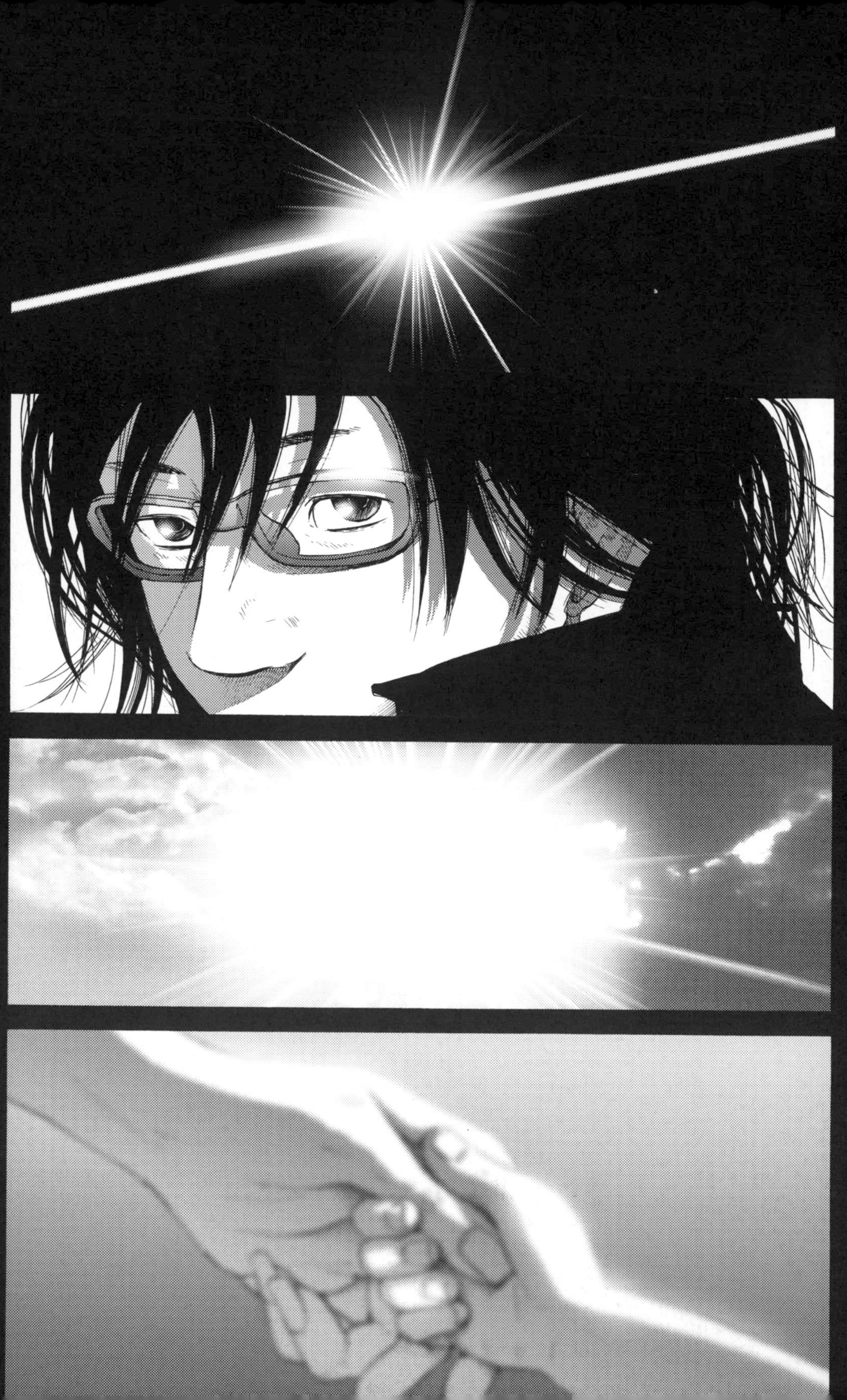

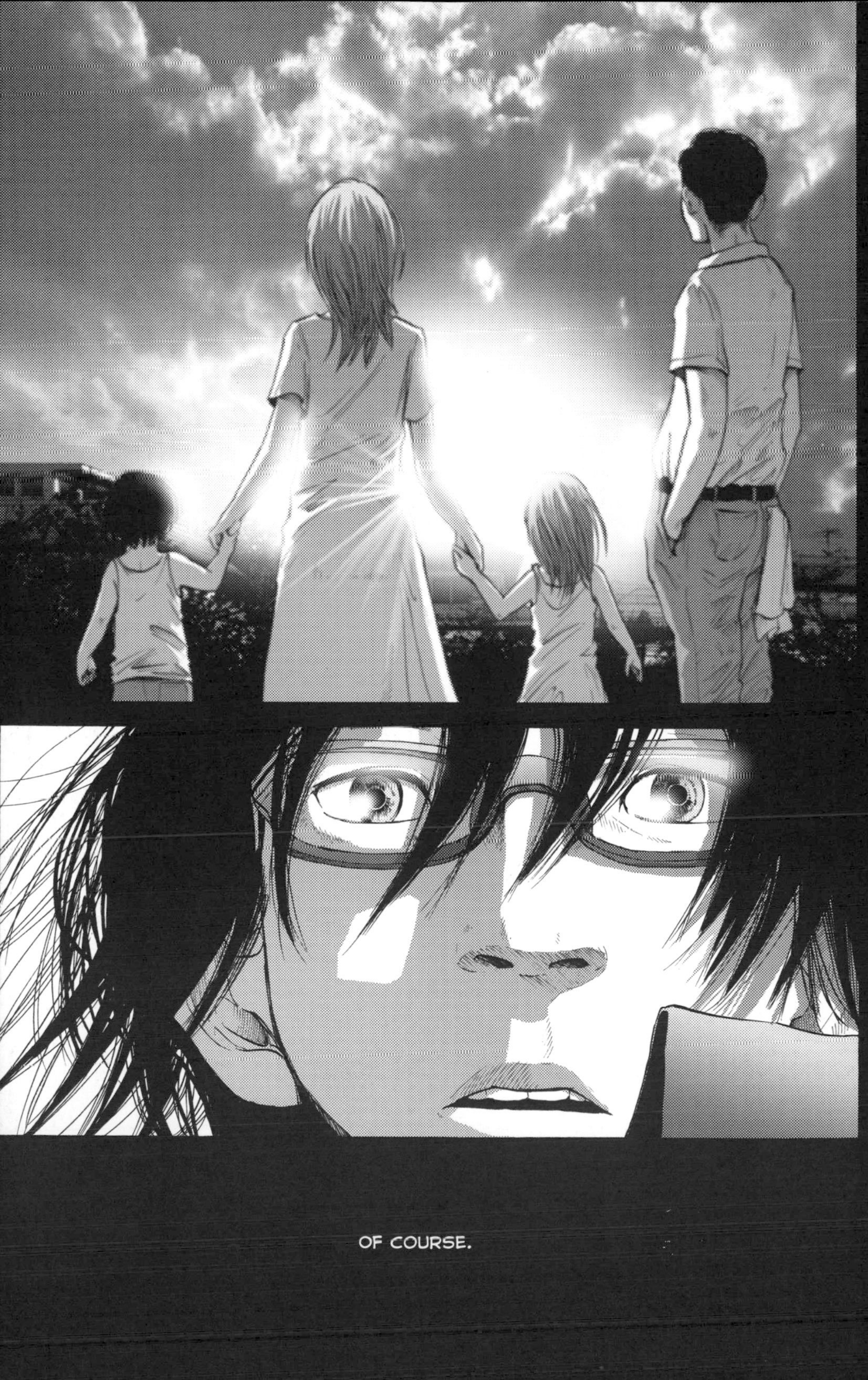
OF COURSE.

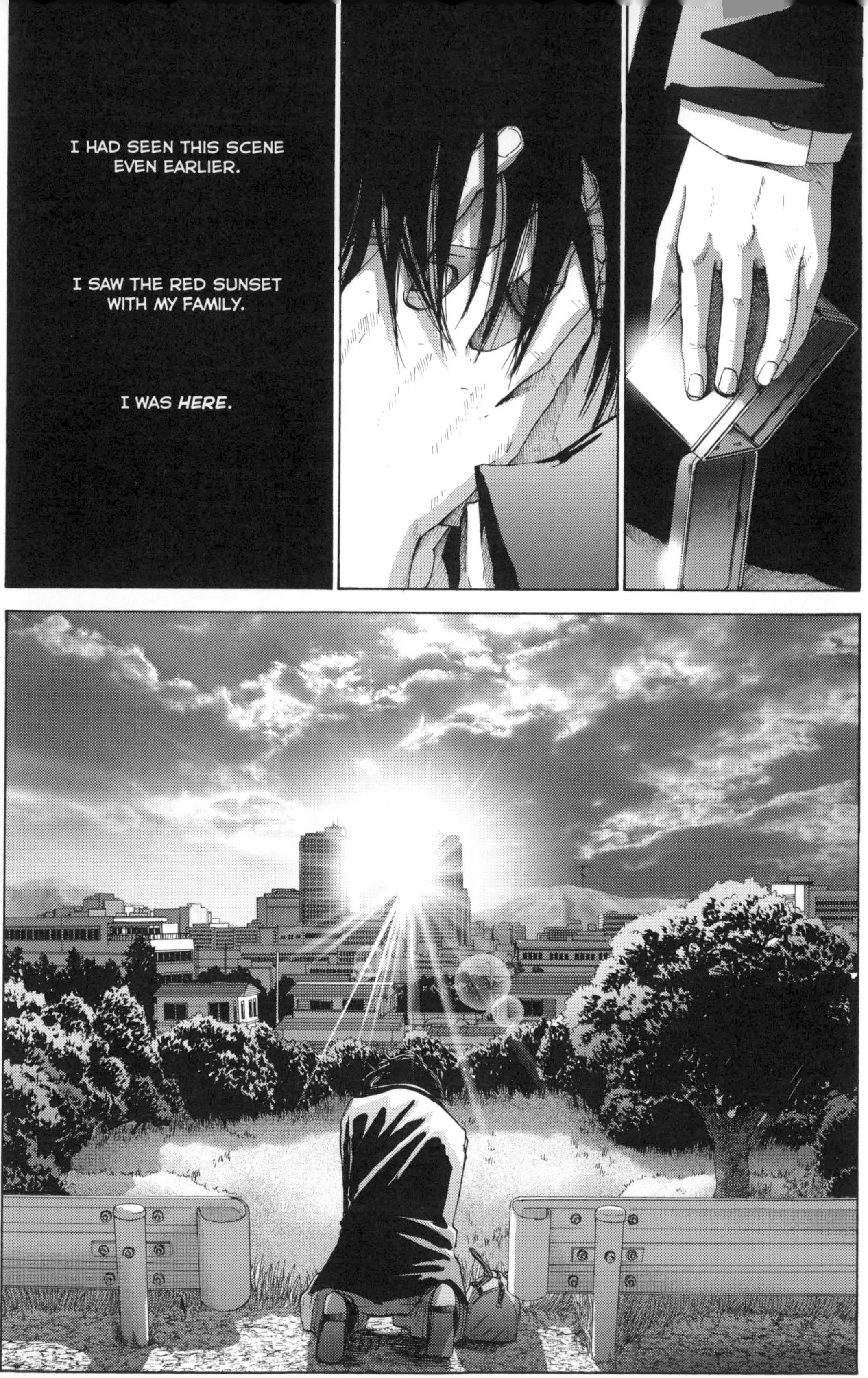
I HAD SEEN THIS SCENE EVEN EARLIER.
I SAW THE RED SUNSET WITH MY FAMILY.
I WAS *HERE*.

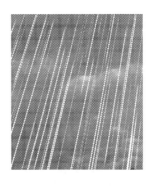

MY FEET STOPPED BEFORE THAT GRAVE SO NATURALLY.

I COULD NOT BE SURE THAT IT WAS MY MOTHER'S GRAVE

AND YET I FELT SOME INCONGRUITY.

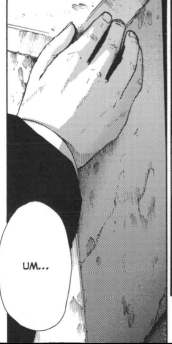

UM...

THE UPPER RIGHT
CORNER OF THE
MEMORIAL STONE
WAS MISSING,
AND UNNATURALLY
ROUNDED.

EXCUSE ME.

IT'S RUDE OF ME TO ASK SOMETHING LIKE THIS OUT OF THE BLUE...

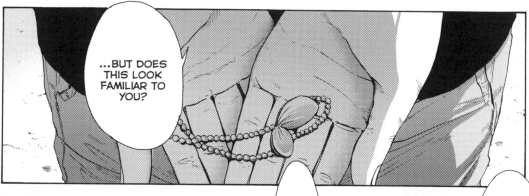

...BUT DOES THIS LOOK FAMILIAR TO YOU?

I GUESS IT DOES.

...UM...

AH...

I DON'T REALLY UNDERSTAND...

...BUT I THINK YOU SHOULD PROBABLY HAVE THIS.

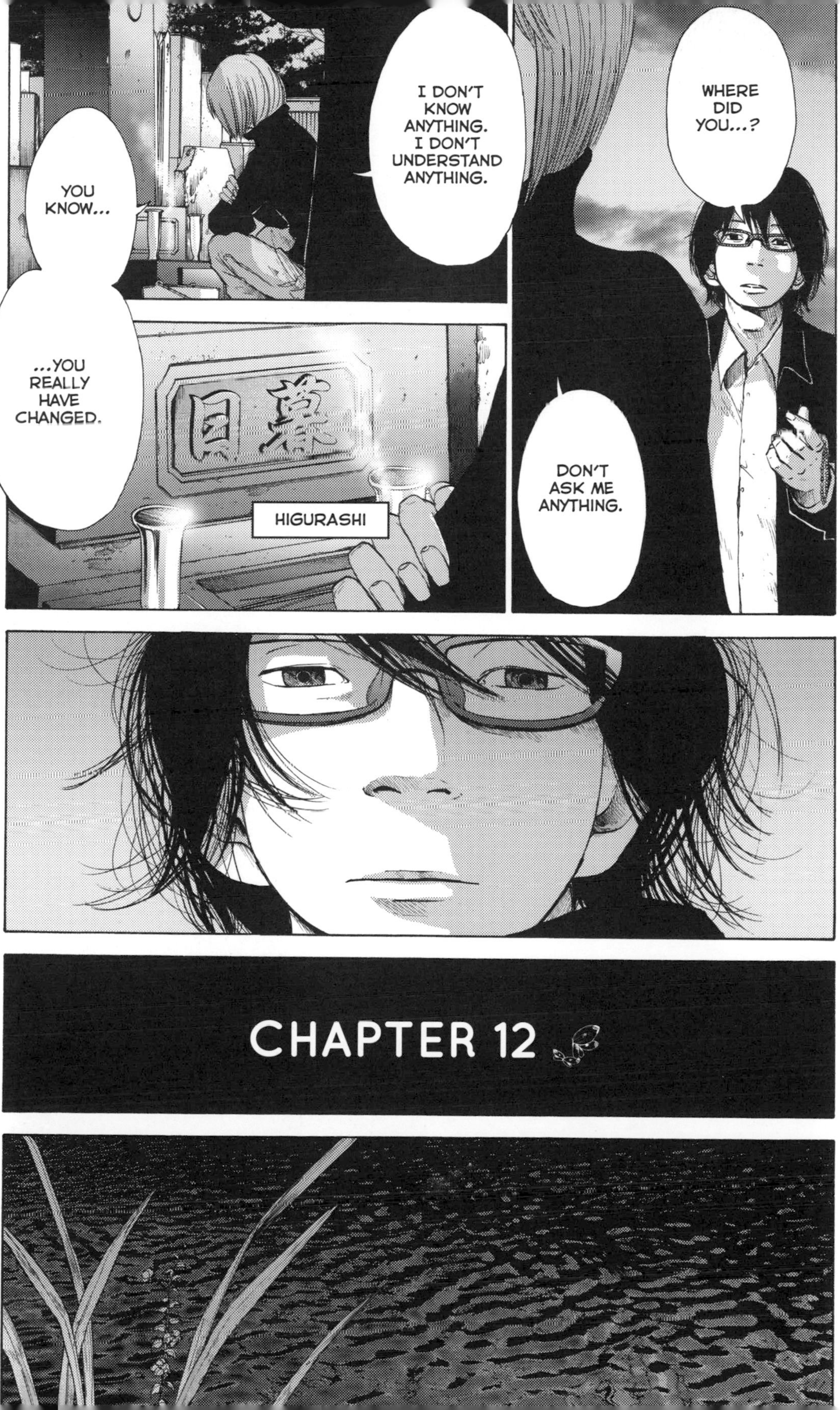
WHERE DID YOU...?
DON'T ASK ME ANYTHING.
I DON'T KNOW ANYTHING. I DON'T UNDERSTAND ANYTHING.
YOU KNOW...
...YOU REALLY HAVE CHANGED.
日暮
HIGURASHI
CHAPTER 12

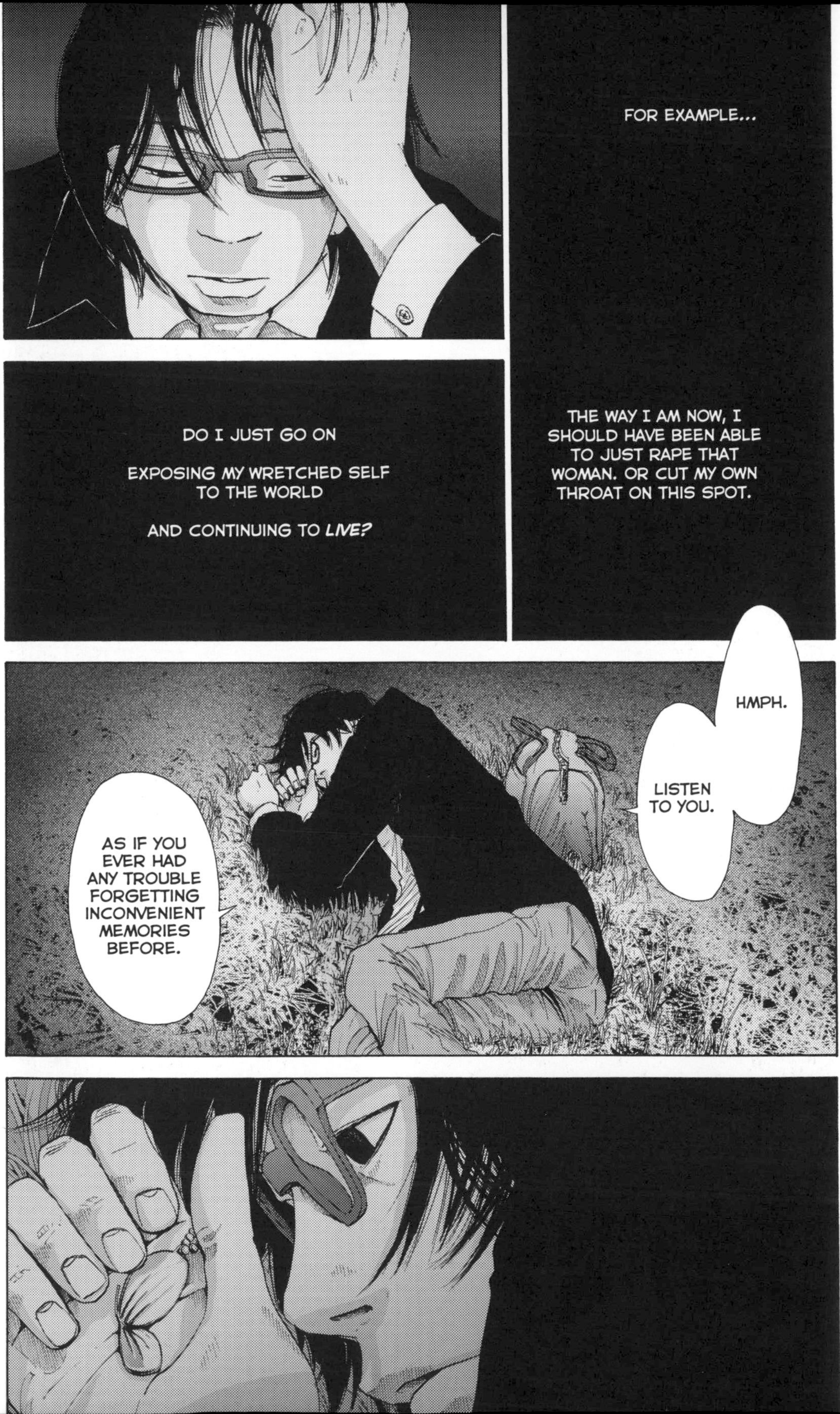
FOR EXAMPLE...
THE WAY I AM NOW, I SHOULD HAVE BEEN ABLE TO JUST RAPE THAT WOMAN. OR CUT MY OWN THROAT ON THIS SPOT.
DO I JUST GO ON
EXPOSING MY WRETCHED SELF TO THE WORLD
AND CONTINUING TO *LIVE?*
HMPH.
LISTEN TO YOU.
AS IF YOU EVER HAD ANY TROUBLE FORGETTING INCONVENIENT MEMORIES BEFORE.

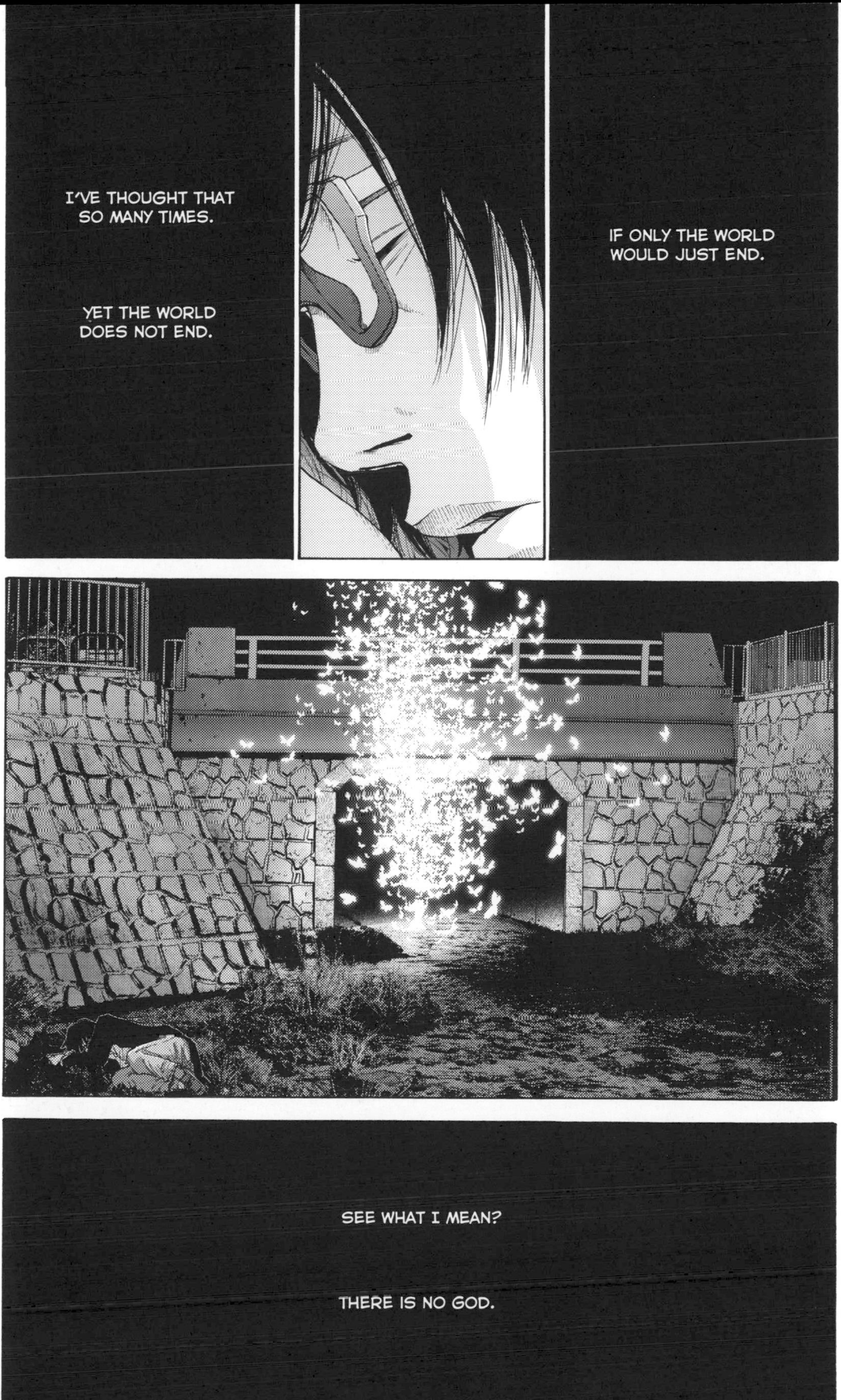
IF ONLY THE WORLD WOULD JUST END.
I'VE THOUGHT THAT SO MANY TIMES.
YET THE WORLD DOES NOT END.
SEE WHAT I MEAN?
THERE IS NO GOD.

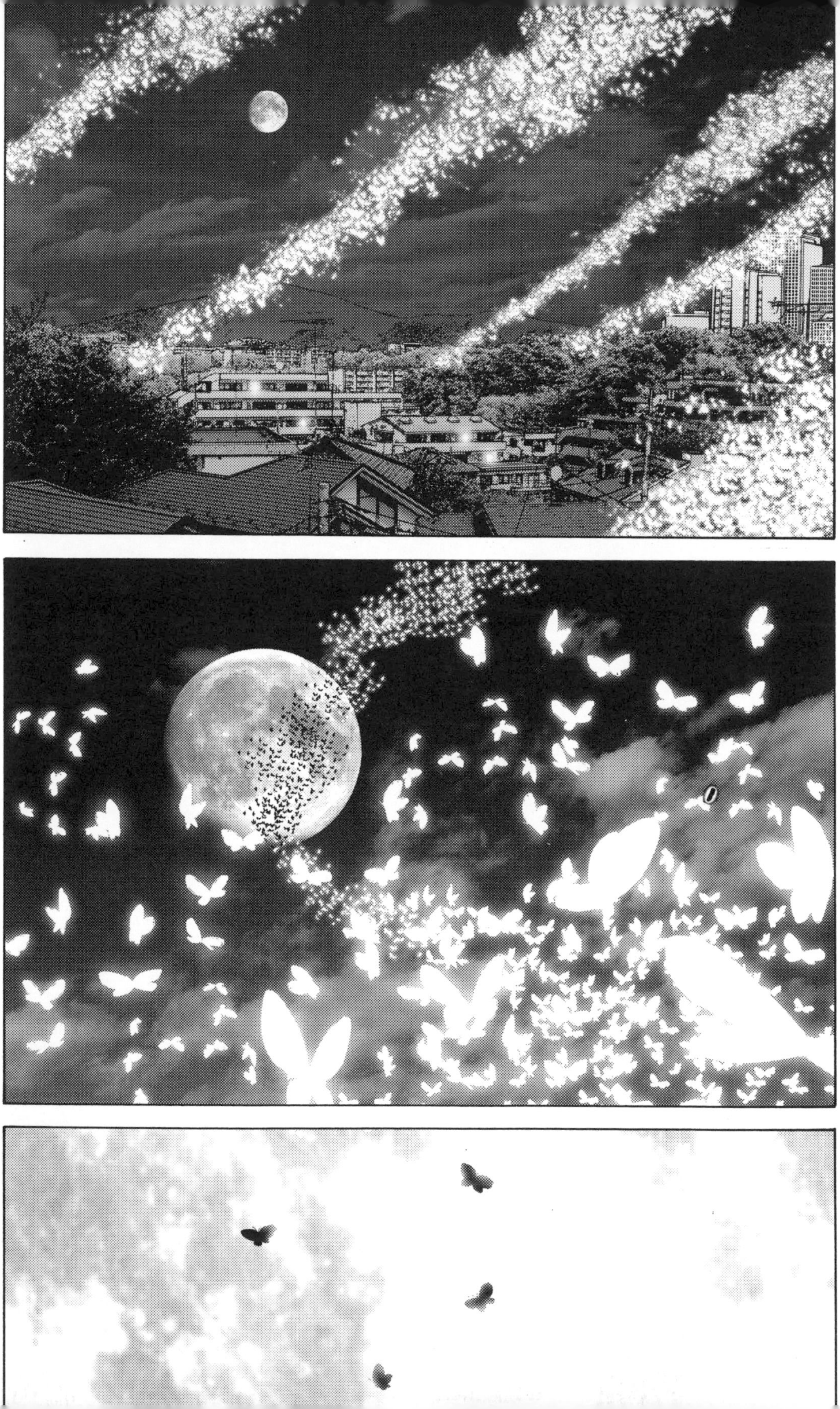

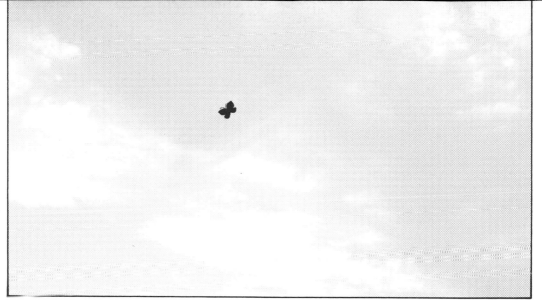

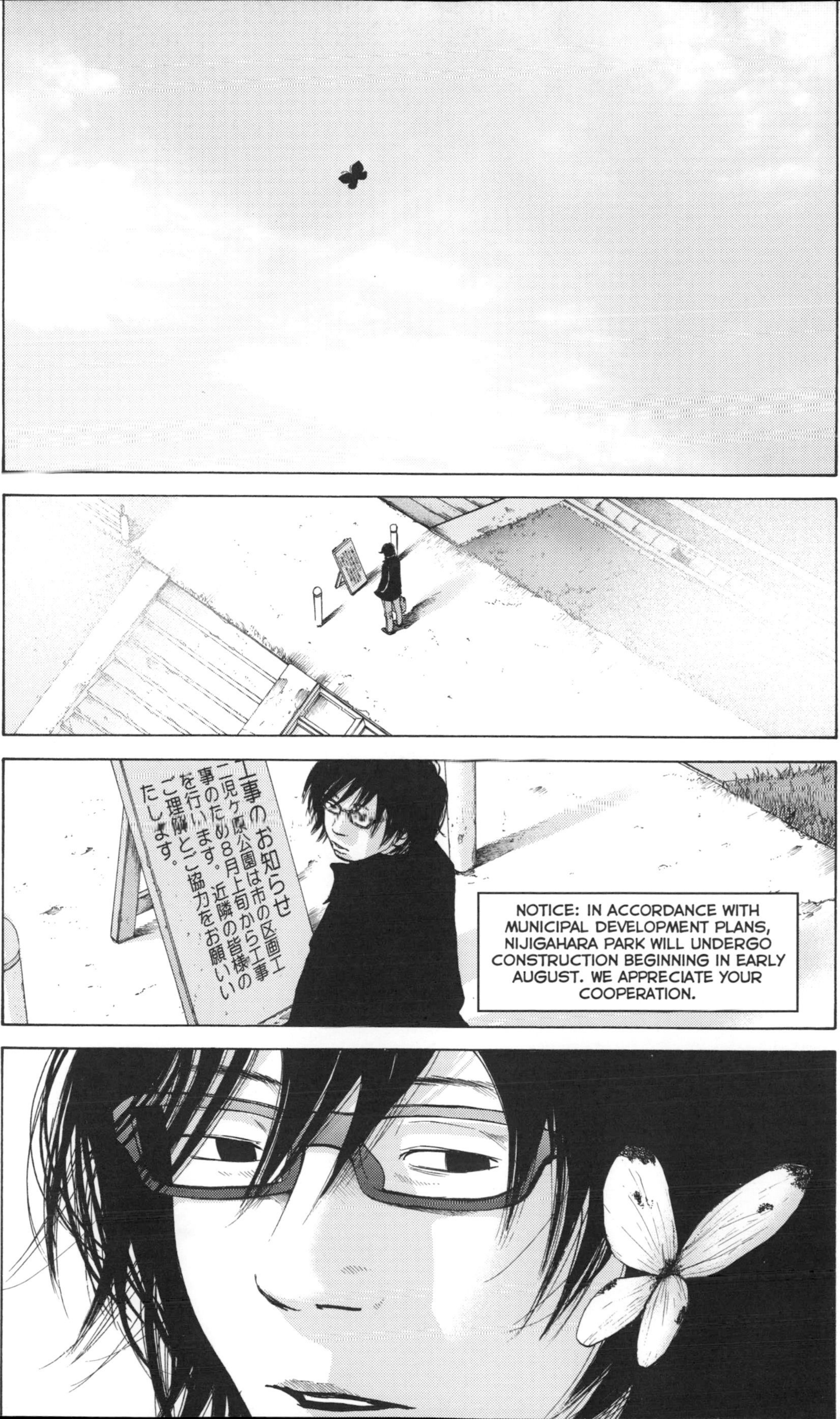
工事のお知らせ
二児ケ原公園は市の区画工事のため8月上旬から工事を行います。近隣の皆様のご理解とご協力をお願いいたします。
NOTICE: IN ACCORDANCE WITH MUNICIPAL DEVELOPMENT PLANS, NIJIGAHARA PARK WILL UNDERGO CONSTRUCTION BEGINNING IN EARLY AUGUST. WE APPRECIATE YOUR COOPERATION.

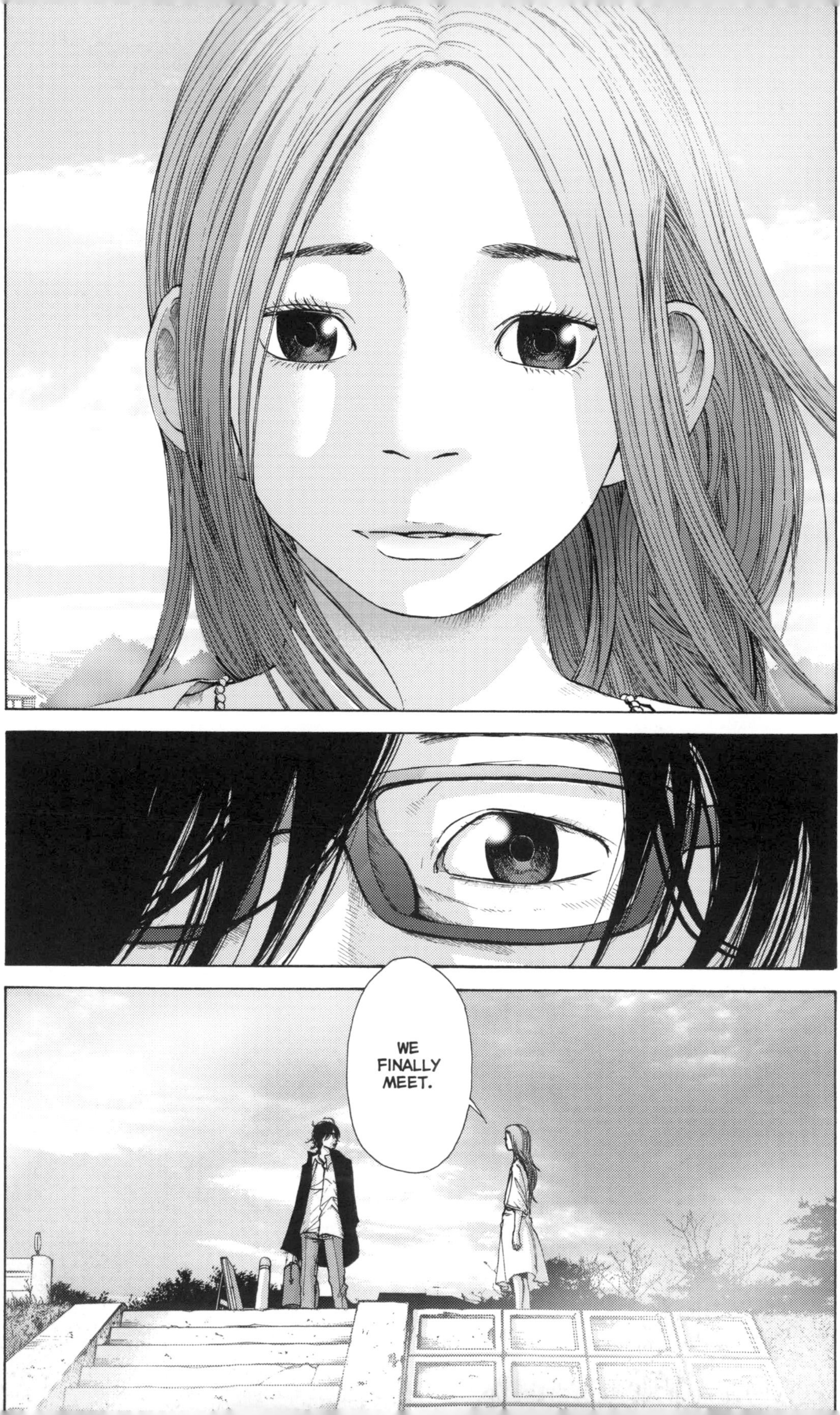
WE FINALLY MEET.

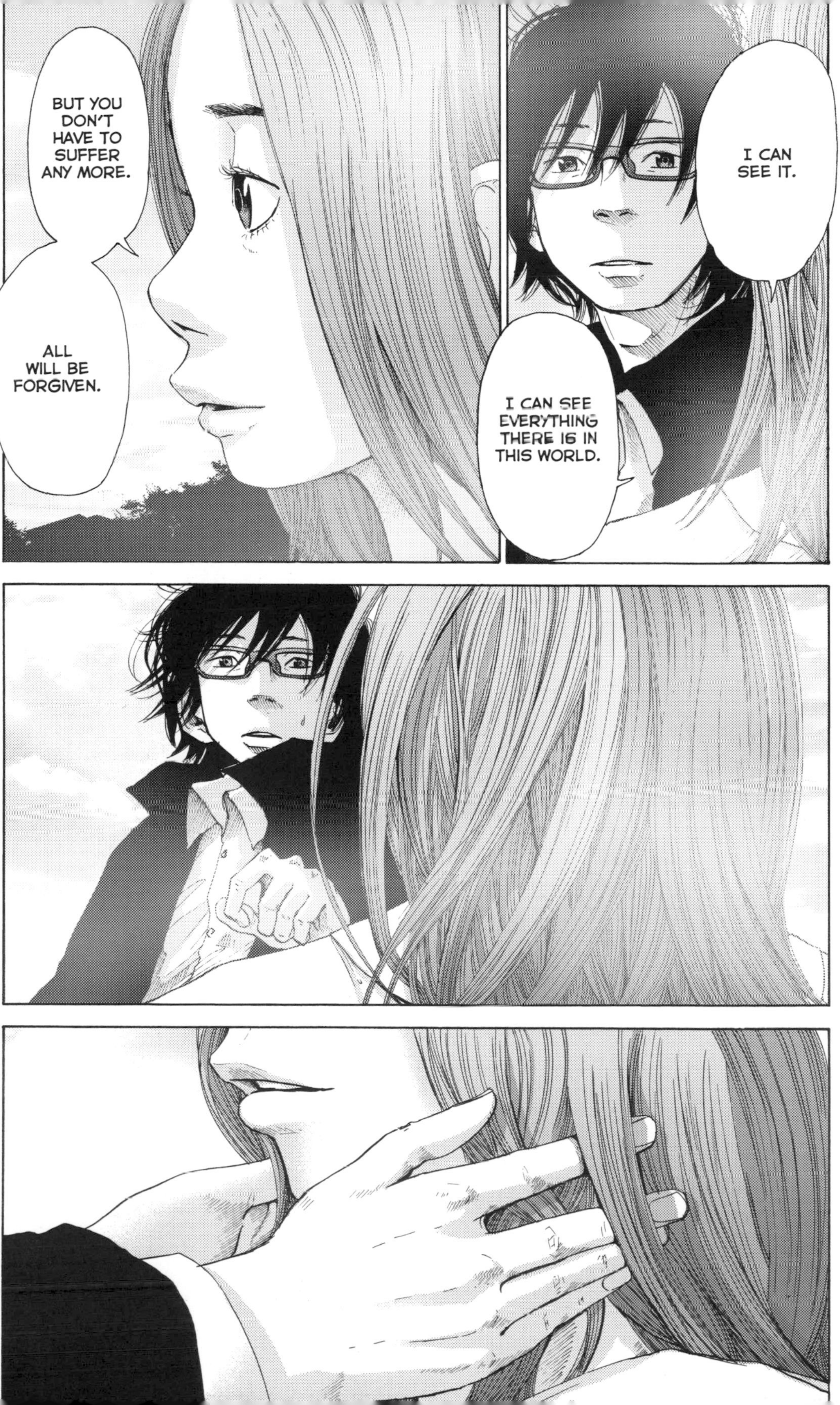
I CAN SEE IT.
I CAN SEE EVERYTHING THERE IS IN THIS WORLD.
BUT YOU DON'T HAVE TO SUFFER ANY MORE.
ALL WILL BE FORGIVEN.

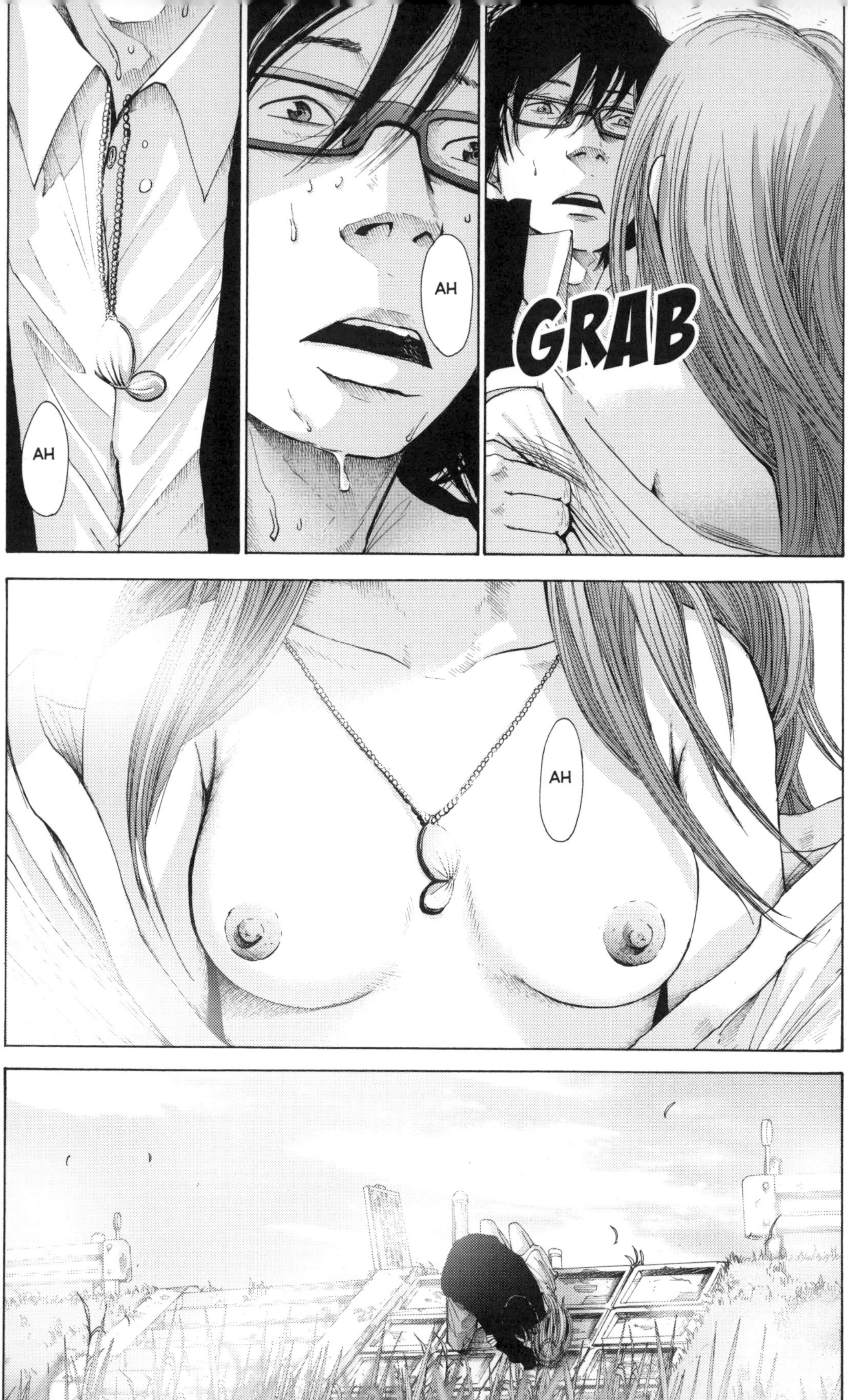
GRAB
AH
AH
AH

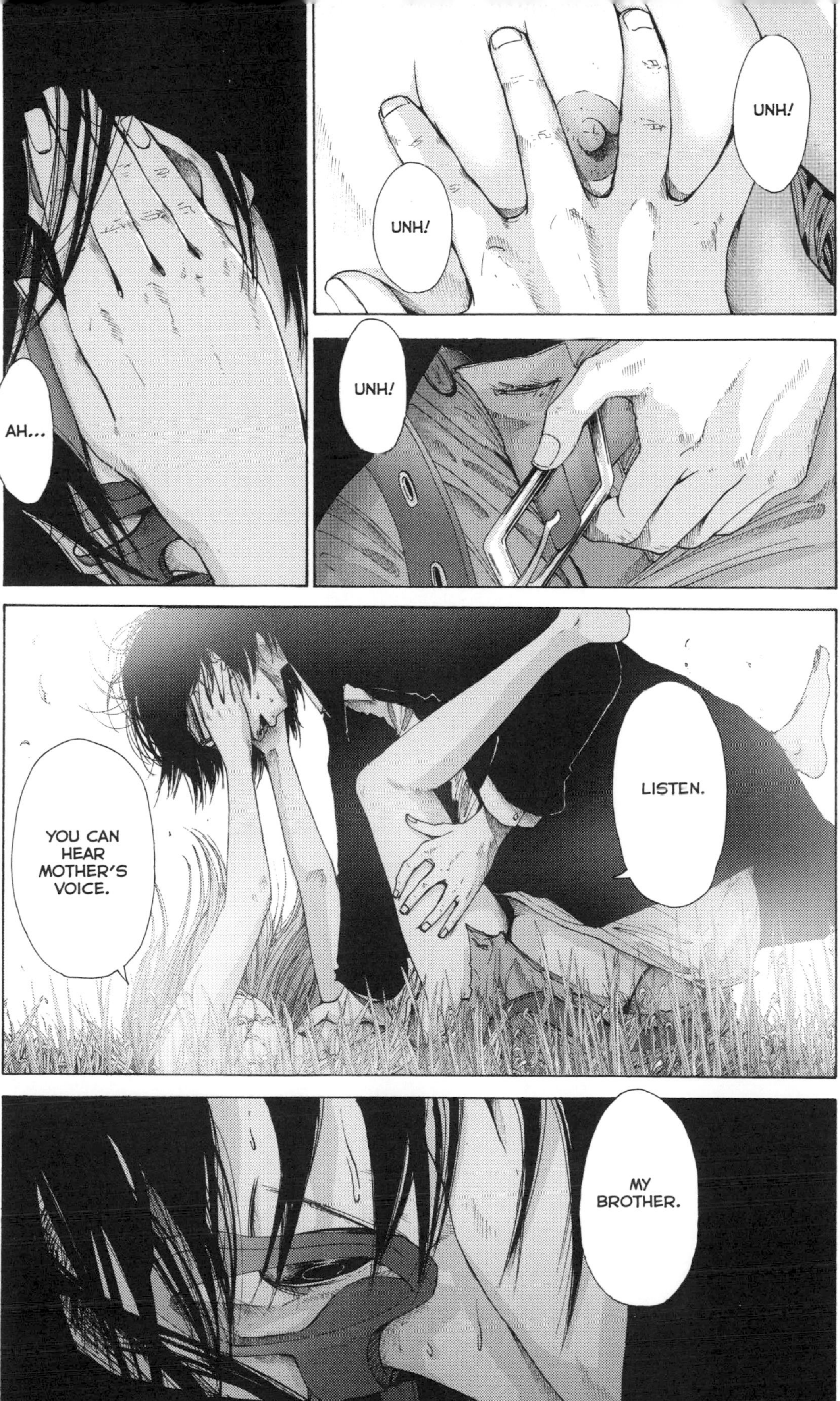
UNH!
UNH!
UNH!
AH...
LISTEN.
YOU CAN HEAR MOTHER'S VOICE.
MY BROTHER.

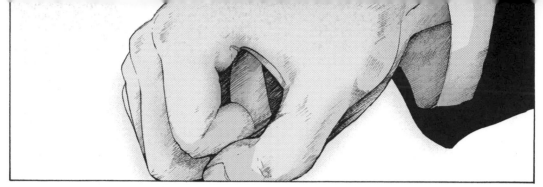

KRAK KRAK KRAK

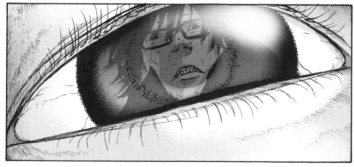

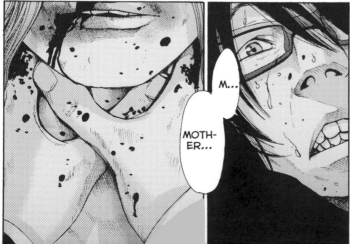

M...

MOTHER...

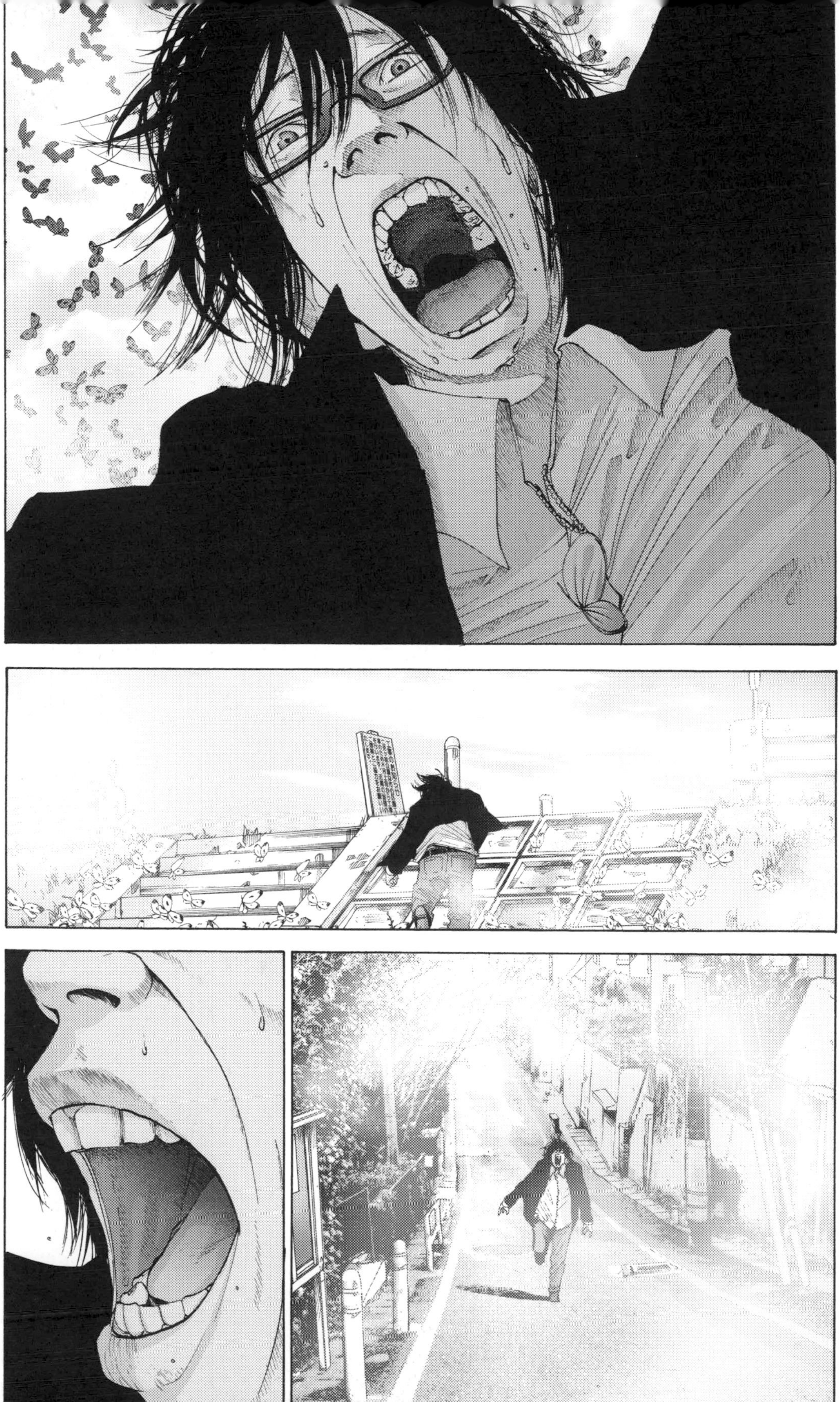

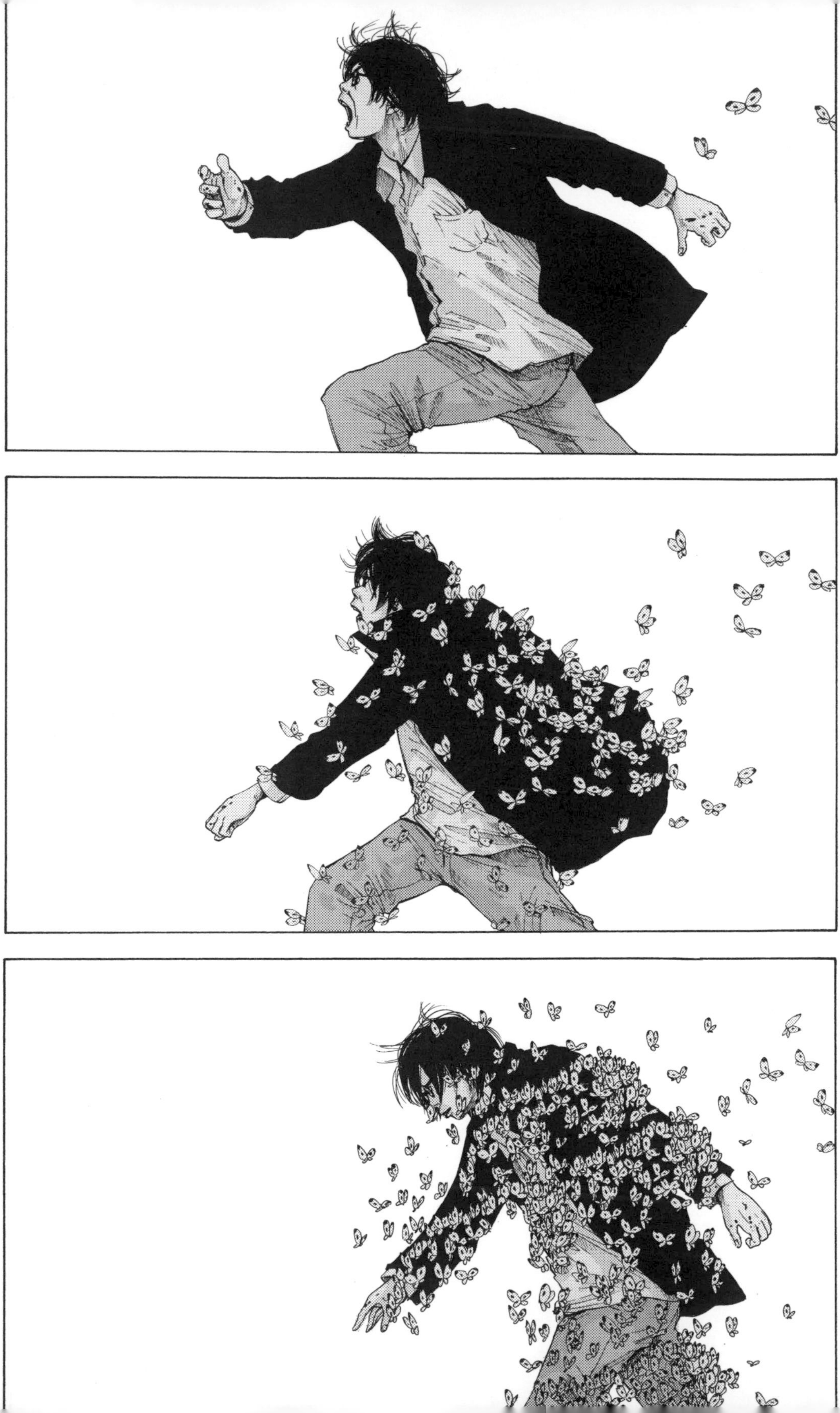

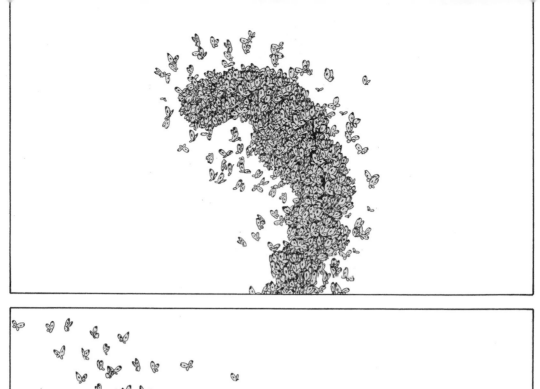

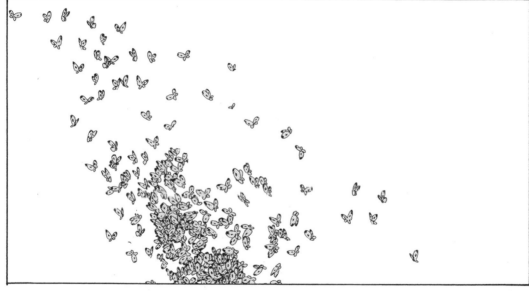

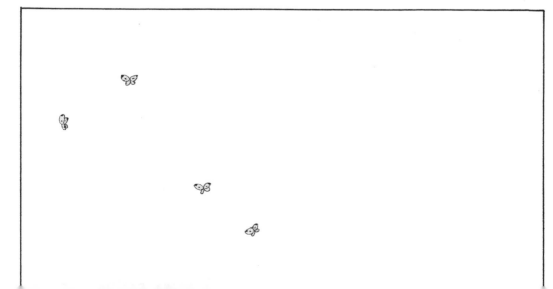

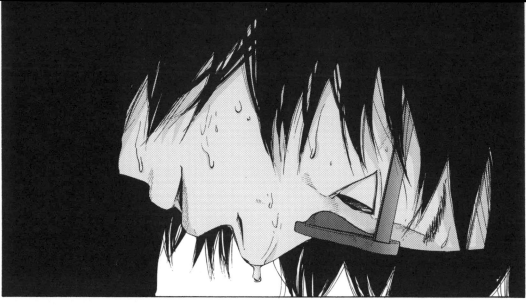

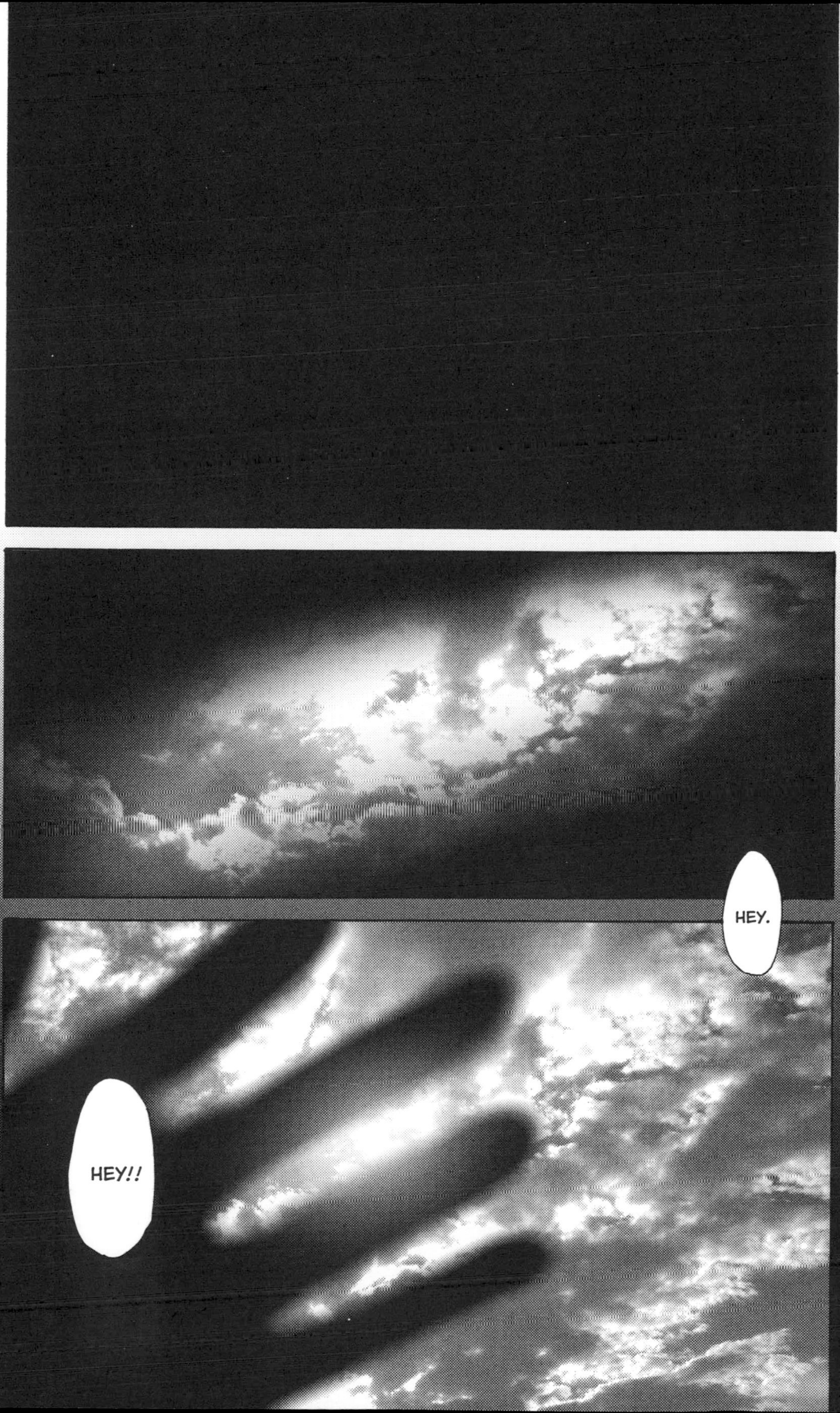
HEY.
HEY!!

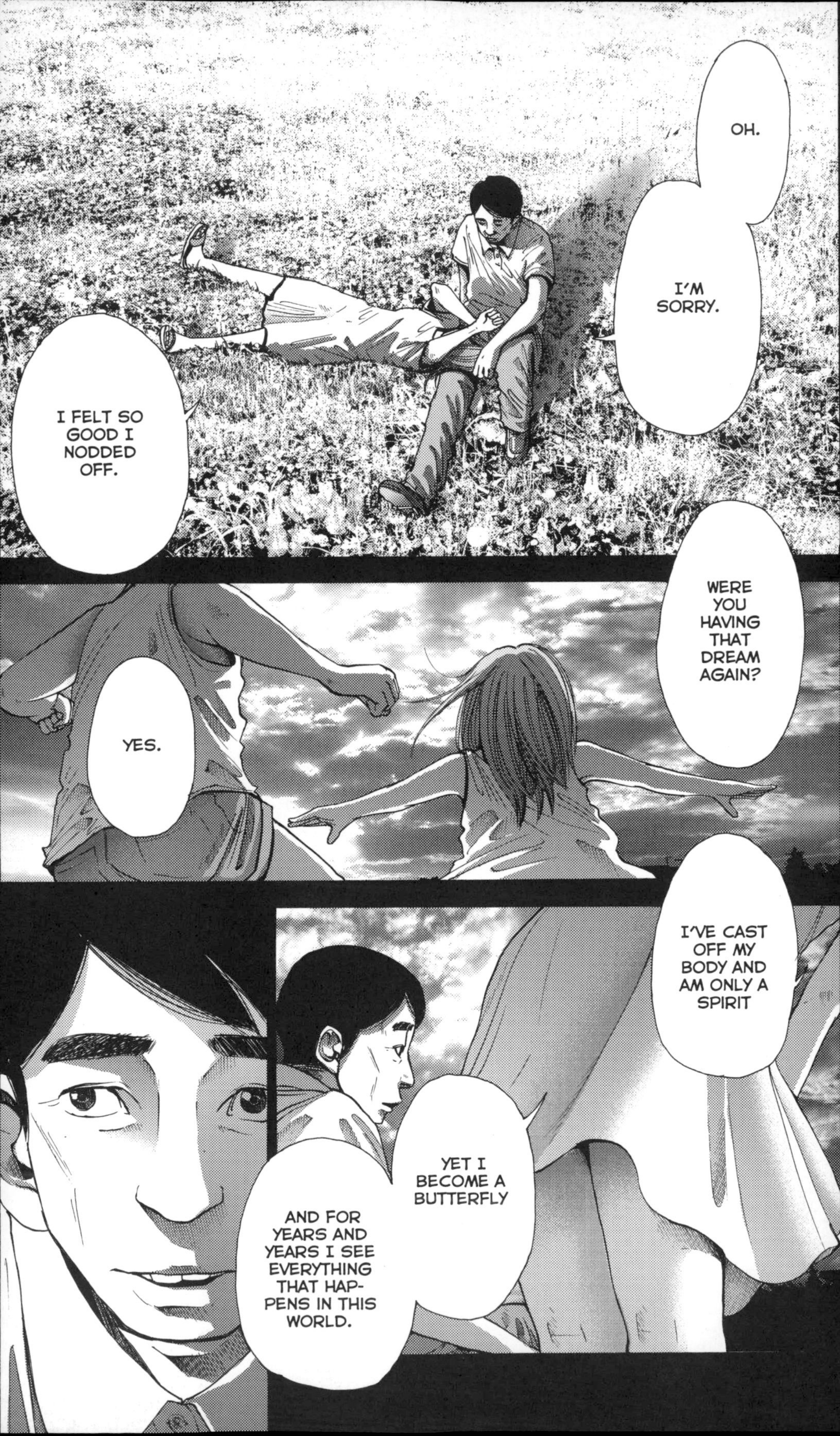
OH.
I'M SORRY.
I FELT SO GOOD I NODDED OFF.
WERE YOU HAVING THAT DREAM AGAIN?
YES.
I'VE CAST OFF MY BODY AND AM ONLY A SPIRIT
YET I BECOME A BUTTERFLY
AND FOR YEARS AND YEARS I SEE EVERYTHING THAT HAP-PENS IN THIS WORLD.

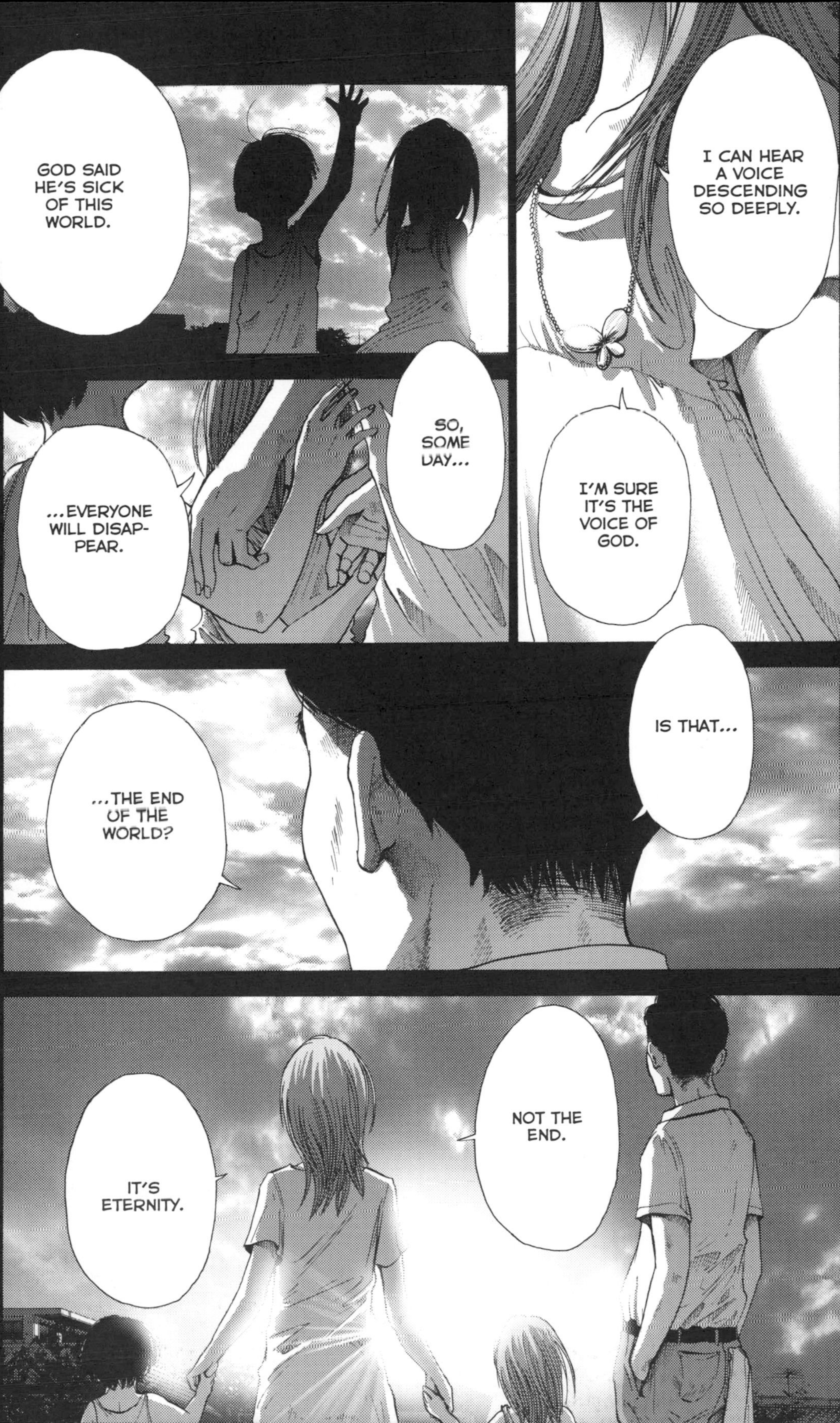
I CAN HEAR A VOICE DESCENDING SO DEEPLY.
I'M SURE IT'S THE VOICE OF GOD.
GOD SAID HE'S SICK OF THIS WORLD.
SO, SOME DAY...
...EVERYONE WILL DISAP-PEAR.
IS THAT...
...THE END OF THE WORLD?
NOT THE END.
IT'S ETERNITY.

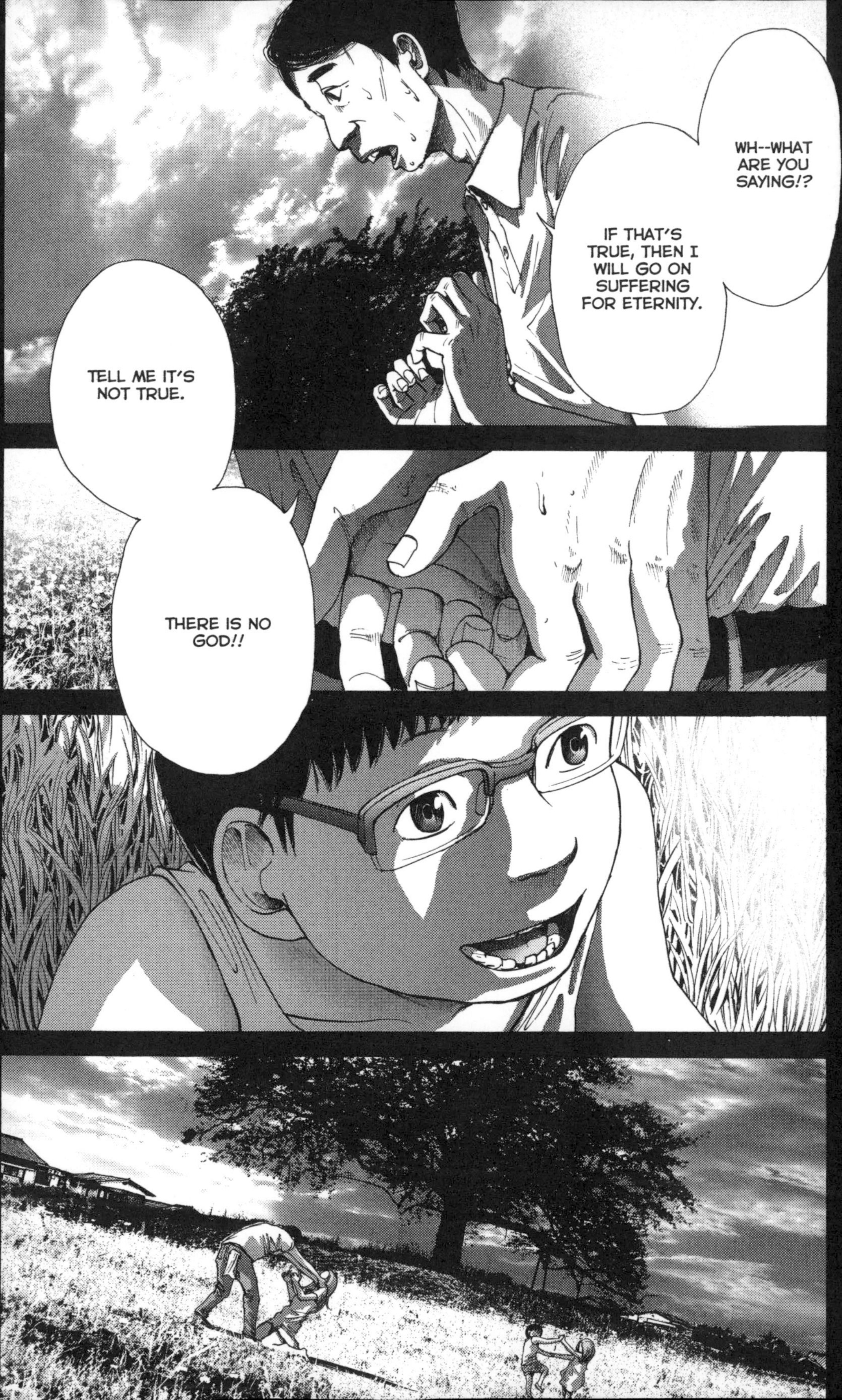
WH--WHAT ARE YOU SAYING!?
IF THAT'S TRUE, THEN I WILL GO ON SUFFERING FOR ETERNITY.
TELL ME IT'S NOT TRUE.
THERE IS NO GOD!!

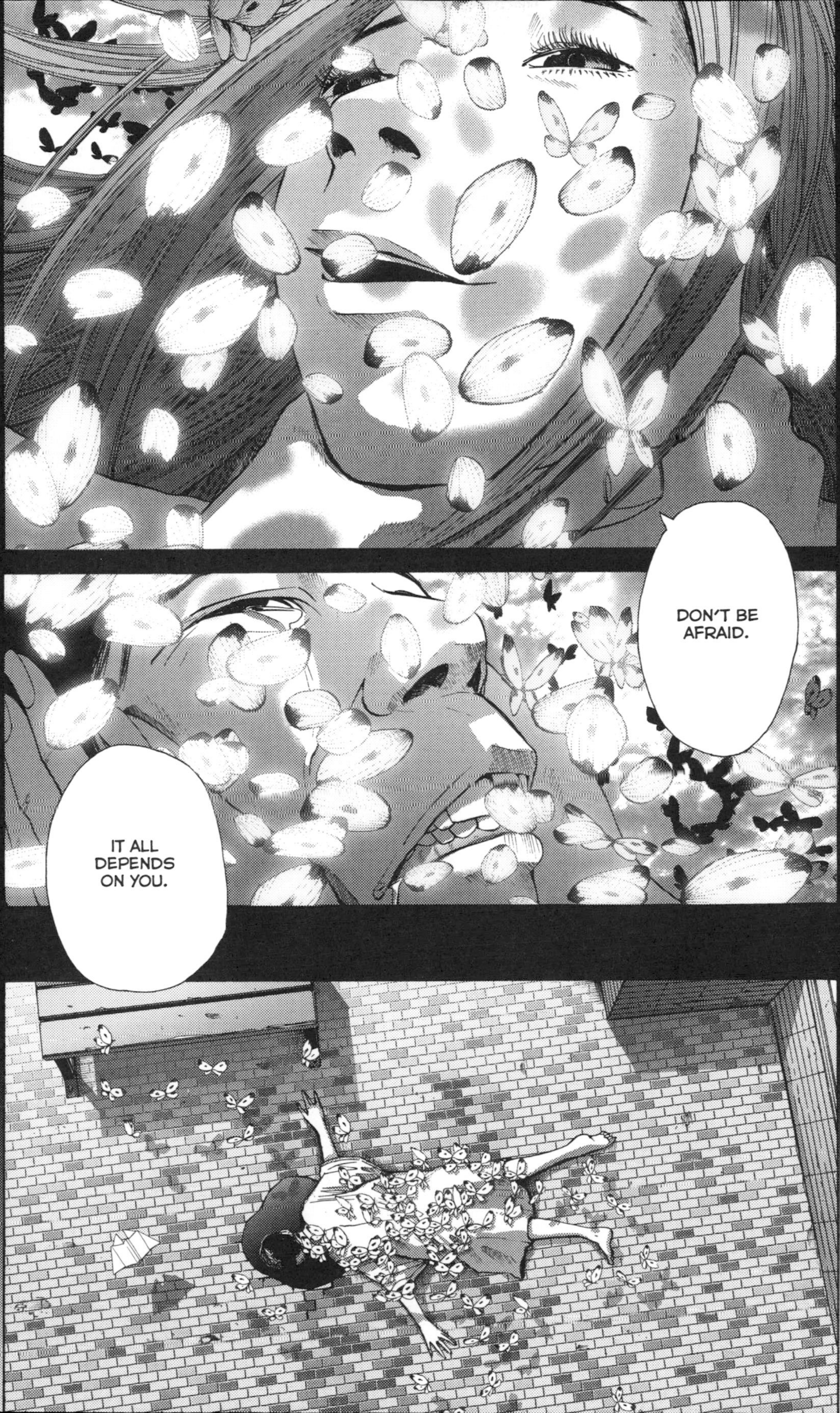
DON'T BE AFRAID.
IT ALL DEPENDS ON YOU.

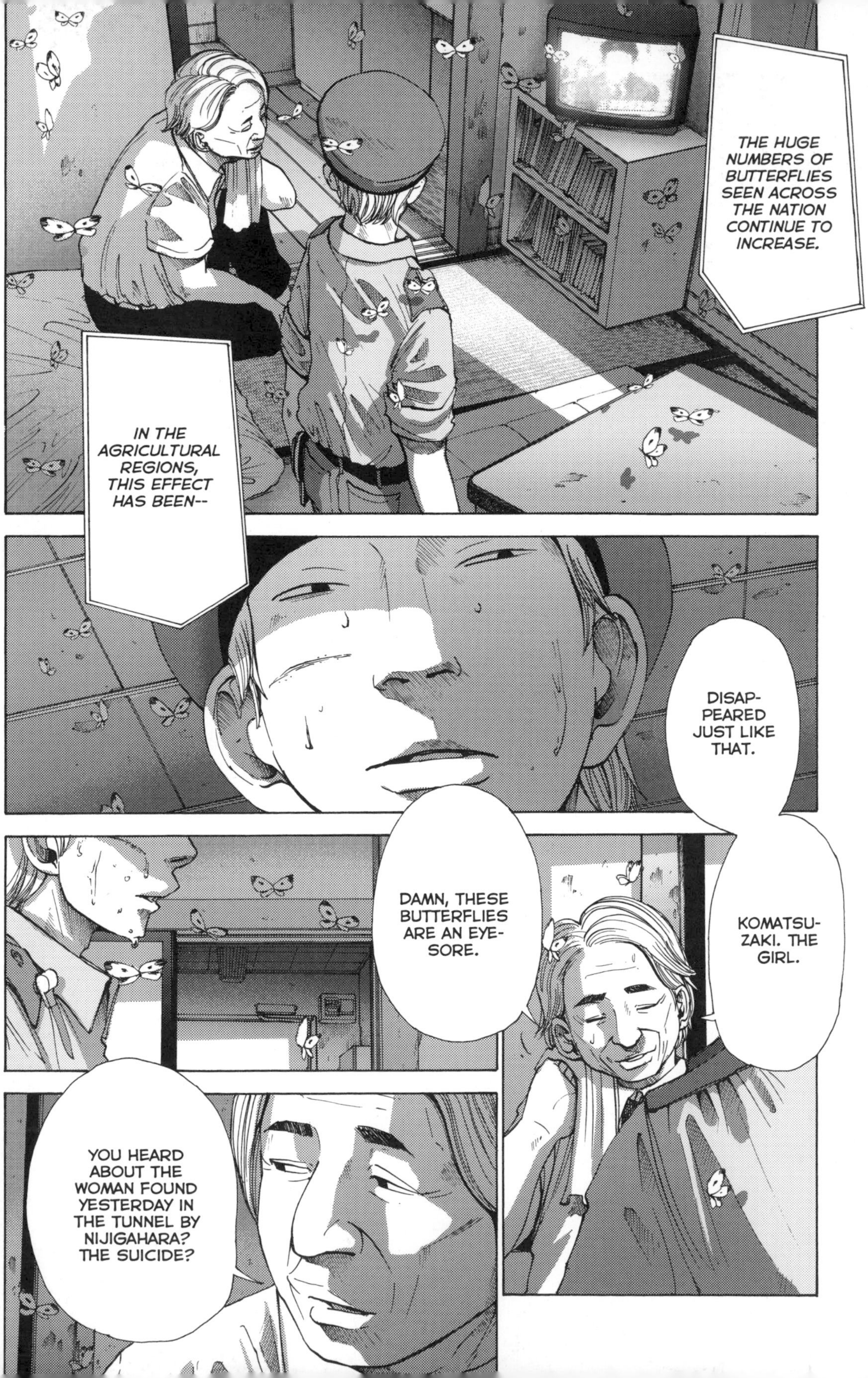
THE HUGE NUMBERS OF BUTTERFLIES SEEN ACROSS THE NATION CONTINUE TO INCREASE.
IN THE AGRICULTURAL REGIONS, THIS EFFECT HAS BEEN--
DISAP-PEARED JUST LIKE THAT.
KOMATSU-ZAKI. THE GIRL.
DAMN, THESE BUTTERFLIES ARE AN EYE-SORE.
YOU HEARD ABOUT THE WOMAN FOUND YESTERDAY IN THE TUNNEL BY NIJIGAHARA? THE SUICIDE?

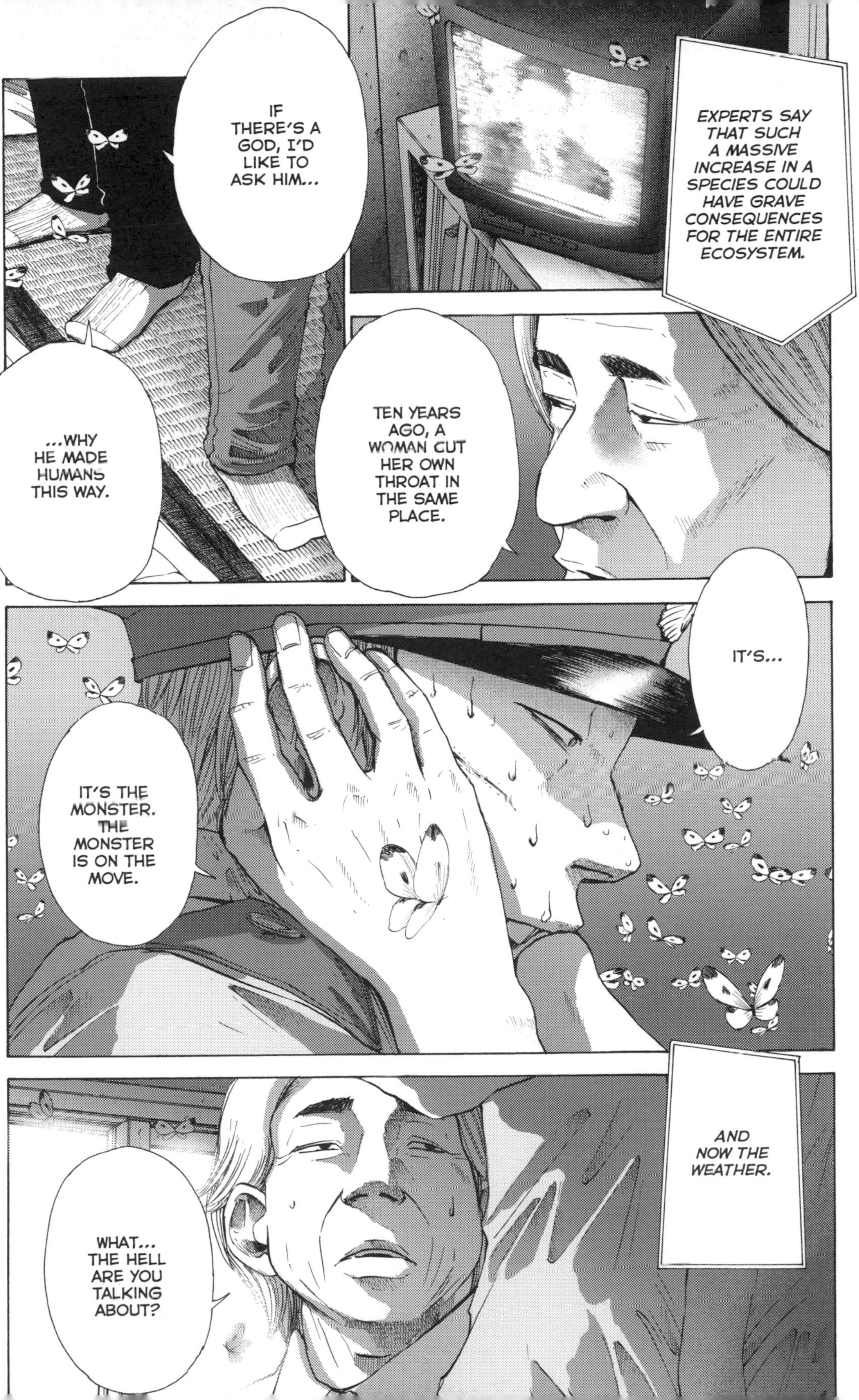
EXPERTS SAY THAT SUCH A MASSIVE INCREASE IN A SPECIES COULD HAVE GRAVE CONSEQUENCES FOR THE ENTIRE ECOSYSTEM.
IF THERE'S A GOD, I'D LIKE TO ASK HIM...
...WHY HE MADE HUMANS THIS WAY.
TEN YEARS AGO, A WOMAN CUT HER OWN THROAT IN THE SAME PLACE.
IT'S...
IT'S THE MONSTER. THE MONSTER IS ON THE MOVE.
AND NOW THE WEATHER.
WHAT... THE HELL ARE YOU TALKING ABOUT?

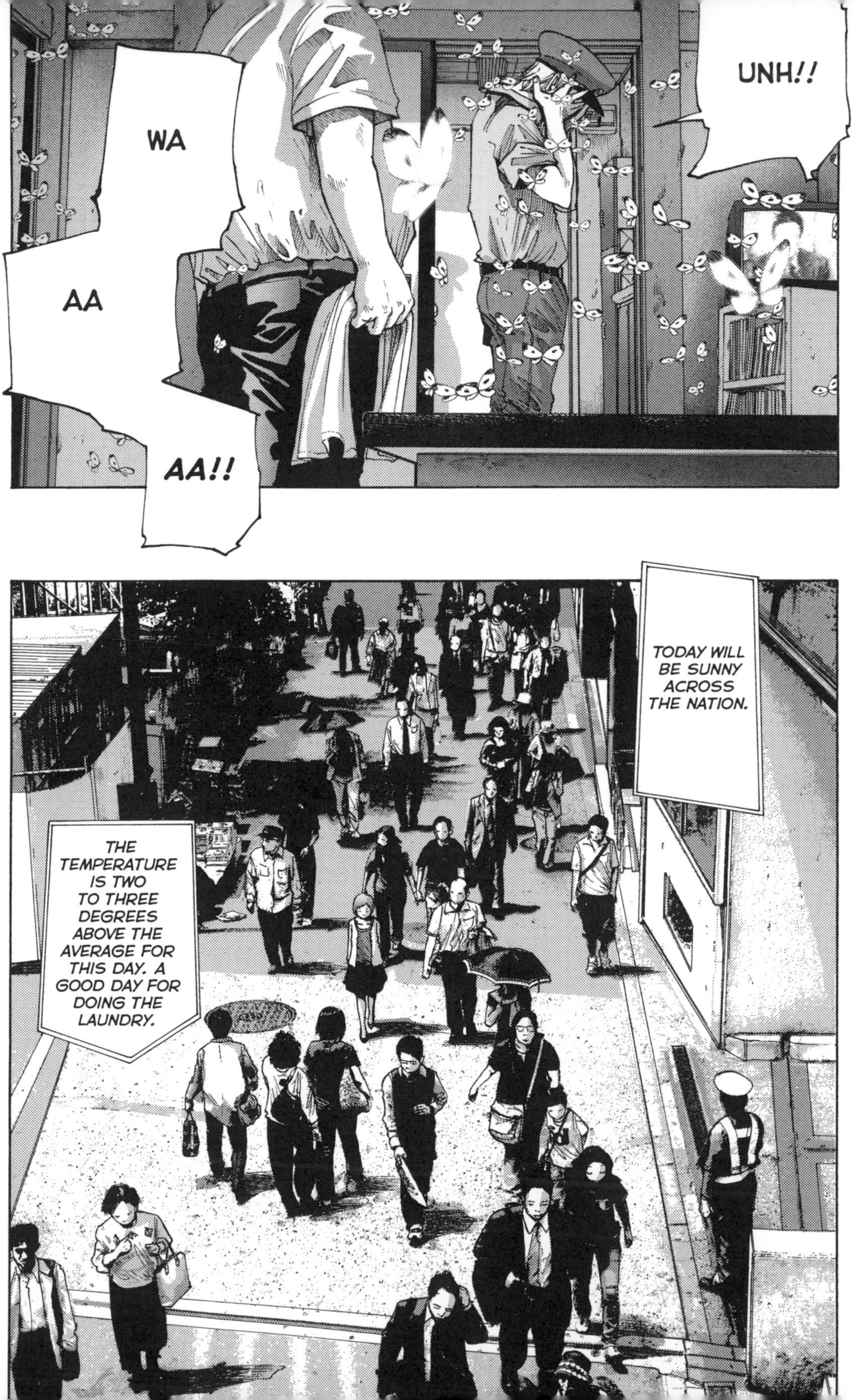
UNH!!
WA
AA
AA!!
TODAY WILL BE SUNNY ACROSS THE NATION.
THE TEMPERATURE IS TWO TO THREE DEGREES ABOVE THE AVERAGE FOR THIS DAY. A GOOD DAY FOR DOING THE LAUNDRY.

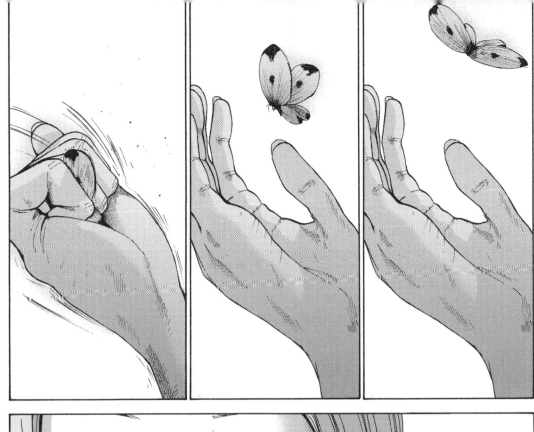

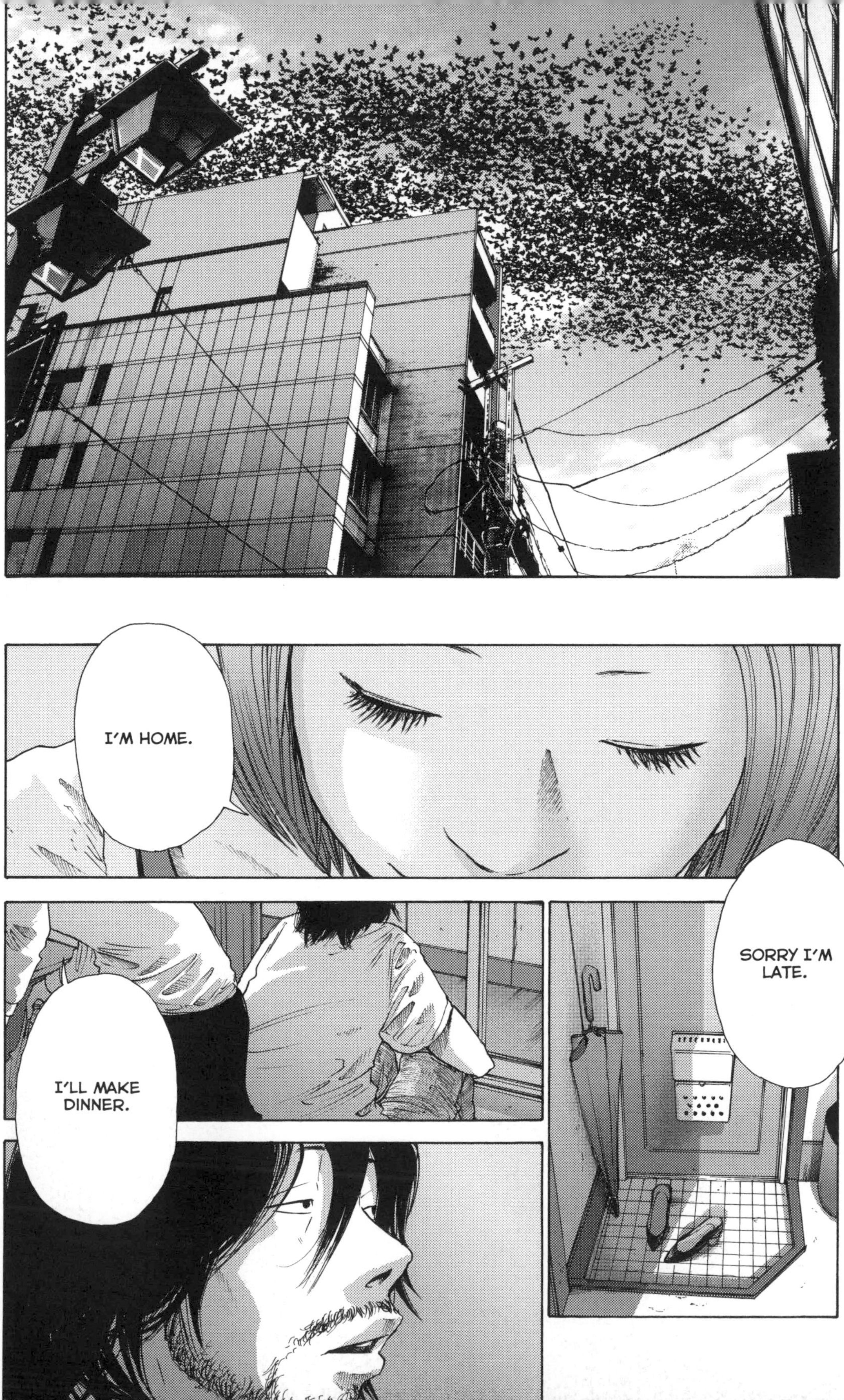
I'M HOME.
SORRY I'M LATE.
I'LL MAKE DINNER.

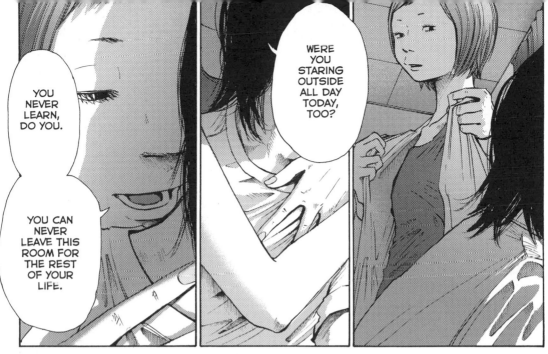

WERE YOU STARING OUTSIDE ALL DAY TODAY, TOO?
YOU NEVER LEARN, DO YOU.
YOU CAN NEVER LEAVE THIS ROOM FOR THE REST OF YOUR LIFE.
GOOD EVENING.

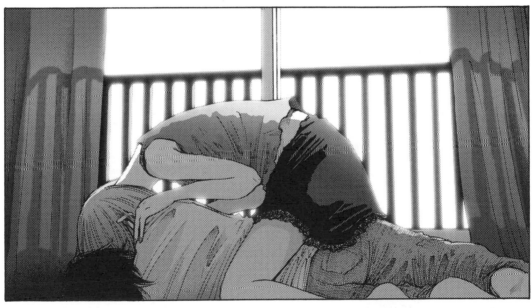

THE MOON IS LOVELY AGAIN TONIGHT.

prism cafe

BUT YOU, BATHED IN THAT MOON-LIGHT...

...ARE BEAUTIFUL BEYOND COMPARE.

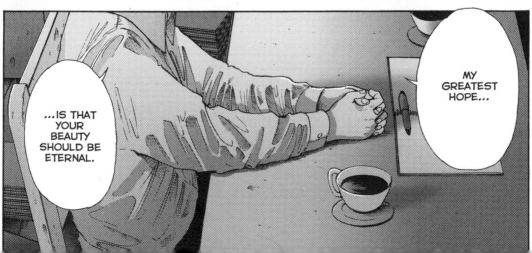

MY GREATEST HOPE...

...IS THAT YOUR BEAUTY SHOULD BE ETERNAL.

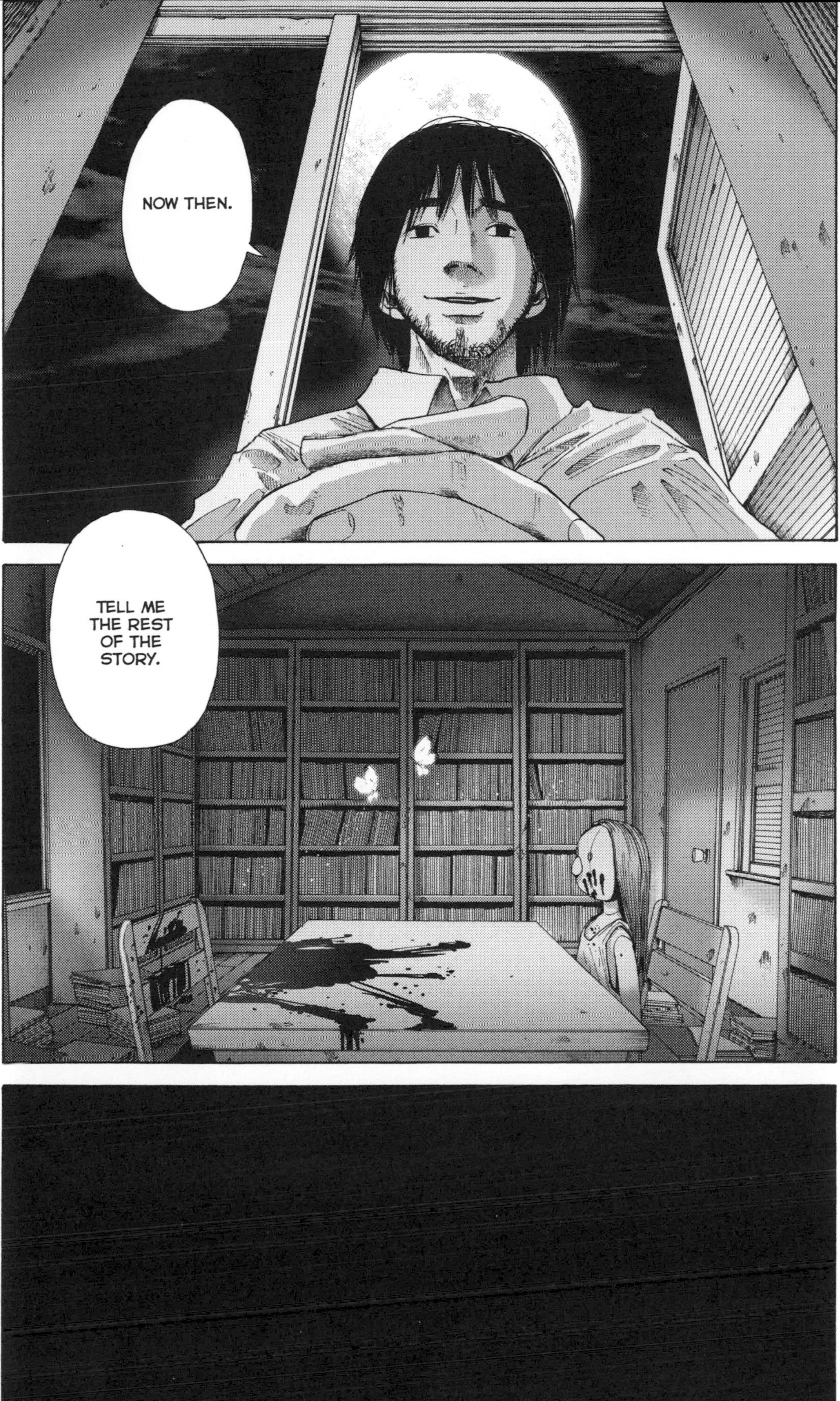
NOW THEN.
TELL ME THE REST OF THE STORY.

HEY.

HEY.

HOW LONG DO YOU
MEAN TO SLEEP?

GET UP NOW.

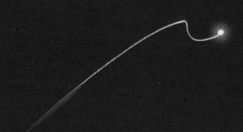

YOU CAN'T FOOL ME.

I KNOW YOU'RE AWAKE.

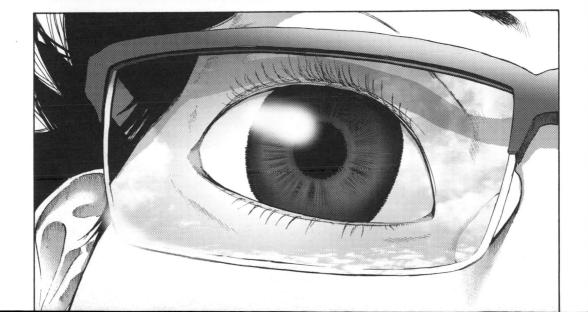

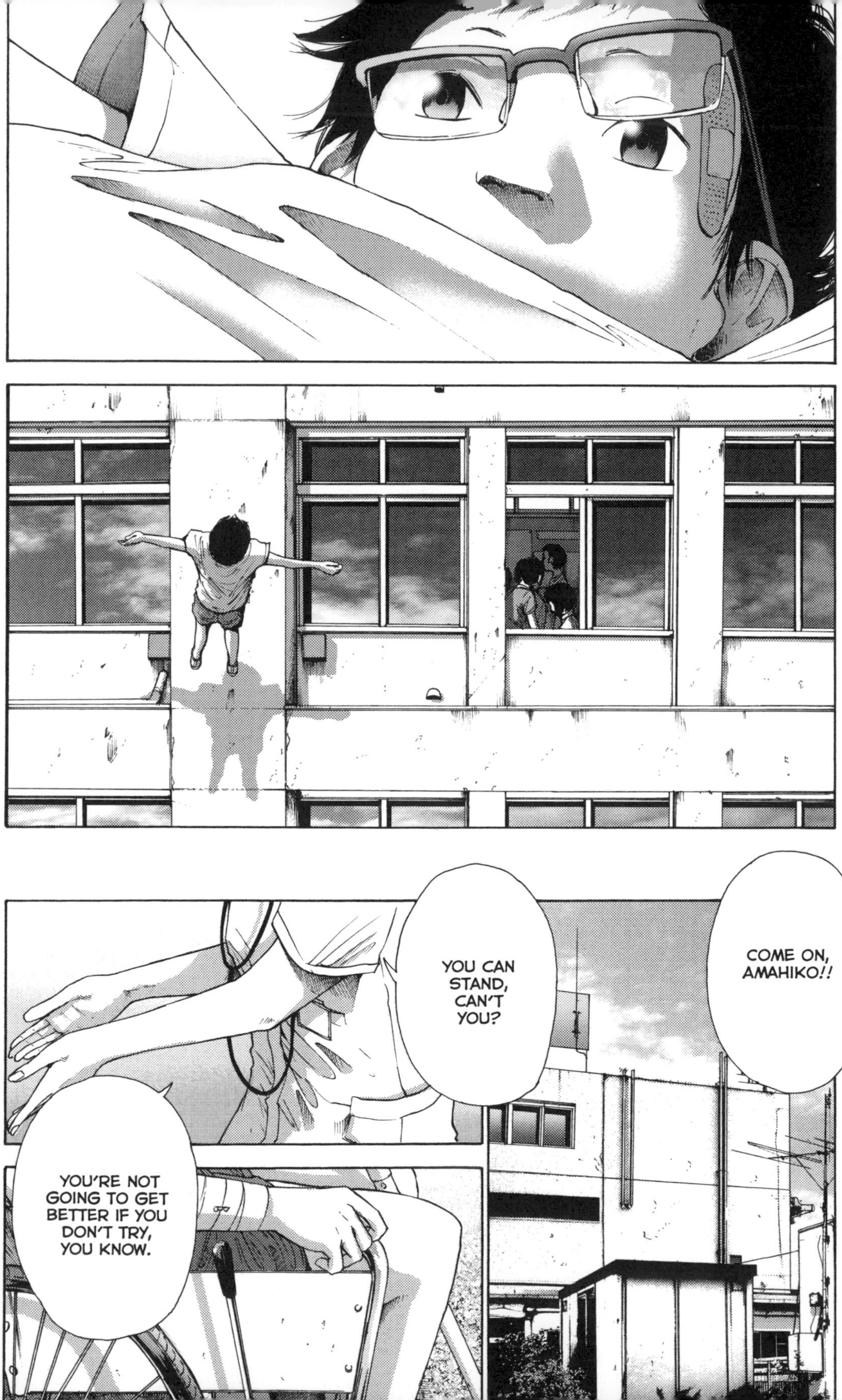
COME ON, AMAHIKO!!
YOU CAN STAND, CAN'T YOU?
YOU'RE NOT GOING TO GET BETTER IF YOU DON'T TRY, YOU KNOW.

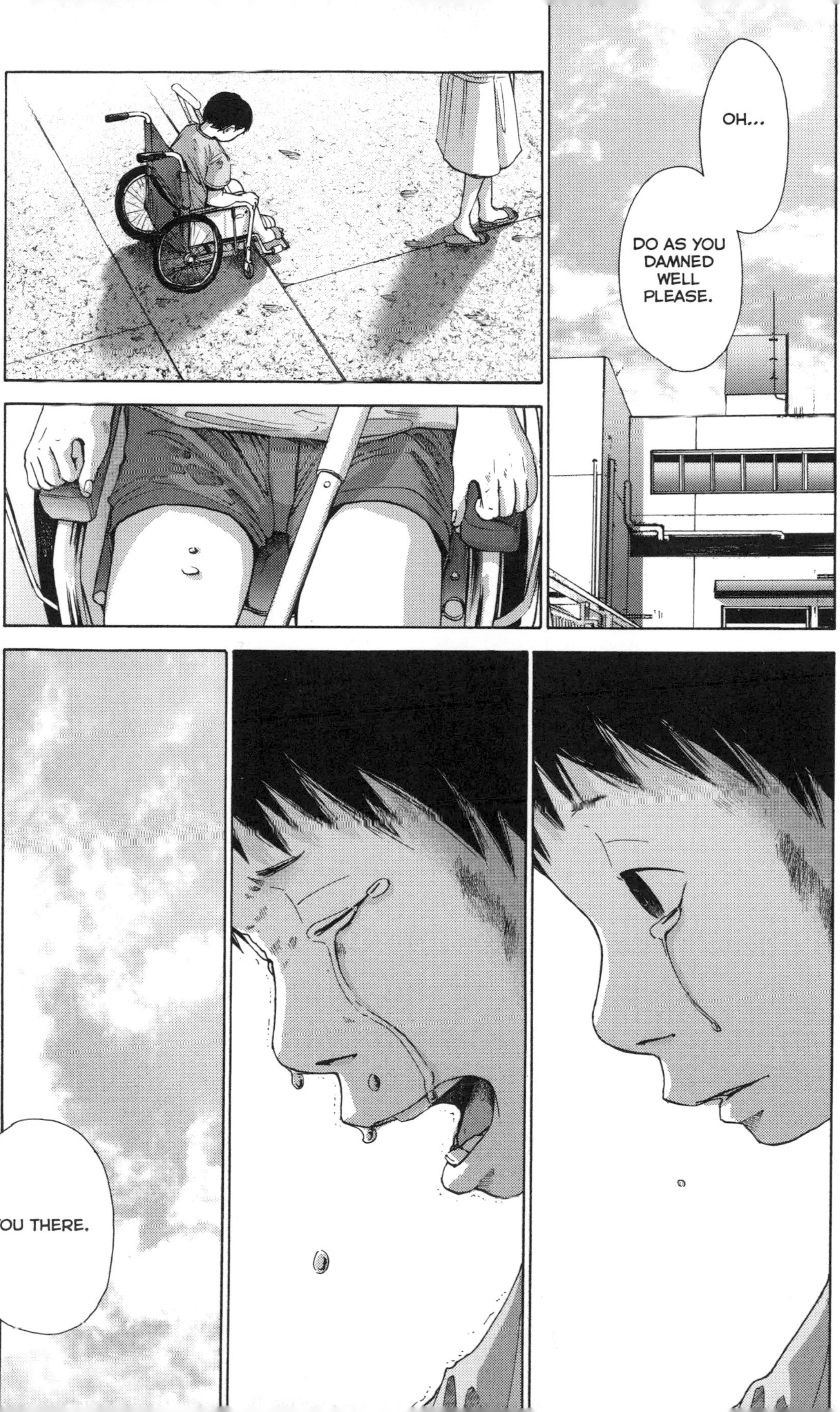
OH...
DO AS YOU DAMNED WELL PLEASE.
YOU THERE.

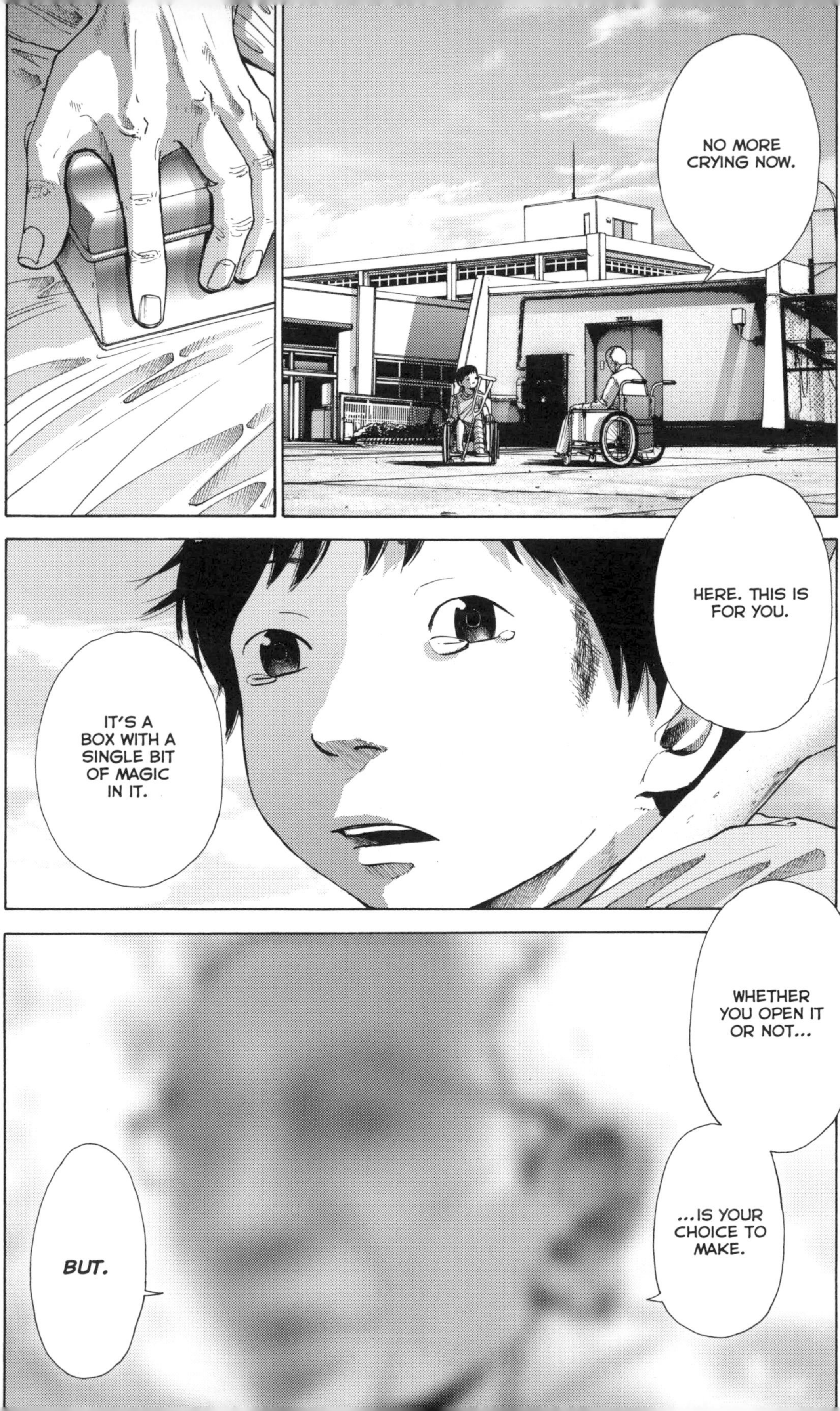
NO MORE CRYING NOW.
HERE. THIS IS FOR YOU.
IT'S A BOX WITH A SINGLE BIT OF MAGIC IN IT.
WHETHER YOU OPEN IT OR NOT...
...IS YOUR CHOICE TO MAKE.
BUT.

NO MATTER HOW AWFUL THE WORLD IS...

...YOU MUST BE STRONG OF WILL.

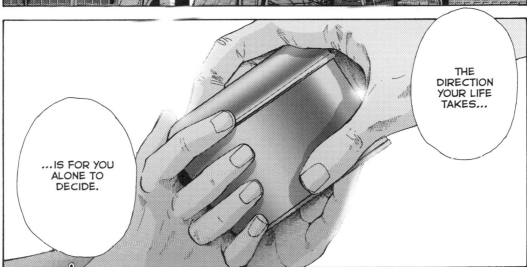

THE DIRECTION YOUR LIFE TAKES...

...IS FOR YOU ALONE TO DECIDE.

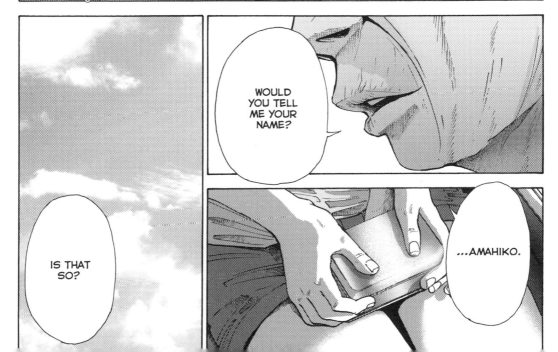

WOULD YOU TELL ME YOUR NAME?

IS THAT SO?

...AMAHIKO.

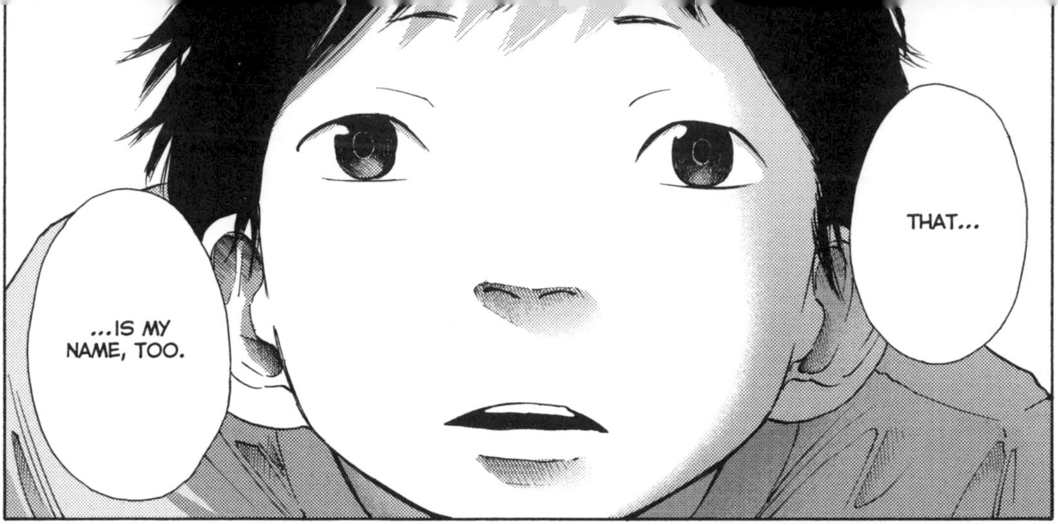
THAT...
...IS MY NAME, TOO.

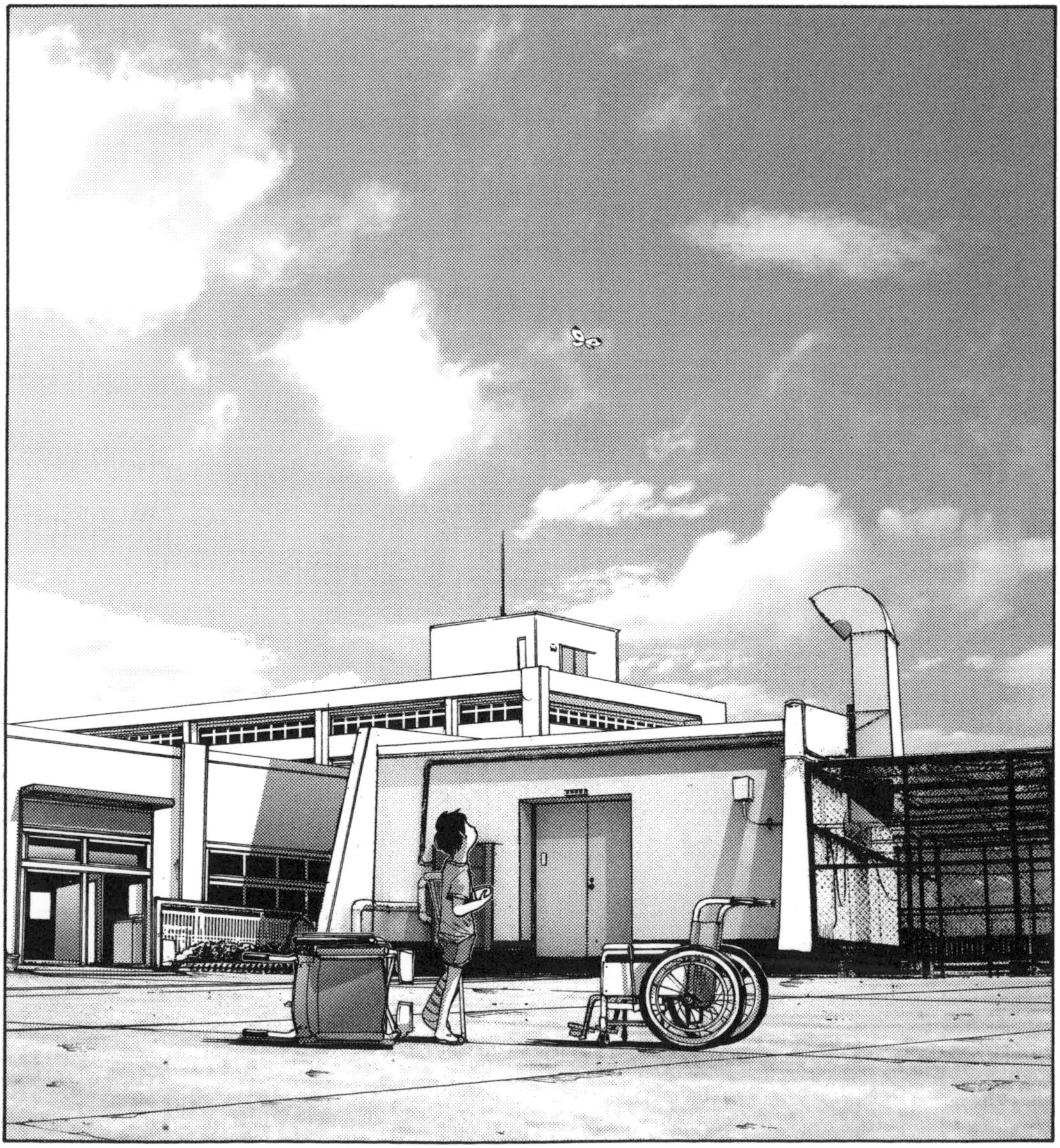

STOP!

THE MANGA IN THIS BOOK IS "UNFLIPPED." MEANING PAGES RUN BACK-TO-FRONT AND PANELS START AT THE TOP RIGHT AND END AT THE BOTTOM LEFT. TURN THIS PAGE AND YOU'LL BE AT THE END OF THE STORY. FLIP THE BOOK AROUND FOR A MUCH MORE SATISFYING READING EXPERIENCE.

PRONUNCIATION GUIDE

VOWELS

a	as in "f<u>a</u>ther"
i	as in "spaghett<u>i</u>"
u	as in "p<u>u</u>t"
e	as in "th<u>e</u>m"
o	as in "p<u>o</u>le"

"Long" vowels are usually indicated by a macron ("ō"), circumflex ("ô") or diaeresis ("ö"), although sometimes the vowel is simply repeated. In personal names, a long "o" is sometimes represented as "oh." In cases where one vowel is followed immediately by a different vowel, but is not in the same syllable, they are often separated by a dash or apostrophe to indicate the end of one syllable and beginning of another. Here are common pairs of vowels that sound to the English-speaker's ear like one syllable (and thus are not separated):

ai	as in "m<u>y</u>"
ei	as in "r<u>ay</u>"
oi	as in "t<u>oy</u>"
ao	as in "c<u>ow</u>"

CONSONANTS *that require clarification*

g	as in "get" (never as in "age")
s	as in "soft" (never like "rise")
t	as in "tale" (never like "d")
ch	as in "church"

ACCENTS

Most English words have "accented" and "un-accented" syllables. This is generally not the case in Japanese, which is more "flat." When English speakers encounter a new word, they tend to accent the first syllable if it has two syllables, the second if it has three, and after that they wing it. If you can't resist accenting a syllable in a Japanese word, accent the first and you'll be fine.

NAMES

Character names are in Japanese order: surname first, given name last.

ASANO Inio was born and raised in the town of Ishioka, in Ibaraki Province. He made his professional debut as a cartoonist while still in high school with the short story "An Ordinary Day." His longer works include *It's a Wonderful World!*, *The City of Light*, *Solanin*, *Goodnight Punpun*, *Perfunctory Boy* and, most recently, *The Girl by the Seaside*. *Solanin* was nominated for an Eisner Award in 2009 and adapted as a live action movie starring MIYAZAKI Aoi and KOHRA Kengo in 2010.

Fantagraphics Books, 7563 Lake City Way NE, Seattle, Washington 98115 | Editor and Translator: Matt Thorn; Supervising Editor: Kristy Valenti; Editorial Liaison: Gary Groth; Design: Emory Liu; Production: Paul Baresh; Production Assistance: Keith Barbalato, Brooke Chin, Tom Graham, Toby Liebowitz, and Sonya Selbach; Associate Publisher: Eric Reynolds; Publisher: Gary Groth | This edition of *Nijigahara Holograph* is copyright © 2014 Fantagraphics Books. All contents copyright © 2006 Inio Asano. Originally published in Japan in 2006 by OHTA Publishing Co. All rights reserved. Permission to reproduce must be obtained from the publisher. | For a free catalog of Fantagraphics Books, call 1-800-657-1100 or visit fantagraphics.com. | Third Fantagraphics Books printing: September 2015 | ISBN 978-1-60699-583-9 | Library of Congress Control Number: 2015940080 | Printed in Singapore